The *Sams Teach Yourself in 24 Hours* Series

Sams Teach Yourself in 24 Hours books pr⸱⸱
answers in a proven step-by-step approa⸱⸱⸱⸱⸱⸱⸱⸱⸱⸱ou. In
just 24 sessions of one hour or less, you wi⸱⸱⸱⸱⸱⸱⸱⸱⸱⸱ task you
need to get the results you want. Let our exp⸱⸱⸱⸱⸱ authors
present the most accurate information to get you ⸱⸱ ⸱able
answers—fast!

Major Languages Covered in These 24 Hours

- QBasic: The perfect beginner's language that operates in a text-based environment so you can concentrate on the language's details. You will learn to write detailed programs in QBasic. Once you learn the fundamentals of a language such as QBasic, you should have little trouble advancing to the next level of languages: Windows languages.

- Visual Basic: Springboard from QBasic into one of the most popular Windows programming languages in use today. Visual Basic uses the QBasic language as a foundation but adds the visual interface required by a true Windows programming language. Visual Basic supports events that occur during Windows operations so that your programs can respond as needed.

- C: One of the most important languages due to its efficient runtime speeds and powerful operators, C single-handedly ousted Pascal as the language of choice in the 1980s. C's small size made it the perfect language for early PCs with limited memory capacities but the mainframe world caught on as well; today, most companies use programs written in C on most of their hardware.

- C++: Master object-oriented programming (OOP) with the most popular OOP-based language in existence. OOP changed the way that programmers organized their code. OOP-based code becomes more self-sufficient, and program maintenance and flexibility improves the programmer's efficiency.

- HTML: Learn how to format Internet Web pages using the language that brought the visual interface to the Internet. HTML is a formatting language that lays out text, graphics, and hypertext links to make Web pages take on the look that you intend.

- Java: Spruce up the Web pages that you design by embedding Java programs that activate the Web pages you provide. Java adds active content to a Web page so that the user can interact with the page but still be free of the download time required by older active Web technologies.

SAMS

Teach Yourself Beginning Programming

in 24 Hours

- Batch and script languages: Control your operating system tasks with these command-based, interactive languages. Collect common operating system tasks into small routines that you execute merely by typing the name of the batch file. Many of today's applications support one or more script languages that enable you to automate common tasks within the application.
- FORTRAN, COBOL, and PL/I: Learn how these mainframe languages brought forth the computerized world. These early languages made it possible for programmers of the first computers to design and create the applications that brought computing power into businesses, universities, and governmental organizations.
- Machine and assembler languages: Learn how programming began by studying the low-level code that only your computer understands. Although you rarely find a need for programs written in these low-level languages, understanding how these languages work will help you understand the more advanced higher-level programming languages that you use everyday.

Standard Controls

Here are just a few of the standard controls you'll be able to place on your applications' windows from most programming languages:

- Command button—Enables the user to indicate a readiness to perform an action such as the termination of a program or the printing of a report
- Label—Holds text, such as titles and prompts
- Text box—Enables the user to enter and edit text or accept default text
- Check box—Provides a way for your user to select one or more options
- Option buttons—Enables the user to select one option from a list of mutually exclusive options
- List box—Provides a list of items from which the user can select
- Combo box—Offers several alternative list box styles, such as a drop-down list box that remains closed to save screen space until the user clicks to open the list box
- Picture box—Holds graphic images from files
- Scroll bars—Available in horizontal and vertical styles so that your users can select from a wide range of choices

SAMS

Greg Perry

Teach Yourself

Beginning Programming

in 24 Hours

SAMS

201 West 103rd St., Indianapolis, Indiana, 46290 USA

Sams Teach Yourself Beginning Programming in 24 Hours

Copyright © 1998 by Sams

All rights reserved. No part of this book shall be reproduced, stored in a retrieval system, or transmitted by any means, electronic, mechanical, photocopying, recording, or otherwise, without written permission from the publisher. No patent liability is assumed with respect to the use of the information contained herein. Although every precaution has been taken in the preparation of this book, the publisher and author assume no responsibility for errors or omissions. Neither is any liability assumed for damages resulting from the use of the information contained herein.

International Standard Book Number: 0-672-31355-3

Library of Congress Catalog Card Number: 98-85492

Printed in the United States of America

First Printing: September 1998

00   99   4   3

Trademarks

All terms mentioned in this book that are known to be trademarks or service marks have been appropriately capitalized. Sams cannot attest to the accuracy of this information. Use of a term in this book should not be regarded as affecting the validity of any trademark or service mark.

Windows is a registered trademark of Microsoft Corporation.

Warning and Disclaimer

Every effort has been made to make this book as complete and as accurate as possible, but no warranty or fitness is implied. The information provided is on an "as is" basis. The authors and the publisher shall have neither liability or responsibility to any person or entity with respect to any loss or damages arising from the information contained in this book.

EXECUTIVE EDITOR
Brian Gill

ACQUISITIONS EDITOR
Ron Gallagher

DEVELOPMENT EDITOR
Scott Warner

MANAGING EDITOR
Jodi Jensen

PROJECT EDITOR
Maureen Schneeberger McDaniel

COPY EDITORS
Kate Givens
Rhonda Tinch-Mize

INDEXER
Charlotte Clapp

TECHNICAL EDITOR
Sundar Rajan

PRODUCTION
Mona Brown
Michael Dietsch
Michael Henry
Ayanna Lacey

Overview

Contents

PART II FUNDAMENTALS OF PROGRAMMING

PART IV PROGRAMMING IN VARIOUS ENVIRONMENTS

HOUR 13 WINDOWS PROGRAMMING CONSIDERATIONS   241

HOUR 14 PROGRAMMING WITH VISUAL BASIC   259

HOUR 15 PROGRAMMING WITH C   279

About the Author

Greg Perry is a speaker and writer on both the programming and the application sides of computing. He is known for his skills at bringing advanced computer topics down to the novice's level. Perry has been a programmer and trainer since the early 1980s. He received his first degree in computer science and a master's degree in corporate finance. Perry is the author or co-author of more than 50 books, including *Sams Teach Yourself Windows 98 in 24 Hours*, *Absolute Beginner's Guide to C*, *Moving from C to C++*, and *Sams Teach Yourself Office in 24 Hours*. He has written about rental-property management and loves to travel. His favorite place to be when away from home is either at New York's *Patsy's* or in Italy because he wants to practice his fractured, broken Italian (if a foreign language were as easy as a computer language, he'd be fluent by now).

Dedication

For my nieces, Jessica and Hannah, who show me how to go fast when rollerblading, and for their baby brother, David, who'll probably out-race us all.

Acknowledgements

The people at Macmillan Computer Publishing make the best books possible in the industry for a good reason: They take their jobs seriously. They want readers to have the best books possible. They accomplish that goal. Among the MCP editors and staff who produced this book, I want to send special thanks to Ron Gallagher and Brian Gill who patiently waited for my slow writing. In addition, Scott Warner turned my words into a readable book. I am grateful to them all.

In addition, Sundar Rajan made this book more accurate. If errors still exist, they are solely mine. Maureen McDaniel rounded out the front-line team to give this text its polish.

My lovely and gracious bride Jayne continues to wait by my side while I finish just "one more page." The best parents in the universe, Glen and Bettye Perry, encourage and support me in every way. Thanks to both of them.

Tell Us What You Think!

As the reader of this book, *you* are our most important critic and commentator. We value your opinion and want to know what we're doing right, what we could do better, what areas you'd like to see us publish in, and any other words of wisdom you're willing to pass our way.

As the Executive Editor for the Programming team at Macmillan Computer Publishing, I welcome your comments. You can fax, e-mail, or write me directly to let me know what you did or didn't like about this book—as well as what we can do to make our books stronger.

Please note that I cannot help you with technical problems related to the topic of this book, and that due to the high volume of mail I receive, I might not be able to reply to every message.

When you write, please be sure to include this book's title and author as well as your name and phone or fax number. I will carefully review your comments and share them with the author and editors who worked on the book.

Fax: 317-817-7070

E-mail: `prog@mcp.com`

Mail: Executive Editor
          Visual Basic Programming
          Macmillan Computer Publishing
          201 West 103rd Street
          Indianapolis, IN 46290 USA

Introduction

Introduction to Programming

Learning how to program computers is easier than you might think. If you approach computers with hesitation, if you cannot even spell *PC*, if you have tried your best to avoid the subject altogether but can do so no longer, the book you now hold contains support that you can depend on in troubled computing times.

This 24-hour tutorial does more than explain programming. This tutorial does more than describe the difference between Visual Basic, C, and Java. This tutorial does more than teach you what programming is all about. This tutorial is a *training tool* that you can use to develop proper programming skills. The aim of this text is to introduce you to programming using professionally recognized principles, while keeping things simple at the same time. It is not this text's singular goal to teach you a programming language (although you will be writing programs before you finish it). This text's goal is to give you the foundation to make you the best programmer you can be.

These 24-hour lessons delve into proper program design principles. You'll not only learn how to program, but how to *prepare* for programming. This tutorial also teaches you how companies program and explains what you have to do to become a needed resource in a programming position. You'll learn all about programming job titles and what to expect if you want to write programs for others.

Who Should Use This Book?

The title of this book says it all. If you have never programmed a computer, if you don't even like them at all, or if your VCR's timer throws you into fits, take three sighs of relief! This text was written for *you* so that, within 24 hours, you will understand the nature of computer program and you will have written programs.

This book is aimed at three different groups of people:

- Individuals who know nothing about programming, but who want to know what programming is all about.

- Companies that want to train non-programming computer users for programming careers.

- Schools—both for introductory language classes, and for systems analysis and design classes—that want to promote good coding design and style and that want to offer an overview of the life of a programmer.

Readers who seem tired of the plethora of quick-fix computer titles cluttering today's shelves will find a welcome reprieve here. The book you now hold talks to newcomers to programming without talking down to them.

What This Book Will Do For You

In the next 24 hours, you will learn something about almost every aspect of programming. The following topics are discussed in depth throughout this 24-hour tutorial:

- The hardware and software related to programming
- The history of programming
- Programming languages
- The business of programming
- Programming jobs
- Program design
- Internet programming
- The future of programming

Can This Book Really Teach Programming in 24 Hours?

In a word, yes. You can master each chapter in one hour or less. (By the way, chapters are referred to as "hours" in the rest of this book.) The material is balanced with mountains of shortcuts and methods that will make your hours productive and hone your programming skills more and more with each hour.

Conventions Used in This Book

Each of the 24 hours ends with question-and-answer sessions and additional quizzes whose answers appear in Appendix A, "Answers to End of Chapter Questions."

This book uses several common conventions to help teach programming topics. Here is a summary of those typographical conventions:

- Commands and computer output appear in a special monospaced computer font.
- Words you type also appear in the monospaced computer font.
- If a task requires you to select from a menu, the book separates menu commands with a comma. Therefore, this book uses File, Save As to select the Save As option from the File menu.

In addition to typographical conventions, the following special elements are included to set off different types of information to make them easily recognizable.

Special notes augment the material you read in each hour. These notes clarify concepts and procedures.

You'll find numerous tips that offer shortcuts and solutions to common problems.

The cautions warn you about pitfalls. Reading them will save you time and trouble.

 Each hour contains new term definitions scattered throughout to explain important new terms.

HOUR 1

Computers as Tools

If you have given up instead of giving in to all the technical manuals and error messages that invade the computer industry, the next 24 hours will show you that not only are computers simple to understand, but they are easy to program as well. Despite the widespread promises of *user-friendly computing*, the mysteries of computers still elude many today. A visit to any bookstore verifies that many people are craving sincere help with computers. Look at your local community college's curriculum and you'll find class after class with titles such as "Introduction to Computers," "Computer Concepts," "PCs for Those Who Can't Even Spell PC," and "PC Programming for Beginners."

The book you now hold promises you these things above all else: to respect your ability to think and learn by teaching to you and not down to you or above your head. This tutorial shows that you don't have to be a wizard to become proficient (or even an expert) with computers. This hour's lesson introduces you to the way computers are used in business and in the home from a programmer's perspective. Without programs, computers would be nothing more than big calculators.

The highlights of this hour include:

- How to determine the true difference between data and information
- What a program is
- What the three most common misconceptions are about computers
- How computers are used in the home
- How computers are used in business
- What makes a successful computer information system

What a Computer Does

Most people today have some understanding of a computer's purpose. A computer helps people balance their books or track their inventory. If you want to begin programming, you have probably used a computer for some time. Nevertheless, as a future programmer, perhaps you should review some fundamental computing concepts before mastering the ins and outs of a new computer language.

At its simplest level, a computer *processes data*. Many businesses call their computer programming departments *data processing departments* because computers process data into meaningful information. You may not have considered the difference between the words *data* and *information* before, but there is a tremendous difference to a computer professional.

NEW TERM *Data* (plural for *datum*, although this book uses *data* for both singular and plural, as is common) is made up of raw facts and figures. *Information*, on the other hand, is processed data. Information has meaning; data, in its raw form, does not. Figure 1.1 shows the fundamental data processing model. Notice that data goes into the computer, the computer processes that data, and meaningful information is the result. The computer and its programs perform the processing of the input; therefore, the program turns data into useful information.

FIGURE 1.1.

Data processing at its most fundamental level.

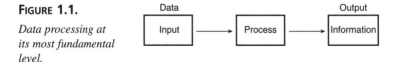

The data is generally input from some input device such as a keyboard. The information generally goes out to an output device such as a screen, printer, or disk file. As you will see throughout these 24 lessons, the computer's input and output can come from many different types of devices.

1

INFORMATION IS USEFUL

Data by itself is not useful to people who need to make decisions with it. People need information—the processed data—to make decisions. The president of a large company is concerned about the payroll for the company's 1,500 workers. When times are good for the company, the president wants to reward the employees accordingly. Therefore, the president might make a request to see the payroll figures for the last three months to analyze exactly where the company can direct more benefits.

Does that president need a list of every individual, down to the lowest paid part-time clerk? Does the president want the weekly payroll figures for 1,500 people for the last three months? Maybe, but that type of data would not be as useful as the total payroll per department, the payroll increases over this time last year, or the average payroll per employee compared to other companies in the same business. Such information, derived from data, is much more useful to the president. A computer with the right program can rapidly produce the kind of payroll figures the president needs. The source for that useful information would come from the detailed payroll data.

NEW TERM The program is the driving force behind any job that a computer does. A *program* is a list of detailed instructions that the computer carries out. The computer cannot do anything without a program. It is the job of the programmer to design and write programs that direct the computer to take raw data and transform that data into meaningful information for the end-user. The *end user* (or just *user*) of the computer is generally the non-technical, non-programming person who needs the results (the information) that the computer provides.

What's data to one person might be information to someone else. To the clerk, the clerk's salary figure is vital and meaningful information; to the company president, it might just be part of a pool of meaningless data.

The programmer is most responsible for guiding the computer. Learning to program computers takes awhile, but it is rewarding. Computer programming offers the advantage of instant feedback, unlike a lot of other jobs you can train for. Before you finish the next 24 hours, you will be writing your own programs and seeing the results. Many programming texts assume that you already understand the background of computers and how they work from a programmer's perspective, but this book guides you through the programming maze and directs you toward working as a programmer.

Common Misconceptions

It seems as though people who like computers love them, but people who don't like computers absolutely abhor them. Most of the time, a person's dislike for computers directly reflects a lack of knowledge about computers. Despite worldwide usage, many people still know very little about computers. To those people, computers and the programs that drive them are nothing more than magic boxes that mere mortals need not understand.

This text aims directly at the heart of the matter: Computers are easy to use and easy to program. A computer is nothing more than a dumb machine that "knows" absolutely nothing. A computer is like a robot that waits on your every command and acts out your instructions exactly as you give them. Of course, sometimes your instructions are incorrect. If they are, the computer goes right ahead and attempts them anyway.

> Don't fear computer programming. Computers are tools to help you get your job done. You can learn to program.

You may have heard horror stories about a computer deleting someone's bank balance because of a bad program. You might believe that someday a computer is going to take over the world. People who often fear the worst with computers simply know little about them. These people fear that the computer somehow can do more than it really is capable of doing. A computer is just a machine, not a replica of a living human being's mind. A computer cannot take over the world any more than a car, an electric drill, or a dishwasher can. (Remember, you can always pull the plug if it does. . .but it won't.)

Most of the misconceptions about computers stem from a lack of understanding how computers work and what computers are physically capable of doing. This book wants to shoot down the myths and improve your understanding of these machines. You'll be programming computers in no time. The computer is nothing more than a tool that helps you do certain types of work. The computer itself is not bad or good. A hammer is a tool you can use for good (to build houses) or for bad (to break things). A computer in the wrong hands can be used for bad, but that isn't the computer's fault any more than it is the hammer's fault if someone misuses it.

Computers are not only useful tools; they are required tools of companies today. Most businesses, schools, and banks would have to close their doors if computers disappeared. There is simply too much data moving from point to point to handle the numerous transactions manually. Consider how difficult and dangerous it would be to control airplanes around major airports without computerized assistance. Computers perform needed analysis for business, produce mailing labels for charities, forecast the weather, improve air traffic control, and keep the kids entertained while teaching them math, science, and reading skills.

The next few sections attack the three most popular computer myths. Have you heard any of them? Did you think some were true?

Myth 1: Only Math Experts Can Program Computers

Thank goodness this is a myth and not reality—thousands of people would be out of work (including most computer book authors!). Computers would be elitist machines used by only the best engineers and scientists; the casual user could not master them. Computers would still be beneficial in some areas, but they would not provide the benefits that so many people can enjoy.

Not only can you be poor at math, but you don't have to like math or even have the desire to learn math to be a good computer programmer. The computer does all the math for you; that's one of its jobs. There are countless expert computer programmers in the world who cannot tell you the area of a circle or the square root of 64. Relax if you thought this myth was reality.

Programming can provide beneficial side effects. It turns out that, as you become a better programmer, you may find your math skills improving. Developing programming skills tends to improve your thinking on the left side of your brain (where doctors believe that math and numeric skills reside). Therefore, being good in math might be a result of programming, but it's not a prerequisite.

> People who favor logic puzzles, crosswords, anagrams, and word-search games seem to adapt well to programming, but again, liking these gaming activities is not a programming prerequisite. You will find that you can learn to program computers, and actually become extremely good at it, without liking math, being good at math, or having any flair at all for puzzles or word games.

Myth 2: Computers Make Mistakes

You might have heard the adage, "To err is human, but to *really* foul things up takes a computer!" This might be accurate, but only in that a computer is so very fast, it duplicates a person's mistakes rapidly.

Computers do not make mistakes—people make mistakes. If you have heard a bank teller tell you that $24 was incorrectly deleted from your savings account because "the computer program made an error," the teller probably has no idea what really happened. People program computers, people run them, and people enter the data that the computer processes.

The odds of a computer randomly fouling up a customer's bank balance are minute. Computers simply do not make random mistakes unless they are programmed incorrectly. Computers are finite machines; when given the same input, they always produce the same output. That is, computers always do the same things under the same conditions. Your job, as you learn to program, will be to reduce the chance of computer mistakes.

When a computer malfunctions, it does not make a simple mistake; rather, it *really* messes things up. When a computer fails, it typically breaks down completely, or a storage device breaks down, or the power goes out. Whatever happens, computers go all out when they have a problem, and it is usually very obvious when they have a problem. The good news is that computers rarely have problems.

| You, and everybody else, will know when a computer is broken. |

Before people invented computers, banks kept all their records on ledger cards. When a teller found a mistake (possibly one that the teller had made), do you think the teller said, "The ledger card made a mistake"? Absolutely not. Computers can have mechanical problems, but the likelihood of small mistakes, such as an incorrect balance once in a while, is just too small to consider.

Myth 3: Computers Are Difficult to Use

If computers were difficult to use, they would also be difficult to program. Computers are getting easier to use, and to program, every day. If you used a microwave or drove a car recently, the chances are good that you used a computer when you did. Yet, did you know you were using a computer? Probably not. The makers of computers have found ways to integrate computers into your everyday life to monitor and correct problems that might otherwise occur without them.

Of course, if you are reading this book, you want to learn enough about computers to write your own programs. Writing computer programs does take more work than using a microwave oven's computerized timer functions. The work, however, primarily involves getting down to the computer's level and learning what it expects.

Not only are computers getting easier to use every day, but you have more opportunities to learn about them than ever before. Cable television channels are loaded with educational shows about using and programming computers. Books and videos on the subject are all around you. There is probably a computer programming class now in session somewhere within 15 minutes of your house as you read this.

Think about the goals of the computer industry. Computer corporations want to make money. They want to make a lot of money, and the more people are buying their computers, the more money the corporations make. When they make more money, they supply more jobs and increase the nation's wealth. Do you think the computer industry wants to *limit* the number of people who can learn to use computers? Not at all. When the computer manufacturers make computers easier to use, more people will use them, more people will buy them, and computers will help more people do their jobs more effectively.

Some of this book explores the ways the computer industry is making computers easier to use and program. Operating environments such as Windows combined with today's word processors, for example, make printing and proofing your letters as easy as pushing buttons. Word processors are only one of the thousands of programs on the market. Manufacturers try to produce programs that are easier to use than the competition's so that you will purchase their product.

USER-FRIENDLY. . .NOT!

Too often, the term *user-friendly* appears in computer literature. In the 1960s and 1970s, when computers sales began their 35+ year boom that has yet to end, and were still difficult to use, someone in marketing (isn't that always the case?) coined the phrase *user-friendly*. *User-friendly* meant that the programs were friendly to the computer user, as opposed to other programs that must have required heavy training and were hard to use (maybe *user-antagonistic* is the opposite of *user-friendly*).

The problem with the label *user-friendly* is that it seems every program ever written since they coined the term is described as user-friendly. Nobody can measure whether a program is user-friendly because people have different likes and dislikes, and people all learn skills differently.

Computer Programs Benefit Many

Computers are wonderful tools that help make the world more productive. Our society is moving away from primarily industrial to more of an informational society. Information is considered a vital corporate asset. Today people have more information at their fingertips than ever before, thanks to computers.

The following sections attempt to give you a glance at the ways computers are being used today in both business and personal computing. While reading through the information, keep one idea firmly planted in your mind: The reason computers are so beneficial is that someone took the time to learn how they work and how to write the programs that do the jobs at hand. A computer without a program is like a blank cassette; a computer is useless without its programs because it is nothing more than a machine that you must direct every step of the way.

Computers in the Home

Walk into any computer store and the salespeople might say that you can use the computer to balance your checkbook and keep your recipes. Although a computer can certainly do those things, it can do much more as well. Actually, keeping all your recipes on the computer can make for one messy machine during flour sifting, and you probably don't want to turn on your computer every time you write a check. Nevertheless, the computer's quick retrieval time makes storing records almost painless.

One of the most beneficial uses of the home computer is for education. Adults as well as children are finding that computers can serve as teaching tutors, giving instant feedback on learning results. Complete computerized encyclopedias are commonplace today. With today's *multimedia* computers (computers that produce sounds and graphics), you can hear and watch people and events as you read about them on the computerized encyclopedia screen (as Figure 1.2 shows).

FIGURE 1.2.

Watch, hear, and read about subjects on your computerized encyclopedia.

The computer could not run a multimedia encyclopedia without programs. Programs cannot exist without programmers.

 If you have children, you might want to develop some learning programs for them once you learn how to write programs. Instead of a store-bought program, you can design a program with your child's specific needs in mind.

The Internet has changed the way people use computers. The Internet, a networked system of computers that you can access from your telephone, enables you to bank and shop from your own home. You can read thousands of magazines and books, search for investment information, and send electronic messages to anyone else on the Internet no matter where they are in the world. The Internet is not a program but the general name given to this loosely networked system of computers, but without programs, you would be unable to access the Internet from your PC.

Probably the most common use of computers in the home today is word processing. As you may already know, a word processor is a computerized typewriter (Remember those? Perhaps your local museum of ancient history may have one on display!), but it is really much more. You can type, edit, move, copy, store, retrieve, and print text of any kind with an ease unmatched by yesterday's typewriters. Today's word processing programs are so powerful, you can integrate both text and pictures and create your own publications at your desk. Figure 1.3 shows a newsletter being created with Word, one of today's most popular word processors.

This 24-hour tutorial is not intended to be a descriptive text of the entire computing industry. This book is going to prepare you for programming computers. If you are reading this book, you probably already use a computer at home or at work, and you might already use a word processor. Nevertheless, it is important, even in a text such as this one, to remind you of that which drives all uses of computers today: computer programs.

This hour shows you that the computer is nothing more than a tool, although it is a special kind of tool. It is one of the most general-purpose tools you will ever use in your life. One minute your kids are learning about the first moon walk on the encyclopedia and the next minute you're preparing a financial analysis for your business. You can use the computer to dial up an online banking service to transfer money from one account to another at 4:15 on a Sunday morning. You can store your family's genealogical history on the same disk that you keep your holiday mailing list.

FIGURE **1.3.**

Creating a publication at home.

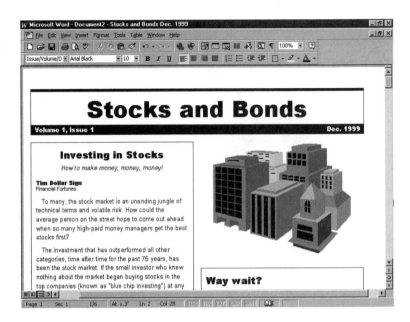

Although there are many programs already written for you to use, sometimes you need a program that fills a specific need and you cannot find one that does exactly what you want. When you are done with this book, you will know exactly what you need to design and write your own programs.

Computers in Business

NEW TERM   Although word processors are the most-frequently used type of program in business as well as home, electronic worksheets (also called *spreadsheets*) come in a close second. An electronic worksheet is a program that acts like a word processor for numbers. Accountants, financial analysts, and other business people use worksheets to perform "what if" analyses, which enable people to look at results given changing conditions.

Worksheets are useful for two reasons. First of all, worksheets are general-purpose programs that perform many different kinds of tasks. You might create one worksheet to compute business cycles and another to schedule employee lunch breaks. In effect, a worksheet is a program that non-programmers can direct to do a specific task.

NEW TERM   Figure 1.4 shows a worksheet being used to calculate payroll amounts. Before worksheets became popular (in the early 1980s), business people would have to hire programmers to write programs that performed specific calculations. Now, a business person can develop her or his own worksheet applications. A worksheet eliminates

1

the need for programming in one respect; that is, a skilled programmer does not have to get involved with the worksheet user. A worksheet enables the non-programmer to program at a higher level—one that does not require knowledge of a computer programming language. By moving the cursor, defining rows and columns, entering calculations, and using the worksheet's built-in *macro language* (a simple and high-level set of worksheet programming commands, explained in Hour 18, "Batch, Macro, and Scripting Languages"), non-programmers can enjoy autonomy with their computers.

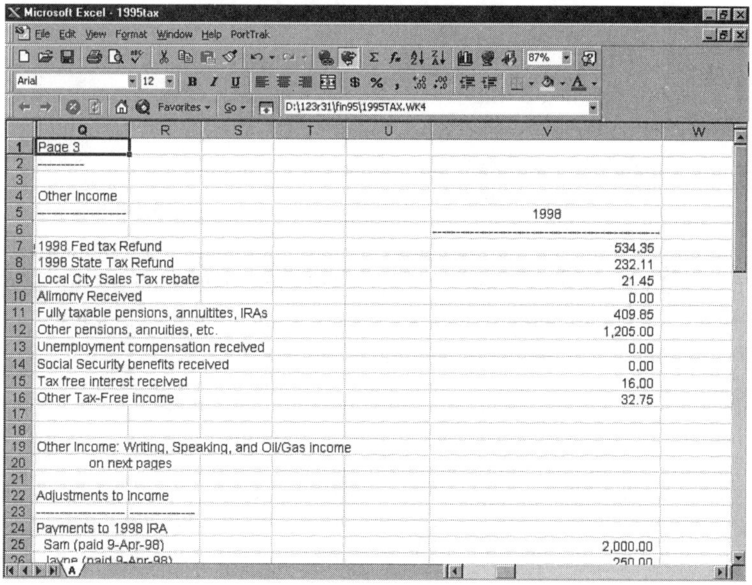

FIGURE 1.4.

Worksheets can be programmed to take the place of some other programs.

Despite its power and programmability by non-programmers, a worksheet is a limited tool. It is great for analyzing numbers of all kinds, but there is an abundance of jobs that worksheets are just too limited to handle. If the computer is to process transactions of any kind, such as printing payroll checks, or if the computer is to interact with the user from a focus point different from a grid of numbers and words (such as is done in educational programs), a worksheet just isn't enough.

NEW TERM Another popular business application is *database management*. One of the jobs that computers do best is process huge amounts of data. Companies can better manage that information when they organize it with a database program. Most database programs offer their own programming language that is generally more high-level (like the worksheet programming languages) than those used by programmers. By using the built-in programming languages of database programs, end-users (the non-programming users of computers) can develop simple applications that manage data in the way they prefer.

The *big three*—word processing, worksheets, and database management programs—compose only a handful of the useful applications in business today. Businesses, non-profit organizations, churches, scientific laboratories, sporting groups, musicians, drafters, engineers, and governmental agencies use computers in their day-to-day processing and would likely have to cease their operations without them. The future of computers lies in the hands of programmers, not end-users, for it is the programmers who write the programs that people use.

Computers in the Job Market

Despite all the popular programs in use by business today, there is still a vast number of programs that businesses need. Programmers will have work for years to come. The transactions of business are too complex and change too rapidly for current programs to fill all the computer users' needs.

Computers do not replace people. If you ever had that notion, or heard someone else say it, think again. The computer industry has created a tremendous number of new jobs. More and more people are needed to design computers, put them together, sell them, fix them, train people for them, and write the programs that drive them. That is where this book fits in; you have a challenging and fun career ahead of you if you want to program computers for a living.

CAN PROGRAMS REPLACE PEOPLE?

Have you ever heard of a computer replacing someone's particular job? Despite the fact that computers generate more jobs than they replace, there may be specific instances where a person was replaced with a computer.

Be careful that you do not blame the computer for this, however. Almost every time, the person whose job was replaced by a computer was unwilling to change or learn more to use the computer. Companies know that people are much more reliable and important to their future than computers. Companies often attempt to find a way to integrate the computer into a person's job, letting the computer take over the tedious chores such as adding lists of numbers and typing lists of names and addresses. By replacing a person's tedious job with the computer, that person can then move into a more enriching job that requires intuitive thinking that computers aren't capable of doing.

The more people learn about computers, the more they can use the computer to enhance their jobs. Computers offer a positive impact on the job market. Rarely has there ever been a one-for-one replacement of an employee with a computer, except in the case where the employee did not want to adapt to the changing world as today's employees must do to remain with globally competing firms. In that case, someone more open to learning new skills would be replacing the employee, not a machine.

NEW TERM Look in your Sunday newspaper's help-wanted professional section. You'll find that there is a severe shortage of computer programmers. Amidst the requests for C programmers, C++ programmers, Visual Basic programmers, systems analysts, senior systems analysts, object-oriented programmers, systems programmers, HTML coders, and application programmers, you may find yourself lost in a sea of uncertainty and *TLAs* (three-letter acronyms) that might, at first, seem hopeless. Do not fret; this book helps direct you toward areas of programming that might be right for you.

Hour 21's lesson, "How Companies Program," explores the chain of computer jobs and describes what each type of programming job is all about. If you are just starting out, you probably won't be able to go to work as the most senior-level programmer, but you will be surprised at the salary your programming skills can bring you.

People and Computers

People and computers can work together very well. A person cannot add a list of 100 numbers in the blink of an eye, but a computer can. A person cannot print 1,000 names and addresses sorted by ZIP code in under a minute, but a computer can. People get bored doing the same jobs over and over, but computers never get bored. Computers can perform varied tasks, from graphic art to scientific calculations, whereas people are often really good at only a handful of different kinds of tasks.

The computer, however, is no match for a human being. People can think, whereas a computer can only blindly follow line by line instructions. Where do those instructions come from? They come from people who write the programs of instructions. People have insight into problems that computers can never achieve. People are intuitive and creative. People think. People can deal with ambiguities far superior to those that the most power- ful computer in the world can. The computer is still years away that can understand a large vocabulary of human speech. Even then the computer will no doubt stumble between different accents and speaking patterns.

Using Programs Takes More Than a Computer

NEW TERM So many people today buy a computer thinking that all of their problems are solved, only to find that the computer offers little or no help at all. Perhaps more computer buyers should be taught that the computer by itself is useless. As a program- mer, it is incumbent upon you to teach others that a computer is useless, but a *computer information system* is useful. It is a computer information system that most people need when they purchase computers, but it is just a computer that they usually end up with.

NEW TERM A *system* is a collection of interrelated parts that work together for a common goal. The human body is a system; the hands, arms, legs, heart, ears, nose, and all the other parts work together to accomplish the common (and miraculous) goal of living. A computer is a system in that a computer's keyboard, printer, screen, and system unit work together to perform the needed task of computing.

A computer information system is more than just a computer. Buyers of computers are not fulfilled by the promise of computing unless they learn that a successful computer information system always consists of the following five components:

- Hardware
- Software
- People
- Data
- Procedures

The following sections look at each component of a computer information system and show you why all five components must be in place before a computer purchase is successful.

The Hardware

NEW TERM *Hardware* has been described as the parts of the computer you can kick. Although it is a sloppy definition, it does make the point that the hardware is the collection of physical components that make up the computer. The screen, printer, and system unit are hardware components. An analogy to stereo systems is useful here. Your stereo hardware is the tuner, amplifier, tape deck, and CD player. As stereo owners do not consider records, tapes, and CDs to be part of the hardware, neither do computer owners consider disks and programs to be hardware components. They fall into the category of *software*, which is discussed in the next section.

The falling prices of computers in the last few years have allowed more and more people to buy and use computers, but the falling prices have also led to many people buying a computer and then asking, "What now?" As mentioned in the previous section, a successful computer installation requires four more components than the hardware alone. Business owners often face a dilemma: only the hardware is affordable, but the hardware is just one-fifth of the equation that makes up a successful computer information system. When an accountant or attorney buys a $1,000 computer and gets it to the office, it is sad to note that the hardware is the least-expensive component of the computer information system.

Figure 1.5 shows a graph that might help illustrate this point. Even if you do not care for graphs, this one is easy to understand. You can see that time is going to the right and dollars are going up the left side of the graph. As time goes by, the cost of hardware steadily becomes cheaper. Today, you can buy more computing power than ever before. It seems that computers are obsolete almost as soon as you buy them because as soon as you do, another one takes its place that does a lot more for less money.

Some people fall into the trap of thinking they should wait to buy a computer and then never get one. If you need a computer, buy one knowing that it might be obsolete soon, but you can still get years of use out of the one you buy. If you keep waiting, you'll never have one. Too many months of waiting are wasted when you could have bought one and used it. As long as you buy one that is fairly advanced at the time (you don't have to be on the bleeding edge—maybe just on the tail end of that edge), the computer you buy should fill your needs nicely for a long time to come.

FIGURE 1.5.

Hardware is going down in price while the cost of other computer information system components is going up.

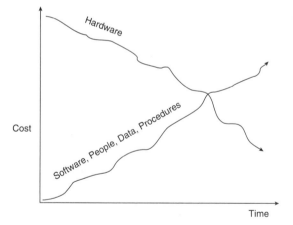

Figure 1.5 also shows another phenomenon that you must consider. The other four components of a successful computer information system are going up in cost over time. Therefore, when businesses buy the hardware, they have shelled out only the beginning of their overall computer costs. The cost of the other components of the computer information system is not hidden from computer buyers, but buyers do not always know what is in store.

Computer hardware cost is analogous to the cost of a stereo. At first you might think you pay much more for your stereo than for your CDs and tapes, but if you had a fire tonight and only could save either your stereo equipment or your records and tapes, which would you choose? Almost everyone would save their records and tapes; they are much harder to replace and much more costly than the actual equipment. You can replace your equipment within a week (and probably with more modern equipment thanks to the computer components in most stereos), but it could take another lifetime to replace all your records and tapes.

The next hour's lesson, "Computer Hardware Unmasked," explains the details of computer hardware from the programmer's perspective.

The Software

NEW TERM Although individual *software* (another term for the programs on computers) is going down in price, companies and individual computer owners invest more and more in software every year. Not only do people purchase new software as it comes out, but they update the older versions of programs they already have.

Businesses and individuals must factor in the cost of software when making computer decisions. Whereas an individual usually buys a computer and is done with the hardware purchasing for a while, software purchasing never seems to end—software changes rapidly. As a future programmer, this is welcome news because you have a secure career. For the uninformed computer purchaser, the cost of software can be staggering.

A business must also factor in the on-staff programmers and the time needed to write the programs it uses. More information on the programming and support staff appears in the next section.

NEW TERM When a company purchases software, it most often purchases a *software license*. If a company wants to buy a word processing program for 100 employees, legally it must purchase 100 copies of the program, or at least buy a *site license* that allows the company to use the software on more than one machine. When a company buys a program, it does not own the program. When you buy a record, you do not own the music; you have only purchased the rights to listen to the music. You cannot legally alter the music, record it, give away recordings of it, and most importantly, you cannot sell recordings that you make of it. The same is true for software that you buy. The license for individual software grants you permission to use the software on one computer at any one time.

The People

If a company sells cars, that company's most important asset is not the cars, but its people (and not the customers, but the employees; the customers will come if the employees do their jobs). If a company sells insurance, the insurance is not the most important asset, but the company's people are.

When a company buys a computer, whether it's a desktop computer or a huge mainframe computer that fills an entire room, the company must consider the cost of the people who will be a part of that computer information system. There will be costs associated with training, programming, and using the computer. There will have to be back-up personnel trained to take over the computer chores if someone else leaves. And as with software, the cost of personnel does not quit; it is an ongoing process. Often, a computer information system can save a company money in efficiency and processing power, but the company may have to hire additional staff, and people are expensive.

The Data

NEW TERM   Look all the way back at Figure 1.1 for a moment and consider this: It is vital that the data going into the computer be as accurate as possible. If bad data comes in, almost assuredly bad information goes out. This is known as *GIGO*, or *garbage-in, garbage-out*. The programmer must constantly be on the look-out for better ways to get data so that it is accurate. The program cannot always determine if the data is bad.

If a company computerizes its payroll, someone must enter the weekly payroll figures, direct the payroll processing programs, and be there to put the checks in the printer. The payroll data that was previously recorded by hand and sent to an accountant must now be accurately entered into the computer.

Some larger companies have complete staffs of 20 or more people whose full-time job is to sit in front of a computer and enter data. Large companies have massive amounts of data. Computers can process that data, but only when it is entered properly and accurately. Oil companies must account for every drop of oil they refine and sell, accounts payable and accounts receivable must be updated every period, and records must be filed. The entry of this kind of data is tantamount to its processing and is a cost that must be factored into the price of a successful computer information system.

> A company's data-entry department not only enters the data needed for its data processing, but it enters the data *twice*. Typically, this is done by two different people. Because of the garbage-in, garbage-out phenomenon, companies help ensure that their data is accurate with double-entry. Once two different people enter the same data, a computer program compares the data for discrepancies. Although errors can still creep in, the chances are slim.

The Procedures

Data processing procedures must be put into place soon after a computer is installed. These procedures generally include everything the computer user does on a daily basis to process the data needed. People change jobs, and the company must do what it can to provide adequate procedures in case someone else has to fill in.

Procedures also include computer security. Both physical security and data security must be maintained. Burglars won't touch desks and lamps, but they will take a computer. Whereas an office did not have to worry much about security before the computer, it now must maintain adequate protection of its computer systems. Although your job as a programmer may not include part-time deputy, you should be on the lookout for potential security problems. Make sure the computers are safely locked in their offices at night. Alarms and locks are now available that companies can install to make their computers more secure. Most insurance companies now offer additional policies that specifically cover computer thefts.

If a phone line is connected to the computer, there is potential for unauthorized callers getting through to the system. Adequate passwords should be assigned. Data protection is equally or more important than the hardware itself. Backup disks of all the data should be made each night and taken off-site (the backups would not be much use if a fire destroyed both the computer files and the backup disks sitting next to the computer).

Data privacy should also be maintained. Although most employees are honest, important company figures such as payroll amounts should be guarded. Don't let employees have direct access to their payroll files, and make sure the person who runs the payroll programs knows the importance of privacy.

Spread the Word

As you go through your programming career, keep in mind that all five components must be in place before a computer information system is successful. Although some companies cannot adapt overnight, most will make an honest effort to put all five components into place, but you must let them know how important the five components are. Your job as a programmer will be more vital to the companies you program for if you can do more than just program; you must learn to be their overall computer consultant, helping them to see the big picture.

1

Summary

Now that you know more about the computer industry as a whole, you have a good idea of where programmers fit into the picture. Computers can do nothing without programs and programmers are responsible for providing those programs.

The next hour explores computer hardware from the programmer's perspective. You need to understand how your hardware internally processes the data that your programs require.

Q&A

Q Once I write a program, is my job finished?

A It is said that a program is written once and modified many times. Throughout this 24-hour tutorial, you will learn the importance of maintaining a program after it is written. As businesses change and computing environments improve, the programs that people use must improve as well. Companies provide upgrades to software as new features are needed. The programs that you write today will have to change in the future to keep up with the competition as well as with new features that your users require.

Q What is the demand for programmers in the future?

A As Hour 21 explains, programming jobs will continue to be more plentiful as the use of computers increases. The demand for programmers has steadily increased over the past several years, and fortunately for the programmers, so have the pay and benefits associated with the programmer's job.

Workshop

The quiz questions are provided for your further understanding. See Appendix A, "Answers to End of Chapter Questions," for answers.

Quiz

1. What is the difference between data and information?
2. True or false: Data to one person may be information to another.

3. What is a program?

4. True or false: Computers never make mistakes.

5. Why should people not fear the computer replacing their jobs?

6. Which is the least expensive component of a computer information system: Hardware, software, people, data, or the procedures?

7. True or false: The price of software, people, data, and procedures is going down over time.

8. How does the term garbage-in, garbage-out apply to computer programs?

9. What department in large companies is responsible for providing most of the data for programs that the programmers write?

10. What are examples of procedures that a company must put into place when installing a computer information system?

Hour **2**

Computer Hardware Unmasked

The computer industry is one of the newest in existence. Medicine, mathematics, and engineering all date back to the early ages, but the first real computer was invented in the 1940s. Although the roots of computing go all the way back to the *abacus* (a mechanical calculating contraption used for addition and subtraction), the first electronic computers are around 50 years old. As a new programmer, you need to understand the trends of the industry to know where it is heading. You must understand the past to understand the future because there are some very obvious trends that have been going on since the first computer was invented. Primarily, computers are getting smaller, cheaper, and faster.

This hour takes you on a journey through the young roots of the computer industry. A different approach is taken from that of a lot of historical computing textbooks. Instead of concentrating on the facts and dates, the patterns of the evolving computer are presented with an emphasis on the programmer's view of this evolution.

The highlights of this hour include:

- Why the computer industry is one of the newest
- How computer technology evolved
- Why advanced technology allowed for the proliferation of computer technology
- What an operating system is
- How the computer's hardware interacts with the operating system
- How client/server technology enables companies to gain synergy with all kinds of computers, both big and small
- What steps a computer goes through when executing a program

The Computer's Background

The early computers were huge. They were known as *first-generation computers*. The first-generation computers, developed in the late 1940s, were *tube-based*. If you have ever looked inside an old television set, you may have seen lots of components that look like little light bulbs. These are tubes—also known as vacuum tubes—and they were the storage and computing mechanisms used in the early computers.

The first-generation computers were so massive, they took up several rooms—almost an entire building. Actually, the computers took up much of the space, and the gigantic air conditioning needed to keep the huge machines cool took the rest. Large power plants were needed to supply the power to the thousands of tubes inside these machines.

 The first-generation computers were incredibly powerful. . .well, they were not quite as powerful as today's solar-powered pocket calculators, but for their time, they were a needed invention. Until electronic computers came along, there was simply no way to compute and process large amounts of data.

The cost, size, and energy requirements kept the first-generation computers out of the hands of most organizations. It was not until the second generation came along that many more people began using them and learning more about computing possibilities. In the late 1950s, second-generation computers were composed of *solid-state technology* and used tiny parts called *transistors*. If you have ever seen the inside of a transistor radio, you may have seen the little colored parts, which are transistors. Transistors were the smaller replacements for vacuum tubes in electronic computers, immediately increasing computers' power, decreasing their size, and lowering their cost. Hundreds of transistors fit in the size of a single vacuum tube. Transistors are also much more reliable than tubes. With them, businesses and schools could finally afford these computing machines.

Do you see the benefits of lower-cost computing? Because more organizations could afford computers, more people had access to computers. A synergy took place because not only was the computer hardware being fine-tuned by leaps and bounds, but also advances in computer software were taking place at unbelievable rates. It was primarily during the second generation of computers that programming languages, such as those you will learn about in this tutorial, were developed.

2

Computers became a tool of business, and the 1960s saw an unbelievable growth of computer uses and jobs. More companies got into the computer business, science fiction stories and movies were produced that showed these computing machines in both good and bad light, and everybody knew that the computer was here to stay.

In the 1960s, NASA decided it wanted to send people to the moon. Imagine that! It had a realistic problem, however. Computers were needed to send people to the moon, and the lightning-fast calculations of computers were needed during the flight. Computers had to be in control of a lot of the operations.

Be aware of how seriously NASA had to take the computers in space missions. Split-second calculations are necessary or the rockets could end up on the sun, and *that* wouldn't be good (unless they went at night, of course).

The problems that NASA faced were not programming problems because there were enough programmers around to take care of the software. The problem was the distance from the earth to the moon. Even though the computers down on earth could control the rocket ship by radio signals, radio signals take time to travel through space. It takes about 3.5 seconds for a radio signal to make the trip from the earth to the moon. By that time (3 seconds is almost an eternity to a computer) the rocket could be in danger if course corrections were required.

NASA could not send rockets into space without on-board computers to control the rockets. Even though the second-generation computers were much smaller and lighter than the first, they were still too large to fit into a rocket ship. Therefore, NASA either had to design smaller computer components or shelve major space projects until it could.

Some NASA genius developed a component, still used today, called the *integrated circuit* (see Figure 2.1). The integrated circuit (also called an *IC* or *chip*) is about the size of a matchbook, black in color, and has silver connections that usually run along two sides, making the IC look like a high-tech black beetle. Whereas the transistor replaced vacuum tubes one-for-one, each integrated circuit replaced thousands of transistors. The entire circuitry of a second-generation computer could be squeezed into the space of a match-book. Computers instantly became dramatically smaller, NASA got to the moon and back with its on-board computers, we got desktop computers, a computer was now available to every person, and the *third-generation computers* were born and have thrived ever since.

FIGURE 2.1.

An integrated circuit chip contains many thousands of parts.

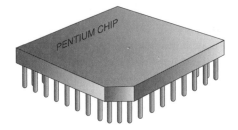

An integrated circuit is an almost magical device. Its designers use laser tools to install and connect the thousands of miniature components onto its wafer body. Integrated circuits are also known as *microprocessors*. Because of the microprocessor's widespread use in today's desktop computers, the term *microcomputer* was coined and the name stuck. Most people who read this book probably are using a microcomputer as their primary computing machine. The microprocessor chip is the actual computer; all other hardware related to the computer exists to send data to and from the microprocessor.

The term *machine* is used in the computer industry to mean *computer*. Unlike most other devices called *machines*, computers have relatively few moving parts. The printer and disk drives have moving parts, but there are few others.

You may be interested in a brief summary of some of the milestones in the computing industry. When you know where technology has been, you'll have a better idea of where, with your help, technology is heading. Table 2.1 offers a glimpse into the computing timeline in case you want some of the historical details.

TABLE 2.1 A BRIEF HISTORY OF COMPUTERS

Approximate Date	Description of Event
3000 B.C.	The abacus was invented and used for quick, manual addition and subtraction calculations.
1645 A.D.	A mechanical adding and subtracting machine called the *Pascaline* (after its inventor, the French mathematician Blaise Pascal) was invented.
1830	Charles Babbage, the *father of computers*, designed the first electronic computer called the *difference engine*. Unfortunately, the difference engine was never actually built, but today's computers are based on it.
1890	The 1890 census was predicted to be so vast that people-power alone could not tabulate it. Therefore, an inventor named Herman Hollerith invented the *punch card*. Census data was punched onto these cards, and tabulating machines churned through them computing the totals. The punch card was the primary input device for 20th century computers through the 1960s.
1937	An electromechanical calculator was built with the help of IBM. Although not truly an electronic computer because all of its parts were mechanical and moving, this *Mark I computer* (as it was named) proved that the theory of computing machines could be a reality and not just theory.
1939	The first vacuum tube calculating machine was invented.
1946	The first true general-purpose, vacuum-tube, first-generation computer, named the *ENIAC*, was invented.
1945–1952	Computers named the *EDSAV* and *EDVAC* were developed that had electronic memories that held both data and programs.
1957	FORTRAN, one of the oldest programming languages still in use today, was developed to aid scientific and mathematical programmers.
1959	The second-generation computers came on the scene.
1960	COBOL was developed to give business programmers the language they needed to write programs.
1964	The first version of BASIC, the most important language for start-up programmers, was written.
1965	The third-generation computers were perfected.

continues

2

TABLE 2.1 CONTINUED

Approximate Date	Description of Event
1976	BASIC was ported to the early microcomputers by Microsoft, a company formed and run by two teenagers out of their garage (one of whom, Bill Gates, still keeps his hand in the computer industry by running Microsoft, Inc., and accepting credit for being America's richest living person in the 1990s).
1976–1978	Two of the most important microcomputers that started the true trend of home computing, the Apple computer and Radio Shack's TRS-80, were invented and sold for a few hundred dollars each. Their low cost and widespread availability probably did more for the microcomputer industry than any other single accomplishment.
1981	The introduction of IBM's first microcomputer, the IBM PC, finally added stability to microcomputers. Until the PC was invented, lots of companies were making lots of incompatible machines. As the IBM PC sold more computers than anybody (including IBM) had predicted, more and more people saw the benefits of sticking to one kind of machine. Programs, data, and add-on parts could be used interchangeably as long as you had an IBM or an IBM-compatible computer.
1982	The American National Standards Institute (ANSI) agreed to a universally accepted standard for the C programming language. C would prove to be the most important computer language of the 1980s, spreading to larger computers and slipping into industries previously owned by the COBOL language stronghold.
1984	The Windows operating system began spurring interest.
1989	The C++ programming language was made available for a wide variety of microcomputers, helping spearhead the *object-oriented programming* (*OOP*) movement that promises to change the way programmers write programs.
1990	Visual Basic began taking shape to provide Windows programming skills without requiring huge investments in time.
1995	Windows 95 and Windows NT became the dominant operating systems of PCs and server computers.

There are expert programmers who have fantastic programming jobs who know less about the history of computers than you know now. There is so much literature that refers to the computer's background and to the different generations of computers that you will only benefit from having this cursory understanding of the computer's short history.

Today's Computers

If you read many texts on today's computers, you will see the terms *fourth-* and *fifth-generation computers* used sometimes. Most computer pundits agree that the distinction between generations after the third is nothing more than opinion. There has not been as obvious and distinct a separation of technology since the third generation as there were with the first three. Nevertheless, every day it seems that computer manufacturers are finding ways to squeeze more parts onto smaller integrated circuits at a fraction of the previous technology's cost.

The future of computer technology seems intent on repeating the previous 50 years. It appears that more and more computing power will be squeezed into smaller, more reliable, faster, and cheaper boxes. More and more people will use computers for more and more uses.

What this means to the programmer is twofold. First, as more people use computers, more programmers are needed to write the programs for the computers. Second, as computers become more powerful and faster, older uses of computers (and therefore, older programs) have to be updated to take advantage of the new hardware. This program *maintenance* becomes the programmer's most important job. Throughout the rest of this 24-hour tutorial, you will learn how important program maintenance is to the computing industry.

HOW FAST IS "FAST ENOUGH"?

Will there be a day when computers don't have to go any faster? Have they already reached that point? Think about this for a moment: If computers were several times faster than today's machines, forecasters could predict the weather with stunning accuracy— much more accurately than today. "So what?" you might still ask. Think about how many lives could be saved if the exact pattern and severity of every hurricane, tornado, and flood could be tracked weeks in advance. You can measure the advantages of working for faster computers in human lives. Completely accurate weather prediction is just one of the many areas, along with space exploration, statistics, economic policy planning, and scientific research, where computers much faster than today's versions would benefit society.

Are you going to be the programmer of the first computer capable of accurately predicting the weather?

2

The Types of Computers

Computers come in all shapes and sizes, but they primarily fall within four broad categories: *supercomputers*, *mainframes*, *minicomputers*, and *microcomputers*. Despite the fact that computers are getting smaller, there is still need for large computers. Businesses, banks, universities, and other large organizations need the power that larger computers bring. Although desktop computers are getting more powerful every day, the larger machines still produce hundreds of times more computing power than smaller ones do.

A few years ago, distinctions among the various kinds of computers were more important than they are today. Today's computing environments, with the exception of home computer users, almost always consist of a collection of several of these computer types networked together in some way.

Computers are designed to be multitasking machines. That is, even though computers can perform only one instruction at a time, they do it so fast that more than one program can run at the same time. On larger computers, more than one person can share the computer and each person thinks he or she is the only person on that computer at the time.

Before delving into the hardware specifics of computers, it will be helpful to define what the four types of computers are all about.

Supercomputers

The most expensive and fastest computers in existence are supercomputers. Supercomputers are so fast that they are best used for scientific applications where heavy mathematical calculations must be swift. The expense of supercomputers and their lack of availability (there are only a few hundred in existence) cause most businesses to turn to the other kinds of computers mentioned in subsequent sections. Supercomputers are so fast, liquid hydrogen, helium, or other gasses are cooled to tremendously cold levels to keep these fast computers running at peak performance. (Heat, caused by resistance in the wiring, will slow a computer.) The cost of supercomputers keeps them in the hands of only a few large government and business organizations.

Mainframes

Mainframe computers are the cornerstone of modern-day, large-business, data processing. When heavy processing and several thousand users must be handled at once, a mainframe is the primary choice for businesses. Mainframe computers require large staffs of maintenance personnel, operators, programmers, and data-entry clerks. They run around the clock, and any *downtime* (machine failure) is costly to the companies that rely on them.

Mainframe computers must be housed in a large room or two because of their large system units and the numerous storage devices attached to them. These rooms are often environmentally controlled, being cooled to keep the computer running at a comfortable level, and the air is filtered to keep as much dust out of the system as possible. Most companies with mainframes have two or more mainframe computers connected to each other, as well as networked to minicomputers and microcomputers. The smaller computers offload some of the workload from the mainframe, leaving the mainframe to handle the more calculation-intensive tasks.

Minicomputers

A minicomputer is generally a multiuser computer that can handle up to 300 users at the same time. A minicomputer typically is no larger than a refrigerator. The minicomputer is not as fast as a mainframe, but it does not cost as much, either. Despite these advantages, the minicomputer has virtually become extinct. As the microcomputer gets more powerful and becomes fast enough to handle more than one user seamlessly, fewer companies replace their outdated minicomputers with additional minicomputers. Today's microcomputer storage capacities rival that of minicomputers, and the cost of the microcomputer is much less than that of the minicomputer.

During the 1970s and 1980s, the minicomputer filled a niche that the microcomputer was not capable of filling at the time. Mainframes were out of reach to a lot of companies, and the microcomputer was not powerful enough for serious multiuser business data processing. Therefore, despite the virtual extinction of minicomputers, programmers owe many of the plentiful programming job openings to minicomputers that made it possible for smaller companies to integrate computers into their business over the past 20 years.

Microcomputers

The microcomputer is the smallest, least expensive, and most popular computer in existence today. Often called *desktop computers*, *PCs*, and *personal computers*, microcomputers have seen a tremendous growth in popularity since the late 1970s and their fast-paced growth seems to be continuing into the future.

The most popular type of microcomputer in use today is known as a *PC-compatible* or, more rarely these days, an *IBM-compatible* computer. The line of PC-compatibles includes a microprocessor from the 80X86 family of processors. Intel is the company that developed the original 8088 (the chip on which the first IBM PC that defined PC-compatibility was based) and has since improved the chip. The improved versions of the chip are named 80286, 80386, 80486, the Pentium, and Pentium II, and new names appear as Intel improves upon the chip's speed and capabilities.

When a manufacturer releases a new processor, that processor is almost always faster and has more components squeezed into a smaller space than the one that came before it. The massive improvements made in chip technology makes for PC speeds that double every two years or so.

Because businesses originally adopted the IBM PC *en masse* instead of Apple's original line of computers named the Apple II, no Apple computer since the IBM PC was introduced has enjoyed as big of a sales share as the PC-compatibles. Apple's current line of microcomputers, the Macintosh line, is a high-quality array of computing power that excels in graphics and usability features. Despite the tremendous features of the Macintosh, however, the PC-compatible rules the world of small computing.

PCs are taken very seriously in the world of business and research. "A PC on every desktop" seems to be the objective of today's management. Laptop and even palm-sized PCs are now small enough to fit in a briefcase, and few business travelers leave town without their PCs. It is also common to see at least one microcomputer in most homes—something almost unheard of a decade ago. Thanks to the productivity of programmers who make the computers perform useful tasks, many homes have a second and even third PC and more homes are linking them together in a home-based network.

Client/Server Computing

Because of the popularity of the PC, and the processing abilities of the mainframe computer, many of today's companies are combining the power of these machines to provide *client/server computing*. The mainframe, the server, provides the huge databases available to the company's PCs (the clients) that are connected together on a network. The users at the PCs can run the programs on the PC's disk, but also pull data from the larger server for processing as well.

Client/server computing is also known as *enterprise computing*. By utilizing client/server technology, a company can increase its overall computing power by adding PCs or by increasing its mainframe or minicomputer server. Many of today's programming languages are well-suited for the client/server model.

2

Because of the wide availability and low cost of PCs, most programmers learn programming on PCs. The focus of this book is programming on the PC, although attention is also devoted to programming on the larger computers. This text assumes that you are learning to program on a PC, but as your skills progress, you someday may be programming in a larger organization. You will not only learn to write programs, but you will also learn how a company goes about designing and writing programs.

Hardware from the Programmer's Perspective

This section gives you a brief overview of computer hardware and how the programmer can direct that hardware in programs. The PC is the primary focus of this discussion. If you will be programming a larger computer, such as a mainframe, all of the same information applies on a much larger scale. All computers, from supercomputers to the smallest PCs, have the same primary components; they all have at least one processor, memory, and input and output devices connected to them.

Understanding PC Hardware

Figure 2.2 shows a typical desktop PC system. Almost every PC has a system unit, monitor, keyboard, mouse, modem, and printer. Long-term storage is achieved through disk drives, CD-ROM, and DVD storage. Larger computers have the same parts, although they usually have more of each and are scattered over a larger area. Some mainframes have as many as 1,000 keyboards, 50 disk drives, and 20 printers attached to them. The programmer has a serious vested interest in all the hardware included with a computer because the programmer's programs must interact with these devices.

The primary component of a PC is the *system unit*. It is in the system unit that the primary memory, power supply, disk drives, and, most importantly, the microprocessor are located. The microprocessor is often called the *CPU* (for *central processing unit*). The CPU is the true computer because it does all the work of processing the data and producing the information needed.

FIGURE 2.2.

The PC contains all the components necessary for storage, processing, input, and output.

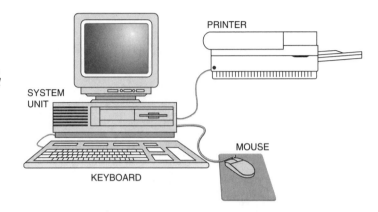

Figure 2.3 shows a high-level diagram of the inside of a typical system unit. The power supply steps down the wall outlet's voltage from 110 volts to around 5 volts. The circuitry inside the computer needs very little voltage to run. A fan next to the power supply keeps the air circulating enough to keep the temperature down. The monitor and printer often consume much more energy than the computer itself.

FIGURE 2.3.

The programmer should understand the inside of a PC's system unit.

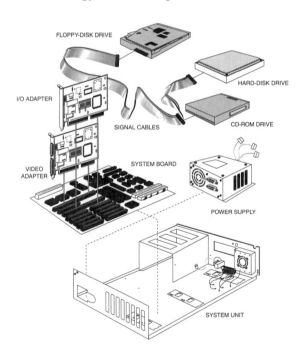

Have you looked in a PC? You won't void the warranty if you do. Your PC's manual should explain how to open the system unit cover. By all means, unplug the power first and properly ground yourself before looking inside. The manual's instructions should guide you. Many people are surprised at how *little* is actually inside these machines that cost as much as $4,000! Despite the constant reduction in PC prices, the cost of a PC goes more toward the research needed to design the PC than to the actual components themselves.

2

Speed Counts

The speed of the CPU is measured in *megahertz*, often abbreviated to *MHz*. The speed determines the number of instruction cycles the CPU can perform in a single second. *Mega* always means million, so a 400MHz CPU can process 400 million instructions per second. The megahertz measurement gives the industry a fairly consistent yardstick to measure and compare CPU speeds. The first IBM PC measured in at a whopping speed of 1.7MHz! The industry thought it had found nirvana when that 8088 CPU hit the shelves. Little did the industry (or even IBM) predict the future impact of that first extremely slow PC.

These megahertz-measured instructions are different from the individual instructions inside the programs that you write. Your programs are considered to be a higher level of instruction that must be broken down to more primitive instructions that the CPU accepts.

In the back of the system unit resides a set of expansion slots that hold electronic circuit cards. These slots enable you to expand the capability of your computer so that you can add storage and additional devices to the computer later. It is in these expansion slots that you can add an expansion card for a *modem*, which lets your computer communicate with other computers via the telephone lines. (Modems also can reside outside your computer as a separate device plugged into one of your PC's expansion ports.)

The devices inside and outside the system unit are often called *peripheral devices*. A device is either an input device, output device, or both input/output device (*I/O device* for short). To know which is which, picture yourself as the program running inside the memory directing the CPU. If data is coming in to you, such as that from a keyboard, the device is an input device. If you are sending information out of the computer, such as to the printer, you are writing to an output device.

The memory of the computer generally resides inside the system unit as well. Memory is housed in small integrated circuit chips (generally smaller than the CPU) inside the computer. The important memory is known as *RAM*, which stands for *random access memory*. When you execute the programs you write, the computer stores those programs in RAM during the program's execution. RAM is volatile; that is, when you turn the computer off, the contents of RAM are automatically erased.

If the different memory measurements such as 640KB and 32MB confuse you, don't be alarmed; there is an easy-to-understand explanation. In computer terminology, KB means 1,024 bytes, although most computer people round the number down to an even 1,000 when discussing memory. (A *byte* is any single character in the computer.) Therefore, 640KB means approximately 640,000 bytes of storage. An MB after a number means megabyte. *Mega* is computer lingo for million. 32MB means approximately 32 million bytes of storage. A *gigabyte* is approximately one billion bytes of storage.

Disks, CD-ROMs, and DVDs hold the long-term storage of your programs and data. These technologies are non-volatile; that is, they retain their memory after the power is turned off because data is stored on them magnetically. If the drive is writeable, such as disks and some CDs, you can store data and the programs that you write there.

The Operating System

The hardware is useless without an operating system. The operating system is the go-between for the hardware and the programs and data. When a program issues a command to write to or read from a device, the operating system carries out the work. Figure 2.4 shows the logical view of the operating system and the rest of the computer's hardware and software.

FIGURE 2.4.

The operating system helps the software communicate with the hardware.

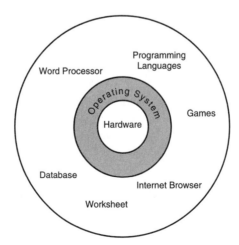

Notice that Figure 2.4 includes, in its outer circle that lists programs, the entry *Programming Languages*. A programming language is just a program that you use to write other programs!

The operating system forms a common interface for programs. Instead of you having to include all the specifics of writing to the disk, moving the read/write disk head, spinning the disk platter, and so on, the operating system makes sure all these tedious chores are done for you. Windows works as the most popular operating system today for PCs and most client/server technologies enable mainframes to communicate with Windows-based PCs. Windows is a *graphical user interface (GUI)* with which you interact using your keyboard and mouse.

> Not every computer supports a windowed environment. Some mainframes, for example, still use text-based operating systems. Other computers, such as the Macintosh, use a GUI but not the PC's Windows as the graphical user interface. Older versions of Windows still in use today, such as Windows 3.1 and other versions that came out prior to Windows 95, were not even true operating systems. These Windows versions were simply outer layers to the computer's native operating system so that the user could interact with the computer using the windowed advantages that the text modes did not provide.

Not only does the operating system form a common interface for programs, but also it forms a common interface for users. No matter which Windows program you use, you will open a file or request help in virtually the same manner using the same windows (called *dialog boxes*). Users depend on interfaces that are uniform because the users can learn how to access a menu in one Windows program and already understand how to access the menu in every other Windows program also.

The operating system contains routines that you, as the programmer, can access and use in your own programs. For example, if you want to read a list of files located in a certain folder on the computer, you can access an operating system routine that returns the list of files for you. Some programming languages rely more heavily on operating system routines than others so the amount of support you can borrow from the operating system is dependent on the language that you use.

The operating system itself is nothing more than a huge program running on your computer. The operating system is always running when your computer is running so that other programs can access the computer's hardware. Without the interface, programs have a difficult time controlling such devices as the disk drives. In some special circumstances, a *utility program*, one that monitors, analyzes, and performs system checks and maintenance, can access devices without the operating system being loaded. To write such programs that don't rely on the operating system takes much more tedious effort, however, than writing typical end-user kinds of programs.

When you write a program to access a peripheral device, such as the screen, your program does not need to bother with the physical characteristics of the screen. Your program doesn't have to know exactly how large the user's screen is, for example, to write to the screen. Your program only needs to, through the instructions that you write, send output to the screen directed through the operating system. The operating system of each user's individual computer takes care of routing the exact, required commands to the computer's screen. The operating system forms a common program interface to all the computer's hardware.

Hardware and Programs

When you run a program that someone (perhaps you) wrote for your computer, the following events take place:

1. You issue a command to start the program. Often, the command is little more than an icon or a menu selection in Windows.

2. Your operating system interprets your command and searches the disk or other storage device (perhaps a CD-ROM or network) for the program.

3. If found, the operating system loads the program from the disk into RAM. The entire program does not have to reside in memory for the program to begin. Most operating systems load only as much of the program as needed. If the requested program is not found, the operating system issues an error message.

4. The program begins *running* or *executing*. In other words, the computer begins following the instructions inside the program.

5. During the program's execution, other programs may be running as well. The user and even the operating system itself can start and stop programs during the execution of other programs.

6. During the program's execution, the program may request that the operating system access peripheral devices and read or write data to those devices.

7. When the program finishes executing, the operating system regains control of the resources reserved by the program, generally RAM memory that is freed up, and the program ceases executing. The computer then returns to the operating system's or to another running program's instructions to determine what happens next.

Keep in mind that only the operating system, in most cases, has control of the computer the entire time that the computer is turned on. As the user operates the machine, various programs begin and end, sometimes executing at the same time. Unless the computer contains multiple CPUs, the computer can perform only one instruction at a time, but the computer operates so fast, it appears that programs are *multitasking* (running at the same time).

PROGRAMS AND FILES

Not every file on every computer disk is a program. The following list details just some of the things that might be stored as a file on your disk: programs, data, operating system–related programs, word processor documents, graphics files, multimedia files that contain sound and video, and setup files that control the way a program loads.

Often, a program interacts with other programs and files. The program files on a disk don't execute until the program is loaded into memory. The program often creates, reads, and writes other files, such as when working with data needed for later retrieval.

In the next hour's lesson, "What Is a Program?," you will learn more about the details that take place during the life of a running program.

Is It Too Late to Start?

Sometimes, beginning programmers fear they are starting too late. Hour 24's lesson, "The Future of Programming," addresses some issues that newcomers to programming must face when deciding to program. Nevertheless, you have not gone too long without learning to program. As a matter of fact, programmers can now produce more powerful programs more quickly than programmers ever could since the invention of computers because of the advanced programming technology available today.

It is true that with easier tools, programmers don't always understand the underlying principles involved, whereas programmers who have been around for a while understand more fundamental concepts. Nevertheless, you don't have to understand how an engine works to drive a car and you don't have to understand exactly how bits of data stream in and out of a microprocessor to learn to program. Therefore, put your programming cap on, set your keyboard in high gear, and prepare your users for the powerful programs that you are going to write.

Summary

Now that you know where the computer industry has been, you will have a good idea of where it is heading. The computers of tomorrow will be faster, cheaper, and smaller than today's, and more people will be needed to program them. Isn't it a good thing that you decided to learn to program when you did? Being one of the newest industries, computing is still evolving rapidly and changing the world as it goes. Windows is making PCs simpler to use and as they get more simple, more people will require them, more programs will be required, and more programmers will be needed.

The next hour explores the structure of a program in more depth. After Hour 3's lesson, you will have a better understanding of what programs can and cannot do.

Q&A

Q Instead of using common program elements, such as the typical Windows menu bar, shouldn't I design new interfaces for the programs I write?

A Look at the most popular programs sold today. Besides games, which are in a category of their own, most programs have the same interface. The bestselling word processor, Microsoft Word, contains a menu and dialog boxes that look almost identical to the bestselling worksheet program, Microsoft Excel. That commonality does not appear because both happen to be made by Microsoft. Microsoft realizes that users want consistency so Microsoft puts the same kind of user interface, with similar menus and online help routines, in all programs. The users, therefore, don't have to learn a new way to control the program every time they use a different program.

You should try to achieve this same uniformity in the programs that you write. You will not be plagiarizing other programs just because your menu structure mimics Microsoft's. You will be doing your users a service. As a matter of fact, Microsoft, the author of Windows, publishes guidelines for writers of Windows programs (available on its Web site at www.microsoft.com, along with scores of other helpful materials for programmers) that state explicitly how to set up menu options, how to organize programs for consistency, and how to design your screens so they have the same look and feel as other Windows programs. You want your users to feel comfortable using your program and that will occur as long as you follow industry standards.

Workshop

The quiz questions are provided for your further understanding. See Appendix A, "Answers to End of Chapter Questions," for answers.

Quiz

1. Why are large computers still needed?
2. How did the introduction of *solid-state technology* enable the proliferation of computers?
3. What is a CPU?
4. True or false: Computers have reached a point where speed is no longer an issue.
5. Why is it important to cool supercomputers down?
6. What is client/server computing all about?
7. How does the operating system tie both hardware and software together?
8. True or false: Windows is just a program.
9. Why should programmers use fairly advanced computers when writing programs for others?
10. What is meant by *program execution*?

2

Hour **3**

What Is a Program?

The words *program* and *programmer* are mentioned throughout each of these 24 lessons and you've undoubtedly heard them before you picked up this book. Before delving into the specifics of programming languages, this hour's lesson attempts to explain what a program really is. A firm grasp of this chapter's material is a prerequisite for moving on to the programming languages later in this book.

As you read this lesson, keep in mind that programming is rewarding, not only financially, but also mentally and emotionally. Programmers often feel the same sense of creative rush that artists and skilled craftspeople feel while honing their projects. Writing a program, however, can be tedious. It is often a detailed task, and ample frustration comes with the territory. The computer's quick feedback on your mistakes often provides a sense of accomplishment that keeps you programming until you get it right.

The highlights of this hour include:

- How programs are like directions for the computer
- Why programs must be detailed

- Why programs must reside in memory instead of remaining on the disk drive when you execute them
- Whether programming is considered an art or science
- What some of the more common programming languages are
- Why computers cannot yet understand a human language
- Which types of errors can occur in programs

Understanding the Need for Programs

When individuals and companies need a program, there are three ways they can obtain one:

- Buy one that's already written
- Buy one and modify it so that the customized version does exactly what they need
- Write their own

There are advantages and disadvantages to each option (see Table 3.1). The first two options are much quicker than the third, and also much less expensive.

TABLE 3.1 ADVANTAGES AND DISADVANTAGES OF OBTAINING PROGRAMS

Option	Advantages	Disadvantages
Buy one	The program can be obtained quickly and inexpensively.	The program may not be exactly what is needed.
Buy and customize one	A usable program that does what is needed can be obtained fairly quickly. Also, the program is relatively inexpensive, depending on the changes needed.	It isn't always possible to modify the program.
Write one	The program (after proper design and testing) does exactly what you want it to do.	This option is very expensive and takes a lot longer than the other options.

Most microcomputer users choose the first option because the programs are fairly inexpensive given their power. Because companies such as Intuit, Microsoft, Borland, and Symantec sell so many of the same versions of programs, they can do so at fairly inexpensive prices. Individual microcomputer users simply don't have the resources that companies have to write every program they need.

Companies, on the other hand, do not always choose the first option, although you may question why. Companies spend many years developing products and services that distinguish themselves from other companies. When a company computerizes any of its record keeping, it is vital that new programs reflect exactly what the company already does. The company should not have to change the way it does business just so it can use programs found in stores or in mail-order software outlets. Purchased programs have to be generic so the producers of the programs can sell them to more than one customer.

The second option, buy a program and customize it, might then seem like the smartest option, but it is chosen least often. If companies could buy a program that is already written, they would have a framework in which to quickly adapt it to their specific needs. The problem is that software is rarely sold; instead, it is *licensed*. When you buy a program, you do not own the program, you only own the right to use it. You cannot legally change it, sell it, or copy it (except for backup purposes).

Not only are there legalities involved, but sometimes you cannot physically change the software either. As you will learn later in this chapter, once a program is written it is translated to a compressed format that programmers can no longer modify.

Therefore, although it is expensive and time-consuming to write programs from scratch, most businesses prefer to do so, keeping large programming departments on hand to handle the programming load. A company might have several members of its data processing staff spend a full year writing a program that is a lot, but not exactly, like one the company could buy. Despite the cost and effort involved, it is worth it to the company not to have to conform to a program they buy from someone else. The program, once written, conforms to the company's way of doing business.

> Some companies have found that they can sell programs they develop to *other* firms doing similar business, thereby recapturing some of their development costs. As you write programs for your company or for individuals, keep in mind the possible subsequent sale of your program to others.

Companies often measure the amount of time it takes to write programs in *people-years*. If it takes two people-years to write a single program, it is estimated that two people could write it in a single year, or one person would take two years. A 20 people-year project would take 20 people one year, or one person 20 years, or ten people two years, and so forth. This measurement is only an estimate, but it gives management an idea of how it should allocate people and time for programming projects.

If you were to become a contract programmer, the people-year measurement is a great tool to use when pricing your service. You might give a customer an estimate of the price per people-year (or, for smaller projects, perhaps you would estimate the job in people-months or -weeks). If you hire programmers to help you finish the program, you may finish early but you can still charge fairly for each person's labor due to the fact that you priced the programming job in people-years and not in calendar time.

Programs, Programs, Everywhere

Why aren't all the programs ever needed already written? Walk into any software store today and you'll see hundreds of programs for sale. There are programs for everything: word processing, accounting, drawing, playing games, designing homes, going online, and planning trip itineraries. It seems as if any program you need is within reach. Because computers have been around for 50 years, you would think that everybody would be about done with all the programming anyone would need for a long time.

If all the programs needed were already written, you would not see the large listings of "Programmer Wanted" ads in today's newspapers. The fact is, the world is changing every day, and businesses and people must change with it. Programs written ten years ago are simply not up-to-date with today's practices. They were also written on computers much slower and more limited than today's machines. As hardware advances are made, the software must advance with it.

 One of the most timely issues facing programmers before the turn of the century is the notorious Year 2000 problem that, perhaps, will affect computers and therefore the businesses that rely on computers (which is just about *every business today*). Hour 24, "The Future of Programming," discusses the ramifications of the Year 2000 problem and how programmers will be affected by this problem both before and after the year 2000 is reached.

There is a tremendous need for programmers, today more than ever. As computers become easier to use, some people believe that programmers will become relics of the past. What they fail to realize is that it takes top-notch programmers to produce those easy-to-use programs. More importantly, it takes programmers to modify and improve upon the vast libraries of programs in use today.

Programs as Directions

If you have ever followed a map into unfamiliar territory, you know what it is like for your computer to follow a program's instructions. With only the map, you feel blind as you move from place to place, turning left and right, until you reach your destination or find that you made a wrong turn somewhere. Your computer, as the previous chapters explain, is a blind and dumb machine waiting for you to give it directions. When you do, the computer acts out the instructions you give it without second-guessing your desires. If you tell your PC to do something incorrectly, it does its best to do so. Recall this definition of a program (from Hour 1, "Computers as Tools"):

A program is a list of detailed instructions that the computer carries out.

The term *detailed* in the previous definition is vital to making a machine follow out your orders. Actually, the job of programming is not difficult; what is difficult is breaking the computer's job into simple and detailed steps that assume nothing.

To get an idea of the thinking involved in programming, consider how you would describe starting a car to someone from the past. Suppose Heath, a cowboy from the old west, appears at your doorstep, bewildered by the sights around him. After getting over the future shock, Heath wants to adapt to this new world. Before learning to drive your car, Heath must first learn to start it. When he is comfortable doing that, you will teach him to drive. Unlike a 16-year-old learning to drive, Heath has not grown up seeing adults starting cars, so he really needs to master this process before going any further. Being the busy programmer you are, you leave him the following set of instructions taped to the car key:

1. Use this key.
2. Start the car.

How far would Heath get? Not very far. You gave correct instructions for starting a car, but you assumed too much knowledge on his part. You must remember that he knows nothing about these contraptions called automobiles and that he is relying on you to give him instructions that he can understand. Instead of assuming so much, these might be better instructions:

1. Attached is the key to the car. You need it to start the car.
2. With the key in hand, go to the car door that is closest to the front door of our home.
3. Under the door's black handle, you will see a round silver-dollar-sized metal part in which you can insert the key (with its rough edge pointing down).

3

4. After sticking the key into the hole as far as it goes, turn it to the right until you hear a click.

5. Turn the key back to the left until it faces the same way as it did when you inserted it and remove the key.

6. Open the door and get into the car. Be sure to sit in front of the round wheel (called a *steering wheel*) on the left-hand side of the front seat.

7. Close the door.

8. On the right side of the column holding the steering wheel, you will see a slot in which you can put the key.

Are you beginning to get the idea? This list of eight items is very detailed, and Heath hasn't even started the car yet. You still have to describe the gas pedal that he must press while he turns the key (in the correct direction, of course), and you don't want to assume that Heath will turn *off* the car when he is done practicing, so you have to give him those directions as well. (Perhaps you should also warn your neighbors to stay off the streets for a while.)

If you are beginning to think this car-starting analogy is going a little too far, consider what you must do to tell a non-thinking piece of electronic equipment—a computer—to perform your company's payroll. A payroll program cannot consist of only the following steps:

1. Get the payroll data.

2. Calculate the payroll and taxes.

3. Print the checks.

To the computer, these instructions lack thousands of details that you might take for granted. It is the detailing of the program's instructions that provides for the tedium and occasional frustration of programming. Programming computers isn't difficult, but breaking down real-world problems into lots of detailed steps that a computer can understand is hard.

A typical payroll program might contain 20,000 or more lines of instructions. Don't let this deter you, however. Most company's large programming projects are written by teams of programmers; you will have plenty of help if you ever write such programs for a living. Also, new programming techniques and programming environments for today's computer languages make programming, even for the individual programmer working alone, much easier than ever before.

There are many design tools that help you take large problems and break them down into detailed components that translate into programming elements. Hour 4, "The Program's Design," explains many of the methods that programmers use to get to a program's needed details. Therefore, instead of jumping ship amid this hour's seemingly horrendous descriptions of the details of programs, keep a stiff upper lip because help is on the way. Also consider this: If programming were truly difficult, there is no way so many computer advances could have been made over the last 50 years.

Programs Are Saved Instructions

The nice thing about programs you write is that you save them to disk after you write them. As with word-processed text, you store the programs you write in disk files. A program is to a computer as a recipe is to a cook. When a cook wants to make a certain dish, he or she finds the correct recipe and follows the instructions. When someone wants to execute a program, she or he instructs the computer to load the program from disk into memory and then run the program's instructions. In the previous hour's lesson, you read a detailed list of steps the computer goes through to execute a single program.

The computer's internal memory is vital for program execution. Your computer's CPU cannot execute a program's instructions directly from the disk. Just as you cannot know what is in a book lying on a table until you read the book's contents into your memory (using your own CPU, your mind), your CPU cannot process a program's instructions until it loads the program from disk into main memory. Figure 3.1 shows the process of loading a program from the computer's disk (or disk-like storage such as a CD-ROM) into memory. As the figure shows, the CPU has direct access to memory, but has no access to the disk drive. The disk is the long-term storage, and the memory is the short-term storage where programs temporarily reside while the CPU executes them.

Keep in mind the difference between the program and its output. The program is a set of instructions, and the *output* is the result of those instructions. A recipe's output is the finished dish, and the program's output is the printed output once the instructions are running.

FIGURE 3.1.

A program must be in memory before the CPU can execute the program's instructions.

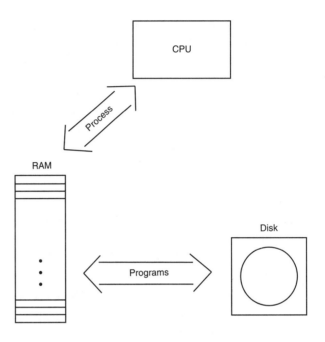

Perhaps a specific example will further help clarify what it means to a programmer for a user to use a program. If you use a word processor, you probably follow steps similar to these:

1. You load the word processing program from the disk into the computer's main memory. When you select the word processing program's name from the menu or select the word processor's Windows icon, you are instructing the computer to search the disk drive for the program and load it into main memory.

2. What you see onscreen is output from the program. You can produce more output by typing text on the screen. Everything that appears onscreen throughout the program's execution is program output.

3. After you type text, you may interact with other devices. You will probably issue a command to print the document (more than likely using the standard Windows File, Print menu option) to the printer and save the document in a data file on the disk.

4. When you exit the word processor, your operating system regains control. The word processing program is no longer in memory, but it is still safely tucked away on disk.

As you can see, the results of a program's execution make up the output. The instructions themselves are what produce those results. Figure 3.2 gives an overview of the program/output process. Modern-day programs produce output in many different ways. Programs play music, talk to other computers over the phone lines, and control external devices. Output sent to the screen and printer still makes up the majority of today's program output.

FIGURE 3.2.

The program comes from disk, executes, and then sends its results to any of the many output devices such as the disk, screen, or printer (or more than one of them from within the same program).

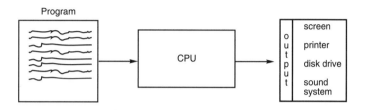

When a program is in memory, it is not there alone. Your operating system always resides in memory. If it did not, you could neither load a program from disk nor run it because the operating system itself is what actually loads programs to and from memory when you issue the correct command. Limited memory often poses a problem for larger programs. You should recall that a program processes data, and the data must be in memory as well as the program before the program can process it easily.

Figure 3.3 shows what a typical computer installation's memory looks like when a program is running. The operating system takes a big chunk, the program must be there too, and, finally, there must be room for data.

FIGURE 3.3.

A typical memory layout shows that the operating system shares memory with executing programs.

The more memory your PC has, the faster your programs run. The extra memory means that the operating system will have to swap less to and from disk as the program operates. Some programs are even contained in memory in their entirety the whole time the program runs. As a programmer, you should run with ample memory, as much as 32MB or 64MB, so that you can properly test your running programs while still keeping your programming environment loaded at the same time.

Art or Science?

NEW TERM   A debate that you often see in computer literature is whether programming is an art or a science. Throughout the years, there have been advances made in programming that, if followed, improve a program's accuracy, readability, and *maintainability* (the process of changing the program later to perform a different or additional set of tasks). Most of these advancements are nothing more than suggestions; that is, programmers don't have to use them to write programs that work.

Two of the most important advances in programming are more philosophically based than engineered. They are *structured programming* and *object-oriented programming*. This book explores these two programming advances thoroughly in the chapters that follow. They both offer suggested ways that a programmer can write a program to make it better. Again, though, these are just suggested approaches to programming; programmers can (and many do) ignore them.

There are many ways to write even the smallest and simplest programs. Just as authors write differently and musicians play differently, programmers each have their own style. Therefore, you would think that programming is more of an art than a science. On the continuum of science to art, you would be more correct than those few who argue that programming is more of a science.

Nevertheless, as more advances are made into developing programming approaches such as structured programming and object-oriented programming, you should see a shift in thinking. With the massive proliferation of computers in today's world, there is a massive education in process to train tomorrow's programmers. Because the programming industry is young (as is the entire computer industry), there are many advancements left to make.

Some of the biggest proponents of moving away from the artful approach to a more scientific approach, using structured and object-oriented programming, are the companies paying the programmers. Companies need to react quickly to changing business conditions, and they need programs written as quickly and as accurately as possible. As advances in computer programming are discovered, more companies are going to adopt policies that require their programmers to use more scientific and time-proved methods of writing better programs.

Speak the Language

The instructions you give in your programs must be in a language the computer under-stands. At its lowest level, a computer is nothing more than thousands of switches flip-ping on and off lightning fast. A switch can have only one of two states; it can be *on* or *off*. Because either of these two states of electricity can be controlled easily with elec-tronic switches, many thousands of them control what your computer does from one microsecond to another.

If it were up to your computer, you would have to give it instructions using switches that represent on and off states of electricity. Actually, that is exactly the way that program-mers programmed the early computers. A panel of switches, such as the one shown in Figure 3.4, had to be used to enter all programs and data. The next time you find yourself cursing errors that appear in programs you write, think of what it would have been like programming 45 years ago.

FIGURE 3.4.

Programmers used a panel of switches to program early computers.

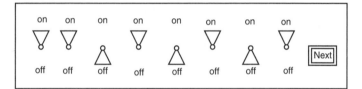

The on and off states of electricity are represented as 1s and 0s at the computer's lowest level. You can control what your computer does if you know the correct pattern of 1s and 0s required to give it commands. You can program a computer simply by issuing 1s and 0s if you have the correct system tools. Of course, programming in 1s and 0s is not much better than flipping up and down switches on the switch panel, so there has to be a better way.

> Computers are not going to learn any human's spoken language any time soon, despite what you might see in science fiction movies. You have to learn a programming language if you want the computer to do what you want.

Computers Cannot Handle Ambiguity

English and all the other spoken languages are too ambiguous to computers. People's brains can decipher sentences intuitively, something a nonthinking machine cannot do. There are some inroads being made into *artificial intelligence*, which is the science of programming computers so they can learn on their own. It also includes programming them to understand a spoken language such as English. Despite recent advancements, artificial intelligence is many years away (if it is even possible for computers to understand simple English commands).

Consider the following sentence:

Time flies like an arrow.

Your mind has no trouble understanding the parts of this sentence. You know that it is an analogy, and the parts of speech make total sense to you. *Time* is a noun that performs an action, it *flies*, and it does so *like an arrow*. If you teach the computer to accept these descriptions of this sentence, it will work fine until it runs into something like this:

Fruit flies like an orange.

Think about this for a moment. Again, you have no problem understanding this sentence, even though it is completely different from the other one. The computer taught to decipher the first sentence, however, is going to throw its cables up in frustration at the second sentence because none of the parts of the sentence are the same. The word *flies* is now a noun and not an action verb. The phrase *like an orange* is no longer a description of the action, but rather both the verb (*like*) and the object receiving the action (*an orange*). As you can see from these two sentences alone, understanding simple sentences that most people take for granted poses a tremendous problem for programmers trying to "teach" a computer to understand a language such as English.

Therefore, computers and people are at opposite ends of the spectrum. People want to speak their own language, but so do computers, which only really understand 1s and 0s. There has to be some kind of go-between. Programming languages were created to try to appease both the computer and the person programming the computer. Programming languages use words similar to those that people use, but they have a highly specific *syntax* (structure, order, grammar, and spelling) that allows little room for the ambiguity that is so prevalent in spoken languages. The computer can take a programming language and translate it to its machine language of 1s and 0s; the human programmer can learn, remember, and use the programming languages more effectively than 1s and 0s because programming languages appear similar to spoken languages, although more precise and simple.

Computers Speak Many Languages

You are going to learn a lot about different programming languages in this 24-hour course. You may have heard of some of the languages before, and you might not have heard of others. Over the years since the first computer language was invented, hundreds of programming languages have been written, but there are only a handful that have pre-vailed over the rest. The following is a list of several programming languages that gained more than obscure notoriety through the years:

Machine Language *	Assembler *
Algol *	PL/I *
PROLOG *	LISP
COBOL *	Forth *
RPG *	RPG II *
Pascal *	Object Pascal *
SNOBOL	ADA *
C *	C++ *
Objective C	FORTRAN *
SmallTalk *	Eiffel
BASIC *	Visual Basic *
APL *	

Each programming language has its own dialects. BASIC has enjoyed tremendous popu-larity in all the following varieties:

BASICA

GW-BASIC (which stands for *Gee-Whiz BASIC*)

Quick BASIC

QBasic

Visual Basic

Before you finish this book, you will be writing programs in QBasic. Hours 8 through 12 teach you QBasic (a simple language that is available on all PCs) and show you how to write complete programs that do what you want them to do.

---

* These languages achieved dominance through either sheer numbers of usage, or in their specific area of expertise. For example, PROLOG is rarely used outside the artificial intelligence field, but has been the language of choice there.

The computer is like a modern-day tower of Babel, indirectly responsible for more programming languages than were ever needed. Most people considered to be "computer experts" might only know a handful of programming languages—from two to five—and they probably only know one or two very well. Therefore, don't let the large number of languages deter you from wanting to learn to program.

There are lots of reasons why there are so many programming languages. Different people have different preferences, some languages are better than others depending on the tasks, and some people only have access to one or two of the languages.

The program that you write is called a *source program* (or *source code*). Throughout this book, when you see the term *source program*, that text is referring to your program before it is compiled.

The Language Translator

Your computer cannot actually understand BASIC, C, Pascal, or any of the other programming languages. You might be confused because the previous section explained that computer languages are important because the computer cannot understand English, or any other languages that people speak. Even so, the computer cannot understand BASIC either, but it is easy for a program to translate BASIC to the actual 1s and 0s that the computer *does* understand.

There are two kinds of language translators: *compilers* and *interpreters*. Both take a programming language such as Pascal and translate it into a form readable by the computer. Each takes a different approach, but their end results are the same; both take programs and convert them into 1s and 0s (called *machine language*), as Figure 3.5 shows.

FIGURE 3.5.

Both interpreters and compilers translate source code into low-level machine language that the computer can understand.

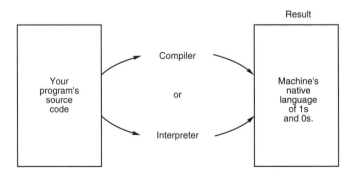

Interpreters

Some programming languages, such as APL and BASIC, come as interpreters (there are also BASIC-like compilers available, such as Visual Basic). Interpreters translate one line at a time, executing each line as it is translated. The name *interpreter* is very descriptive. You are familiar with the way computer interpreters work because you already understand the way human interpreters work.

Suppose someone gives you a book written in a foreign language that you don't understand. In order to understand the book, you could hire a human interpreter to read the book to you. The interpreter reads a line, translates it, and then reads the next line to you. The only drawback to interpretation (as opposed to compilation, which the next section describes) is that the interpreter must re-interpret lines that you want read again. Interpretation is slower than compilation. Figure 3.6 shows the position of the human interpreter between you and the book. Keep this in mind as you read about the computer interpreters.

FIGURE 3.6.

An interpreter translates one line at a time.

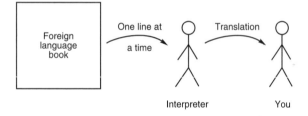

A programming language interpreter acts like the human interpreter in that it can be a slow process, interpreting one line at a time. Computers often perform repetitive tasks, such as printing several hundred payroll checks. If you have an interpreted programming language, the interpreter takes each line of the program, translates it, and then executes it. This process makes repetitive tasks run very slowly.

Here is a section from a BASIC program. You will learn more about the BASIC language specifics later in the book, but for now all you need to know is that these three lines repeat 50 times:

```
FOR i = 1 TO 50
  PRINT i
NEXT i
```

The reason the interpreter is slow is that every time it repeats a line, it must first interpret the line again. Therefore, these three lines of code are interpreted 50 times as well as run 50 times.

Interpreters do offer some advantages over compilers. Interpreted languages are a little easier to learn for beginning programmers. The process of compiling programs is historically more difficult than interpreting them (although many of today's compilers are almost as easy as to use as interpreters). The time from running the program to seeing the results is quicker when you use an interpreter. This quick feedback is helpful for beginners learning to program.

Compilers

Instead of hiring an interpreter to read the foreign language book to you, you might be better off asking the translator to *compile* the book for you. The translator can sit down and write out all the interpretation for you, without reading it to you while doing so. Although it takes much longer to prepare, you then can read the compiled version and refer to it as often as necessary.

Figure 3.7 shows the process of compiling the volume. The nice thing about having the compiled book is that you don't need the interpreter once the book is compiled.

FIGURE 3.7.

After compiling the book, you no longer need the translator.

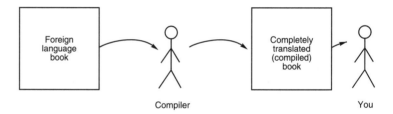

Compiling a program takes an extra step over interpreting a program. You must request the compiler to compile the program and then wait for the results. Only after fully compiling the program will any of it work. Most beginning programmers have enough difficulties learning about the program's interaction with hardware, operating system, and the language itself, without having to learn compiler commands as well.

Most businesses prefer compiled programming languages because, once compiled, the programs run much faster than they would if they were interpreted. In the previous three-line BASIC example, the three lines only have to be compiled into machine language one time. After the compiler is finished, the code executes the 50 repetitions without any translation at all.

Businesses prefer compiled programs over interpreted ones for security as well. Once compiled, a program cannot easily be changed. When you buy a program that is already written, the chances are good that it is compiled. You can run it, but you cannot see the source program itself.

Some of today's programming languages, such as Visual Basic, enable you to run programs interpreted as well as compiled. Therefore, you get the testing advantages of an interpreted language, and, after you complete the testing, you get the speed and security of a compiled language.

Accuracy Is Everything

You are now well aware that the computer is a machine that cannot deal well with ambiguity. A programmer's plague is the collection of errors that show up in code. Programmers must ensure that they do not write programs that contain errors, although this is not always as easy as it might seem.

NEW TERM   In computer terminology, a program error is known as a *bug*. When breaking the programming problem into detailed instructions, programmers often leave things out or code the wrong thing. When the program runs, errors creep in because of the bugs in the code.

3

THE FIRST BUG

The term *bug* has an interesting origin. The late U.S. Navy admiral, Grace Hopper, one of the early pioneers of computer hardware and software (she helped design and write the first COBOL compiler), was working on a military computer system in the early 1950s. While printing a report, the printer stopped working. Admiral Hopper and her coworkers set out to find the problem.

After spending lots of time without finding any problems in the program or data, Admiral Hopper looked in the printer and noticed that a moth had lodged itself in the wires of the printer, keeping the printer from operating properly. As soon as the *bug* (get it?) was removed, the printer worked perfectly. The moth did not fare as well, but it did go down in computer history as the first computer bug.

NEW TERM   *Debugging* is the process a programmer goes through to exterminate the bugs from a program. As a programmer writes a program, he or she often runs the program in its unfinished state (as much as can be run) to catch as many bugs as possible and keep them out of the finished program. Often, the majority of the bugs can only be found after the program is completely written.

Beginning programmers often fail to realize how easy it is for bugs to creep into code. Expect them and you will not be surprised. Many early programming students have taken a program into the instructor saying, "the computer doesn't work right," when in reality, the program has a bug or two. When you begin to write your first programs, expect to have to correct some problems. Nobody writes a perfect program every time.

Depending on the length of a program, the time it takes the programmer (or programmers) to correct the problems is often almost as long as the time taken to write the program originally. Some errors are very difficult to find.

There are two categories of computer bugs: logic errors. To learn the difference, take a few moments to find the two errors in the following statement:

There are two errrors in this sentence.

Need a clue? Not yet; look again for the two errors before going further.

The first error is obvious. The word *errrors* is misspelled; it should be *errors*. The second problem is much more difficult to find. The second problem with the statement is that the entire premise of the statement is incorrect. There is only *one* error in the statement, and that error is the misspelled word *errrors*. Therefore, the logic of the statement itself is in error.

NEW TERM This problem demonstrates the difference between a *syntax error* and a *logic error*. The syntax error is much easier to find. Syntax errors are commonly misspelled programming language commands and grammatical problems with the way you used the programming language. Logic errors occur when your program is syntactically correct, but you told it to do something that is not what should really be done.

Compilers and interpreters locate your program's syntax errors when you try to compile or run it. This is another reason why syntax errors are easier to spot: Your computer tells you where they are. When a computer runs into a syntax error, it halts and refuses to analyze the program further until you correct the syntax error. Figure 3.8 shows a QBasic program that stopped because of a syntax error. The QBasic interpreter stops and highlights the exact line where the error occurred.

Suppose you're writing a program to print invoices for your company's accounts receivable. Because of an error, the computer prints all the invoices with a balance due of –$1,000. In other words, according to the invoice, every customer has a $1,000 credit. Your computer did its job, acting out your program's instructions. The program obviously contained no syntax errors because it ran without stopping. The logic errors, however, kept it from working properly.

Extensive testing is critical. The programmer wants to get all the errors out so the program will work correctly when the user finally uses it. The larger the program, the more difficult this is. Exterminating program bugs is just part of the daily job programmers tackle.

FIGURE 3.8.

QBasic finds a syntax error and refuses to continue until you fix the problem.

The error occurred here.

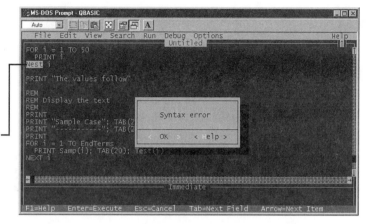

There is one other kind of error, a *runtime error*. Runtime errors are actually almost always caused by a logic mistake because the programmer failed to predict and therefore handle a potential problem. Runtime errors can occur if a program attempts to write to a disk without first checking to ensure that the disk door is closed and that a disk is inside the drive. A runtime error can occur, for instance, if the program divides by zero (division by zero is undefined mathematically). The more you program, you more you will learn to head off potential runtime errors that can occur.

Summary

There are several ways to obtain programs for computers, but to really make computers do what you want, you have to write the programs yourself. Most programs that you purchase are merely licenses to use but not customize the programs. Companies need programs that enable them to do business the way the company prefers and not force a business to change its practices to conform to the program. Before you can program, you must learn a programming language. Programs often contain errors so you will need to test your program before distributing the program to users.

The next hour describes some of the background needed for proper program design.

Q&A

Q **How much of a program consists of avoiding and handling possible errors that can occur at runtime?**

A The last thing you want is for a user, whether that user works for your company or purchases your program, to run into a bug that you failed to catch. If you put more effort into catching all bugs, predicting bugs that can occur, and handling them in the program, your users will be much happier and you will be a more successful programmer. To avoid problems, you will have to put extensive error-handling routines in your programs. Some programs include more code to avoid errors than they have code that performs the required goal of the program.

Workshop

The quiz questions are provided for your further understanding. See Appendix A, "Answers to End of Chapter Questions," for answers.

Quiz

1. What are the three ways to acquire a new program?

2. Why do businesses often write their own programs, despite the extra expense required?

3. Why must programmers know a programming language?

4. Why do computers not understand human language?

5. What is the only language that computers really understand internally?

6. True or false: To be useful, a programmer should know at least five programming languages.

7. Why is RAM-based internal memory so important to a running program?

8. What kinds of bugs appear in programs?

9. Which kinds of bugs are the easiest to locate?

10. Which produces faster programs: a compiler or an interpreter?

HOUR 4

The Program's Design

Programmers learn to develop patience early in their programming careers. They learn that proper design is critical to a successful program. Perhaps you have heard the term *systems analysis and design*. This is the name given to the practice of analyzing the problem and then designing the program from that analysis. Complete books and college courses have been written about systems analysis and design. This chapter attempts to cover the highlights, letting you see what mainstream computer programmers go through before writing programs.

The highlights of this hour include:

- Why program design is so important
- What three steps are required when writing a program
- What is meant by *output definition*
- Why top-down design is better than bottom-up design
- What a flowchart is
- What the symbols in flowcharts mean
- When pseudocode has an advantage over flowcharting
- What the final step in the programming process is

Understanding the Need for Design

When a builder begins to build a house, he doesn't pick up a hammer and begin on the kitchen's frame. The designer must design the new house before anything can begin. As you will soon see, a program must also be designed before it is written.

A builder must first find out what the purchaser of the house wants. Nothing can be built unless the builder has an end result in mind. Therefore, the buyers of the house must meet with an architect. They tell the architect what they want the house to look like. The architect helps the buyers decide by telling them what is possible and what isn't. During this initial stage, the price is always a factor that requires both the designers and the purchasers to reach compromise agreements.

After the architect completes the plans for the house, the builder must plan the resources needed to build the house. Only after the design of the house is finished, the permits are filed, the money is in place, the materials are purchased, and the laborers hired can any physical building begin. As a matter of fact, the more effort the builder puts into these preliminary requirements, the faster the house can actually be built.

The problem with building a house before it is properly designed is that the eventual owners may want changes made after it is too late to change them. It is very difficult to add a bathroom in the middle of two bedrooms *after* the house is completed. The primary idea is to get the owners to agree with the builder on the final house. When the specifications are agreed to by all the parties involved, there is little room for disagreement later. The clearer the initial plans are, the fewer problems can occur down the road because all parties agreed on the same house plans.

Program Design

Sure, this is not a book on house construction, but you should always keep the similarities in mind before writing a program of any great length. You should not go to the keyboard and start typing instructions into the program before designing it any more than a builder should pick up a hammer before the house plans are determined.

> The more up-front design work that you do, the faster you will finish the final program.

Thanks to computer technology, a computer program is easier to modify than a house. If you leave out a routine that a user wanted, you can add it later more easily than a builder can add a room to a finished house. Nevertheless, adding something to a program is never as easy as designing the program correctly the first time.

The program maintenance that takes place after the program is written, tested, and distributed is one of the most time-consuming aspects of the programming process. Programs are continually updated to reflect new user needs. Sometimes, if the program is not designed properly before it is written, the user will not want the program until it does exactly what she wants it to do.

Computer consultants learn early to get the user's acceptance, and even the user's signature, on a program's design before the programming begins. If both the user and the programmers agree on what to do, there is little room for argument when the final program is presented. Companies with internal data processing departments also require that their programming staffs come to a written agreement with the users who want them to write the programs. Company resources are limited; there is no time to add something later that should have been in the system all along. Most of this hour's lesson explains how to go about producing the design that you and your users agree to.

There are three steps you should perform when you have a program to write:

1. Define the output.
2. Develop the logic to get to that output.
3. Write the program.

Notice that writing the program is the *last* step in writing the program. This is not as silly as it sounds. Remember that physically building the house is the last stage of building the house; proper planning is critical before any actual building can start. You will find that actually writing and typing in the lines of the program is one of the easiest parts of the programming process. If your design is well thought out, the program practically writes itself; typing it in becomes almost an afterthought to the whole process.

The rest of this chapter explores these three components of program design.

Step 1: Define the Output

Before beginning a program, you must have a firm idea of what the program should produce. Looking back at the fundamental model of programming (repeated in Figure 4.1), you see that the output is the last thing produced, but it is the *first thing you must design.* Just as a builder must know what the house should look like before beginning to build it, a programmer must know what the output is going to be before writing the program.

FIGURE 4.1.

Data processing at its most fundamental level turns data into information.

A program's output consists of more than just printed information. Anything that the program produces and the user sees is considered output that you must define. You must know what every screen in the program should look like and what will be on every page of every printed report.

The output definition is more than a preliminary output design. It gives you insight into what data elements the program should track, compute, and produce. Defining the output also helps you gather all the input you need to produce the output.

Some programs produce a huge amount of output. Don't skip this first all-important step in the design process just because there is a lot of output. Because there is more output, it becomes more important for you to define it. Defining the output is relatively easy—sometimes even downright boring and time-consuming. The time you need to define the output can take as long as the third step, which is typing in the program (the second step, however, is the *most* time-consuming). You will lose that time and more, however, if you shrug off the output definition at the beginning.

One of the benefits of the Windows operating system is its visual nature. Before Windows, programming tools were limited to text-based design and implementation. Designing a user's screen today means starting a programming language such as Visual Basic, drawing the screen, and dragging objects to the screen that the user will interact with, such as an OK button. Therefore, you can quickly design *prototype screens* that you can send to the user. After the user sees the screens that he will interact with, he'll have a much better feel for whether you understand the needs of the program.

The output definition consists of many pages of details. You must be able to specify all the details of a problem before you know what output you need. One of the best approaches for specifying the details of a problem is top-down design.

Top-Down Program Design

NEW TERM The most important design available is top-down design. With top-down design, you produce the details needed to accomplish a programming task. *Top-down design* is the process of breaking down the overall problem into more and more detail, until you finalize all the details.

The problem with top-down design is that programmers tend not to use it. They tend to design from the opposite direction (called *bottom-up design*). When you ignore top-down design, you impose a heavy burden on yourself to remember every detail that will be needed; with top-down design, the details fall out on their own. You don't have to worry about the petty details if you follow a strict top-down design because the process of top-down design takes care of producing the details.

> One of the keys to top-down design is that it forces you to put off the details until later. Top-down design forces you to think in terms of the overall problem for as long as possible. Top-down design keeps you focused. If you use bottom-up design, it is too easy to lose sight of the forest for the trees. You get to the details too fast and lose sight of your program's primary objectives.

Performing a Real-World Top-Down Design

You can learn about top-down design more easily by relating it to a common real-world problem before looking at a computer problem. Top-down design is not just for programming problems. Once you master top-down design, you can apply it to any part of your life that you must plan in detail. Perhaps the most detailed event that a person can plan is a wedding. Therefore, a wedding is the perfect place to see top-down design in action.

What is the first thing you must do to have a wedding? First, find a prospective spouse (you'll need a different book for help with that). When it comes time to plan the wedding, the top-down design is the best way to approach the event. The way *not* to plan a wedding is to worry about the details first, yet this is the way most people plan a wedding. They start thinking about the dresses, the organist, the flowers, and the cake to serve at the reception. The biggest problem with trying to cover all these details from the beginning is that you lose sight of so much; it is too easy to forget a detail until it's too late. The details of bottom-up design get in your way.

The Top-Down Design Steps

Here is the three-step process necessary for top-down design:

1. Determine the overall goal.
2. Break that goal into two, three, or more detailed parts. Too many more details make you leave out things.
3. Put off the details as long as possible. Keep repeating steps 1 and 2 until you cannot reasonably break down the problem any further.

What is the overall goal of a wedding? Thinking in the most general terms possible, "Have a wedding" is about as general as it can get. If you were in charge of planning a wedding, the general goal of "Have a wedding" would put you right on target. Assume that "Have a wedding" is the highest-level goal.

 The overall goal keeps you focused. Despite its redundant nature, "Have a wedding" keeps out details such as planning the honeymoon. If you don't put a fence around the exact problem you are working on, you'll get mixed up with details and, more importantly, you'll forget some details. If you're planning both a wedding and a honeymoon, you should do two top-down designs, or include the honeymoon trip in the top-level general goal. This wedding plan includes the event of the wedding itself—the ceremony and reception—but doesn't include any honeymoon details. (Leave the honeymoon details to your spouse so you can be surprised. After all, you have enough to do with the wedding plans, right?)

Now that you know where you're heading, begin breaking down the overall goal into two or three details. For instance, what about the colors of the wedding, what about the guest list, what about paying the minister. . .*oops,* too many details! The idea of top-down design is to put off the details for as long as possible. Don't get in any hurry. When you find yourself breaking the current problem into more than three or four parts, you are rushing the top-down design. Put off the details. Basically, you can break down "Have a wedding" into the following two major components: the ceremony and the reception.

Using the Top-Down Design

The next step of top-down design is to take those new components and do the same for each of them. The ceremony is made up of the people and the location. The reception includes the food, the people, and the location. The ceremony's people include the guests, the wedding party, and the workers (minister, organist, and so on—but those details come a little later).

The top-down design naturally produces a triangular result, the first part of which appears in Figure 4.2. There are a lot of details left to put in, but that is the point; you should put off the details as long as possible. The details fall out on their own as you divide the tasks into more parts. By making sure your overall goal includes the general idea of where you want to head, the details will eventually come.

Soon, you will run out of room on the page. That's okay; use more sheets of paper. You can number the sheets and put the page number of each in the box "above" that page in the top-down design. Actually, keeping track of the pages is not as important as you might think. The first page is your focus page that makes sure you are working toward the goal you really want. Keep breaking down each of the succeeding detail pages until you can go no further. You will find that no detail is left out at the end.

FIGURE 4.2.

The early part of planning a wedding using top-down design includes the most general goals.

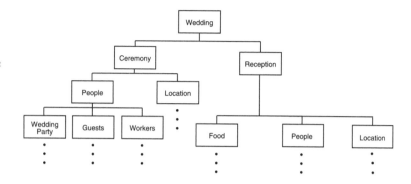

Don't worry about the time-order of the details yet. The top-down design's goal is to produce every detail you need (eventually), not to put those details into any order. You must know where you are heading and exactly what is required before considering how those details relate to each other and which come first.

Eventually, you will have several pages of details that cannot be broken down any further. For instance, you'll probably end up with the details of the reception food, such as peanuts for snacking. (If you start out listing those details, however, you could forget many of them.)

Moving to a more "computerized" problem, assume you are assigned the task of writing a payroll program for a company. What would that payroll program require? You could begin listing the payroll program's details, such as this:

- Print payroll checks.
- Calculate federal taxes.
- Calculate state taxes.

What is wrong with this approach? If you said that the details were coming too early, you are correct. The perfect place to start is at the top. The most general goal of a payroll program might be "Perform the payroll." This overall goal keeps other details out of this program (no general ledger processing will be included, unless part of the payroll system updates a general ledger file) and keeps you focused on the problem at hand.

Consider Figure 4.3. This might be the first page of the payroll's top-down design. Any payroll program has to include some mechanism for entering, deleting, and changing employee information such as address, city, state, ZIP code, number of exemptions, and so on. What other details about the employees do you need? At this point, don't ask. The design is not ready for all those details.

FIGURE 4.3.

The first page of the payroll program's top-down design would include the highest level of details.

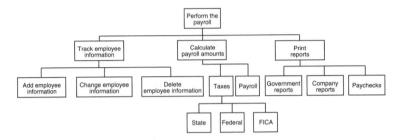

There is a long way to go before you finish with the payroll top-down design, but Figure 4.3 is the first step. You must keep breaking down each component until the details finally appear. Only after you have all the details ready can you begin to decide what the program is going to produce.

Only when you and the user gather all the necessary details through top-down design can you decide what is going to comprise those details.

Tools for Output Definition

The details stemming from the top-down design are not all output. Many of the details are procedures the final program must perform. For instance, one of the details of a payroll program would probably be "Compute net pay." Computing net pay causes no output to appear. Elsewhere in the top-down design, somewhere under payroll reports, would be the "Print net pay on the paycheck" detail. That detail would be output.

You must make sure that the output consists of and looks exactly like what the user wants to see in the final program. It is your job to meet with the user and define every single element of the program's output. This is called *output definition.*

As mentioned in the previous section, you can create a prototype, or model of your program's proposed output, using many of today's programming tools. Figure 4.4 shows a window from the Windows-based programming language called Visual Basic. The programmer required no programming language to design this screen. The programmer can create this screen in a matter of minutes and then show the screen to the user immediately afterward.

FIGURE 4.4.

Your users can work with the prototype to ensure that the output includes all necessary items.

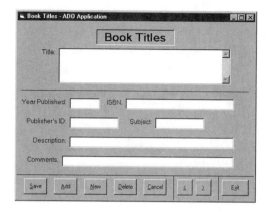

One of the biggest advantages of prototyping user screens during the design stage, using visual tools that are now available, is that once you and the user agree to a screen design, you can easily port that designed screen into the final program. In other words, the prototype can become an actual screen in the final product. If you don't use these interactive design tools, but prefer (or are required as mentioned later in this section) to use paper-based design tools for the program's output, you will have to enter the paper design into the computer when you write the program. Your time is better spent if the design itself can become part of the program immediately.

The prototype is only an empty shell that cannot do anything but simulate user interaction until you tie its pieces together with code. Your job as a programmer has only just begun once you get approval on the screens, but the screens are the first place to begin because you must know what your users want before you know how to proceed.

If you use a visual programming tool such as Visual Basic, which more and more programmers do these days, teach your users how to prototype their own screens! A knowledge of programming is not required to design the screens. Your users, therefore, will be able to show you exactly what they want. The prototyped screens are interactive, as well. That is, your users will be able to click the buttons and enter values in the fields even though nothing happens as a result of that use. The idea is to let your users try the screens for a while to make sure they are comfortable with the placement and appearance of the controls.

Sometimes you cannot use visual prototyping tools. This could occur because your users don't have enough power on their PCs or available disk space to run your programming environment. In addition, you may not have the license to install the programming environment on the user's PC. Also, if you are writing a program for users who know very little about computers, those users may be more inclined to adapt to your program design if you initially show them paper designs of what the screens will look like and let the user mark up the paper designs and make changes as they see necessary.

There are several paper-based tools that can help you define the output. Graph paper is useful for sketching out the details of each screen and report. Consider Figure 4.5. From this figure, you can determine how many lines and spaces separate the elements on the screen. In a visual environment such as Windows, there is no longer one-character per space and per line as there used to be in text-based operating environments, but the graph paper does give your users some idea of the screens they will use, and the graph paper is less formidable than a screen might be initially.

FIGURE 4.5.

Graphing the output elements helps indicate their final placement in the program.

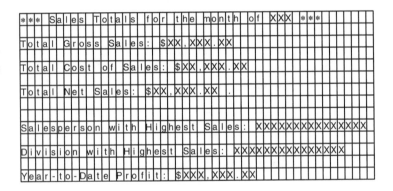

Given the flexibility of today's word processors, and given that even beginning computer users often use a word processor for their letters, you can work with your users on the initial screen content using a word processor. The word processor will not be as confrontational as a visual design tool might be and word processors run on low-powered PCs. Perhaps the word processor isn't a great final design tool, but you can sit there with your users and sketch out, using the word processor's commands and tools, the initial screen contents that the user needs to see. When the screens are completed, you can print them and save them to your own disk for later reference.

Be sure to include data-entry screens as part of your output definition. This may seem contradictory, but input screens require that your program place *prompts* (questions and titles of the data required) on the screen, and you should plan where these input screen elements go. For example, Figure 4.4 was little more than a data-entry screen where a bookstore could enter new book data. (In addition, the same screen provides output of existing books.) Although the end user will enter the required data book elements (called *fields*), defining the data-entry screen's layout before writing the program that produces the screen greatly speeds the completion of your program.

In conclusion, all output screens, printed reports, and data-entry screens must be defined in advance so you know exactly what is required of your programs. You also must decide what data to keep in files and the format of your data files. As you progress in your programming education, you will learn ways to lay out disk files in formats they require.

Working with Users

Unless you will be the final user of your program, you have to talk with the users and define the output, as the previous section discussed. Often, users have only a vague idea of what they want the program to do. You have to help them define what it is the program will do and what the output is going to be as well.

Some end users who want programs written have no idea what the computer is capable of doing. You'll learn to develop some professional guidance counseling skills as you design programs for them. You must be able to hone the user's overall program requests into meaningful and concrete pieces.

The output definition is one of the best tools you can use to define the user's program requests. Continually show the user your output designs and ask questions such as, "Is this what you wanted?" and "Does this report contain everything you need?" If you are writing programs for a company, the company often has strict requirements as to what each report should contain. In some companies, every page of every computer-generated report needs to contain the date and time the report was printed. You have to delve into the output standards within a company to find out what it requires.

When working with users, give them as many prototypes to work with as you can. When you write a program that displays output and data-entry screens and lets the user fill in the blanks with the keyboard, the underlying program doesn't have to do anything with the data entered by the user. Just by working with the screens, the user will have a very good idea about whether the program contains all the necessary elements.

Be sure to get some final written agreement from the user, even an informal one, that the output definition is correct. This vital step, required before starting the logic development, contractually binds the user (and you) to the output definition. When you present the final program later, the user won't be able to argue that it doesn't produce the results he wanted.

What do you do with all the details of the top-down design and output definition? You must now move them into some kind of time-order logic that your program can follow to produce the details. That is where design tools such as flowcharts and pseudocode come in.

Step 2: Develop the Logic

After you and the user agree to the goals and output of the program, the rest is up to you. Your job is to take that output definition and decide how to make a computer produce the output. You have taken the overall problem and broken it down into detailed instructions that the computer can carry out. This doesn't mean that you are ready to write the program—quite the contrary. You are now ready to develop the logic that produces that output.

The output definition goes a long way toward describing *what* the program is supposed to do. Now you must decide *how* to accomplish the job. You must order the details that you have so they operate in a time-ordered fashion. You must also decide which decisions your program must make and the actions produced by each of those decisions.

Flowcharts

Flowcharts and related logic-development tools are the staple item of computer professionals. Sadly, flowcharting is rarely taught these days because of the amount of material that most programming courses cover. The complexity of programs requires that you somehow find a way to depict the logic of a program before writing it. Flowcharting seems archaic but programmers who don't use tools such as flowcharting find themselves less productive than they otherwise could be.

It is said that a picture is worth a thousand words, and the flowchart provides a pictorial representation of program logic. The flowchart doesn't include all the program details but represents the general logic flow of the program. The flowchart provides the logic for the final program. If your flowchart is correctly drawn, writing the actual program becomes a matter of rote. After the final program is completed, the flowchart can act as documentation to the program itself.

The flowchart describes the middle box of the input-processing-output model for computer programs.

Flowcharts are made up of industry-standard symbols. You can buy plastic flowchart symbol outlines, called *flowchart templates*, at an office supply store to help you draw better-looking flowcharts instead of relying on freehand drawing. Figure 4.6 shows you a typical flowcharting template. There are also some programs that guide you through a flowchart's creation and print flowcharts on your printer.

FIGURE 4.6.

You can purchase a plastic flowchart template to draw better-looking flowcharts.

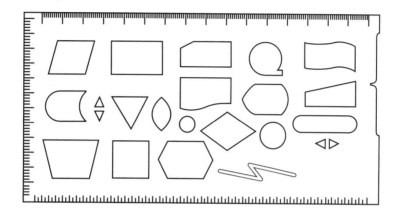

Only after learning to program can you learn to flowchart a program, yet you must flowchart (or use one of the other kinds of related logic development tools) before writing programs. This "chicken before the egg" syndrome is common for newcomers to programming. When you begin to write your own programs, you'll have a much better understanding of the need for flowcharts.

4

As you can see from the flowchart template, there are many possible flowcharting symbols. Nevertheless, only a handful are used often. This chapter teaches you about the most common flowcharting symbols. With the ones you learn about here, you can write any flowchart that you'll ever need. The remaining symbols are simply refinements of those you learn here.

Figure 4.7 describes the flowcharting symbols used in this chapter. You should take the time to learn these symbols because they are extremely common in the programming literature that you will come across. As with top-down design, you can use flowcharts to help map out any event, not just computer programs. There are many noncomputer "how-to" books on the market that use these very same flowcharting symbols. A general perusal of five current programming magazines and periodicals at the time this hour's lesson is being written showed at least one flowchart in every issue looked at.

FIGURE 4.7.

You only need to learn the common flowcharting symbols and their meanings.

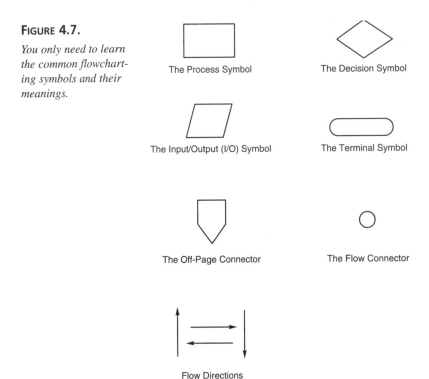

The Process Symbol

The Decision Symbol

The Input/Output (I/O) Symbol

The Terminal Symbol

The Off-Page Connector

The Flow Connector

Flow Directions

The flowcharting symbols have nothing to do with the top-down design's boxes. Remember that the top-down design was the tool you used to produce the program's needed details. Flowcharts provide the logic needed to produce those details.

Table 4.1 describes each of these symbols and how to use them.

TABLE 4.1 FLOWCHARTING SYMBOLS AND THEIR USAGE

Symbol	Description
Process	Contains a description of what is being done. Use a process symbol when straight processing of data is taking place, such as a calculation or program initialization.
Decision	Use when the program must make a decision based on two outcomes, such as printing either to the screen or to the printer, depending on where the user requested the printing.

Symbol	Description
Input/Output	Use for any input or output the program does, such as asking the user a question, or printing a report. (The slanted shape of the I/O symbol gives you a clue as to what it means; the slash in *I/O* slants the same way.)
Terminal	A terminal symbol with the word *Begin* or *Start* written in it always begins every flowchart. A terminal symbol with the word *End* or *Finish* written in it always ends every flowchart. When you refer to the flowchart later, there will be no question where it begins or ends.
Off-page	Put an off-page connector at the bottom of any flowchart that is continued to another page. Put the next page's page number inside the off-page connector. Put an off-page connector at the beginning of each page that concludes a previous page's flowchart. Put the previous page's number inside the off-page connector that begins the new page of the flowchart.
Flow connector	Use when one logic flow of the flowchart is to merge with existing logic. You typically see an alphabetic letter inside the flow connectors. A matching flow connector (one with the same letter) indicates the reentry point to the existing logic.
Flow direction	These arrows connect every symbol in the flowchart and indicate the direction of the program flow.

The Rules of Flowcharting

Although every programmer draws flowcharts differently, there are some distinct rules that you should acquaint yourself with before going further. These rules are almost universally followed, and therefore you should understand them so the flowcharts you write will be readable by others. With each rule, you will see an example that both follows and breaks the rule so you can get an idea of how to use the rule.

- Rule #1: *Use standard flowcharting symbols.* If you stick to the conventional symbols, others can understand your flowchart's meaning, and you can understand theirs. Figure 4.8 shows the right and wrong ways to follow this rule.

- Rule #2: *The flowchart's logic should generally flow from the top of the page to the bottom of the page, and from left to right.* If your flowcharts don't follow this standard, they could become disorganized and hard to follow. Figure 4.9 illustrates the proper flow direction of flowcharts. Notice that the flow direction arrows point in the direction that the logic follows.

FIGURE 4.8.

Use standard, conventional flowcharting symbols.

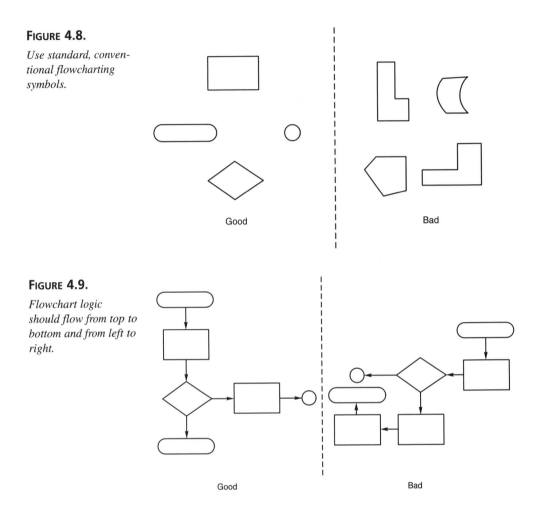

FIGURE 4.9.

Flowchart logic should flow from top to bottom and from left to right.

Some flowcharts have no need to move to the right because they describe sequential program logic, but most have some kind of flow going in either of the two recommended directions. There might be times when a proper flowchart seemingly breaks this rule; you will see one shortly. Because of repetition in logic, the flowchart might have areas that go back up and to the left to repeat sections of the logic, but eventually the logic must continue in the preferred directions. The *overall* logic must flow from top to bottom and from left to right.

- Rule #3: *The decision symbol is the only symbol that can have more than one exit point, and it always has two.* Most flowcharting symbols have one entry point and one exit point. The direction flow arrows indicate the entry and exit points. The decision symbol always has two exit points because, at that place in the logic, one of two things takes place, and the next flow of logic is determined by the result of that decision. Figure 4.10 illustrates this rule.

FIGURE 4.10.

Only the decision symbol can have more than one exit point, and it has exactly two.

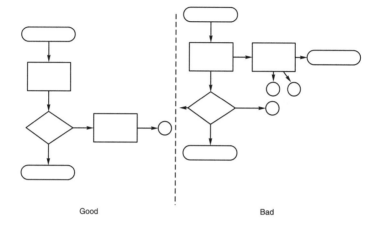

Good   Bad

- Rule #4: *A decision symbol should always ask a yes-or-no question.* A flowchart's decision should always have two and only two outcomes (hence, Rule #3's two-exit reasoning). You will see the decision in the symbol itself. Most flowcharting symbols have words in them that describe what is taking place at that point in the flowchart. Figure 4.11 illustrates this rule.

FIGURE 4.11.

A decision symbol should always ask a yes-or-no question.

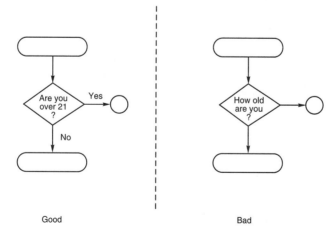

Good   Bad

Clearly label the exits of each decision symbol as well. Because the exits are the result of a yes-or-no question, label the exits *Yes* or *Y* and *No* or *N* so you know what the exits indicate.

You might wonder if it is reasonable to expect all decisions to have only two possible results. There are times when your program must choose between one of many values, based on the data it receives. However, multiple decision symbols will take care of any number of possibilities. When you were a child, you may have played Twenty Questions, a game in which someone thinks of an object or person, and you can only ask yes-or-no questions to determine what the object is. Ask enough yes-or-no questions, and you can determine anything. The same concept applies to decisions in a program. In the lessons about programming that begin in Part III, "Hands-On Programming," you will see how to direct programs to handle more than two possibilities.

- Rule #5: *Instructions inside the symbols should be clear English descriptions, not computerese or programming language statements.* You should develop a flowchart before you write a program. You should not include programming statements inside flowcharting symbols. If you were ready for the programming language at this point, you wouldn't need to take the time flowcharting.

The flowchart is your own development of the logic. You will eventually convert the flowchart into programming language statements, but only after you are clear that the flowchart performs the logic you need—and not before.

An Example Flowchart

As with the top-down design wedding plans, it may be helpful to see a common everyday problem described with a flowchart before seeing a more traditional flowchart for a computer program. Always keep in mind that the logic dictates what the machine does, so you cannot leave out any details.

Figure 4.12 shows the flowchart for calling a friend on the telephone. To keep the example reasonable, the flowchart includes the important aspects of the problem, but there are many other ways to write the same flowchart. See if you can follow the flowchart. The direction arrows show you how to do it. Follow the flowchart several times, from start to finish, given each of these different scenarios:

1. Assume your phone is dead when you begin the call.
2. Assume your friend is home and answers the phone.
3. Assume your friend's phone is busy.
4. Assume nobody is home at your friend's house.
5. Assume your friend is not home, but her roommate answers.

Notice that the flowchart doesn't leave out the details of an actual phone call. It tries not to assume too much either. Calling a friend, to you, might just mean picking up the phone and calling, but when you flowchart the details, you begin to see how much you take for granted.

FIGURE 4.12.

You can flowchart the actions that you take when calling a friend on the telephone.

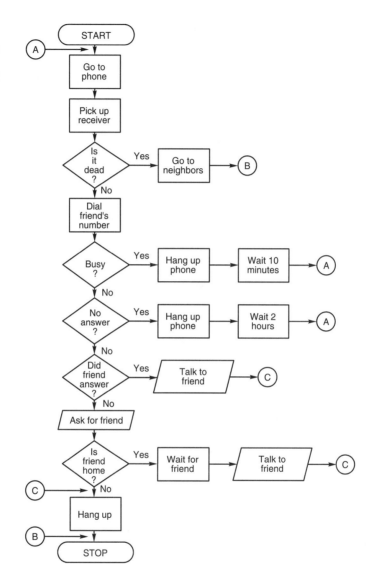

Can you see how using a flowchart for detailing a program's logic helps you to organize and select program details that are required? In Hour 3, "What Is a Program?," you learned how important it is to break up a program's goals into several detailed steps. The flowchart helps you do just that.

Notice also how the connector symbols work to keep the flowchart clean and tidy. There are several places where parts of the flowchart repeat. For example, if the friend's phone is busy, the connector circle with the *A* directs the flow back up to the top of the flowchart. Repetitive logic such as this might appear to go up the flowchart, breaking the second flowcharting rule, but it doesn't because the repeating logic eventually continues down and to the right when the friend's phone is finally answered.

Real-World Flowchart Solutions

Moving to a problem that uses a computerized solution, suppose you have to flowchart the logic of many payroll systems with overtime. You have to detail the procedure necessary to compute net pay given the possibility of time-and-a-half and double overtime. Before getting the flowchart, try to decipher these details:

- If an employee works 40 hours or less, the employee gets paid an hourly rate times the number of hours worked.

- If an employee works between 40 and 50 hours, the employee gets paid the regular pay rate times 40 hours, plus time-and-a-half (1.5 times the hourly rate) for those hours between 40 and 50.

- If an employee works more than 50 hours, the employee gets double time (2 times the hourly rate), plus 10 hours of time and a half (for those hours between 40 and 50), and 40 times the regular hourly rate for the first 40 hours.

Even though you can follow these details if you have to, the flowchart provides a much easier way of depicting the logic. Follow the flowchart in Figure 4.13. Take any number of hours worked and follow those hours through the flowchart. The flowchart keeps you on the right path of logic flow without the details that don't apply. Trying to write a program from the previous three-point list is much more difficult than writing a program from the flowchart.

Pseudocode

NEW TERM   Despite the power and ease of flowcharting, some companies prefer another method for logic description called. Pseudocode, sometimes called *structured English*, is a method of writing logic using sentences of text instead of the diagrams necessary for flowcharting.

Flowcharts take a lot of time and paper to draw. Even though flowcharting programs are available to help you draw and place the symbols, they are often limited and don't offer the flexibility that a lot of programming logic needs. Therefore, you must often resort to drawing flowcharts by hand. When you finish a flowchart and realize that you left out two critical symbols, you have to redraw much of the flowchart. Because of their nature, flowcharts take lots of time to draw, and some companies don't want their programmers taking the time to flowchart when pseudocode can take its place and is more time efficient.

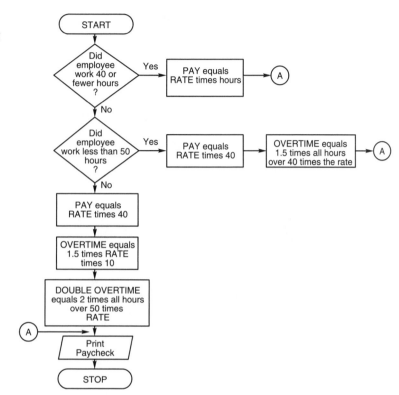

FIGURE 4.13.

Flowcharting a payroll routine helps you determine the logical order.

The only tool you need for pseudocode is a word processor. Word processors offer the power to insert, move, and delete text. Because pseudocode requires no drawing, it is faster than flowcharting by hand and easier to maintain. In addition, many programmers find it easier to convert pseudocode logic to the final program code.

As with flowcharts, there is no way to teach some pseudocode techniques unless you have been programming for a while. The term *pseudo* means false; therefore, *pseudocode* literally means *false code*. The more you know about programming languages, the more you will adapt to pseudocode, so just read the next example and try to get a feel for pseudocode.

Pseudocode doesn't have any programming language statements in it, but it also is not free-flowing English. It is a set of rigid English words that allow for the depiction of logic you see so often in flowcharts and programming languages. As with flowcharts, you can write pseudocode for anything, not just computer programs. A lot of instruction manuals use a form of pseudocode to illustrate the steps needed to assemble parts. Pseudocode offers a rigid description of logic that tries to leave little room for ambiguity.

Here is the logic for the payroll problem in pseudocode form. Notice that you can read the text, yet it is not a programming language. The indention helps keep track of which sentences go together. The pseudocode is readable by anyone, even by people unfamiliar with flowcharting symbols:

```
For each employee:
  If the employee worked 0 to 40 hours then
    net pay equals hours worked times rate.
  Otherwise,
    if the employee worked between 40 and 50 hours then
      net pay equals 40 times the rate;
      add to that (hours worked -40) times the rate times 1.5.
    Otherwise,
      net pay equals 40 times the rate;
      add to that 10 times the rate times 1.5;
      add to that (hours worked -50) times twice the rate.
  Deduct taxes from the net pay.
Print the paycheck.
End the problem.
```

Step 3: Write the Program

After the output is defined and the logic determined to get that output, you must go to the computer and generate the code—the programming language statements—you need to get there. This means that you must learn a programming language first. As mentioned earlier, there are many programming languages, and writing programs is no easy task for beginners, but you will soon be writing them with skill and expertise.

The program writing takes the longest to learn. After you learn to program, however, the actual programming process takes less time than the design if your design is accurate and complete. The nature of programming requires that you learn some new skills. The next few hourly lessons describe the programming process and give you the background of many of the popular programming languages available today.

Summary

A builder doesn't build a house before designing it, and a programmer should not write a program without designing it as well. Too often, programmers rush to the keyboard without thinking through the logic. A badly designed program results in lots of bugs and maintenance. This lesson described how you can ensure that your program design matches the design that the user wants. After you complete the output definition, you can organize the program's logic using top-down design, flowcharts, and pseudocode.

The next hour begins a new part of this 24-hour tutorial that introduces you to the fundamentals of programming.

Q&A

Q At what point in the top-down design should I begin to add details?

A Put off the details as long as possible. If you are designing a program to produce sales reports, you would not enter the printing of the final report total until you had completed all the other report design tasks. The details do fall out on their own when you can no longer break a task into two or more other tasks.

Q Once I break the top-down design into its lowest-level details, don't I also have the pseudocode details?

A The top-down design is a tool for determining all the details your program will need. The top-down design doesn't, however, put those details into their logical execution order. The pseudocode dictates the executing logic of your program and determines when things happen, the order they happen in, and when they stop happening. The top-down design simply determines everything that might happen in the program.

Workshop

The quiz questions are provided for your further understanding. See Appendix A, "Answers to End of Chapter Questions," for answers.

Quiz

1. Why does proper design often take longer than writing the actual program?
2. Where does a programmer first begin determining the user's requirements?
3. True or false: Proper top-down design forces you to put off details as long as possible.
4. How does top-down design differ from pseudocode?
5. Why can you not always use visual design tools with users?
6. How many values can a flowchart decision symbol produce?
7. What kind of question should a decision symbol include?
8. True or false: You can flowchart both program logic as well as real-world procedures.
9. How does pseudocode differ from a flowchart?
10. What is the final step of the programming process (before testing the final result)?

Hour 5

The Programming Process and Structured Techniques

Now you are familiar with the steps to take before programming. In this hour's lesson, you begin the programming process, starting to learn about specific languages and to write your own programs. You now know that two steps must always precede writing the program—defining the output and developing the logic. After you develop the logic, you can write the program, using one of the many available programming languages.

To finish the programming process, you must write, test, and distribute the program. Of course, all three steps assume that you know a programming language. The rest of this book completes the programming process that began with the design of the program output and the development of the logic.

The highlights of this hour include:

- What it takes to write programs
- What an editor is

- What the difference is between a line editor and a full-screen editor
- Why structured programming is so important
- What the three structured-programming constructs are
- What steps are necessary for testing a program
- What the difference is between desk checking and beta testing
- Why parallel testing is so critical

Using an Editor

NEW TERM An *editor* is the tool you use to type programs into your computer. An editor is like a word processor in that it enables you to type lines of code, edit them, move and copy them, and save them to the disk. For this reason, editors are often referred to as *text editors*. An editor is unlike a word processor, however, in that it doesn't perform *word wrapping*. When you come to the end of a line in a word processor, the word processor moves the cursor and the partial word at the end of the line to the next line. Word wrap would be detrimental to computer programs.

Remember that programming languages must be concise. Programming statements can't run together like printed speech. Using some programming languages, you can put more than one programming statement on a single line, but this practice isn't recommended because it makes reading the program more difficult for you and others. The harder a program is to read, the more difficult that program will be to maintain and update in the future.

Editors fall into the following two categories: line editors and full-screen editors. The next two sections describe each one.

Programmers are sometimes fanatical about their editors, often thinking the editor they use is the only one anyone should consider when doing *serious* programming. Generally, whatever editor you feel comfortable with is the one you should use. Familiarize yourself with both kinds of editors because each offers advantages over the other in certain situations.

Line Editors

Many programmers feel that line editors are an ancient relic of the past, useful only for those old teletype terminals that were considered the cutting edge in 1965. Another group of programmers, however, says that they are more productive using a line editor than any other kind.

Using a line editor, you can enter and edit program text. What differentiates a line editor from a full-screen editor is that the line editor lets you work on only a single line at a time. Line editors don't let you use the cursor-movement keys (generally the up-arrow, down-arrow, left-arrow, and right-arrow keys) to move around the screen, making changes to several lines one after the other, as does a full-screen editor. Instead, you must specifically tell the editor which line you want to change. You can make changes to that line only. Then you must designate another line you want to edit.

The most popular line editor in use today is still the UNIX-based version named *vi* (for *visual*). vi is available for microcomputers and is used by many UNIX programmers who have moved to the microcomputer environment.

LINE EDITORS AREN'T FOREVER

Even those programmers who prefer line editors to full-screen editors have to agree that more and more programmers are moving to full-screen editors (described in the next section). Full-screen editors are considered easier to learn and use, especially because they mirror the actions of many word processors.

Be careful not to dismiss line editors as something you can ignore. The advantage of line editors is that they are almost always available, no matter what computer you use. Some dial-up computer systems don't allow full-screen editors because the modem connection doesn't permit full-screen control from a remote site (although even modem connections that don't permit full-screen control are becoming less common). Therefore, even if you don't fully master a line editor, you should spend some time learning a few commands from one so that you can use one quickly if you ever need to.

5

Full-Screen Editors

The tedium of line editors causes many programmers to switch to a full-screen editor and stay there. Many of today's full-screen editors have pull-down menus and mouse capabilities. If you've used a word processor, you might not need to learn any editor commands to use a full-screen editor. As long as you can use the menus and find the Help key, you can do almost anything you want with a program file.

Figure 5.1 shows a QBasic program being entered. Many programming languages today come with their own full-screen editors. Because QBasic has been supplied with every operating system since MS-DOS 5.0's release, you can write QBasic programs if you have a PC.

You will learn all about QBasic's editor when you begin to write QBasic programs, starting in Hour 9, "Input and Output."

FIGURE 5.1.

*QBasic uses a
full-screen editor.*

In Figure 5.1, you see many elements common to most full-screen editors. The large editing window in the middle of the screen is where you enter and make edits to the program. Across the top of the screen is a row of menu options. Unlike a line editor, such as the old Edlin that used to come with MS-DOS, you don't have to memorize a bunch of commands to use a full-screen editor; you only have to select from menus.

Most of the time when you are in an editor, you are typing and changing the program's text. With full-screen editors, you can use the arrow keys to move the cursor around the screen, inserting and deleting text as you would with a word processor. When you want to perform more than typing and changing characters and words, you can resort to the menu, which has commands for saving and loading programs to and from the disk, searching and replacing text, and moving and copying blocks of text (a *block* is one or more characters).

New Term Most of today's full-screen editors offer *pull-down menus*. Figure 5.2 shows the File pull-down menu. When you select File (by selecting with the mouse, if you have one, or pressing Alt+F), QBasic opens a list of all the File menu's options (sometimes called a *submenu* because it's a menu produced from the main menu). When you see a pull-down menu, you can either select one of its options (by moving the menu highlight with the arrow keys or selecting with the mouse) or eliminate the menu altogether by pressing the Esc key.

One of the biggest advantages of integrating program editors with program interpreters and compilers is their ease of use. Before integration (back when line editors were the *only* kind of editors available), you had to start an editor, enter the program, save the file, exit the editor, compile the program you just typed (which means learning another set of commands), and if the program had errors, you had to go back into the editor and correct the errors.

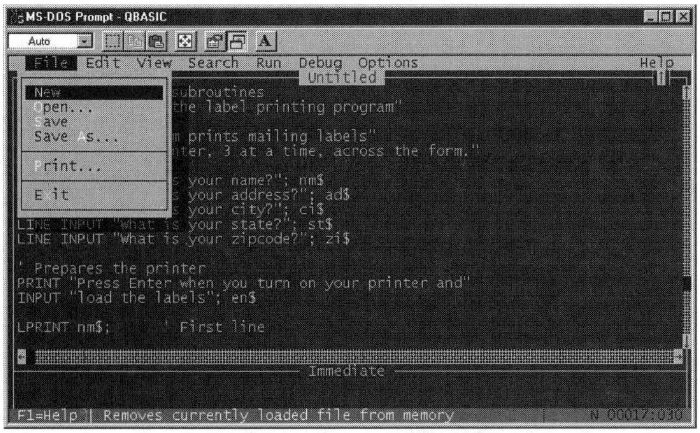

Figure 5.2.

*Most full-screen
editors come with
helpful pull-down
menus.*

With an integrated editor and programming language, as you'll use with QBasic, you can use the same set of menu commands and a common environment to enter the program, interpret it (or compile it), and run it, all from the same place. This simplicity means that beginners can concentrate more on the program's contents and less on all the other commands needed to get the program working. After you enter the program, you can use the menus to translate the program into machine language and run it without leaving the full-screen environment. You can view the program output and instantly switch with one keystroke back to the program that produced the output. (You can continue switching back and forth as many times as you like.) If the output has errors, you can easily find the errors and change the source code.

Some of the most powerful integrated full-screen editors and programming languages are Microsoft's Visual Basic and Visual C++, and similar compilers from other companies. These full-screen editors and compilers offer the usual fare of powerful editing and compiling menu options and advanced programming tools such as debuggers and profilers.

New Term With a *debugger* you can run a program one line at a time, inspecting pieces as it runs. Rather than try to figure out what's wrong at the lightning-fast execution speed at which programs normally run, you can examine the output at your own pace. A *profiler* is a program that monitors the execution of your program, looking for sluggish code that might be optimized for speed or size. Many of today's compilers are optimizing compilers that try to take your code and turn it into the fastest possible machine code, but there is always room for improvement. On average, 5% of a program takes 95% of the program's execution time. The profiler can help you improve the speed and efficiency of your program.

If you are writing programs for the Windows environment, as most PC programmers do today, it helps to perform the program writing, testing, and debugging within a single

5

Windows programming environment such as Visual Basic. Figure 5.3 shows the Visual Basic screen with its full-screen editor in the middle window. The Visual Basic screen looks busy, and it is, but as you'll learn in Hour 14, "Programming with Visual Basic," Visual Basic is not as complex as it first appears.

FIGURE 5.3.

The Windows-based Visual Basic programming environment includes an editor.

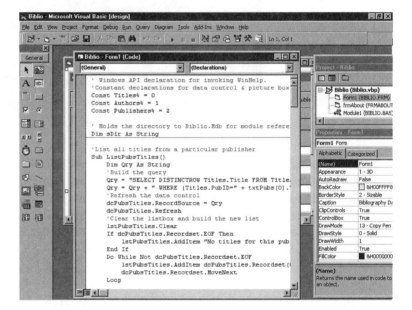

Structured Programming

In the late 1960s, programming departments began to wallow in programming backlogs that built at tremendous rates. More people were writing more programs than ever, but many programmers had to be hired to maintain the previously written programs.

Learn to write readable and maintainable programs. By using a conscientious approach (instead of the old "throw a program together" approach that some programmers use), you help ensure your future as a programmer for many years. Companies save money when a programmer writes code that is easily maintained.

When you finish a program, you are finished only for the time being. That program's assumptions about the job it performs will change over time. Businesses never remain constant in this global economy. Data processing managers began recognizing that the programming maintenance backlog was beginning to take its toll on development. Programmers were pulled away from new projects in order to update older projects. The maintenance was taking too long.

During the maintenance crisis of the 1960s, data processing people began looking for new ways to program. They weren't necessarily interested in new languages but in new ways to write programs that would make them work better and faster and, most importantly, make them readable so that others could maintain the programs without too much trouble. Structured-programming techniques were developed during this time.

Structured programming is a philosophy stating that programs should be written in an orderly fashion without a lot of jumping to and fro. If a program is written to be easily read, the program can be changed more easily. People have known for many years that clear writing style is important, but it became obvious to computer people only after nearly 20 years of using nonstructured techniques.

There is some debate as to exactly when beginning programmers should be introduced to structured programming. Some people feel that programmers should be trained in structured programming from the beginning. Others feel beginners should learn to program any way that gets the job done, and then they should adapt to structured programming.

You now understand flowcharts and pseudocode, so you can see what structured programming is all about with those tools. Then, when you learn a programming language in the last half of this book, you will be thinking in the structured-programming mode and will naturally fall into a structured-programming pattern from the beginning.

A well-written and easily read program doesn't necessarily mean it's structured. Structured programming is a specific approach to programming that generally produces well-written and easily read programs. Nothing can make up for a programmer rushing to finish a program by what he thinks is the fastest way. You often hear "Later, I'll make it structured, but for now, I'll leave it as it is." *Later* never comes. People use the program until one day, when changes have to be made, the changes take as long as, or longer than, it would take to scrap the entire program and rewrite it from scratch.

Structured programming includes the following three constructs:

- Sequence
- Decision (also called *selection*)
- Looping (also called *repetition* or *iteration*)

NEW TERM   A *construct* (from the word construction) is a building block of a language and one of the language's fundamental operations. As long as a programming language supports these three constructs (most do), you can write structured programs. The opposite of a structured program is known as *spaghetti code*. Like spaghetti that flows and swirls all over the plate, an unstructured program—one full of spaghetti code—flows all over the place with little or no structure. An unstructured program contains lots of *branching*. A branch occurs when a program goes this way and that with no order. The first list of directions to the grocery branched on its very first statement.

JUMPING AROUND

Most programming languages enable you to branch with a GOTO statement. The GOTO works like it sounds; it tells the computer to go to another place in the program and continue execution there. Having to search a program for the next instruction to execute makes you break your train of thought.

Some programmers and programming textbooks warn you to completely stay away from the GOTO statement. The GOTO statement by itself isn't bad when used conservatively, but it can wreak havoc on a program's readability if you overuse it.

The three structured-programming constructs aren't just for programs. You will find that you can use them for flowcharts, pseudocode, and any other set of instructions you write for others. The three structured-programming constructs ensure that a program doesn't branch all over the place and that any execution is controlled and easily followed.

The following three sections explain each of the three structured-programming constructs. Read them carefully and you'll see that the concept of a structured program is easy to understand. Learning about structure before learning a language should help you think of structure as you develop your programming skills.

Sequence

NEW TERM   *Sequence* is nothing more than two or more instructions, one after the other. The sequential instructions are the easiest of the three structured-programming constructs because you can follow the program from the first statement to the last within the sequence. Figure 5.4 shows a flowchart that illustrates sequence.

Here is pseudocode that matches the sequence of the flowchart:

```
Get the hours worked.
Multiply the hours by the rate.
Subtract taxes to compute net pay.
Print paycheck.
```

Because computers must have the capability of making decisions and performing repetitive tasks, not all your programs can consist of straight sequential logic. When sequence is available, however, it makes for straightforward program logic.

FIGURE 5.4.

The sequence structured-programming construct executes the program in order.

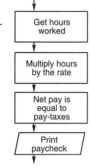

Decision (Selection)

NEW TERM You have seen the *decision* construct before. The decision symbol in a flowchart is the point at which a decision is made. Any time a program makes a decision, it must take off in one of two directions. Obviously, a decision is a break from the sequential program flow, but it's a controlled break.

By its nature, a branch must be performed based on the result of a decision (in effect, the code must skip the code that is not to execute). A decision, however, as opposed to a straight branch, ensures that you don't have to worry about the code not performed. You won't have to go back and read the part of the program skipped by the decision. (Based on new data, the program might repeat a decision and take a different route the second time, but again, you can always assume that the decision code not being executed at the time is meaningless to the current loop.)

Figure 5.5 shows a flowchart that contains part of a teacher's grading program logic.

5

FIGURE 5.5.

The decision structured-programming construct offers one of two choices.

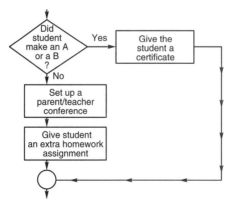

Here is the pseudocode for the decision shown in the flowchart:

```
If the student makes an A or B,
  give the student an achievement certificate.
Otherwise:
  set up a parent-teacher conference;
give the student extra homework.
```

Looping (Repetition and Iteration)

NEW TERM   Perhaps the most important task of computers is *looping* (the term for repeating or iterating through lines of program code). Computers repeat sections of a program millions of times and never become bored. Computers are perfect companions for workers who have lots of data to process, because the computer can process the data, repeating the common calculations needed throughout all the data, and the person can analyze the results.

Looping is prevalent in almost every program written. Rarely do you write a program that is a straight sequence of instructions. The time it takes to design and write a program isn't always worth the effort when a straight series of tasks is involved. Programs are most powerful when they can repeat a series of sequential statements or decisions.

Figure 5.6 shows a flowchart that repeats a section in a loop. Loops only temporarily break the rule that says flowcharts should flow down and to the right. Loops within a flowchart are fine because eventually the logic will stop looping.

> Be aware of the dreaded *infinite loop*. An *infinite loop* is a never-ending loop. If your computer goes into an infinite loop, it continues looping, never finishing, and sometimes it's difficult to regain control of the program without rebooting the computer. Loops should always be prefaced with a decision statement so that eventually the decision triggers the end of the loop and the rest of the program can finish.

Here is the pseudocode for the flowchart:

```
If there are more customers,
  do the following:
    calculate the next customer's balance;
    print an invoice.
Otherwise,
  print the total balance report.
```

As you can see, eventually there won't be any customers, and the loop (beginning with do) will stop looping so that the rest of the logic can take over.

FIGURE 5.6.

The looping structured-programming construct repeats parts of the program.

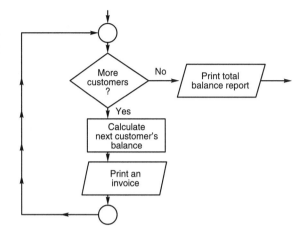

None of these structured-programming constructs should be new to you because you saw them in Hour 4, "The Program's Design." As long as you keep these three constructs in mind while you write flowcharts, pseudocode, and the eventual program, and as long as you resist the temptation to start branching all over the program, you will write well-structured, easy-to-maintain programs and ensure your position as a programmer for many years.

Testing the Program

When you finish writing the actual program code, you aren't completely done with the program. You must turn to the task of debugging the program. You want to eliminate as many bugs from the program as possible. For obvious reasons, you don't want the user to do this. You don't want the user of your program finding all kinds of mistakes that you made. Therefore, you must thoroughly test the program.

Here are the typical testing steps that programmers should follow before distributing a final version of a program to users:

1. Perform desk checking.

2. Perform a beta test.

3. Compare the results of the beta test against the old system's parallel test results.

 Most programmers go through a series of desk checks on their programs. *Desk checking* is the process of sitting in front of a computer and checking the program by using as many different scenarios of data as possible to find weak spots and errors in the code. During desk checking, programmers should try extreme values, type bad input, and generally try their best to make the program fail. Programmers should also try every option available in the program, using different combinations to see what happens in all situations.

NEW TERM When desk checking is completed and programmers are as confident as they can be about the program's correctness, programmers should set up a group of users to try the program. This is known in the industry as the *beta testing* stage. The more beta testers (test users of the program) you find to test the program, the better the chance that errors will be found. Users often try things the programmer never thought of while writing the program.

BETA TESTING NOW EXISTS ON A GRAND SCALE

More and more companies are openly inviting the public to help beta test products. Microsoft, for example, is extremely open about distributing beta test copies of its applications and operating systems long before the final release is available for sale. Most of these beta versions are available for download over the Internet. These beta test products give reviewers and testers an early peek at the software, which also helps Microsoft because these testers can inform Microsoft of bugs they find.

As the beta audience grows, so does the time a company takes for the test. The problem is that today's software is highly complex, taking as many as 100 programmers to produce a product such as a new version of Windows. A large-scale beta test is about the only way that these companies can discover some of the bugs that must be fixed before the product is released.

NEW TERM The user should never abandon an old system and switch to the new program right away. *Parallel testing* should be performed. For instance, if you write a payroll program to replace the manual payroll system for a dry cleaner, the dry cleaner shouldn't receive a copy of your program and use only that. Instead, the dry cleaner should continue its manual payroll system and use your program at the same time. Although this means that payroll takes a little longer each pay period, you can compare the results of the program with those of the manual system to see whether they match.

Only after several pay periods of well-matched parallel testing should the user feel confident enough to use the program without the manual backup.

During this testing period, programmers might have to make several changes to the program. Expect that changes will be necessary, and you won't feel disappointed or lose your programming confidence. Programmers rarely write a program correctly the first time. It usually takes many attempts to make programs correct. The thorough testing described in this section doesn't ensure a perfect program. Some errors might appear only after the program is used for a while. The more testing you do, the less likely that errors will creep up later.

Learning the Program Language

One important step has been left out of this book so far. That is the step of learning the language itself. The rest of this book is devoted to describing the various programming languages available. You will have hands-on practice with an introductory language called QBasic, and you will learn about other languages as well.

Most programming books jump right in and start teaching a language in the first chapter. There is nothing wrong with this approach, but somewhere along the way, you need to learn to design programs. That is the purpose of this book. At this point, you have a good grasp of programming fundamentals, and you understand more about what professional programmers do in their programming environments.

It is now time for you to take the plunge into the world of programming languages and begin to see what you will face as you learn a programming language.

Summary

The programming process requires more than sitting at the keyboard. Proper design is important, as are structured-programming techniques and proper testing. An editor is a tool that you use to enter programs into the computer, just as you use a word processor to create documents. With the editor, you can enter, change, delete, move, copy, and save (to disk) program text. Although two kinds of editors exist, the full-screen editor is much more common these days than the line-editor. Most of today's programming languages come with their own editor built in to the programming environment.

You and others can maintain a well-written program. Because of the changing world and the high maintenance of programs, you should attempt to learn structured-programming techniques that help clarify programs. The three structured-programming constructs that you now know are sequence, decision, and looping.

The next hour describes the early programming languages so that you will understand how today's languages evolved.

5

Q&A

Q How much testing is enough?

A You can never test too much, but resources and the user's request for the program certainly bear on the decision to stop testing. If you know bugs exist in the program, you must remove them, so testing will help ensure that you've fixed all that you can fix.

Q What tools are available to help me test my program?

A Most of today's integrated debuggers are highly efficient at helping you spot and remove errors in your programs. Hour 22's lesson, "Debugging Tools," explores the way that you can use a debugger to locate problems, examine values, and test programs.

Workshop

The quiz questions are provided for your further understanding. For the answers, see Appendix A, "Answers to End of Chapter Questions."

Quiz

1. Why should you avoid using a word processor for program editing?
2. What are the two kinds of editors?
3. Which editor is the most popular today?
4. What takes the place of memorized commands in today's full-screen editors?
5. What is a debugger?
6. What is a profiler?
7. What is the opposite of spaghetti code?
8. What are the three structured-programming language constructs?
9. Why can excess branching be bad?
10. What is the difference between parallel testing and beta testing?

HOUR **6**

Programming Languages: The Early Years

With this hour's lesson, you can step into the ranks of the few, the proud, the people of tomorrow, by developing an understanding of several programming languages. This lesson focuses on the earlier programming languages, many of which are still in use today. You will learn how programming languages began and how they have evolved over the years.

To understand how programming languages work, you must learn how computers store programs and data at the machine's lowest level. This chapter teaches you a little *binary representation* (with which you can impress your friends at the next cocktail party you attend). After you see how computers actually do things at their lowest level, you'll move up to learn about some of the many high-level programming languages.

The highlights of this hour include:

- What is meant by a bit
- How many bits are in a byte

- What the ASCII table is for

- How a computer actually does math

- What kinds of programs are best suited to the FORTRAN language

- Why COBOL, one of the earliest languages, is still used today

- Why a company might adopt FORTRAN instead of COBOL, or vice versa

- How PL/I failed

- When APL is used

- Why someone would want to learn ADA

Storing Programs and Data

While typing away in your program editor, what do you think happens when you press the keys? Does the letter A go somewhere inside the computer's memory when you press the A key? It must, or else the computer could never remember your program's contents. The computer does store the A, but not in the format you might first expect. The computer only stores a representation of the letter A. For all intents, the A is in memory, but it does not look like you think it should.

Your computer's memory is made up of many characters of storage. As you learned in Hour 2, "Computer Hardware Unmasked," when you purchase a computer with 32MB of memory, you get a computer with approximately 32 million characters of storage. Although the number is rounded down slightly because of the way computer memory is measured, you can store approximately 32 million characters and not a lot more. Think of a cassette tape; a 60-minute tape cannot hold 90 minutes of music no matter how hard you try to squeeze 90 minutes of music on it.

Remember that your computer is nothing more, at its lowest level, than thousands of switches turning electricity on and off. Each character in your computer is represented by a combination of on and off switches. Programmers generally refer to an on switch as a *1* and an off switch as a *0*. Because these switches have only two values, programmers call the 0s and 1s *binary digits*, or *bits* for short. There is a total of eight bits for every character in your computer, and eight bits are known as a *byte*. Therefore, every character of storage takes eight bits to represent (eight on and off switches), and therefore, a character is a byte.

The reason it takes eight switches to represent one character is that if there were fewer, there wouldn't be enough combinations of on and off states to represent all the characters possible (uppercase, lowercase, digits, and special characters such as %, ^, and *).

Understanding the ASCII Table

NEW TERM Years ago, somebody wrote the various combinations of eight 1s and 0s, from 00000000 to 11111111, and assigned a unique character to each one. The table of characters was standardized and is known today as the *ASCII table* (pronounced *ask-ee*). Table 6.1 shows a partial listing of the ASCII table. ASCII stands for *American Standard Code for Information Interchange*. Some ASCII tables use only the last seven bits (called the *7-bit ASCII table*) and they keep the far left-hand bit off. 7-bit ASCII tables cannot represent as many different characters as can today's 8-bit ASCII tables.

TABLE 6.1   SAMPLE ASCII VALUES

Character	ASCII Code	Decimal Equivalent
Space	00100000	32
0	00110000	48
1	00110001	49
2	00110010	50
3	00110011	51
9	00111001	57
?	00111111	63
A	01000001	65
B	01000010	66
C	01000011	67
a	01100001	97
b	01100010	98

Each ASCII value has a corresponding decimal number associated with it. These values are shown at the right of the eight-bit values in Table 6.1. Therefore, even though the computer represents the character ? as 00111111 (two off switches with six on switches), you can refer, through programming, to that ASCII value as 63 and your computer will know you mean 00111111. One of the advantages of high-level programming languages is that they often let you use the easier (for people) decimal values and the programming language converts the value to the eight-bit binary value used inside the computer.

6

As you can tell from the ASCII values in Table 6.1, every character in the computer, both uppercase and lowercase letters, and even the space, has its own unique ASCII value. The unique ASCII code is the only way the computer has to differentiate characters.

New Term Every microcomputer, and the few minicomputers still in existence, uses the ASCII table. Mainframes use a similar table called the *EBCDIC table* (pronounced *eb-se-dik*). The ASCII table is the fundamental storage representation of all data and programs that your computer manages.

The Nature of ASCII Codes

Think back to the internal storage of single characters described earlier in the previous section. When you press the letter A, that A is not stored in your computer; rather, the ASCII value of the A is stored. As you can see from the ASCII values in the previous table, the letter A is represented as 01000001 (all eight switches except two are off in every byte of memory that holds a letter A).

> The ASCII table is not very different from another type of coded table you may have heard of. Morse code is a table of representations for letters of the alphabet. Instead of 1s and 0s, the code uses combinations of dashes and dots to represent characters.

As Figure 6.1 shows, when you press the letter *A* on your keyboard, the *A* does not go into memory, but the ASCII value of 01000001 does. The computer keeps that pattern of on and off switches in that memory location as long as the *A* is to remain there. As far as you are concerned, the *A* is in memory as the letter *A*, but now you know exactly what happens.

Figure 6.1.

The A is not an A after it leaves the keyboard.

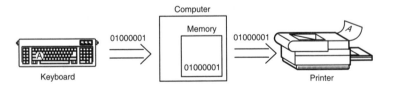

If you print the program you just typed, and the computer is ready to print the "character" stored in that memory location, the computer's CPU sends the ASCII code for the A to the printer. Just before printing, the printer knows that it must make its output readable to people, so it looks up 01000001 in its own ASCII table and prints the A to paper.

From the time the A left the keyboard until right before it printed, it was not an A at all, but just a combination of eight 1s and 0s that represents an A.

Understanding Binary Arithmetic

At their lowest level, computers cannot subtract, multiply, or divide. Neither can calculators. The world's largest and fastest supercomputers can only add—that's it. It performs the addition at the bit level. Binary arithmetic is the only means by which any electronic digital computing machine can perform arithmetic.

The computer makes you think it can perform all sorts of fancy calculations because it is lightning-fast. The computer can only add, but it can do so very quickly.

Suppose you want the computer to add seven 6s together. If you asked the computer (through programming) to perform the calculation:

$6 + 6 + 6 + 6 + 6 + 6 + 6$

the computer would return the answer 42 immediately. The computer has no problem performing addition. The problems arise when you request that the computer perform another type of calculation, such as this one:

$42 - 6 - 6 - 6 - 6 - 6 - 6 - 6$

Because the computer can only add, it cannot do the subtraction. However (and this is where the "catch" comes in), the computer can *negate* numbers. That is, the computer can take the negative of a number. It can take the negative of 6 and represent (at the bit level) negative 6. After it has done that, it can *add* –6 to 42 and continue doing so seven times. In effect, the internal calculation becomes this:

$42 + (-6) + (-6) + (-6) + (-6) + (-6) + (-6) + (-6)$

NEW TERM Adding seven –6s produces the correct result of 0. In reality, the computer is not subtracting. At its bit level, the computer can convert a number to its negative through a process known as *2's complement*. A number's 2's complement is the negative of its original value at the bit level. The computer has in its internal logic circuits the ability to rapidly convert a number to its 2's complement and then carry out the addition of negatives, thereby seemingly performing subtraction.

6

After the computer can add and simulate subtraction (through successive adding of negatives), it can simulate multiplying and dividing. To multiply 6 times 7, the computer actually adds 6 together seven times and produces 42. Therefore,

6×7

becomes this:

$6 + 6 + 6 + 6 + 6 + 6 + 6$

To divide 42 by 7, the computer subtracts 7 from 42 (well, it adds the *negative* of 7 to 42) until it reaches 0 and counts the number of times (6) it took to reach 0, like this:

$42 + (-7) + (-7) + (-7) + (-7) + (-7) + (-7)$

The computer represents numbers in a manner similar to characters. As Table 6.2 shows, numbers are easy to represent at the binary level. After numbers reach a certain limit (256 to be exact), the computer will use more than one byte to represent the number, taking as many memory locations as it needs to represent the extent of the number. The computer, after it is taught to add, subtract, multiply, and divide, can then perform any math necessary as long as a program is supplied to direct it.

TABLE 6.2   THE FIRST 20 BINARY NUMBERS

Number	Binary Equivalent
0	00000000
1	00000001
2	00000010
3	00000011
4	00000100
5	00000101
6	00000110
7	00000111
8	00001000
9	00001001
10	00001010
11	00001011
12	00001100
13	00001101
14	00001110

Number	Binary Equivalent
15	00001111
16	00010000
17	00010001
18	00010010
19	00010011
20	00010100

The first 255 binary numbers overlap the ASCII table values. That is, the binary representation for the letter A is 01000001, and the binary number for 65 is also 01000001. The computer knows by the context of how your programs use the memory location whether the value is the letter A or the number 65.

To see an example of what goes on at the bit level, follow this example to see what happens when you ask the computer to subtract 65 from 65. The result should be 0, and as you can see from the following steps, that is exactly what the result is at the binary level:

1. Suppose you want the computer to calculate the following:

   65
   -65

2. The binary representation for 65 is 01000001 and the 2's complement for 65 is 10111111 (which is –65 in *computerese*). Therefore, you are requesting that the computer perform this calculation:

   01000001
   +10111111

3. Because a binary number cannot have the digit *2* (there are only 0s and 1s in binary), the computer carries 1 anytime a calculation results in a value of 2; 1 + 1 equals 10 in binary. Although this can be confusing, you can make an analogy with decimal arithmetic. People work in a base-10 numbering system. (Binary is known as base 2.) There is no single digit to represent 10; we have to reuse two digits already used to form ten, namely *1* and *0*. In base 10, 9 + 1 is 10. Therefore, the result of 1 + 1 in binary is 10 or "0 and carry 1 to the next column."

   01000001
   +10111111
   100000000

6

4. Because the answer should fit within the same number of bits as the two original numbers (at least for this example—your computer may use more bits to represent numbers), the ninth bit is discarded, leaving the 0 result. This example shows that binary 65 plus binary negative 65 equals 0, as it should.

Remembering the First Programs

NEW TERM
The earliest computers were not programmed in the same way as today's computers. It took much more effort to program them. The early computers' memories held only data and not programs. The concept of programming those early computers was vastly different because the programs were *hard-wired* into the machine. The programs were physically wired by experts to generate and process the data. The first computer programmers had never heard of using a keyboard, editor, and compiler; the first programmers were hardware experts, not software experts.

NEW TERM
Programming these computers was very difficult. To make a change, the hardware programmer had to reroute the wires that made the program do its thing. It wasn't long before a man by the name of John von Neumann invented the *shared-program* concept. He demonstrated that a program could be stored in memory along with the data. After the programs were in memory and out of the wired hardware, the programs were much easier to change. John von Neumann's breakthrough was one of the most important and lasting advances in the entire computing history; we still use his shared-program concept in today's machines.

Programming early computers took a tremendous effort because they had to be programmed in the machine's native 1s and 0s. Therefore, the first few instructions to a computer might look like this:

```
01000110
11000100
10111011
00011101
    .
    .
    .
```

Whenever a programmer wanted to add two numbers, move values in memory, or whatever, the programmer had to refer to a table that described the proper patterns of 1s and 0s for the desired instructions. Flipping the switches and programming the machine took hours, but it was a giant leap forward from hard-wired computer programming.

Simplifying Machine Language

Instead of typing 1s and 0s, the programmer can type names associated with each instruction in the machine language. Therefore, the instructions from the previous section might look something like this:

```
ADD A, 6
MOV A, OUT
LOAD B
SUB B, A
   :
```

These commands are cryptic, but they are a lot easier to remember than the 1s and 0s. The words are called *mnemonics*, which means the words are easy-to-remember abbreviations for the instructions. ADD A, 6 is a lot easier to remember when you need to add 6 to the value of a memory location named A than is 01000110.

NEW TERM   Of course, the computer could not understand the mnemonics, but a translator program called an *assembler* was written to be the go-between for the programmer's mnemonics and the 1s and 0s to which they were translated. Figure 6.2 shows how the assembler acts as the go-between for the human programmer at the keyboard and the machine. A huge leap forward was made when the assembler language became the primary means by which programmers entered instructions into the computer. This second programming language (the first was the native 1s and 0s machine language) allowed for much faster program development. The software revolution was begun just a few years after the computer hardware was born.

FIGURE 6.2.

The assembler translates mnemonics into 1s and 0s.

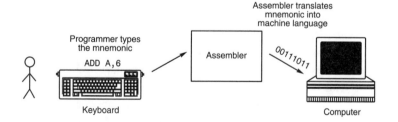

Low-Level Programming

These first two programming languages—machine language and assembler language—are called *low-level programming languages*. The computer doesn't need to translate much to convert assembler to machine language because each assembler instruction has a one-to-one correlation with a machine-language instruction (a machine-language instruction may take more than one byte of memory, though). Although low-level languages are not used as much today as the high-level programming languages (Visual Basic, C, and

C++, for example), you can still program today's computers using low-level languages. For instance, if you have a PC, you can use a program called an assembler to enter machine language code directly into the computer's memory locations.

 NEW TERM Your car probably has a computer in it, as well as your VCR and watch. Many of these devices require *embedded programming*, meaning that the instructions are burned right into the chips of the computer and not stored on any kind of disk storage. Often, these kinds of devices are expensive, so to reduce their cost, the makers use machine language to program them to eliminate all extra overhead and to use as small and inexpensive a device as possible.

> Today's machine language programmers don't use binary 1s and 0s, but what they do use is almost as cryptic, especially to the uninitiated in the ways of low-level languages. By converting the binary values to *hexadecimal* values (also known as *base 16*), machine language programs are slightly easier to work with.

There are only a few modern assembler language translators on the market today, and most of those are only available by mail order because of their low demand in retail outlets. The most common is Microsoft's Macro Assembler, although with most of Microsoft's visual programming products, such as Visual C++, you can access assembler from the high-level programming language. These machine language product elements still require complexity that most programmers never need to master.

Security Is an Issue

With today's online and networked computer environments, security becomes an issue when dealing with machine-level code. The operating system, such as Windows 95, Windows 98, or Windows NT, attempts to protect from inadvertent (or attempted) security violations by protecting memory from direct modifications. These operating systems buffer memory so that a low-level program cannot change the contents of a system area of memory without proper system permission. Therefore, you may not even be able to access some areas of memory when working with a low-level programming product.

Getting Closer to English

High-level programming languages evolved from the complexity of the low-level languages. After assembler language was made available, more companies began using computers. With the beginning of widespread use of computers came the need to write more complex software applications to support those companies. The low-level machine and assembler languages were too inefficient for the quick turnaround that the companies needed. High-level languages were developed to add one more layer between the programmer and the hardware. That extra layer meant that more work was required by the computer to translate a high-level language into machine language, but the programmers were free from the job of low-level coding. Two of the earliest high-level programming compilers were FORTRAN and COBOL. Both are still in widespread use today.

Using the FORTRAN Language

FORTRAN stands for *Formula Translator*. As its name implies, it is used for mathematical and scientific applications. FORTRAN works very well with high-precision numbers and offers an excellent library of built-in trigonometric routines that aid the scientific developer.

Over the years, programmers have added to the FORTRAN language, giving it more character-manipulation capabilities. The early versions of FORTRAN existed to solve mathematical computations without much regard for the cosmetics of how the results looked. FORTRAN compilers still exist today, both for mainframes as well as in PC versions, and modern FORTRAN compilers work better with character data (often called *character string* data because strings of characters make up words and sentences) than the older versions did, but they still retain their mathematical capabilities.

Listing 6.1 shows a sample FORTRAN program. It is not the goal of this lesson, or of this book, to teach you FORTRAN. FORTRAN is not regarded as a beginner's language (although it is not as difficult as many of the others; after you learn QBasic, you can pick up FORTRAN relatively easily because QBasic's early roots were originally based on FORTRAN). The program in Listing 6.1 is an example of a payroll computation that you can study.

LISTING 6.1 FORTRAN CAN HELP CALCULATE PAYROLL

6

```
 1: *
 2: * Calculate payroll amounts and print the net pay
 3: *
 4: * Print a title
 5:       WRITE(6,10)
 6:    10 FORMAT(1H1, 2X, '** PAYROLL COMPUTATION **'//)
 7: *
 8: * Initialize overtime to 0
 9: *
10:       TOVRTM = 0.0
```

continues

LISTING 6.1   CONTINUED

```
11: *
12: * Get hours worked and other pay data from user
13: *
14:       WRITE(6, 20)
15:    20 FORMAT('WHAT WERE THE HOURS WORKED? ')
16:       READ(5, 21) HRS
17:    21 FORMAT(F4.1)
18:       WRITE(6, 22)
19:    22 FORMAT(/'WHAT IS THE HOURLY RATE? ')
20:       READ(5, 23) RATE
21:    23 FORMAT(F7.2)
22:       WRITE(6, 24)
23:    24 FORMAT(/'WHAT IS THE TAX RATE? ')
24:       READ(6, 25) TAXRTE
25:    25 FORMAT(F7.2)
26: *
27: * Calculate the results
28: *
29: * Overtime is left at 0.0 or is double pay
30: * depending on the hours the employee worked
31:       IF (HRS .LT. 40.0) GOTO 100
32:       TOVRTM = (HRS - 40.0) * RATE * 2.0
33:       GROSS = 40.0 * RATE
34:       GOTO 200
35:   100 GROSS = HRS * RATE
36:   200 GROSS = GROSS + TOVRTM
37:       TNET = GROSS * (1.0 - TAXRTE)
38: *
39: * PRINT THE RESULTS
40: *
41:       WRITE(6, 300) HRS, RATE, TAXRTE, GROSS, TNET
42:   300 FORMAT(//'Hours: ', F4.1, 2X, 'Rate: ', F7.2,
43:      1    2x, 'Tax rate: ', F7.2, 2x, 'Gross: $', F10.2,
44:      2    2x, 'Net: $', F10.2)
45:       END
```

Notice that FORTRAN is a high-level language, easier to read than its assembler language precursor shown earlier, but still not extremely obvious to nonprogrammers. Although you may not understand everything in the program, you can see some words you recognize such as WRITE and FORMAT. You should begin to see that high-level programming languages are closer to spoken language than either the 1s and 0s or the mnemonics of the low-level languages.

FORTRAN is not known as a large language. It has relatively few commands (as opposed to COBOL and modern-day QBasic-like languages), although its compactness causes some confusion if you don't know the language. FORTRAN is not regarded as a *self-documenting* language, a sometimes-overused term applied to languages that offer some readability for nonprogrammers. Nevertheless, FORTRAN appears to have its foothold in the scientific community, and it will for some time. In fairness, FORTRAN has lost ground over the years to PL/I, Pascal, and then to C and C++, but its superior math capabilities keep FORTRAN far from obsolescence.

> FORTRAN, like most programming languages in widespread use over the years, has been standardized by the ANSI committee. ANSI is the American National Standards Institute, an organization that attempts to sift through all the versions of programming languages and offers a standard set of commands for each one it adopts. Language vendors don't have to follow the ANSI standard, but if the companies don't, they risk losing customers who believe in the advantages that standards provide. Most companies prefer to program in an ANSI standard language; by doing so, they help ensure that new programmers will be versed in the same version as those that came before them.

Using the Business of COBOL

Grace Hopper, the U.S. Navy admiral who is credited with discovering the first computer bug (refer to Hour 3, "What Is a Program?," for a refresher if you need it), is also known as the author of COBOL. In 1960, Admiral Hopper and her team of programmers decided they needed a language for the business side of computing (even the Navy has to meet a payroll and pay its bills). FORTRAN was taking care of the scientific side of things, but the FORTRAN language was never designed to handle business transactions. Programmers were also discovering that FORTRAN's cryptic nature slowed down programming maintenance chores.

Admiral Hopper's team developed *COBOL*, an acronym for *Common Business Oriented Language*. The COBOL design team's primary goal was to develop a self-documenting language that could process a large amount of business data such as inventory and personnel records. A sample of their achievement is shown in Listing 6.2. This is a program that performs the very same processing as its FORTRAN counterpart in Listing 6.1, yet the COBOL listing is almost twice as long. Take a few minutes to peruse the listing and become familiar with the nature of COBOL.

6

All COBOL programs are separated into four divisions. The identification division describes the program. The environment division describes the computer system running the program. The data division describes the format of all data in the program. The procedure division contains the code that processes the data. See if you can find these four divisions in Listing 6.2.

LISTING 6.2 COBOL Is Better than FORTRAN at Business Applications

```
 1: IDENTIFICATION DIVISION.
 2: PROGRAM-ID.     'PAYROLL'
 3:
 4: ENVIRONMENT DIVISION.
 5: INPUT-OUTPUT SECTION.
 6: FILE-CONTROL.
 7:    SELECT GET-DATA, ASSIGN TO KEYIN.
 8:    SELECT OUT-DATA, ASSIGN TO DISPLAY.
 9:
10: DATA DIVISION.
11: FILE SECTION.
12: FD  GET-DATA
13:     LABEL RECORDS ARE OMITTED.
14: 01  GET-REC.
15:     02 AMOUNT        PICTURE 9(5)V2.
16:
17: FD  OUT-DATA
18:     LABEL RECORDS ARE OMITTED.
19: 01  OUT-REC.
20:     02 FILLER        PICTURE X(80).
21:
22: WORKING-STORAGE SECTION.
23: 01  ARITHMETIC-DATA.
24:     02 TOT-OVR       PICTURE 9(5)V2 VALUE ZERO.
25:     02 HOURS         PICTURE 9(3)V1 VALUE ZERO.
26:     02 RATE          PICTURE 9(5)V2 VALUE ZERO.
27:     02 TAX-RATE      PICTURE 9(5)V2 VALUE ZERO.
28:     02 GROSS-PAY     PICTURE 9(5)V2 VALUE ZERO.
29:     02 NET-PAY       PICTURE 9(5)V2 VALUE ZERO.
30: 01  OUT-LINE-1.
31:     02 FILLER        PICTURE X(28)
32:        VALUE 'What were the hours worked? '.
33:     02 FILLER        PICTURE X(52) VALUE SPACES.
34: 01  OUT-LINE-2.
35:     02 FILLER        PICTURE X(25)
36:        VALUE 'What is the hourly rate? '.
37:     02 FILLER        PICTURE X(55) VALUE SPACES.
38: 01  OUT-LINE-3.
39:     02 FILLER        PICTURE X(22)
```

```
40:         VALUE 'What is the tax rate? '.
41:    02 FILLER        PICTURE X(58) VALUE SPACES.
42: 01  OUT-LINE-4.
43:    02 FILLER        PICTURE X(17)
44:         VALUE 'The gross pay is '
45:    02 OUT-GROSS     PICTURE $ZZ,ZZZ.99.
46:    02 FILLER        PICTURE X(53) VALUE SPACES.
47: 01  OUT-LINE-5.
48:    02 FILLER        PICTURE X(15)
49:         VALUE 'The net pay is '
50:    02 OUT-NET       PICTURE $ZZ,ZZZ.99.
51:    02 FILLER        PICTURE X(55) VALUE SPACES.
52:
53: PROCEDURE DIVISION.
54: BEGIN.
55:    OPEN INPUT GET-DATA.
56:    OPEN OUTPUT OUT-DATA.
57:
58:    MOVE OUT-LINE-1 TO OUT-REC.
59:    WRITE OUT-REC.
60:    READ GET-DATA.
61:    MOVE AMOUNT TO HOURS.
62:
63:    MOVE OUT-LINE-2 TO OUT-REC.
64:    WRITE OUT-REC.
65:    READ GET-DATA.
66:    MOVE AMOUNT TO RATE.
67:
68:    MOVE OUT-LINE-3 TO OUT-REC.
69:    WRITE OUT-REC.
70:    READ GET-DATA.
71:    MOVE AMOUNT TO TAX-RATE.
72:
73:    IF HOURS > 40.0
74:       THEN COMPUTE TOT-OVR = (40.0 - HOURS) * RATE * 2
75:            COMPUTE GROSS-PAY = 40.0 * RATE + TOT-OVR
76:    ELSE
77:       COMPUTE GROSS-PAY = HOURS * RATE.
78:    COMPUTE NET-PAY = GROSS-PAY * (1.0 - TAX-RATE).
79:
80:    MOVE GROSS-PAY TO OUT-GROSS.
81:    MOVE OUT-LINE-4 TO OUT-REC.
82:    WRITE OUT-REC.
83:
84:    MOVE NET-PAY TO OUT-NET.
85:    MOVE OUT-LINE-5 TO OUT-REC.
86:    WRITE OUT-REC.
87:
88:    CLOSE GET-DATA, OUT-DATA.
89:    STOP RUN.
```

6

Admiral Hopper's crew wanted COBOL to be self-documenting so that nonprogrammers could understand it. Can you figure out what Listing 6.2 is doing just by reading the code? If you get lost in the program's silver-dollar words, don't be dismayed. Instead of being self-documenting, COBOL ended up being very *wordy*. There is so much that gets in the way of the working code that most people would probably agree (even those COBOL fans, of whom there are still many thousands) that COBOL does not achieve a self-documenting effect. Nevertheless, it shines as the world's premiere business language of choice, and has for almost 40 years.

COBOL is still one of the most common languages in use today, although newer programs in other languages are slowly replacing COBOL code in larger organizations. Most large (and some smaller) businesses still use COBOL in their data processing shops, a trend that C++ and other languages are beginning to change, and a trend that PL/I (described next) fought and failed at a few years ago. It will take a long time before COBOL is done away with entirely in today's business data processing departments.

Can't They Make COBOL Easier?

Part of COBOL's wordiness problem might be solved if a COBOL compiler vendor allowed some shortcuts. For example, the very first line in Listing 6.2's program, IDENTIFICATION DIVISION. is required, period and all, in every COBOL program in the world. If the line is required in every program, why is it required at all? Why not do away with it? Or at least allow for an abbreviated form?

Fans of the language argue that adding shortcuts would violate the ANSI standard COBOL, and they are correct if ANSI did not adopt the abbreviated version; ANSI probably would have done so before now if there were ever a possibility of shortcuts being added. Also, despite the fact that COBOL is wordy, lots of people know it; changing the language would do nothing but make it more difficult to relearn for those currently using it.

If you want to have a career in programming, you should plan to make COBOL the second or third language you learn. Having at least a cursory knowledge of COBOL in your mind's toolkit goes a long way in today's data processing world. To learn COBOL as quickly as possible, you should remember that there are still PC versions of the language available. When you do learn COBOL, learning with the quick response time of a PC might be easier than learning via a mainframe for your first time. (COBOL's home environment is in the mainframe world, and that is where COBOL is used most.) By learning COBOL, you will better understand current programs still in use, and will be more in demand when companies decide to replace older code with newer code.

ANSI standard COBOL compilers were never plentiful on the PC platform. The microcomputer's limited memory and speed, until recent years, could not support production-level COBOL programming. Smaller languages such as Pascal and C filled the smaller microcomputer programming niche quite nicely. Beginning in the early 1990s, however, PCs became quite capable of handling full ANSI-COBOL compilers containing not only the COBOL language itself, but also support programs such as built-in editors, debuggers, and profilers.

Other Languages Through the Years

After FORTRAN and COBOL gained ground, there was no turning back the software industry. Languages began appearing all over the place. Companies would develop their own in-house programming languages that, supposedly, supported their environment better than the big two languages, FORTRAN and COBOL.

PL/I

So many languages began appearing that the programming community started becoming fragmented, wallowing in the sheer number of possibilities, unable to decide which language was the best to use for any given project. At least, that was the scenario that IBM saw when it decided to create "the only programming language anyone would ever need." IBM saw (or tried to create, there is debate today, even amongst IBMers) a need for a programming language that did it all. The new language would be the best scientific language. It would be the best business language. It would solve any and every programmer's needs.

NEW TERM   IBM created the PL/I programming language to solve the problem of too many languages. *PL/I* stands for *Programming Language I*. IBM designed PL/I by taking the best of the COBOL language, the best of FORTRAN, and the best of some other programming languages of the time. The end result, at least in terms of sales, was never achieved; IBM never had the success with PL/I it had hoped for. Instead of being the only programming language anyone would ever need, PL/I became just another programming language amidst many.

The primary problem with PL/I was that it was too good; it was massive. IBM did make use of the best of every programming language of the day, but in doing so, it created a huge language that required massive computing resources to run. During the 1960s, not enough businesses had enough computer power to devote 100 percent of the CPU's time to PL/I compiles. Also, PL/I took too long for programmers to learn. The language was so large that programmers rarely mastered it.

6

Today, there are companies with PL/I programs in use, and some companies still program in PL/I, but the language never caught hold as IBM hoped. Listing 6.3 shows part of a PL/I program that performs the same routine as the FORTRAN and COBOL listings you saw earlier. In this example, the code looks more like its COBOL counterpart than FORTRAN, but much of PL/I differs from COBOL. The differences become more apparent as you begin programming scientific and other nonbusiness applications.

LISTING 6.3 A SAMPLE PL/I PROGRAM THAT MIMICS EARLIER COBOL AND FORTRAN LISTINGS

```
 1: PAYROLL: PROCEDURE OPTIONS (MAIN);
 2: DECLARE OVRTIM    FIXED DECIMAL (2);
 3: DECLARE HOURS     FIXED DECIMAL (5,2);
 4: DECLARE RATE      FIXED DECIMAL (9,2);
 5: DECLARE TAXRATE   FIXED DECIMAL (9,2);
 6: DECLARE GROSS     FIXED DECIMAL (9,2);
 7: DECLARE NETPAY    FIXED DECIMAL (9,2);
 8:
 9: BEGIN: GET LIST(HOURS, RATE, TAXRATE);
10:    IF HOURS < 40 THEN
11:        OVRTIM = (HOURS - 40) * RATE * 2
12:        GROSS = 40 * RATE
13:    ELSE
14:        OVRTIM = 0
15:        GROSS = HOURS * RATE;
16:    NETPAY = GROSS * (1 - TAXRATE);
17:    PUT LIST (OVRTIM, HOURS, RATE, TAXRATE, GROSS, NETPAY);
18: END PAYROLL
```

Although part of the PL/I language offers some interesting programming concepts, aspiring computer programmers should assign a low priority to learning PL/I. Unless you want to program for a company that you know uses PL/I, which is rare, you'll be more marketable and your time will be better spent if you learn Visual Basic, C, or COBOL (after first learning an introductory language such as QBasic).

Perhaps another reason for PL/I's decline is that it was never ported to a microcomputer environment. Originally, the microcomputer didn't have the memory or disk space for a language as large as PL/I. Although today's PCs would have no trouble running PL/I, other languages such as C and Visual Basic have taken hold in the PC arena and a PL/I compiler would have little chance of success.

RPG

Another programming language that has been around for many years is RPG. RPG stands for *Report Program Generator* and exists in newer versions named RPG II and RPG III. As its name implies, RPG began as a report-writer only. It was originally intended to be a language that nonprogrammers (shades of COBOL's ideals) could use to generate reports from data in disk files.

NEW TERM RPG is unlike most other programming languages. The languages you have seen so far are *procedural languages*. That is, they offer individual instructions that the computer follows in a sequential manner until the job is done. RPG does not have typical commands, and its logic is nonprocedural. (Some of the later versions of RPG do offer limited procedural capabilities.) An RPG program is one that is written using codes that follow strict column placements. Nonprogrammers, and even veteran programmers who are inexperienced in RPG, have a difficult time deciphering RPG programs. To make matters worse, there are several nonstandard versions of RPG in widespread use.

Listing 6.4 shows a sample RPG program. The placement of the codes must be exact. If you shift any line of the program to the right or left a few spaces, the program doesn't work. As you might imagine, an RPG program is difficult to follow and extremely difficult to get right the first time you write one.

LISTING 6.4 AN RPG PROGRAM CAN PERFORM BUSINESS DATA PROCESSING

```
 1: F*    PAYROLL PROGRAM
 2: FOUTP    IP  F    80            KEYBOARD
 3: FINP     O   F    80            SCREEN
 4: IREPORT  AA  01                      1    10RATE
 5: I                                    8    30HOURS
 6: I                                   12    40TAXRATE
 7: C        *PY01        IFGT '40'
 8: C        OVTIM        MULT     RATE*2
 9: C        OVTIM        MULT     HOURS
10: C                     END
11: C        *GROSS       IFLE '40'
12: C        GROSS        MULT     RATE * HOURS
13: C                     END
14:          OOUTP        H   100 1P
```

NEW TERM RPG programmers used *RPG specification sheets* to write RPG programs. These sheets are similar to graph paper, with cells labeled for the different RPG commands. By writing out the program using specification sheets, the programmer can help ensure accurate column placement for his or her RPG programs.

Programmers primarily used RPG on minicomputers when minicomputers were popular. RPG was probably used on more minicomputers than any other programming language. (There have only been a couple of RPG compilers available for microcomputers over the years, and their sales collapsed from severe lack of interest.) Many predict that RPG will go away with the final minicomputer.

In the meantime, RPG is used on the minicomputers still in use; you should be aware of its report-generating capabilities. If you ever work on a minicomputer, you will almost assuredly run across an RPG program.

APL and ADA

Two other programming languages, APL and ADA, have also been used a lot over the years. *APL* (which stands for *A Programming Language*) is a highly mathematical programming language developed by IBM. APL is a language as different from COBOL and FORTRAN as is RPG. An APL program consists of many strange symbols (housetops, curved arrows, triangles, and so forth) and requires special hardware to generate its symbols. Because of the hardware restriction and its slow speed compared to other programming languages (APL is almost always run in an interpreted mode and rarely compiled), it is losing favor even by those who were fans in the past.

Another problem with APL is that it is difficult to maintain due to its cryptic nature. Companies are finding that a more natural procedural language makes for more productive long-term programming teams than APL allows.

ADA, named after Lady Augusta Ada Byron (daughter of the poet Lord Byron and girl-friend of Charles Babbage, the father of computers), is used almost exclusively by the Department of Defense and other governmental contracts, although even the government is using ADA less and less. In the 1970s, the American government thought it best to standardize on a programming language so that all its programs would be consistent and governmental programmers would be familiar with the language of all in-house code. Experts view ADA as a mediocre programming language that is difficult to learn (keep in mind, the government put its blessing on ADA as the language of choice, but governments have never been known for being extremely efficient or logical). One wonders why the Department of Defense, which designed and wrote the first COBOL compiler years earlier, chose to use something besides COBOL when almost every company at the time had adopted COBOL and was having tremendous success using it.

Because the government standardized on the ADA programming language early (it was the Department of Defense that designed ADA in 1979), the ANSI committee adopted an

ANSI ADA standard shortly after ADA's release. As long as you learn to program in ADA using an ANSI ADA compiler, you are assured of knowing a language still used in some governmental contracts. Notice, in *some* governmental contracts, because even ADA has fallen prey to more modern languages such as C++.

You might want to learn ADA if you someday work for a company that writes or maintains software for the government. The government doesn't do all its own programming. Because so few nongovernmental employees know ADA, ADA programmers are often in demand, especially for aviation, defense, and space applications. In addition, as the government converts to other languages such as C++, programmers who can understand ADA are in demand because these are the programmers who can best make the conversion needed.

Summary

Understanding the inner workings of your computer is a prerequisite for becoming a master programmer. Only after learning about what is "under the hood" can your programming skills blossom. Computer programming has come a long way since the early days of wiring panels and switches. High-level languages such as COBOL and FORTRAN offer a much easier approach to making computers do what you want them to do.

The next hour offers a look at some of the newer programming languages (those developed within the last 25 years).

Q&A

Q We've reached the second millennium; how important is it really to understand bits and bytes?

A Many programmers have great jobs these days and don't know much about the internal bits in computers. Certainly, the hardware manufacturers and maintenance personnel must understand the low-level hardware because that understanding is needed for hardware to work with other hardware. In addition, programmers who work in a communications environment must understand bits and bytes to be effective.

6

Think for a moment about that last sentence. Do many programmers today work in a communications environment? As you will see beginning in Hour 19, "Internet Programming Concepts," online programming is one of the hottest programming jobs around. In addition, global communications technology is rapidly expanding and improving and that requires people to program new equipment and computers that help exchange information over communications lines. Therefore, one of the most important reasons to understand the internal workings of your PC, the bits and bytes, is precisely because of the second millennium and all the added communications technology that advances every day.

Workshop

The quiz questions are provided for your further understanding. See Appendix A, "Answers to End of Chapter Questions," for answers.

Quiz

1. How many characters are there in a bit?
2. How many characters are there in a byte?
3. How many bits in a byte?
4. What table does a PC use for translating characters?
5. Which simple mathematical operation is the only math operation the computer can actually perform?
6. What is the name of the low-level language that replaced the 1s and 0s of machine language?
7. What is considered the best programming language for business?
8. Which is more self-documenting: COBOL or FORTRAN?
9. Why did the popular APL language fall away so quickly?
10. Which language did the government develop for its required contracts?

Hour 7

Programming Languages: Modern Day

Programming languages have come a long way since the original COBOL compiler in the early 1960s. With each new programming language comes the promise of faster learning time and more maintainable code. Some of the newer languages look similar to those presented in the previous chapter. Being newer doesn't always mean that the programming languages have to differ greatly from the ones people already know. As a matter of fact, the closer a new language is to an existing one, the faster programmers can get up to speed with it and use it. (This may have been the thinking of the designers of C++, which is a close relative of C yet is light-years ahead of C in what it can accomplish.)

The trend toward *graphical programming languages* has been astounding. Programmers and non-programmers are able to produce working programs simply by moving graphical objects around on the screen. Their popularity is a direct result of the popularity of graphical user interfaces (GUIs) such as the Macintosh computer systems, Windows, and IBM's OS/2 operating environments. The procedural languages don't lend themselves well to the needs of the graphical environment. Many graphical user interface programmers today tend to mix GUI programming with procedural languages, using the best each has to offer.

This hour focuses on the programming languages that have been popular for the last few years. Because microcomputer use has grown so much during this time, most of these languages are available on microcomputers, and some are used exclusively in microcomputer environments.

The highlights of this hour include:

- What Pascal's strengths are
- Why C is known as a high low-level language
- What programming operators are
- Which advantages C++ offers over C
- How beginners can use a BASIC language to begin programming right away
- Which Windows programming tool is simple to use
- Why some companies prefer one language over another

Structured Programming with Pascal

In 1968, Niklaus Wirth wrote the first Pascal compiler. Pascal was named after the French mathematician Blaise Pascal. Pascal is a good general-purpose programming language, offering support for scientific work as well as business. Pascal's input/output capabilities are not as advanced as other programming languages used in business, such as COBOL, so it was never a contender for removing COBOL from its business perch. Nevertheless, Pascal is a solid language that does many things well.

Pascal's biggest advantage is that it supports the structured programming concept so well. The three structured programming constructs—sequence, decision, and looping (see Hour 5, "The Programming Process and Structured Techniques," for a review of the structured programming constructs)—are integrated into the design of Pascal. Pascal was a language that Niklaus Wirth designed specifically to address the goals of structured programming. Pascal's control statements offer several ways to accomplish structured programming constructs within a program.

Spaghetti code is almost non-existent in Pascal programs. Unlike most programming languages, some versions of Pascal don't contain a GOTO statement that allows the unconditional branching and jumping other languages provide.

During the 1970s, it was thought that Pascal would become "the only programming language you would ever need." Can you remember where you have heard that before? The previous chapter mentioned that same prediction for PL/I. As with PL/I, Pascal never achieved that lofty goal. Pascal's usage seemed to shrink as quickly as it grew. The 1970s saw a tremendous growth in Pascal and the 1980s saw it decline. Today, Pascal is rarely used in business and engineering. Pascal is used mostly as a teaching tool for programming and on home computers by people who still enjoy the language.

There is a lot of debate as to why Pascal lost ground to other programming languages when it had such a strong start. Perhaps the competition from C and C++ languages (the use of which grew tremendously in the 1980s at the expense of Pascal) was just too strong for Pascal to retain its lead.

Listing 7.1 shows a sample Pascal program. Don't expect to understand the code in full. You should be able to see where data is initialized and where it is output to the screen, however.

PASCAL IS A FREE-FORM LANGUAGE

Unlike FORTRAN and COBOL, Pascal (as are all of the modern-day languages) is *free form*. That means that you can put as many blank lines and spaces in the program (called *whitespace*) as you like to make the program more readable. Pascal programmers often indent lines of code that go together and add blank lines between sections of their programs to help clarify the parts of the programs and make them easier to modify later.

LISTING 7.1 PASCAL SUPPORTS STRUCTURED PROGRAMMING CONSTRUCTS WELL

```
 1: { Typed constant arrays with records
 2:    that hold people's statistics }
 3: PROGRAM People;
 4: USES Crt;
 5: TYPE PersonTypes  = (Employee, Vendor, Customer);
 6:      PersonString = STRING[9];
 7:      PersonRecord = RECORD
 8:                       Name:    PersonString;
 9:                       Balance: WORD;
10:                     END;
11:    PersonNameArray = ARRAY[PersonTypes] OF PersonRecord;
12: CONST People: PersonNameArray =
13:                ((Name: 'Sally'; Balance: 323.56),
14:                 (Name: 'Ted';   Balance:   0.00),
15:                 (Name: 'John';  Balance: 1212.37));
16: VAR Person: PersonTypes;
```

continues

7

LISTING 7.1 CONTINUED

```
17:
18: {The primary output routine appears next }
19: BEGIN
20:    CLRSCR;
21:    WRITELN( '*** People in System ***'):
22:    WRITELN;
23:    FOR Person := Employee TO Customer DO
24:      WITH People[Person] DO
25:        BEGIN
26:          WRITELN( Name, ' has a balance of $',
27:                    Balance, '.');
28:          WRITELN;
29:        END;  {with}
30: END.  {People}
```

For many years, one of Pascal's biggest promoters in the PC industry was Borland International. Borland, now called Inprise, achieved the reputation of being the premiere supplier of Pascal programming products in the mid-1980s since its first Pascal language, Turbo Pascal 1.0, was released. Turbo Pascal, which became Borland Pascal with the Windows version, grew into a complete programming environment that included comprehensive graphics and database support libraries. Some feel that without Borland's support of Pascal in the 1980s, the language would have died away completely before 1990. Thanks to Borland, there is still a small base of Pascal programmers and support publications available. Despite Borland's massive efforts to propel the language, Pascal is mostly a fond memory even to those programmers who used Pascal exclusively in the 1980s.

Many colleges and universities still require their programming students to take a Pascal course early in the curriculum. Pascal's structured programming support is so strong that educators feel that, although the mainstream computer world may not use Pascal, budding programmers learn a lot about how to program correctly with this language. By learning Pascal, you develop good programming habits that should stay with you as you move into other programming languages. Therefore, Pascal is still strong today at the educational level, and probably will be for some time to come.

Inprise developed a new programming language in the 1990s called Delphi that it hoped would take over where its Pascal product left off. Delphi is a visual language that enables programmers to produce Windows applications with little programming effort. Delphi has a loyal following, not unlike die-hard Pascal programmers who still use the language. Inprise developed Delphi to compete with Microsoft's Visual Basic (described later in this hour), but Visual Basic is used much more than Delphi today.

Reviewing the Background of C

In Hour 15, "Programming with C," you will learn many details about the C language itself. As a preview, this hour discusses the background of C and show you how C fits in with the rest of programming languages in use today.

The C language was developed at Bell Laboratories by two men named Brian Kernighan and Dennis Ritchie, men whose programming language made their names as famous in the computer industry as Charles Lindbergh is in aviation. In 1972, Bell Laboratories needed to write a new operating system. Until that point, all operating systems were written in assembler language because the high-level programming languages were not efficient enough given the lack of computer power. The problem with the low-level programming of assembler language is that the code is difficult to maintain. As the operating systems were updated, programmers dreaded the nightmares that updating assembler code brought.

 The operating system that resulted from this endeavor was called UNIX, which is still in widespread use today on minicomputers.

Bell didn't want its new operating system to be as difficult to maintain as previous ones were, but there was simply no high-level language at the time that could do the job. Therefore, it set out to write a new programming language, one that would be as easy to maintain as high-level programming languages tend to be, and one that was almost as efficient as assembler code.

Kernighan and Ritchie (known in the industry as simply K&R) made several attempts, finally coming up with the C programming language. (The story goes that their first two attempts, A and B, failed, but the third time was a charm.)

New Term C is known as a *high low-level language*, meaning that it supports all the programming constructs of any high-level language, including structured programming constructs, but also compiles into extremely tight and efficient code that runs almost as fast as assembler language. Bell Labs ended up with an operating system that was efficient but still easy to maintain and update.

The Success of C

C's popularity grew rapidly. Companies liked the idea of having more efficient programs. A C program might run up to ten times faster than an equivalent COBOL program. Although C has not displaced COBOL, it has come close to doing so in programming

7

departments. The C programming language is the language that most people want to learn. Scan any computer bookshelf and you'll see scores of titles on the C programming language.

The computer industry never saw such a widespread acceptance and movement toward a single programming language than C in the late 1980s and early 1990s. Critics of C quickly become pundits. Schools are facing a huge number of enrollments in their C classes. The sales of C (and C++) book titles continue to set records. Many companies have moved all their programming departments to straight C (and C++) data processing shops. The help-wanted ads in the programming newspaper sections all seem to want C (and C++) programmers. It has reached a point where if you don't know C, you had better learn it fast.

MODERN-DAY SOFTWARE IS C-BASED!

Most of the PC programs you use are now written in C or C++, whereas they used to be written in assembler. Popular spreadsheets and word processors are almost always coded in C these days to gain as much efficiency as possible while still being maintainable.

Almost all Windows programs sold on store shelves are written in C because the internal Windows routines that Windows programs must integrate with are written in C and designed to be executed from a C program. As graphical user interfaces continue to grow in usage, so, it appears, will the need for C programmers.

C is not necessarily a good choice for your first computer language. A BASIC-like language, although a very different language from C, makes a good introduction to C. Because the next few lessons of this book teach you the fundamentals of QBasic programming, you might find that C can be your next step after this book. If so, plan to take it easy and don't expect to master C within a week or two. (Lesson 15, "Programming with C," and Lesson 16, "Programming with C++," begin to teach you C and C++ so you'll know where you are headed with these two cousin languages.)

Whatever your programming goals are, plan to make C the language you eventually learn. Over the next few years, it appears that the jobs in C (and its successor C++, described later in this hour's lesson) will remain plentiful.

Understanding the C Language

A quick look at C will help take some of the possible mystery of the language away. Some consider C to be a cryptic programming language. C can be cryptic if it is not written and documented well. C is a free-form language and allows comments so you can describe what is going on inside the program. This helps alleviate some of the cryptic nature of C programs. C programs are not necessarily difficult to follow; a well-written C program is easier to understand than a badly written COBOL program, even though COBOL is supposedly a self-documenting programming language and readable by nonprogrammers.

C is known as a programming language "written for programmers by programmers." Many programming languages have lots of rules that restrict the programmer. C lets programmers get away with much more than other programming languages allow. In doing so, programmers must keep a sharp eye out for logic errors. Because the C compiler checks for fewer errors, programmers assume more responsibility to ensure that their code is accurate.

C is a language that has few words and numerous operators. The C programming language has only 32 commands. Languages such as COBOL and QBasic have well over a hundred commands, but C tries to be more succinct.

NEW TERM C has more operators than any other programming language with the exception of the scientific APL language described in the previous hour. An *operator* is usually a special character that performs some operation on data. Not all operators are mathematical, but the primary math operators are the most obvious way to learn about operators because you are already used to them. In the expression 5 + 6, the plus sign (+) is an operator. Most programming languages use the four operators shown in Table 7.1 as their primary math operators, which look much like other languages' operators. C is no exception.

TABLE 7.1 C's PRIMARY MATH OPERATORS

Operator	Example	Description
+	5 + 6	Performs addition
–	10 – 4	Performs subtraction
*	4 * 7	Performs multiplication
/	27 / 9	Performs division

The asterisk is used in programming languages for multiplication because the small letter x is often available for other things, most notably for naming data values. There is no division symbol on computer keyboards, so the forward slash almost universally indicates division.

As you learn a programming language, you will learn how the command names work and how the operators manipulate the data. Unlike with most languages, learning how C's operators work is of utmost importance. Most of your time learning C will be spent

7

working with C's operators. It is the large number of operators that make people think that C is a cryptic or mathematical language. Actually, C's operators are not all mathematical. A complete list of C's operators contains some that have nothing to do with mathematical operations. Many of them take the place of commands used by other languages. This abundant use of operators in C makes it very efficient and succinct.

Listing 7.2 shows a sample C program. As you can probably gather, a C program looks a lot like the other programs you have seen in this and the previous chapter. Learning more than one programming language is more of an exercise in spotting how they are similar instead of how they are different. Look through the program and see if you can determine its purpose.

LISTING 7.2 A SAMPLE C PROGRAM CAN BE CRYPTIC BECAUSE OF THE OPERATORS

```
 1: /* Letter guessing game */
 2: #include <stdio.h>
 3: #include <time.h>
 4: #include <stdlib.h>
 5: main()
 6: {
 7:    int tries = 0;
 8:    char compAns, userGuess;
 9:
10:    /* Save the computer's letter */
11:    srand(time(NULL));  /* Randomize the random-number generator */
12:    compAns = (rand() % 26) + 65;   /* Generate a random letter */
13:
14:    printf("I am thinking of a letter...");
15:    do {
16:      printf("What is your guess? ");
17:      scanf(" %c", &userGuess);
18:      tries++;   /* Add 1 to the guess counter */
19:      if (userGuess > compAns)
20:        { printf("Your guess was too high");
21:          printf("again...");
22:        }
23:      if (userGuess < compAns)
24:        { printf("Your guess was too low");
25:          printf("again...");
26:        }
27:    } while (userGuess != compAns);  /* Quit when a
28:                                        match is found */
29:
30:    /* User got it right, announce it */
31:    printf("*** Congratulations!  You got it right! ");
32:    printf("It took you only %d tries to guess.", tries);
33:    return 0;
34: }
```

This C program is a letter-guessing game. The computer generates a random letter and loops until the user correctly guesses the letter. You don't have to understand any of the C instructions (lines of program instructions are often called *statements*) to get a good idea of how this program works. You can read the text throughout the program and figure out a lot just from the text. The instructions themselves are not all extremely cryptic. printf obviously prints something on the screen. The program has ample comments (descriptions that are not C instructions, but are notes to people looking at the program); C comments always appear between /* and */. As you can see, C programs are not always as cryptic as touted, but to really master C, learning another language first is most helpful.

C++: A Better C

In a way, C is losing ground as the most popular language of today, but its close cousin and successor, C++, is gaining much of that support all the time. C++ is a newer version of C. It was designed by a Swedish programmer named Bjarne Stroustrup in the early 1980s. The advantage that C++ has over other new languages is that it is based on C. As a matter of fact, many C++ programs look exactly like C programs, because most of C++ is C. C++ offers a few additional commands and operators but is mostly just another way to program in C.

OOPS, IT'S OOP

The biggest reason for the current success of C++, as well as the reason you should learn it, is that it contains *object-oriented programming* capabilities. Object-oriented programming (called *OOP* for short) is a different way of writing programs that helps programmers write programs more quickly and with fewer errors. OOP also helps speed the program maintenance process later. Hour 16 explains more about object-oriented programming with C++.

C++ is a more restrictive language than regular C. C++ doesn't give the programmer the freedom that C allows, but C++ also doesn't let as many hidden errors creep into the code because it is more strict than C.

The C++ language adds only a few more commands and operators to regular C. The popularity of C++ is attributed to its object-oriented capabilities and its more restrictive nature. Listing 7.3 shows you the C++ version of the letter-guessing game. As you can see, it looks very similar to C code.

7

LISTING 7.3 A SAMPLE C++ PROGRAM LOOKS A LOT LIKE C

```
 1: // Letter guessing game
 2: #include <iostream.h>
 3: #include <time.h>
 4: #include <stdlib.h>
 5: main()
 6: {
 7:    int tries = 0;
 8:    char compAns, userGuess;
 9:
10:    // Save the computer's letter
11:    srand(time(NULL));  // Randomize the random-number generator
12:    compAns = (rand() % 26) + 65;   // Generate a random letter
13:
14:    cout << "I am thinking of a letter...";
15:    do {
16:      cout << "What is your guess? ";
17:      cin >> userGuess;
18:      tries++;   // Add 1 to the guess counter
19:      if (userGuess > compAns)
20:         { cout << "Your guess was too high";
21:            cout << "again...";
22:         }
23:      if (userGuess < compAns)
24:         { cout << "Your guess was too low";
25:            cout << "again...";
26:         }
27:    } while (userGuess != compAns);  // Quit when a
28:                                     // match is found
29:
30:    // User got it right, announce it
31:    cout << "*** Congratulations!  You got it right! ";
32:    cout << "It took you only " << tries << " tries to guess.";
33:    return 0;
34: }
```

Learning the BASICs

This discussion on specific languages concludes with an explanation of BASIC to spring-board your thoughts into the hour's lesson, which teaches you a modern-day version of BASIC called QBasic. BASIC was originally developed at Dartmouth College for teaching beginners how to program. The FORTRAN programming language was a little too complex for students to learn quickly enough to use it in their studies. John Kemeny and Thomas Kurtz, who taught at Dartmouth, used FORTRAN as a basis for creating BASIC. *BASIC* stands for *Beginner's All-purpose Symbolic Instruction Code*, a name that is more foreboding than the language itself.

BASIC is typically run in an interpreted environment, although modern-day versions of BASIC can be compiled. By being interpreted, beginners can concentrate on the programming language and not worry about the details of compiling a program. As with any interpreted language, interpreted BASIC programs run slower than compiled programs, so interpreted BASIC programs are not used much in business.

Over the years, BASIC has been distributed in many different forms. The original BASIC language had very little structure and had a strict set of coding rules. It was thought that the strict rules would take away some of the ambiguity present in other programming languages and speed the beginner's learning of the language. Listing 7.4 shows a version of a program written in the original BASIC language. You can tell from the use of GOTO statements that the language was not very well structured and provided avenues for spaghetti code. Also, each line required a line number. The common practice was to increment the line numbers by tens so you could insert up to nine more lines between existing lines if you had to later.

LISTING 7.4 THE ORIGINAL BASIC LANGUAGE REQUIRED LINE NUMBERS

```
 1: 10  REM Letter-guessing game in BASIC
 2: 20  REM Generate a random number from 65 to 90
 3: 30  REM (ASCII 65 is A and ASCII 90 is Z)
 4: 40  NUM = (INT(RND * 26)) + 65
 5: 50  CA$ = CHR$(NUM)
 6: 60  CLS
 7: 70  PRINT "*** Letter Guessing Game ***"
 8: 80  PRINT
 9: 90  PRINT "I am thinking of a letter..."
10: 100 INPUT "What is your guess"; UG$
11: 110 TR = TR + 1
12: 120 IF (UG$ > CA$) THEN GOTO 150
13: 130 IF (UG$ < CA$) THEN GOTO 180
14: 140 GOTO 210
15: 150 PRINT "Your guess was too high"
16: 160 PRINT "Try again..."
17: 170 GOTO 200
18: 180 PRINT "Your guess was too low"
19: 190 PRINT "Try again..."
20: 200 GOTO 100
21: 210 REM Here if guess was correct
22: 220 PRINT "*** Congratulations!  You got it right!"
23: 230 PRINT "It took you only"; TR; "tries to guess."
24: 240 END
```

7

The output of this program appears below. Try to follow the program to see how the output was produced. This will prepare you for the next chapter, where you learn how to

write your own BASIC programs. As you look through the program, try to answer these
questions: Where is the program's remark? (A remark is a statement that comments the
program. Remarks are ignored by BASIC when you run the program. Remarks are there
for you to document the code so someone looking through the program listing has a better idea what the program is supposed to do.) Where is the program's loop? What BASIC
command produces output?

OUTPUT

```
*** Letter Guessing Game ***

I am thinking of a letter...
What is your guess? A
Your guess was too low
Try again...
What is your guess? Z
Your guess was too high
Try again...
What is your guess? M
Your guess was too low
Try again...
What is your guess? V
Your guess was too high
Try again...
What is your guess? S
*** Congratulations!  You got it right! It took you
➥only 5 tries to guess.
```

Although BASIC began as a language for beginners and is still quite useful for introducing programming, today's versions of BASIC rival Pascal and C by providing a rich
assortment of structured programming elements. Here are a few of the names of BASIC
as it has evolved through the years:

- BASICA (for *BASIC Advanced*)
- GWBASIC (for *Gee Whiz BASIC*)
- Power BASIC
- Turbo BASIC
- QuickBASIC (a compiled BASIC)
- QBasic (which began shipping with MS-DOS starting with Version 5.0 of DOS)
- Visual Basic (both a DOS-based version and a Windows version appeared,
  although the Windows version is the only one still sold)

One of the biggest factors in BASIC's success was Microsoft's adoption of BASIC.
Microsoft has offered many versions of BASIC through the years, improving the language with each version it releases. Microsoft was one of the first companies to offer a
compiled BASIC (QuickBASIC) for PCs. Microsoft is the company that supplied QBasic

(an interactive structured version of BASIC that you will learn starting in the next hour) in DOS 5.0 and all later versions. Microsoft also distributes Visual Basic, a graphical programming tool with which you can write customized Windows programs (described in the next section as well as in Hour 14, "Programming with Visual Basic").

With QuickBASIC, BASIC left the ranks of amateur programming languages and moved into the category of a well-written, structured, compiled programming language that rivaled both Pascal and C.

Listing 7.5 shows a QuickBASIC version of the letter-guessing game you saw earlier in the chapter. Notice that there are no line numbers and that the program is free-form and easy to follow, features that the rigid BASICs of old could not have boasted. QuickBASIC is almost C-like or Pascal-like in its appearance. (Fortunately, Visual Basic, the best-selling version of the BASIC language today, retains the QuickBASIC advantages while adding Windows programming abilities.)

LISTING 7.5 A SAMPLE QUICKBASIC PROGRAM IS MORE FREE-FORM THAN BASIC

```
 1: ' Newer BASIC allows the more succinct ' for a remark instead of
    ' REM
 2: ' A letter-guessing game
 3:
 4: num = (INT(RND * 26)) + 65    ' Generate a random number from
                                   ' 65 to 90
 5:                               ' (ASCII 65 is A and ASCII 90
                                   ' is Z)
 6: compAns$ = CHR$(num)    ' Converts the number to a letter
 7: tries = 0
 8:
 9: CLS    ' Clear the screen
10: PRINT "*** Letter guessing game ***"
11: PRINT
12: PRINT "I am thinking of a letter..."
13:
14: DO
15:    INPUT "What is your guess"; userGuess$
16:    tries = tries + 1
17:    IF (userGuess$ > compAns$) THEN
18:       PRINT "Your guess was too high"
19:       PRINT "Try again..."
20:    ELSE
21:       IF (userGuess$ < compAns$) THEN
22:          PRINT "Your guess was too low"
23:          PRINT "Try again..."
24:       END IF
25:    END IF
```

7

continues

LISTING 7.5   CONTINUED

```
26: LOOP WHILE (userGuess$ <> compAns$)    ' Quit when a match is
                                           ' found
27:
28: ' User got it right, announce it
29: PRINT "*** Congratulations!  You got it right!"
30: PRINT "It took you only"; tries; "tries to guess."
31: END
```

Microsoft won industry favor with its QuickBASIC compiler. Finally, there was a compiler for BASIC—not just a compiler, but an integrated full-screen editor as well. Most BASIC versions before QuickBASIC included their own line editor or limited full-screen editor. Many people feel that Microsoft's integrated full-screen editor played as important a role in QuickBASIC's success as the improved language itself. Microsoft helped ensure its leadership in the BASIC arena when it introduced QBasic, an interpreted version of BASIC that now comes supplied with every version of MS-DOS. If you have MS-DOS 5.0 or later, you have QBasic. Its sheer numbers of machines around the world (almost every PC uses a version of MS-DOS) means that QBasic is available to almost anyone with a PC. QBasic is the language of choice for most beginning programmers in the world, and this book is no exception. You will start learning QBasic in the next lesson.

One of BASIC's strongest assets is its support for string data. *String data* consists of characters, words, and sentences, as opposed to numeric data. BASIC has many built-in routines that can left-justify strings, right-justify strings, and pick out one or more characters from strings. These string capabilities are not nearly as easy in C, Pascal, COBOL, or FORTRAN as they are in BASIC.

Graphical Programming with Visual Basic

Perhaps the most impressive programming language of all is Visual Basic. Visual Basic is really less of a programming language and more of a collection of graphical controls with which you build either interpreted or compiled BASIC programs. Visual Basic is a Windows programming environment that you can use to write Windows programs. When you first start Visual Basic, you see the screen shown in Figure 7.1. As you can see from the screen, the term *visual* is an extremely accurate description.

Don't let the randomness of the Visual Basic screen frighten you. As you learn more about Visual Basic in Hour 14, you'll better understand how the different parts of the screen fit together and you'll learn ways to make the screen look more like the way you prefer. Visual Basic lets you rearrange and hide certain parts of the screen so that you can customize the look and feel of the screen and make it appear exactly as is best for you.

FIGURE 7.1.

The opening screen of Visual Basic opens the windows needed for graphical programming.

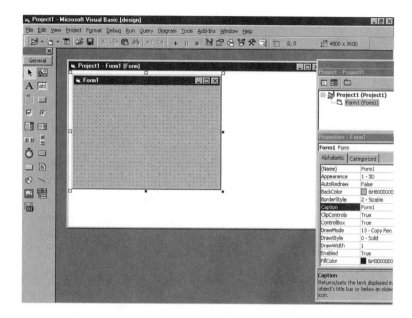

Windows programs are inherently difficult to write for both beginners and advanced programmers who are not used to its environment. In addition to this hour, you will learn more about writing for the Windows programming environment in Hour 13, "Windows Programming Considerations."

Writing a Windows program from scratch, especially for beginning programmers, was a nightmare until Visual Basic came along. Visual Basic takes care of all the petty details of the Windows application, enabling the user to resize the program's window, select from a menu, click with the mouse, or press a key. Visual Basic ensures that the proper task occurs when it is called for.

Visual Basic is one of the first Windows programming environments to offer both an interpreter and a compiler. You can learn Visual Basic and test programs in the interpreted mode and then compile the tested program for distribution to users. In addition to all the Windows-related software that stays in memory during the operation of Windows, the bookkeeping that Windows continually performs can slow down a Visual Basic program. Windows must monitor several activities that a normal non-Windows MS-DOS program didn't have to worry about in pre-Windows days. The Visual Basic compiler didn't appear until version 5, so Visual Basic didn't make major progress into programming departments until Microsoft released Visual Basic as both an interpreter and a compiler.

Visual Basic was the first Windows programming tool that enabled a novice to create simple Windows programs without knowing C. Before Visual Basic, most Windows

7

programs were written in C using Microsoft's *Software Developer's Kit* (*SDK*). The only prerequisite to learning Visual Basic is knowing how Windows applications work in general. If you are familiar with one or two applications in Windows, such as the Word word processor, you know all you need to know to begin writing programs in Visual Basic.

Graphically Oriented

Some programming camps are divided over the use of Visual Basic versus a more "serious" language such as C++ for the Windows environment. Because the Visual Basic system does so much of the work for the programmer, the programmer has less to worry about. However, the argument says that the programmer also has less control over the final program than she or he would have if writing the program using a language such as C++. The movement towards Visual Basic, away from such Windows languages as Visual C++, is helping to prove the case that Visual Basic can indeed be used successfully and taken seriously as a Windows programming system.

Don't fall into the trap of thinking that programming environments such as Visual Basic are object-oriented even though such languages work with objects on the screen. Visual Basic is graphically oriented, but it is not an object-oriented language. Hour 16's lesson helps explain what determines whether or not a programming language is object-oriented.

Games Are the Exceptions

Walk into any computer store today and look for MS-DOS versions of software. You simply won't find them. Everything sold today for the PCs requires Windows, and most are requiring at least Windows 95. One glaring exception that may raise a question or two from you is games. Many extremely popular and current games will not work under any Windows environment, but take over your system and even reboot your system to a DOS-only environment once again to run.

The problem for games is their intensive requirement for computing resources. Not only must a game deal with the normal programming requirements of calculations, disk files, and user interaction, but a game also must provide fast-action color video and sound. The extra layer of Windows between the code and the hardware makes for sluggish games. Despite the fact that Windows is more efficient than ever, that hardware is faster than ever, and that Microsoft provides new interfaces into multimedia programming with Windows, many game makers opt to forego the Windows environment and write in the machine's native mode once again.

Most of these game makers write in C, C++, or assembler language to achieve their efficiencies needed by the games. Despite the fact that Windows is by far the most popular environment in use today, non–Windows-based languages will still be required for some time.

Which Language Is Best?

There are so many programming languages in the world that you might wonder which is best. The answer to that is difficult, if not impossible to determine. Which music is the best? Which period of art is the best? Which car is the best? The answer is a resounding "It depends." The best programming language depends on the job that you need to perform.

If you really want to know which language is the best to learn first, this book has already answered that question. BASIC (or preferably its derivative QBasic) is the best all-purpose language for beginning programmers. That's the author's opinion, but one supportable in about 3,000 students he's taught at the college level. The next hour's lesson begins to develop your programming skills by teaching you QBasic.

Most people will need more power than QBasic can supply. Once they master an introductory language such as QBasic, many people move onto Visual Basic, C, or C++. The current jobs available require that you know C, C++, or Visual Basic, and COBOL in mainframe-based departments. If you feel that you would like to work in large organizations programming mainframes, you should learn COBOL as soon as you feel you are ready (once you get comfortable with QBasic). However, most people have access to microcomputers, and the PC is nice to learn programming with because it offers quick feedback and you can learn to program at home. As you learned earlier in this chapter, C and C++ are high-demand languages these days, and Visual Basic is making a strong impact in corporate programming departments as well.

The languages you know often determine the language in which you program. If you are working on a rush project (as most data processing projects are), you won't have time to master a new language, so if Visual Basic is all you know at the time, that is the language you will probably use.

It is hard to determine how many programming languages a "good" programmer should know. Some highly paid, highly skilled programmers know only a single language, but most know several. You will find that you prefer some programming languages over others and you will become truly expert in only one or two, although you may learn several over the years.

The language a company uses to write a particular application is determined by many factors. The company might have only one or two compilers. If so, its applications will be written using one of those compilers. Mainframe compilers can cost several thousand dollars, so it is difficult for companies to move around from language to language looking for the best one. Often, the language currently owned is made to work.

7

The type of application also helps determine the best language to use. A mainframe scientific application would still be best done in FORTRAN if the choice were between FORTRAN and COBOL. COBOL would be the mainframe language of choice for processing a large amount of business transactions.

 Companies generally prefer programming languages that are common over those that are more obscure. For instance, there is an object-oriented programming language called Actor that is a very good language, but only a handful of programmers know it. C++ would be a much wiser selection if someone else might have to maintain the program in the future.

The best thing to remember about high-level programming languages is that they are general-purpose enough to use when writing almost any application. COBOL might be a lousy choice for scientific applications, but you can make it work if COBOL is all you have to use.

Whatever you end up using, programming is a rewarding career and fun, as well. Get ready to join the ranks of programmers. Turn the page to begin Hour 8's lesson so you can start writing programs immediately.

Summary

As programming languages mature, they become easier to use. Most of today's programming languages include integrated environments and offer support for structured programming. Today's graphical user interfaces such as Microsoft Windows require more complex programming tools, but easy-to-use languages such as Visual Basic ease even beginning programmers into the graphical world of programming.

Programming language popularity changes over time. Pascal, the language of choice for PCs in the early 1980s, now works as a tool to learn structured techniques in schools but that's about as much as it's used. C and C++ virtually took over PC programming in the 1980s and 1990s, although Visual Basic is taking some of the shine away from these languages due to Visual Basic's BASIC roots that make it a simpler language to learn and use.

The next hour teaches you the QBasic language.

Q&A

Q Which is more powerful, Visual Basic or C++?

A Even Visual Basic pundits would agree that C++ is a more powerful language just about any way you view things. Although you can write any Windows program in Visual Basic, the C++ language offers more flexibility and more integration with the Windows environment. Windows-based C++ compilers such as Visual C++ let the C++ programmer create the most advanced Windows programs sold today.

Q Why learn Visual Basic if Visual C++ is better?

A With Visual C++'s power comes responsibility. C++ is more difficult to learn than Visual Basic. In addition, C++ is harder to maintain in many cases. It is true that, if written properly using its full object-oriented programming technology (which you'll learn about in Hour 16), a C++ program should be easier to maintain than a Visual Basic program. In reality, however, Visual Basic's ease of use and simpler language constructs provides advanced Windows programming to beginning and intermediate programmers, as well as to programming departments that want to produce programs that are easy to maintain.

Workshop

The quiz questions are provided for your further understanding. See Appendix A, "Answers to End of Chapter Questions," for answers.

Quiz

1. Which language seems to provide the best support for structured programming techniques?
2. Which language replaced Pascal as the language of choice for PCs?
3. Why were both Pascal and C popular for earlier PCs?
4. What is the improved C language called?
5. How do C and C++ compensate for their small command vocabularies?
6. Which language was the first popular language to offer object-oriented programming?
7. True or false: Visual Basic provides both an interpreter and a compiler.
8. Which language served as the original Windows programming language?
9. Which environment, Windows or DOS, does Visual Basic operate within?
10. True or false: The best language to use is C++.

7

HOUR 8

Your First Language: QBasic

This hour provides your first exposure to the specifics of a programming language. It begins by taking you through a QBasic programming session. You then learn how to store QBasic data and see the results of calculations. After you finish this lesson, you will be able to write your own QBasic programs.

Although you cannot become a programming expert in a single hour, this lesson lays the groundwork for your future as a programmer. All the programming concepts you learn here carry over to any other language you learn in the future.

The highlights of this hour include:

- How to install QBasic
- How to enter and run a QBasic program
- What to do when errors occur
- What variables are, and why their names are important

- What the difference is between string and numeric variables
- How QBasic performs math
- How to print results

Getting Started

If you use Windows 3.1 or if you are one of the few who has never moved to the Windows operating environment, you can start QBasic more easily than those who use Windows 95 and later operating systems. If you work in DOS, simply type QBASIC at the DOS prompt to start QBasic.

If you use Windows 3.1, you may have an icon labeled QBasic in your Main program group. If not, select the MS-DOS icon in your Main program group and type QBasic at the DOS prompt that appears.

> If you use a Windows environment, no matter which version of Windows you use, press Alt+Enter to maximize the DOS session to full screen. You can press Alt+Enter once again to return the DOS session to a smaller window. The advantage of the full-screen session is that you can read the screen better but the smaller window provides a DOS menu that you can access.

Many QBasic programmers were sad when they first upgraded to Windows 95 only to find that the new version of Windows didn't include QBasic. The days of old seemed past. Fortunately, Microsoft did *not* do away with QBasic in Windows 95, and even Windows 98 includes QBasic. The only requirement is that you install QBasic yourself because no option in Windows 95 or Windows 98 installs QBasic for you.

Installing QBasic

To install QBasic, follow these steps:

1. Insert your Windows CD-ROM in your CD-ROM drive.
2. Start Windows Explorer. You can right-click over the Windows Start button and select Explorer or press the Windows+E key if you have a Windows-based keyboard with the Windows logo on it.
3. Click the plus sign next to the Windows CD-ROM entry in Explorer's left pane to expand the list of files stored on the CD.
4. Open the Tools folder.

5. Select the oldmsdos folder. As Figure 8.1 shows, this folder contains the two files needed for QBasic.

FIGURE 8.1.

You can install QBasic yourself from Windows 95 or Windows 98.

The two QBasic files

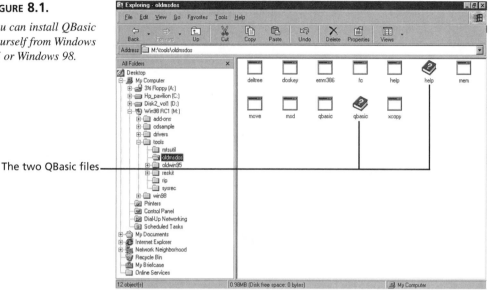

6. Select both QBasic icons (you can select them by drawing a circle around them with your mouse).

7. With the icons selected, click the plus sign to expand your C: drive contents. Click only the plus sign and not the icon or the selected QBasic files will disappear from view.

8. Scroll the left pane until you see your Windows folder appear.

9. Click the plus sign (not the Windows icon) to expand your Windows folder.

10. Drag both the selected QBasic files to the Command folder located in your left pane's Windows folder. This copies both files to the Windows folder and makes QBasic available from any folder.

You now have everything you need to start QBasic from your hard disk.

Starting QBasic

To start QBasic, follow these steps:

1. Click the Windows Start button.

2. Select Run.

3. Type QBasic in the Run dialog box that appears.

4. Press OK to close the Parameters dialog box if one appears. This dialog box lets you pass environment information to a QBasic program, which is rarely done these days because QBasic is normally not used for production-level programs where a compiler is more appropriate. The QBasic screen, shown in Figure 8.2, appears. (Your QBasic window may appear fully maximized without the DOS toolbar at the top.)

FIGURE 8.2.

You have successfully started QBasic.

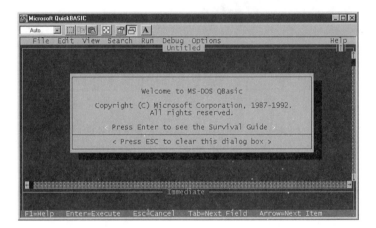

5. Press your Esc key to get rid of the opening title messages.

Using the QBasic Editor

Remember that you must use an editor to write your programs. The editor is the word processor–like entry screen from which you type the program's code. The QBasic editor is more than an editor; it is also a QBasic interpreter. From within the QBasic editor, you can write a program, run it, change it, view its output, and save your program to a disk for long-term storage. The QBasic editor/interpreter combination is a precursor to the Visual Basic environment that includes both the editor, debugger, interpreter, and compiler.

QBasic even includes its own debugging tool, available from the Debug menu, to help you locate errors. Hour 22's lesson, "Debugging Tools," explains how to use the Debug menu.

Although programming languages are all different, as you learn QBasic and others, you will see that almost all programming languages have a lot in common with other languages. They all have ways to print output and to get values from the keyboard and a disk. They all have commands that loop by repeating one or more statements. They all can make decisions. Some perform these actions more elegantly and naturally than other programs do. What is important, though, is that every time you learn a new programming language, the next one becomes even easier to learn. QBasic is a great place to start your programming career. Even if you don't end up programming in QBasic for a living, you will find the programming skills that you develop with QBasic very useful.

Working with the QBasic Editor

Familiarize yourself with the QBasic environment by going through a sample QBasic session. You are given a program to type in and run. Just to keep things interesting, the program contains an error that you must fix before the program will run correctly.

Keep the following points in mind as you work with the QBasic editor:

- Use the arrow keys to move the cursor around the screen.
- The Insert key turns Insert mode on and off (when you first begin QBasic Insert mode is on). When Insert mode is on, existing characters are pushed to the right as you type the new characters. When Insert mode is off (called *Overtype mode*), the characters you type replace those they walk on.
- The Delete key deletes the character under the cursor. Whenever you delete characters, the ones to the right move over and fill in the gap left by the deleted characters.
- You can use the PageUp and PageDown keys to scroll the screen. Use them when your program is too long to fit within a single screen. This scrolling action works like a camera panning a scene.
- Select text by holding down Shift while moving the cursor or select with your mouse by dragging the mouse pointer across the text you want to select. The Edit menu contains the usual Copy, Cut, and Paste commands.
- Common combination keystrokes work to move the cursor around the screen. Home and End move the cursor to the beginning or end of the current line. Ctrl+Home and Ctrl+End move the cursor to the beginning or end of the program. Ctrl+left arrow and Ctrl+right arrow move your cursor to the beginning of the previous or next word on the line.

Running Your First QBasic Program

Follow these steps to enter and run your first QBasic program.

1. Start QBasic. You will see the QBasic startup screen.

2. Press the Esc key to clear the Help option from the editing window. (Later, you might want to view some of the Help screens available from this opening screen.)

3. Type the program in Listing 8.1 into QBasic. (The blank lines are optional, as are the indented lines. The extra whitespace makes the program more readable.) Press Enter at the end of each line. Word wrap will not occur because you are using a text editor and not a word processor.

> If you type an obvious error, such as misspelling part or all of a statement, Visual Basic will recognize the error and display a message box as soon as you press Enter at the end of the line (see Figure 8.3). QBasic attempts to highlight the offending part of the statement, although sometimes QBasic doesn't highlight exactly where the error occurred. You can click OK to close the message box and fix the error before continuing. (Step 6 demonstrates a syntax error that the editor cannot find until you run the program.)

FIGURE 8.3.

The QBasic editor can find some errors as you enter the program.

 LISTING 8.1   YOUR FIRST QBASIC PROGRAM LETS YOU PRACTICE WITH THE QBASIC EDITOR

```
1: REM My first QBasic program
2: BEEP
3: REM Ask the user for his or her first name
4: CLS
5: INPUT "What is your first name"; nm$
```

```
 6: PRINT
 7:
 8: REM Sound the siren!
 9: FOR up = 1000 TO 1500 STEP 25
10:     SND up, 3
11: NEXT up
12:
13: REM Print the name down the screen
14: col = 1
15: FOR row = 1 TO 24
16:     LOCATE row, col
17:     PRINT nm$
18:     col = col + 2
19: NEXT row
20: END
```

4. Make sure that the program you type looks exactly like the one in step 3. Double-check it to ensure that it is correct. QBasic cannot read your mind, and accuracy counts in programming. However, you can type the commands in either upper- or lowercase. QBasic automatically converts commands that you type in lowercase to uppercase.

5. Run the program by choosing Run, Start from the pull-down menu. You can also use the Shift+F5 key combination as a shortcut key to run programs; it is faster than using the menu. All the menu options have their shortcut key equivalents next to them on the menu. (Some menu options, however, don't have shortcut key equivalents.) The Alt key is always the key you press to access the menus.

6. Because the program contains an error, it won't run. QBasic spots the error and displays a message box. Anytime QBasic displays an error message, you have two options. You can get more help about the error message by choosing Help inside the error message box. QBasic's online help appears to guide you toward resolving the error (see Figure 8.4). Click OK to get rid of the help message when you are through reading it. If you don't need more help, choose OK to remove the error message box. Either way, QBasic highlights the place in the code where it found the error. As you can see, QBasic doesn't like the command SND.

7. There is no SND command in QBasic. The command should be SOUND. Change the line so that it looks like this:

   SOUND up, 3

FIGURE 8.4.

QBasic offers help with the error.

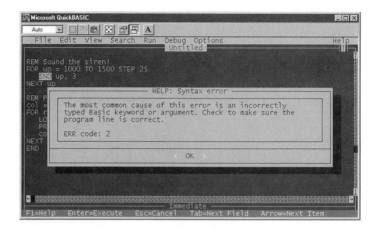

8. Run the program again. When you do, the screen clears and QBasic beeps. Then it asks you for your first name. After typing your name, a siren sounds and your name appears down and across the screen as shown in Figure 8.5. QBasic always displays the `Press any key to continue` message before returning to your program so that you can see the final results of the output screen.

FIGURE 8.5.

The result appears when you run your first QBasic program.

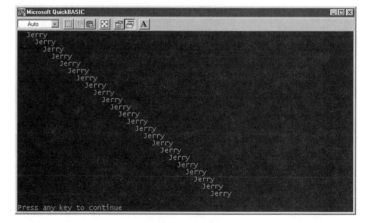

When your screen returns to the program editing window, you can go back and view the output screen by selecting View, Output Screen from the menu or by pressing the F4 shortcut key. The output screen enables you to view code and switch to see the output in the same session.

8

9. If you want to save the program so you can run it later, select File, Save. Then type a filename such as FIRST.BAS, and press Enter. All QBasic programs should have the .BAS filename extension. The first part of the filename follows the pre-Windows 95 DOS file-naming rule that says the first part of the filename must be from 1 to 8 characters long.

QBasic doesn't support long filenames.

Congratulations! You have just successfully typed, corrected, and run your first QBasic program. Now learn the specifics of the language so that you can write your own programs from scratch.

Delving into QBasic

It is now time to develop an understanding of the QBasic language. Throughout these 24 hours, you learn about the importance of writing programs that are easy to maintain. The programs you write should not only work, but also be easy to read. Very likely, you or someone else may need to update your program later. Having code that is clear makes that task much easier.

There is yet another advantage to writing clear, well-documented programs. You will finish your programs faster and they will have fewer errors. Being organized always pays off when programming.

Remarking Code

Some of the most important statements you can put in QBasic programs are completely ignored by QBasic. They are remarks documenting what the program is doing. The QBasic program you typed earlier had four remarks. A QBasic remark is any statement that begins with REM.

The QBasic interpreter completely ignores *remarks*. Remarks appear in programs for the benefit of people who look at the programs. The remarks exist solely to document the program, telling in plain English what the program is about to do. For example, you can see from the four remarks exactly what the program is doing without knowing anything about QBasic except the REM statement.

Many programmers like to begin a program with a remark that states the programmer's name and the date on which the program was written. This is especially important if you are one among many programmers in a data processing department. When others have to modify programs, they can track down the original programmer in case they have questions. Every time you change a program, you can add a remark describing the change. Such a change log is important when several people work on a team and the other team members may have to correct a bug that appears due to a change. Listing 8.2 shows the first few lines of a program that includes a good set of remarks at the beginning of the code.

LISTING 8.2 REMARKS HELP DESCRIBE THE PROGRAM AND THE PROGRAMMER

```
1: REM
2: REM Program written by Sally K. Yarnell
3: REM Original programming date: 6-9-98
4: REM Updated on: 7-2-98: Added support for Payroll Report #4-E
5: REM Updated on: 12-1-98: Added support for new tax law 439T3
6: REM Updated on: 3-16-99: Added support for estimated sales report
```

QBasic allows a shortcut for remarks. You can use an apostrophe (') in place of REM. Listing 8.3 shows the same program you saw earlier with the shortcut remark in place of REM. As you can see from Listing 8.3, the shortcut remarks can go to the right of QBasic statements; they don't have to reside on lines by themselves as REM statements do.

LISTING 8.3 THE QBASIC PROGRAM WITH SHORTCUT REMARKS

```
 1: ' My first QBasic program
 2: BEEP
 3: ' Ask the user for his or her first name
 4: CLS
 5: INPUT "What is your first name"; nm$
 6: PRINT                         ' Print a blank line
 7:
 8: ' Sound the siren!
 9: FOR up = 1000 TO 1500 STEP 25 ' Loop to control the siren
10:     SOUND up, 3               ' Sound a tone on the speaker
11: NEXT up                       ' End of the sound loop
12:
13: ' Print the name down the screen
14: col = 1
15: FOR row = 1 TO 24             ' Loop several times
16:     LOCATE row, col           ' Position the cursor
```

```
17:    PRINT nm$              ' Print the user's name
18:    col = col + 2
19: NEXT row                  ' End of the printing loop
20: END
```

Not all lines require remarks. Use them to clarify what your code is doing. Some programmers insert a remark every three or four lines; for them that is sufficient. The best number of remarks is however many it takes to clarify the program code you write.

The following is not a helpful remark:

```
PRINT SalesTotal     ' Print the Sales Total
```

Such a remark simply echoes the statement itself. The remark is redundant; the code is fairly self-documenting thanks to the well-named value called `SalesTotal`. Consider the following remark, however:

```
PRINT SalesTotal     ' Total includes one-time allocation expense
```

This remark does tell more about the statement than the statement can do. Although code previous in the program might explain that the total doesn't include the one-time expense, this remark helps remind the reader that the total may contain something special. Such remarks are extremely useful indeed.

> Remember that remarks are for programmers and not for users. The user never sees the remarks. The remarks remain in the program listing itself to describe what is happening in the code.

Storing Data

As its definition implies, data processing means that your programs process data. That data must somehow be stored in memory while your program processes it. In QBasic programs, as in most programming languages, you must store data in *variables*. You can think of a variable as if it were a box inside your computer holding a data value. The value might be a number, character, or string of characters.

> Actually, data is stored inside memory locations. Variables keep you from having to remember which memory locations hold your data. Instead of remembering a specific storage location (called an *address*), you only have to remember the name of the variables you create.

Your programs can have as many variables as you need. There is a limit to the number of variables a single program can have, but the limit depends on the type of data you are holding. (Anyway, the number is so large that you will not run out of variables in your program.) Variables have names associated with them. You don't have to remember which internal memory location holds data; you can attach names to variables to make them easier to remember. For instance, Sales is much easier to remember than the 4376th memory location.

You can use almost any name you want, provided that you follow these naming rules:

- Variable names must begin with an alphabetic character such as a letter.
- Variable names can range in length from 1 to 40 uppercase or lowercase characters.
- After the first alphabetic character, variable names can contain numbers. There are a few special characters that can also be part of variable names (such as ., &, and ^), but some other special characters are not allowed (such as (, *, and +). It's safer to stay with letters and numbers.

> Avoid strange variable names. Try to name variables so that their names help describe the kind of data being stored. Balance99 is a much better variable name for your 1998 balance value than X1y96a, although QBasic doesn't care which one you use.

Here are some examples of valid and invalid variable names:

Valid	Invalid
Sales93	Sales-93
MyRate	My$Rate
ActsRecBal	93ActsRec
row	REM

> Don't assign a variable the same name as a QBasic command or QBasic will issue an invalid variable name error message.

Variables can hold numbers or character strings. If you follow the naming rules just listed, the variables can hold numbers.

8

There is one special character that is useful to use at the end of variable names. If you put a dollar sign ($) at the end of a variable name, the variable can hold one or more alphabetic or special characters. Therefore, the following variables can hold characters, words, and even sentences:

nm$

Company$

show$

Employee$

VARIABLE SUFFIXES

You might see suffix characters other than the dollar sign from time to time. The suffix characters indicate specific kinds of data that the variable can hold. The dollar sign is the most common suffix in QBasic and the only one discussed in this text. Nevertheless, other suffix characters exist, such as # and !, that indicate the kind of number the variable can hold.

Assigning Values

The majority of QBasic program statements use variable names. QBasic programs often do little more than store values in variables, change variables, calculate with variables, and output variable values.

When you are ready to store a data value, you must name a variable to put it in. You must use an assignment statement to store values in your program variables. The assignment statement includes an equal sign (=) and an optional command LET. Here are two sample assignment statements:

sales = 956.34

LET rate = .28

The LET keyword is optional and requires more typing if you use it. Therefore, most programmers save typing time and leave off the LET from their assignment statements. Probably, no good reason exists to use LET; old versions of BASIC (in the 1960s) required it, so programmers who learned it then might still use it and you should know what LET does in case you run across an assignment statement that uses it. Keep in mind that Visual Basic is fully compatible with the QBasic programming language. Therefore, you might even see a LET statement in a Visual Basic program.

Think of the equal sign in an assignment statement as a left-pointing arrow. Whatever is on the right side of the equal sign is sent to the left side to be stored in the variable there. Figure 8.6 shows how the assignment statement works.

FIGURE 8.6.

The assignment statement stores values in variables.

If you want to store character string data in a variable, you must enclose the string inside quotation marks. Here is how you store the word *QBasic* in a variable named lang$:

```
lang$ = "QBasic"    ' Enclose strings in quotation marks
```

After you put values in variables, they stay there for the entire run of the program, or until you put something else in them. A variable can hold only one value at a time. Therefore, the two statements

```
age = 67
age = 27
```

result in age holding 27, because that was the last value stored there. The variable age cannot hold both values.

You can also assign values of one variable to another and perform math on the numeric variables. Here is a short program that stores the result of a calculation in a variable and then uses that result in another calculation:

```
pi = 3.1416
radius = 3
area = pi * radius * radius
halfArea = area / 2
```

QBasic zeroes all variables for you. This means that when you name a variable, QBasic assumes that the value of the variable is 0 (zero) until another value is assigned to it. Therefore, if you want a variable to begin with a zero, you don't have to assign a zero to it. QBasic also empties all variables that hold character information (those with a trailing dollar sign suffix) and stores *null strings* or *empty strings* in them to indicate that nothing has yet to be assigned to the variables.

After you store values in variables, you must have a way to display them on the screen and printer. The next few sections describe how to output your data values.

Looking at Values

The PRINT statement outputs data to the screen. PRINT is used in almost every QBasic program because displaying data on the screen is so important. Your users must be able to see results and read messages from the programs they run. Figure 8.7 shows an illustration of what PRINT does.

FIGURE 8.7.

PRINT sends output to the screen.

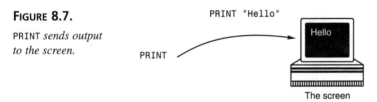

There are several ways to use PRINT. The easiest way to print words on your screen is to enclose them in quotation marks after the PRINT statement. The following two statements print names on the screen:

```
PRINT "Sally Brown"
PRINT "John Wilson"
```

These statements produce the following output:

```
Sally Brown
John Wilson
```

The quotation marks never appear around printed strings; the marks simply enclose the character strings to be printed. Whatever appears inside quotation marks prints exactly as it appears inside the quotation marks. The PRINT statement

```
PRINT "5 + 7"
```

doesn't print 12 (the result of 5 + 7). Because quotation marks enclose the expression, the expression prints exactly as it appears inside the quotation marks. This PRINT statement produces this output:

OUTPUT   `5 + 7`

If, however, you print an expression without the quotation marks, QBasic prints the result of the calculated expression:

```
PRINT 5 + 7
```

which does print 12. Variables printed without quotation marks print as well. Listing 8.4 contains code with output statements so you can see the results of calculations.

LISTING 8.4 PRINT SENDS OUTPUT OF CALCULATIONS AND OTHER DATA TO THE SCREEN

```
 1: ' Program that calculates and prints the area
 2: ' of a circle and half circle
 3: pi = 3.1416          ' Mathematical PI
 4: radius = 3           ' Radius of the circle
 5: area = pi * radius * radius    ' Compute circle area
 6: halfArea = area / 2            ' Compute half the circle area
 7: PRINT "The area of a circle with a radius of 3 is"
 8: PRINT area
 9: PRINT "The area of one-half that circle is"
10: PRINT halfArea
11: END
```

Don't be confused by the name PRINT. PRINT sends output to the screen and not to the printer.

The END statement at the end of QBasic programs is optional. Most programmers put the END statement there so that others looking at the program know when they have reached the end instead of wondering if there might be another page to the program.

Here is the output you see if you run the program in Listing 8.4:

```
1: The area of a circle with a radius of 3 is
2: 28.2744
3: The area of one-half that circle is
4: 14.1372
```

Notice that each PRINT statement causes a new line to be printed. Follow the program and see how its output is produced.

Hour 9, "Input and Output," covers the output of values as well as the input of user data. You will learn more about how QBasic can format data to look any way you want it to look.

Clearing the Screen

Before your program displays anything onscreen, you probably want a blank screen. If your program doesn't first clear the screen before printing to it, all previous output will be on the output screen that appears when you run the program.

8

Remember that QBasic is a DOS-based language. If you don't maximize your QBasic screen, you can, through your QBasic program, clear only the DOS window running your program. If part of Windows appears in the background, that background will not be cleared.

It is very easy to clear the screen in QBasic. The CLS statement is all you need. When QBasic reaches a CLS statement in your program, it clears the contents of the output screen. It is always a good idea to clear the screen at the beginning of any program.

The following short program erases the screen and prints a message at the top of the cleared screen:

```
CLS
PRINT "QBasic is fun!"
```

Be sure your programs erase the screen if you write programs that display critical data. For example, if you write programs for a payroll department, you might want to make sure that your programs always clear the screen before their END statement. The cleared screen ensures that sensitive payroll figures aren't left onscreen for unauthorized eyes to see.

Performing Math with QBasic

QBasic performs mathematical calculations in the same way as most programming languages. It uses the same primary math operators for addition, subtraction, multiplication, and division that you saw in the previous chapter, as well as some additional ones unique to QBasic. Table 8.1 lists the QBasic math operators with which you should familiarize yourself.

TABLE 8.1 QBASIC MATH OPERATORS

Operator	Description
( )	Groups expressions together
^	Exponentiation
*, /, }, MOD	Multiplication, division, integer division, and modulus
+, -	Addition and subtraction

The order of the operators in Table 8.1 is important. If more than one of these operators appears in an expression, QBasic doesn't always calculate the values in a left-to-right order. In other words, the expression:

```
v = 5 + 2 * 3
```

stores the value 11 in v, not 21 as you might first guess. QBasic doesn't perform calculations in a left-to-right order, but rather in the order given in Table 8.1. Because multiplication appears before addition in the table, QBasic computes the 2 * 3 first, resulting in 6; it then computes the answer to 5 + 6 to get the result of 11.

> The order in which operators are evaluated is often called operator precedence. Every programming language except APL computes expressions based on a precedence table. Different programming languages might use different operators from the ones shown in Table 8.1, although almost all of them use parentheses and the primary math operators (*, /, +, and -) in the same way as QBasic does.

Parentheses have the highest operator precedence. Any expression enclosed in parentheses is calculated before any other part of the expression. The statement:

```
v = (5 + 2) * 3
```

does assign the value of 21 to v because the parentheses force the addition of 5 and 2 before its sum of 7 is multiplied by 3.

The exponentiation operator raises a number to a particular power. In the following statement, 100 is placed in the variable x because 10^2 means raise 10 to the second power (10 times 10):

```
x = 10 ^ 2
```

You can also raise a number to a fractional power with the ^ operator. For example, the statement:

```
x = 81 ^ 0.5
```

raises 81 to the one-half power, in effect taking the square root of 81. (If this math is getting deep, have no fear; some people program in QBasic for years and never need to raise a number to a fractional power. But if you need to, you can thanks to QBasic.)

Division is handled three different ways in QBasic. The forward slash (/) produces normal division. The statement:

```
d = 3 / 2
```

8

puts 1.5 into d. The back slash (\) performs *integer division.* An integer is a whole number, and integer division always produces the whole number result of the division (the decimal portion is discarded). Therefore, the statement:

```
d = 3 2
```

puts 1 into d, and the .5 is ignored.

One of the strangest QBasic operators is not a symbol—it looks more like a command. It is the MOD operator. The MOD operator returns the integer remainder from a division. For example, the statement:

```
m = 20 MOD 3
```

puts a 2 in m, because 20 divided by 3 is 6 with a remainder of 2. There are some specialized math operations that require modulus (integer remainder) arithmetic, and QBasic supplies the MOD operator to meet that need.

To sum up (pardon the pun) math operators, Listing 8.5 contains a program that prints the result of calculations that use all the QBasic operators described in this lesson. The output of the program is shown in Figure 8.8 after the program listing.

LISTING 8.5 QBASIC CALCULATIONS FOLLOW THE ORDER OF OPERATOR PRECEDENCE

```
 1: ' Program to demonstrate the QBasic math operators
 2: num1 = 12
 3: num2 = 5
 4: CLS
 5: PRINT "num1 is "; num1
 6: PRINT "num2 is "; num2
 7: ' Print the result of several calculations using 12 and 5
 8: value = num1 + num2
 9: PRINT "num1 + num2 equals"; value
10: value = num1 - num2
11: PRINT "num1 - num2 equals"; value
12: value = num1 * num2
13: PRINT "num1 * num2 equals"; value
14: value = num1 / num2
15: PRINT "num1 / num2 equals"; value
16: value = num1 num2
17: PRINT "num1 num2 equals"; value
18: value = num1 MOD num2
19: PRINT "num1 MOD num2 equals"; value
20: value = num1 ^ num2
21: PRINT "num1 ^ num2 equals"; value
22: value = num1 + num2 * 4
23: PRINT "num1 + num2 * 4 equals"; value
24: value = (num1 + num2) * 4
25: PRINT "(num1 + num2) * 4 equals"; value
26: END
```

FIGURE 8.8.

Viewing the output of the calculations.

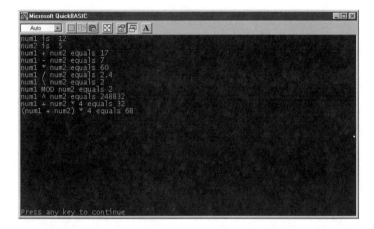

You don't have to be a math expert to use QBasic; it does all the math for you. You only have to understand how QBasic performs the math so that you can properly set up the equations you need to calculate.

Summary

QBasic is one of the best implementations of BASIC that beginning programmers can use. As you learned in this hour, writing programs in the QBasic programming language is not only easy, but it can be fun as well. The programs in this hour showed you how to store data in variables and output results to the screen. The results of math calculations follow a predefined order. You have freedom, however, to override that order with the use of parentheses.

The next hour explains how to produce fancier output and also describes how to get values into variables from the user at the keyboard.

Q&A

Q In QBasic, do I have to know all the values that I will assign to variables when I write the program?

A Data comes from all sources. You will know some of the values that you can assign when you write your programs, but much of your program data will come from the user as you'll see in the next hour, or from data files as discussed in Hour 11, "Managing Data and Disk Files." This lesson assigned all its data to variables just to familiarize you with the way that QBasic assignment statements and calculations work.

Q What kinds of data can variables hold?

A Variables can hold many kinds of data, such as numbers, characters, and character strings. As you learn more about programming, you will see that numeric data comes in all formats and, to master a programming language well, you must also master the kinds of numeric data that are available. Some programming languages, such as Visual Basic, support variables that hold time and date values as well.

Workshop

The quiz questions and exercises are provided for your further understanding. See Appendix A, "Answers to End of Chapter Questions," for answers.

Quiz

1. What must you first do to use QBasic with Windows 95 or Windows 98?

2. What two ways do QBasic help you locate errors (not counting the debugger)?

3. What is a remark used for?

4. What does a variable do?

5. True or false: `PRINT` prints to the screen or printer.

6. How many data values can a variable hold at one time?

7. What does the dollar sign suffix do for variables?

8. Why doesn't QBasic compute calculations in a left-to-right order?

9. True or false: QBasic supports long filenames.

10. What statement erases the QBasic output screen?

HOUR 9

Input and Output

Input and output are the cornerstones of programs that interact in any way with the outside world. In the previous hour, you learned how to produce output on the screen with the PRINT statement. You can do more with PRINT than just output data. With PRINT and the various options that go along with it, you can also format your output.

The opposite of PRINT is INPUT. Whereas PRINT sends output to the screen, INPUT receives input from the user at the keyboard. The INPUT statement is the primary way that your program has of interacting with the user. You'll often see both PRINT and INPUT statements together in pairs within code so that the PRINT can request the data that INPUT needs.

The highlights of this hour include:

- Why you need to improve upon the PRINT statement's appearance
- How to space multiple output values on the same line
- How the comma separator differs from the semicolon output separator
- What internal functions are

- How to jump to the next tab stop onscreen
- When to use SPC() to space output properly
- What the purpose of INPUT is
- Why prompts for data input are so important
- How to format data as currency values

Advanced Printing

The PRINT statement can do far more than just print data values. You can use PRINT to output formatted data in columns that form tables of information. In addition, you can control the spacing of the values. The next several sections show you ways to use PRINT to display your program's output so that it looks exactly the way you want it to look.

Using the Semicolon

In the previous hour's lesson, you learned how to print values one line at a time. The following statement prints three numbers on three different lines:

```
PRINT 15
PRINT 20
PRINT 25
```

Here is the output produced by these PRINT statements when you run the program:

 OUTPUT
```
15
20
25
```

If you want to print several different values on the same line, you can do so by separating them with semicolons. Therefore, the statement

```
PRINT 15; 20; 25
```

prints all three values on a single line, like this:

```
 15 20 25
```

QBasic always includes a space for a number's sign. Positive numbers don't display plus signs in front of them; the plus sign is implied. Negative numbers, however, always appear with the minus sign. If the three values that you print are negative, a minus sign appears before each number without any leading space.

Using the semicolon, you can improve a program introduced in the previous lesson that calculated and printed the area of a circle. By making the values appear directly after the descriptions of the calculations instead of on the next line, your output will make more sense than before. Listing 9.1 shows the improved program.

INPUT   **LISTING 9.1** USE THE SEMICOLON TO SEPARATE PRINTED VALUES ON THE SAME LINE

```
1: ' Program that calculates and prints the area
2: ' of a circle and half circle
3: pi = 3.1416          ' Mathematical PI
4: radius = 3           ' Radius of the circle
5: area = pi * radius * radius     ' Compute circle area
6: halfArea = area / 2             ' Compute half the circle area
7: PRINT "The area of a circle with a radius of 3 is"; area
8: PRINT "The area of one-half that circle is"; halfArea
9: END
```

Here is the output from this program:

OUTPUT
```
The area of a circle with a radius of 3 is 28.2744
The area of one-half that circle is 14.1372
```

The semicolon can also go at the end of a PRINT:

```
PRINT "Sally ";
```

so that a subsequent PRINT will continue the output on the same line as the previous one. Often, you might want to print the results of several calculations on a single line. By printing each one with a trailing semicolon at the end, you can print them as you calculate them throughout the program and still ensure that they all print next to each other.

Printing with Commas

NEW TERM   The comma acts similarly to the semicolon in that it lets you print values together on the same line with a single PRINT statement. Unlike the semicolon, which causes the values to print directly after one another, the comma causes the next value to print in the next *print zone*.

There is one print zone for every 14 columns of your computer screen. Figure 9.1 shows how your screen is divided into five print zones. Each comma in a PRINT causes the next value to print in whichever print zone comes next.

You must take into account the extra space that the imaginary plus sign consumes when printing numbers, but strings are never printed with leading or trailing spaces.

9

FIGURE 9.1.

The print zones appear every 14 columns of your screen.

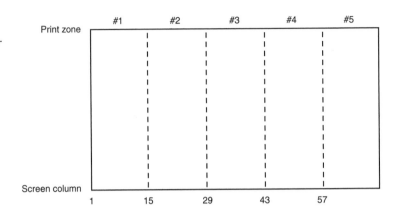

The following PRINT demonstrates the use of the comma:

```
PRINT 15, 20, 25
```

This PRINT prints the 15 (after a leading space), and then the 20 in column 15, and then the 25 in column 29, like this:

```
 15            20            25
```

The comma is useful for printing a table of values. The comma ensures that the columns of the table line up under each print zone. In the following program, the names print starting in the same four columns, even though the names are of different lengths.

```
' Illustrates the use of commas
PRINT "Sam", "Jesse", "Charles", "Susan"
PRINT "Christine", "Ron", "Jayne", "Martha"
PRINT "Johnny", "Thomas", "Francis", "Kerry"
PRINT "Kim", "Barbara", "Lea", "William"
END
```

Here is the output from this code:

Sam	Jesse	Charles	Susan
Christine	Ron	Jayne	Martha
Johnny	Thomas	Francis	Kerry
Kim	Barbara	Lea	William

As you work with more data and print several values at a time, you will appreciate the help that the print zones offer when you want your data to line up in columns.

Printing Blank Lines

To print a blank line, you only need to place a PRINT statement on a line by itself. A blank line appears in middle of the output from the following three statements:

```
PRINT "First line"
PRINT
PRINT "Last line"
```

Here is the output that these three PRINT statements produce:

```
First line

Last line
```

Controlling Spacing

New Term You can format the PRINT statement's output by including either SPC() or TAB(). Each of these is known as an *internal function* (sometimes called an *intrinsic function* or just *function*). A function is a built-in routine that does work for you. The parentheses hold a value that controls the way the function works.

SPC() prints as many blank spaces as the value inside the parentheses requires. TAB() prints as many blank spaces as needed to move the next printed character to the column indicated inside the parentheses. Although these functions perform similar work, you can quickly understand them by seeing them in use.

Consider Listing 9.2 which uses SPC() and the semicolon (;) to print two strings on the same line. SPC(5) tells the PRINT statement to skip five blanks before the text string begins printing in the sixth column. If you end a PRINT statement with a semicolon, the next PRINT prints where the current one left off rather than print on the next line, as would happen without the semicolon.

INPUT   **LISTING 9.2** USE SPC() TO SEPARATE VALUES

```
1: strName$ = "QBasic"
2: PRINT "*"; Spc(5); strName$;   ' Notice semicolon.
3: PRINT Spc(2); strName$
```

The output will appear onscreen as follows when execution of the program reaches these lines:

OUTPUT   `*       QBasic  QBasic`

The code forces PRINT to skip 5 spaces before the first QBasic appears. After two more spaces, the second PRINT also prints QBasic.

If you use TAB() instead of SPC(), QBasic moves to the column argument located inside the parentheses and prints the next data item there. SPC() forces the next print to begin a certain number of spaces over, whereas TAB() forces the next print to begin in a specific column. Study Listing 9.3 for an example.

LISTING 9.3 CONTROL THE PRINT STATEMENT'S SPACING WITH THE TAB() AND SPC() FUNCTIONS

```
1: strName$ = "QBasic"
2: PRINT "*"; TAB(5); strName$; TAB(20); strName$
3: PRINT "*"; SPC(5); strName$; SPC(20); strName$
```

In the second line, TAB() keeps the printing in specific columns, but the third line's SPC() moves the printing over by a certain number of spaces.

Here is the output from this code:

```
*    QBasic    QBasic
*      QBasic                    QBasic
```

Printing to the Printer

You can send output to the printer as well as to the screen. The LPRINT statement sends data to the printer in the same way that PRINT works. If you LPRINT strings inside quotation marks, they print on the printer exactly as they appear in the quotation marks. If you print variables and expressions without quotation marks, QBasic prints the values of those variables and expressions.

Using the semicolons and commas inside the LPRINT causes the printed values to appear either next to one another or in the next print zone, respectively. The following code prints the names in columns on the printer:

```
' Illustrates the use of commas
LPRINT "Sam", "Jesse", "Jackson", "Susan"
LPRINT "Christine", "Ron", "Jayne", "Martha"
LPRINT "Johnny", "Thomas", "Francis", "Kerry"
LPRINT "Kim", "Barbara", "Lea", "William"
END
```

Often, your programs will print both to the screen and the printer. Therefore, similar output statements appear next to each other with one set directing the output to the screen and the other set to the printer.

Getting Keyboard Data with INPUT

INPUT statement is the opposite of PRINT. As Figure 9.2 shows, INPUT receives values from the keyboard. Those values typed by the user go into variables. In the previous chapter, you learned how to assign values to variables. You used the assignment statement because you knew the actual values. However, you don't often know all the data values when you write your program.

Think of a medical reception program that tracks patients as they enter the doctor's office. The programmer has no idea who will walk in next, and so cannot assign patient names to variables. The patient names can be stored in variables only when the program is run.

When a program reaches an INPUT statement, it displays a question mark and pauses until the user types a value and presses the Enter key. Here is an INPUT statement:

```
INPUT age      ' Wait for user to type a value
```

FIGURE 9.2.

INPUT *receives values from the keyboard at program runtime.*

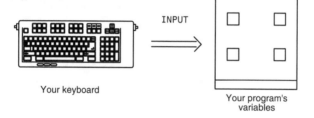

Your keyboard

INPUT

Your program's variables

When program execution reaches this statement, the computer displays a question mark onscreen. The question mark is a signal to the user that something is being asked and a response is desired. How does the user know what the question is? It is the programmer's responsibility to include before every INPUT statement a PRINT statement that asks the user for whatever type of value is needed. The PRINT statement prompts the user for the input. A prompt message is a question that you ask before a user's input is expected. The prompt message puts a complete question before the INPUT question mark. Consider these three lines from a program:

```
PRINT "What is your age";
INPUT age
PRINT "Thank you!"
```

When the computer reaches the first PRINT, it prints the message as usual. The semicolon at the end of the PRINT keeps the cursor on the same line so that whatever is printed next appears after the question. Do you remember what INPUT does? It prints a question mark. Because of semicolon, the question mark appears after the question, and the user sees this:

```
What is your age?
```

The words appear because of PRINT, and the question mark appears because of INPUT. The program doesn't continue to the next PRINT statement until the user answers the question by typing a value and pressing Enter.

> Resist the temptation to put a question mark inside your program's prompt questions. If you do, the INPUT will repeat the question mark, and your messages will look like this is on the screen:
>
> What is your age??

Follow the program in Listing 9.4 and study the output that appears below it. You can see how a variable with no value is filled by an INPUT statement.

INPUT **LISTING 9.4** INPUT RECEIVES A VALUE FROM THE USER AT THE KEYBOARD

```
1: ' Demonstrates the INPUT statement
2: '
3: PRINT "Before the INPUT, the variable named x is"; x
4: PRINT
5: PRINT "What value do you want x to have now";
6: INPUT x
7: ' x now has the value entered by the user
8: PRINT
9: PRINT "After the INPUT, x is"; x
10: END
```

QBasic zeroes all variables for you when a program begins. This means that the value of x is zero until you give it a value via INPUT. Here is a sample output from the program. The user typed 27 for the value of x.

OUTPUT
```
Before the INPUT, the variable named x is 0

What value do you want x to have now? 27

After the INPUT, x is 27
```

> QBasic waits at the INPUT statement as long as it takes for the user to type a value in response to the INPUT statement. The INPUT is finished only when the user presses the Enter key.

Inputting Strings and Multiple Variables

Any type of variable, numeric or string, can be entered with INPUT. For example, these lines wait for the user to enter a string value:

```
PRINT "What is your first name";
INPUT first$
```

If the user types the name in response to the question, the name is put into the first$ variable.

9

> If the user only presses Enter, without entering a value in response to INPUT, QBasic puts a value called *null* into the variable. A null value is a zero for numeric variables, or an empty string for string variables. An empty string— a string variable with nothing in it—is literally zero characters long.

A single INPUT statement can gather more than one value if your application requires it. You can list more than one variable, separating them with commas, after the INPUT statement. The following INPUT statement waits for the user to type three values:

```
PRINT "What are your first name, age, and salary";
INPUT first$, age, salary
```

Here is a sample run of these statements:

```
What are your first name, age, and salary? Fred, 41, 1904.95
```

Notice that the user has to know that commas are required between the values entered. If no commas are typed, the user receives an error message saying Redo from start—a none-too-descriptive advisory. The error message informs the user that the values were not entered in the expected format. One of the drawbacks to gathering multiple values in a single INPUT is that the user does not always know how to enter the values. It is safer and more expedient to ask for each value individually. For example:

```
PRINT "What is your first name";
INPUT first$
PRINT "How old are you";
INPUT age
PRINT "What is your salary";
INPUT salary
```

This set of three INPUT statements is far less likely to generate errors when the program is run. The user only has to enter the three values one at a time; there is no worry about putting commas between them. Notice how the following program output leads the user through the questions one at a time:

```
What is your first name? Fred
How old are you? 41
What is your salary? 1904.95
```

> **CONSIDER YOUR DATA**
>
> One design factor that you should consider when writing a program is the style of user
> input. You must remember that people who know very little about computers might use
> your program. The user of a program should not need to know how your program
> works. Write your programs so that a user must enter values one at a time when prompt-
> ed, not two or more values following a single INPUT. Multivalued INPUT statements are
> prone to cause errors.

Combining PRINT and INPUT

You have seen the importance of printing an INPUT prompt message with a PRINT before
your INPUT statements. Your programs should not display an INPUT's question mark without printing a message beforehand telling the user what kind of input you expect. The
designers of QBasic realized the importance of displaying a prompt along with every
INPUT in your program. They added a feature to the INPUT statement itself to include the
prompt message along with the input. Instead of having pairs of PRINT-INPUT statements
throughout your program, you can have single INPUT statements that both prompt the
user and receive input.

A simple example shows how the prompt message works. The following statements
should be old hat to you by now. The PRINT asks the user a question, and the INPUT gets
the user's answer.

```
PRINT "What is the month number (i.e., 1, 5, or 11)";
INPUT monNum
```

The PRINT displays a prompt that tells the user what input is expected.

Here is an equivalent statement. It does the same thing as the previous PRINT-INPUT, but
in a single line of code:

```
INPUT "What is the month number (i.e., 1, 5, or 11)"; monNum
```

This is what the user sees when QBasic reaches this line in the program:

```
What is the month number (i.e., 1, 5, or 11)?
```

The user can then answer the question, in effect supplying the variable monNum with a
month number, and the program then continues with the rest of its execution.

> Some questions cannot be asked in a single INPUT prompt. Therefore, there
> might be times when you have to put extra PRINT statements before an
> INPUT to fully describe the input you expect. Here is an example that does
> just that:
>
> ```
> PRINT "You must now enter the last four digits of your "
> INPUT "extended zipcode.  What are those four digits"; eZip
> ```

9

Listing 9.5 shows a program that a small store might use to compute totals at the cash
register. The INPUT statements in this program are required; only at runtime will the customer purchase values be known. As you can see, getting input at runtime is vital for
"real-world" data processing.

INPUT

LISTING 9.5 YOU CAN USE INPUT TO SIMULATE A CASH REGISTER PROGRAM FOR
A SMALL STORE

```
 1: ' Demonstrates INPUT by asking the user for several values
 2: ' at a store's cash register and prints a total of the sales
 3: CLS        ' Clear the screen
 4: PRINT , "** Mom and Pop's Store **"
 5: PRINT
 6: INPUT "How many bottles of pop were sold"; pop
 7: popTotal = pop * .75
 8: INPUT "How many bags of chips were sold"; chips
 9: chipTotal = chips * 1.25
10: INPUT "How many gallons of gas were sold"; gas
11: gasTotal = gas * 1.19
12:
13: ' Calculate total sale and add 7% sales tax
14: fullSale = popTotal + chipTotal + gasTotal    ' Total sale
15: sTax = .07 * fullSale
16: netSale = fullSale + sTax
17:
18: ' The following INPUT gets a null value just to pause the program
19: INPUT "Press Enter when you are ready for the invoice..."; ans
20: ' Print an invoice on the screen
21: PRINT
22: PRINT
23: PRINT , "** Invoice Mom and Pop's Store **"
24: PRINT
25: PRINT "*************************************************"
26: PRINT pop; "bottles of pop:", popTotal
27: PRINT chips; "bags of chips:", chipTotal
28: PRINT gas; "gallons of gas:", gasTotal
29: PRINT "-----------------------------------------------"
30: PRINT "Total sale:", fullSale
```

continues

LISTING 9.5 CONTINUED

```
31: PRINT "Sales tax:", sTax
32: PRINT "Final total:", netSale
33: PRINT
34: PRINT "Thank the customer!"
35: END
```

Figure 9.3 shows the result of running this program. As you can see, the program would be helpful for a small store.

FIGURE 9.3.

Running the cash register program produces this output.

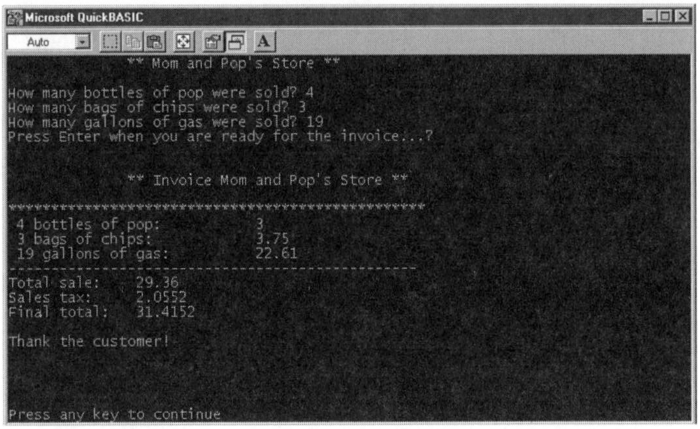

```
** Mom and Pop's Store **
How many bottles of pop were sold? 4
How many bags of chips were sold? 3
How many gallons of gas were sold? 19
Press Enter when you are ready for the invoice...?

           ** Invoice Mom and Pop's Store **
********************************************************
 4 bottles of pop:        3
 3 bags of chips:         3.75
 19 gallons of gas:       22.61
-------------------------------------------------------
Total sale:    29.36
Sales tax:      2.0552
Final total:   31.4152

Thank the customer!


Press any key to continue
```

Using the USING Clause

There is one problem with the program in Listing 9.5; it doesn't print to exactly two decimal places, which a program calculating dollars and cents should do. You can use an additional option on the PRINT (or LPRINT) statement, called USING. The USING option describes how you want your data printed. There is so much to the USING option that it would take an entire hour's lesson to explain it thoroughly. At this point in your programming career, you probably just need USING to print two decimal places for dollars and cents. Currency printing is probably what most QBasic programmers use USING for.

> QBasic doesn't respect the Windows International settings. If your country uses a comma where North America uses a decimal point, and you've set the proper Windows settings for your country, your QBasic code still will use the decimal point.

Here is a PRINT statement that ensures the variable total prints to two decimal places:

```
PRINT USING "#####.##"; total
```

The #####.## might look strange to you. It is a picture clause describing how the next variable should look. If there were three pound signs after the decimal point, three decimal places would result, even if they all happened to be zeros. If total does not have five digits before the decimal point, leading spaces appear in the number.

9

When you use PRINT USING, QBasic follows the pattern in your USING string and ignores the way it would normally print values. Therefore, there is no automatic space before positive numbers if you print them with a USING string.

Listing 9.6 has several PRINT USING statements that show you how to have the output results printed in various formats.

LISTING 9.6 VARIOUS PRINT USING OPTIONS CAN HELP DEMONSTRATE THE

INPUT   STATEMENT

```
1: ' Printing with PRINT USING
2: PRINT 2223.329     ' Extra blank for the imaginary plus
3: PRINT USING "####.##"; 2223.329
4: PRINT USING "####.#"; 2223.329
5: PRINT USING "####.#   ###.#   ##.###"; 2223.329; 12; 12
6: PRINT USING "#####,.##"; 2223.329
7: END
```

The output from the program is as follows:

OUTPUT
```
 2223.329
2223.33
2223.3
2223.3    12.0    12.000
 2,223.33
```

Notice that PRINT USING determines how the printed number will appear and that PRINT USING does *not* leave room for an imaginary plus sign before positive values as the regular PRINT statement does.

The last PRINT USING shows you that putting a comma immediately before the decimal point in a USING string instructs QBasic to insert a comma at every third digit in the number. Printing numbers with commas helps the user read the value more easily.

Listing 9.7 shows the same cash register program you saw earlier. Because of the PRINT USING statements, the program prints all of its output to two decimal places, ensuring that the output is properly rounded to dollars and cents before being printed. Figure 9.4 shows the resulting output with the better look of the currency amounts.

INPUT   **LISTING 9.7** YOU CAN IMPROVE THE LOOK OF DOLLAR VALUES

```
 1: ' Demonstrates INPUT by asking the user for several values
 2: ' at a store's cash register and prints a total of the sales
 3: CLS       ' Clear the screen
 4: PRINT , "** Mom and Pop's Store **"
 5: PRINT
 6: INPUT "How many bottles of pop were sold"; pop
 7: popTotal = pop * .75
 8: INPUT "How many bags of chips were sold"; chips
 9: chipTotal = chips * 1.25
10: INPUT "How many gallons of gas were sold"; gas
11: gasTotal = gas * 1.19
12:
13: ' Calculate total sale and add 7% sales tax
14: fullSale = popTotal + chipTotal + gasTotal    ' Total sale
15: sTax = .07 * fullSale
16: netSale = fullSale + sTax
17:
18: ' The following INPUT gets a null value just to pause the program
19: INPUT "Press Enter when you are ready for the invoice..."; ans
20: ' Print an invoice on the screen
21: PRINT
22: PRINT
23: PRINT , "** Invoice Mom and Pop's Store **"
24: PRINT
25: PRINT "************************************************"
26: PRINT USING "## bottles of pop: ###.##"; pop; popTotal
27: PRINT USING "## bags of chips:  ###.##"; chips; chipTotal
28: PRINT USING "## gallons of gas: ###.##"; gas; gasTotal
29: PRINT "------------------------------------------------"
30: PRINT USING "Total sale:  ####,.##"; fullSale
31: PRINT USING "Sales tax:    ###,.##"; sTax
32: PRINT USING "Final total: ####,.##"; netSale
33: PRINT
34: PRINT "Thank the customer!"
35: END
```

FIGURE 9.4.

The output looks much better with PRINT USING.

Whenever you have to get user data that might have commas in it, such as an address, use LINE INPUT instead of INPUT. Whenever you suspect that the user might type a comma as part of the input value, you would have to use LINE INPUT to get the user's value. LINE INPUT is exactly like INPUT, except that you can get only one input string value with it. That string value may include any character. A comma, however, is not allowed in the INPUT statement because it would be the separating character if you were inputting more than one variable with a single INPUT.

The following statement fills a single string variable from the user and the user can type commas during the input if desired:

```
LINE INPUT "What is your address? "; addr$
```

If you want the user to enter a last name separated from the first name with a comma, LINE INPUT would be required in the name prompt as well.

> LINE INPUT will not generate an automatic question mark for you, so you must put a question mark at the end of the prompt if you use it.

Summary

Mastering proper input and output can mean the difference between a program your users like to use and one they hate. If you properly label all input that you want so that you prompt your users through the input process, the user will have no questions about the proper format for your program. Getting the input data's format correct is important for QBasic because, unlike Windows programs, a QBasic program doesn't allow for fancy data-entry text boxes and edit fields that many Windows controls allow.

The next hour describes how to use the QBasic language to control a program's execution. A QBasic program can actually make decisions based on the data supplied to it.

Q&A

Q Does an INPUT USING statement exist?

A No. The USING clause is only for output because it is output that you need to format. Data comes in all formats but you will want to display data in certain formats that might differ slightly from their native format.

Q How can I format output values that I send to the printer with LPRINT?

A Use the USING clause! LPRINT works exactly like PRINT, and that means that you can issue LPRINT USING commands that mimic their PRINT USING counterparts.

Workshop

The quiz questions and exercises are provided for your further understanding. See Appendix A, "Answers to End of Chapter Questions," for answers.

Quiz

1. Why does a blank often appear before values that your program prints?
2. True or false: QBasic leaves the extra blank before both positive and negative numbers.
3. What does the semicolon do inside a PRINT statement?
4. What is an internal function?
5. What is the difference between the SPC() function and the TAB() function?
6. What does the USING clause do?
7. What statement gets the user's entered values?
8. How can you enter commas as input if the commas appear inside the value being entered?
9. True or false: One INPUT statement can receive more than one value from the user at the keyboard.
10. Why is it important to prompt the user for input?

HOUR 10

Data Processing with QBasic

This hour's lesson extends your knowledge of QBasic by showing you how to compare values and repeat sections of QBasic programs. A user's responses or calculated data can control the flow of your program. This lesson teaches you how to write programs that make decisions. The code sometimes needs to repeat sections to complete the processing of several data values. You'll learn how to create a loop to do just that.

With the concepts that you learn in this lesson, you can write powerful programs to do what you need done. You will find yourself thinking of new ideas and new ways to use your computer.

The highlights of this hour include:

- How QBasic makes decisions
- What the IF statement does
- How the ELSE statement affects decisions

- How to repeat sections of code
- What the difference is between the various kinds of loop statements QBasic supports
- How you can flowchart logic needed for looping and decision statements

Comparing Data with IF

The structured programming decision construct is very easy to implement in QBasic. The decision construct is represented in flowcharts by a decision symbol that always has two exits. Likewise, a QBasic decision statement always has two possibilities. To decide which path to take in a QBasic program, you must use the IF statement. Most programming languages have an IF statement that works exactly like QBasic's.

Listing 10.1 shows you an example of a program that contains an IF statement. Even though you have never seen QBasic's IF before, you will probably have little trouble figuring out what this program does.

INPUT

LISTING 10.1 USE AN IF STATEMENT WHEN YOU WANT YOUR PROGRAM TO MAKE A DECISION

```
 1: ' Deciding how much of a bonus to pay a salesperson
 2: INPUT "What is the salesperson's name"; sName$
 3: INPUT "What were the total sales made last month"; sales
 4:
 5: IF (sales < 5000) THEN
 6:     bonus = 0
 7:     daysOff = 0
 8: ELSE
 9:     bonus = 25
10:     daysOff = 2
11: END IF
12:
13: PRINT
14: PRINT sName$; " earned a bonus of"; bonus;
15: PRINT "and gets"; daysOff; "days off."
16: END
```

Look at the following two sample runs of the program. Pay attention to the fact that the program produces a different bonus depending on the salesperson's total sales. The first sample run follows:

```
What is the salesperson's name? Jim
What were the total sales made last month? 3234.43
Jim earned a bonus of 0 and gets 0 days off.
```

The salesperson did not get a bonus because the sales were not high enough. Consider the difference in the following:

```
What is the salesperson's name? Jane
What were the total sales made last month? 5642.34

Jane earned a bonus of 25 and gets 2 days off.
```

The program offers complete control over one of two options via the IF statement. Figure 10.1 shows you the flowchart of this program. The decision symbol is represented by the IF statement in the program.

FIGURE 10.1.

The flowchart's decision symbol illustrates the nature of the salesperson program's IF statement.

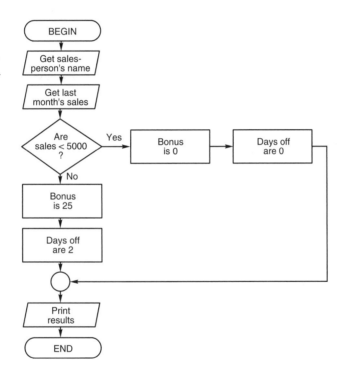

10

The IF works just like it reads. *If* the statement to the right of the IF is true, the block of statements following IF executes. Notice that the word THEN is required. *If* the statement to the right of IF is not true, the block of statements following ELSE executes instead. The ELSE clause is optional; without it, you are testing to see whether you will execute a single block of statements. For example, the following is an IF statement that prints a message only if the statement to the right of IF is true. If it is not, and there is no ELSE, the program continues on the line after END IF:

```
IF (age < 18) THEN
    PRINT "You are not old enough"
END IF
```

The END IF always marks the end of the IF set of statements. Whatever the result of the IF is, the statements following END IF always execute after the IF finishes.

> The parentheses around the statement to the right of the IF are not required, but they clarify what exactly is being tested. This statement to the right of IF, typically enclosed within parentheses, is called a *relational test*.

Writing the Relational Test

The IF statement reads just as it does in plain English: *If something is true, do one thing; otherwise do something else.* You do not always add an *else* after a spoken *if*, and you do not have to have one in QBasic either. Consider the following statements:

If I make enough money, I'll retire early.

If you're out late, call me, or else you'll get in trouble.

If you're in town, we'll eat dinner together.

As a programming language, QBasic is fairly strict about how you make the IF test. The relational test, the statement to the right of the IF, always includes one of the symbols from Table 10.1.

TABLE 10.1 IF STATEMENT RELATIONAL OPERATORS

Operator	Description	Example
<	Less than	IF (sales < maxSales) THEN
>	Greater than	IF (amount > 100.00) THEN
=	Equal to	IF (age = 21) THEN
>=	Greater than or equal to	IF (grade >= 90) THEN
<=	Less than or equal to	IF (price <= 1.00) THEN
<>	Not equal to	IF (year <> 1998) THEN

You learned about the math operators in Hour 8, "Your First Language: QBasic." QBasic supplies these relational operators so you can test certain conditions with an IF statement. There are always two possibilities with the relational operators. Something is either less than something else, or it is not. Something is either greater than something else, or it is not. Something is either equal to something else, or it is not.

> The two possibilities, which the relational operators enable, provide the means for duplicating the two-legged decision symbol in a flowchart. A decision symbol has two possible outcomes, and so does the IF. IF is either true or false.

The statements following the THEN and ELSE can be any QBasic statements. When the ELSE contains an IF in its block, you must combine the ELSE and IF into a single statement: ELSEIF. This language rule of QBasic is easier to understand than it first appears. Listing 10.2 contains a set of IF statements that prints first, second, third, or fourth depending on the number entered by the user.

INPUT   **LISTING 10.2** AN IF WITHIN THE ELSE MUST BECOME AN ELSEIF STATEMENT

```
 1: ' Prints a description based on user's number
 2: INPUT "How many years have you been in school"; years
 3: IF (years = 1) THEN
 4:    PRINT "This is your first year"
 5: ELSEIF (years = 2) THEN
 6:    PRINT "This is your second year"
 7: ELSEIF (years = 3) THEN
 8:    PRINT "This is your third year"
 9: ELSEIF (years = 4) THEN
10:    PRINT "This is your fourth year"
11: ELSE PRINT "You did not enter 1, 2, 3, or 4"
12: END IF
13: END
```

As this program shows, you can test whether the user enters acceptable data by using the IF. This is known as input validation. You can validate some input values to make sure the user entered what you expected. For instance, you can check an age to make sure it is greater than 0. There is not always a way to determine whether the user's input value is exactly correct, but you can check to see if it is reasonable.

Using the SELECT CASE Statement

There is a special type of decision statement in QBasic called the SELECT CASE statement. The SELECT CASE statement is useful for testing several conditions. Although each condition has only two possibilities, as with IF conditions, SELECT CASE can replace a series of IF statements within another IF statement, as in the program in Listing 10.2.

SELECT CASE is extremely easy to understand. Listing 10.3 shows a rewritten version of the program you saw in Listing 10.2.

LISTING 10.3 USING SELECT CASE TO SELECT FROM SEVERAL TESTS IMPROVES
UPON EMBEDDED IF STATEMENTS

INPUT

```
 1: ' Prints a description based on user's number
 2: INPUT "How many years have you been in school"; years
 3:
 4: SELECT CASE years
 5:    CASE 1
 6:       PRINT "This is your first year"
 7:    CASE 2
 8:       PRINT "This is your second year"
 9:    CASE 3
10:       PRINT "This is your third year"
11:    CASE 4
12:       PRINT "This is your fourth year"
13:    CASE ELSE
14:       PRINT "You did not enter 1, 2, 3, or 4"
15: END SELECT
16: END
```

In this program, there are five possible cases. The user could enter 1, 2, 3, 4, or something else. The case that matches the user's input executes, but the other cases do not. SELECT CASE is often useful for replacing the slightly more complicated IF within IF statements.

Use IF statements when you must select from one or two relational conditions. If there are several more relational conditions to test for, a SELECT CASE is generally easier to write and understand.

Looping Statements

Looping statements are another important feature of any programming language. QBasic supplies several statements that control loops. Your computer will never get bored. It will loop over and over, quickly repeating statements as long as you need it to.

Loops have many uses. You might need a loop to ask the user for several people's data, to calculate a combined total, or to print several lines of data. QBasic's three primary looping statements are

- FOR...NEXT loops
- DO...UNTIL loops
- DO...WHILE loops

The following sections describe each of these looping statement.

Using the FOR...NEXT Loop

The FOR...NEXT loop is actually a loop of statements enclosed between the FOR and the NEXT statement. Before you look at the FOR...NEXT statement, an analogy to things in everyday life might be helpful. As with the IF, the FOR loops are natural ways of expressing an idea. Consider the following description:

```
For each of today's invoices:
```
- check the accuracy of the invoice,
- add the total amount to the daily sales total.
- Look at the next invoice.

You can sense from this description of invoice totaling that a repetitive process happens. If there are five invoices, the process repeats for each of those five invoices.

The computer's FOR loop works just like the for each concept in the invoice description (that's why it's called FOR). To ease you into the method of FOR loops, Listing 10.4 shows a simple loop that explains the FOR and NEXT statements.

INPUT LISTING 10.4 USE FOR AND NEXT TO CONTROL A COUNTING LOOP

```
1: ' First FOR...NEXT Program
2: ' This program prints the number 1 through 5
3: CLS
4: FOR i = 1 TO 5
5:    PRINT i
6: NEXT i
7: END
```

Here is the output from Listing 10.4's program:

```
1
2
3
4
5
```

The FOR and NEXT statements work in pairs; they enclose one or more statements. The statements inside the FOR...NEXT loop repeat until the loop finishes. The loop is controlled by the FOR statement's variable. In Listing 10.4's program, the control variable is i (you can use any variable name). The FOR statement is saying the following: *For each i (with i having a value of 1 the first time, 2 the second time, and so on until it gets to 5), perform the statement between FOR and NEXT.*

As you can gather from Listing 10.4, the FOR...NEXT loop automatically increments (adds one each time to) the control variable. The body of the FOR loop (the statement or statements between the FOR and NEXT) loops once for every increment of the variable until the variable reaches its final value specified in the FOR statement.

Listing 10.5 shows a program that does exactly the same thing as Listing 10.4, but without using a FOR loop. You can see that the FOR loop makes repetitive statements much easier to code. (Consider how much easier it would be to use a FOR...NEXT statement to print the numbers from 1 to 200, instead of writing two hundred lines of code to print those numbers if you used the method in Listing 10.5.)

INPUT   **LISTING 10.5** PRINTING WITHOUT A FOR...NEXT LOOP GETS TEDIOUS

```
 1: ' Prints from 1 to 5 without a FOR...NEXT statement
 2: CLS
 3: i = 1
 4: PRINT i
 5: i = 2
 6: PRINT i
 7: i = 3
 8: PRINT i
 9: i = 4
10: PRINT i
11: i = 5
12: PRINT i
13: END
```

You do not have to print the value of the loop variable as done in Listing 10.5. Often, a FOR loop controls a set of statements, determining the number of times those statements repeat, without using the control variable for anything else. Listing 10.6, controlled by a FOR loop, prints a message 15 times.

INPUT   **LISTING 10.6** PRINTING A MESSAGE SEVERAL TIMES IN A LOOP IS EFFICIENT

```
1: ' Message-printing program
2: CLS
3: FOR i = 1 TO 15
4:    PRINT "Happy Birthday!"
5: NEXT i
6: END
```

Another example will make this clearer. Look at the program in Listing 10.7. A teacher might use it to print a grade sheet. The program asks the teacher how many test scores are to be entered. It uses that answer to loop through a series of statements asking for the next child's name and grade. As the teacher enters the data, the values are printed to the printer. At the end of the program, there is a complete listing of names and grades. (In Hour 17, "Program Algorithms," you will learn how to program an accumulator to add all the grades together and to print a class average.)

LISTING 10.7 A TEACHER'S GRADE-PRINTING PROGRAM IS EASY TO FOLLOW WHEN
INPUT YOU USE A LOOP

```
 1: ' Grade-printing program
 2: CLS
 3:
 4: PRINT , "** Grade-listing Program **"
 5: PRINT
 6: INPUT "How many tests are there today"; numTests
 7: PRINT
 8:
 9: LPRINT "** Grades for the Test **"
10: LPRINT
11: LPRINT "Name", , "Grade"
12: FOR i = 1 TO numTests
13:   INPUT "What is the next student's name"; sName$
14:   PRINT "What is "; sName$; "'s grade";
15:   INPUT grade
16:   LPRINT sName$, , grade
17: NEXT i
18: END
```

10

Figure 10.2 shows the output that the program in Listing 10.7 produces. If the teacher has five students, the FOR loop will loop five times. If the teacher says there are ten students, the program loops ten times. Because the teacher's input value controls the FOR loop, the program is of general purpose and able to handle any number of students.

The following is a listing of the program's output if the names and scores are entered in the session as shown by Figure 10.2:

OUTPUT
```
** Grades for the Test **

Name                    Grade
Joe Santiago             87
Kim Moore                98
Eddie Kerry              56
Maggie Smith             73
Carl Jones              100
```

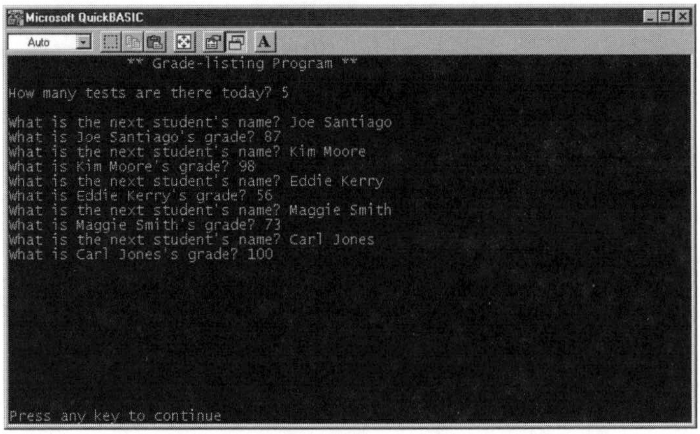

FIGURE 10.2.

Running the grade-printing program displays the loop.

Controlling the FOR Loop

There are additional ways you can control a FOR loop. You can make the control variable increment by a value other than 1 each time through the loop. You can also make the count variable count down instead of up. By adding the STEP option to the FOR statement, you can make the control variable change to a different value by either a positive or negative amount.

Listing 10.8 shows you a program that counts down from 10 to 1 and then prints Blast Off! at the end of the loop. To carry out the countdown, a negative STEP value had to be used. The FOR statement says that a loop is requested, with i looping from 10 to 1. Each time through the loop, –1 is added to i, which causes the descending count.

INPUT   **LISTING 10.8** COUNTING DOWN FROM 10 TO 1 IS SIMPLE WITH A FOR LOOP

```
1: ' A countdown program
2: CLS
3:
4: FOR i = 10 TO 1 STEP -1
5:    PRINT i
6: NEXT i
7:
8: PRINT "Blast Off!"
9: END
```

Here is the output from the program:

OUTPUT
```
10
 9
 8
 7
 6
 5
 4
 3
 2
 1
Blast Off!
```

You can specify any value for a STEP amount. Listing 10.9 shows you a program that prints the even numbers below 15 and then the odd numbers below 15. Two loops control the counting. The first one begins counting at 2, and the second one begins counting at 1. Each loop adds a STEP value of 2 to the initial FOR value to produce the sets of even and odd numbers.

10

INPUT

LISTING 10.9 PRINT THE FIRST FEW EVEN AND ODD NUMBERS USING THE STEP OPTION

```
 1: ' Print the first few even and odd numbers
 2: CLS
 3:
 4: PRINT "Even numbers from 2 to 14:"
 5: FOR number = 2 TO 15 STEP 2
 6:    PRINT number
 7: NEXT number
 8:
 9: PRINT "Odd numbers from 1 to 15:"
10: FOR number = 1 TO 15 STEP 2
11:    PRINT number
12: NEXT number
13: END
```

Figure 10.3 shows the output from this program.

You can also cause a FOR loop to exit early with the EXIT FOR statement. There might be times when you expect to loop for a fixed number of times, as specified by the FOR control variable. Then, because of special input from the user, you have to exit the FOR loop early. The EXIT FOR statement exits a FOR loop whenever QBasic encounters it in your program. Listing 10.10 shows how EXIT FOR works. In Hour 11, "Managing Data and Disk Files," you learn how to use EXIT FOR when you want to prompt the user for disk data.

FIGURE 10.3.

Printing some even and odd numbers.

INPUT   **LISTING 10.10** THE EXIT FOR STATEMENT TERMINATES A FOR LOOP EARLY

```
 1: ' Using EXIT FOR to quit a FOR loop earlier
 2: ' than its natural conclusion.
 3: CLS
 4: FOR i = 1 TO 100      ' Would normally loop 100 times
 5:    PRINT i              ' Prints the numbers from 1 to at most 100
 6:    INPUT "Continue (Y/N)"; ans$   ' See if user wants to continue
 7:    IF (ans$ = "N") THEN
 8:       EXIT FOR                    ' Quit early if user wants
 9:    END IF
10: NEXT i
11: PRINT "That's all folks!"
12: END
```

Here is a sample run of this program. Notice that the FOR loop would have run 100 times, printing the numbers from 1 to 100, if the user had not stopped the process early by entering N in response to the prompt as indicated in the following:

```
1
Continue (Y/N)? Y
2
Continue (Y/N)? Y
3
Continue (Y/N)? Y
Continue (Y/N)? N
That's all folks!
```

The FOR loop offers much loop control, but it is designed to count through the control loop's value. Not all your loops can be determined by a counting variable. Sometimes you need loops that loop while a certain condition is true or until a certain condition is met.

> The variable after NEXT is optional. Both of the following FOR...NEXT loops
> are identical:
>
> ```
> FOR i = 1 TO 10
>   PRINT i
> NEXT i
>
> FOR i = 1 TO 10
>   PRINT i
> NEXT
> ```
>
> Notice the variable named i does not appear after the final NEXT but the
> variable is implied.

You can nest one loop inside another. Such nested constructs can seem rather advanced to beginning programmers, but the nested loops are simple to understand if you consider what happens when you need to perform a loop more than once. You *could* write the loop twice, back to back, or you could enclose the loop inside another loop that executes its body twice. Hour 17, "Program Algorithms," explains nested loops in more detail.

Using the DO...WHILE Loop

The DO...WHILE loop supplies a way to control loops through a relational test. The loop's relational test uses the same relational operators used with IF statements (refer to Table 10.1 for a complete listing of relational operators).

Suppose the teacher with the grade-printing program doesn't know exactly how many students took the test, and doesn't want to take the time to count them. Because the total number of tests must be specified to control the FOR loop properly, another method is required. Listing 10.11 shows you the same program, but controlled by a DO...WHILE loop. Notice that the DO...WHILE continues looping while a certain condition is true. The condition is the teacher's answer in response to having more tests to enter.

INPUT

LISTING 10.11 YOU CAN CONTROL THE GRADE PRINTING WITH A DO...WHILE LOOP

```
1: ' Grade-printing program using DO...WHILE
2: CLS
3:
4: PRINT , "** Grade-listing Program **"
5: PRINT
6:
7: LPRINT "** Grades for the Test **"
8: LPRINT
```

continues

LISTING **10.11** CONTINUED

```
 9: LPRINT "Name", , "Grade"
10: DO
11:    INPUT "What is the next student's name"; sName$
12:    PRINT "What is "; sName$; "'s grade";
13:    INPUT grade
14:    LPRINT sName$, , grade
15:    INPUT "Are there more grades (Y/N)"; ans$
16: LOOP WHILE (ans$ = "Y")
17: END
```

This program keeps looping until the teacher indicates that there are no more grades to
enter. Notice that the body of the loop is enclosed between the DO and LOOP WHILE statements, and that the WHILE is followed by a relational test, the result of which (true or
false) determines whether the loop repeats again or quits.

Using the DO...UNTIL Loop

The DO...UNTIL loop is similar to the DO...WHILE loop you saw in the preceding section.
DO...WHILE loops as long as the relational condition is true; DO...UNTIL loops as long as
the relational condition is false.

The choice of DO...WHILE versus DO...UNTIL depends on your application. You can use
both interchangeably in most programs; just be sure to reverse the conditional test being
performed. The following is a DO...WHILE loop:

```
DO
    PRINT "A"
    INPUT "Again"; ans$
LOOP WHILE (ans$ = "Y")
```

The same code using a DO...UNTIL loop follows:

```
DO
    PRINT "A"
    INPUT "Again"; ans$
LOOP UNTIL (ans$ = "N")
```

The tests being performed in the two sets of loops are the opposite of each other. The
first program loops while a certain condition is true; the second loops until a certain condition is true. Figure 10.4 shows a flowchart of each set of loops. The decision symbol's
question is different for each one, but the logic used is the same.

Listing 10.12 shows you how to use the DO...UNTIL loop to control a number-guessing
game. The computer keeps asking the user for a number until the user's number matches
the computer's number.

INPUT **LISTING 10.12** A NUMBER-GUESSING GAME CAN USE THE DO...UNTIL LOOP TO
MAKE GUESSES

```
 1:  ' Number-guessing game
 2:  CLS
 3:
 4:  compNum = 47     ' The computer's number
 5:
 6:  PRINT "I am thinking of a number..."
 7:  PRINT "Try to guess it."
 8:  PRINT
 9:
10:  DO
11:     INPUT "What is your guess (between 1 and 100)"; guess
12:  LOOP UNTIL (guess = compNum)
13:
14:  PRINT "You got it!"
15:  END
```

10

FIGURE 10.4.

*Flowcharting the
two DO loops.*

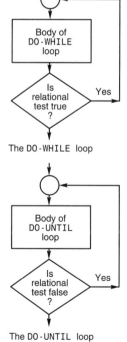

The DO-WHILE loop

The DO-UNTIL loop

Figure 10.5 shows a sample run of this program. DO...UNTIL is the perfect control statement because the program must keep looping, asking for another number, until the user enters the correct number.

FIGURE **10.5.**

Guessing the computer's number takes luck.

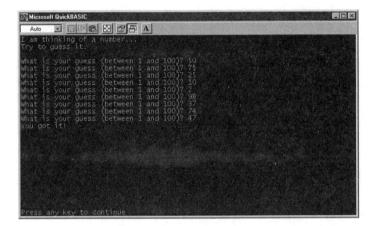

Listing 10.12's program is rather dull and requires no skill but pure guessing. In Hour 17, "Program Algorithms," you will learn how to add some data-checking steps to turn the program into a game that mixes luck and some skill to make things interesting.

QBasic actually supports two pairs of DO...WHILE and DO...UNTIL loops. Instead of putting the conditional test at the bottom of the loops, you can place the test at the top. The following are two examples of such loops:

```
DO WHILE (A < B)
   INPUT "How many years to go"; B
LOOP

DO UNTIL (A < B)
   INPUT "How many years to go"; B
LOOP
```

The placement of the conditional tests determines if the body of the loop executes at least one time. The previous versions of the loops that you learned earlier in this hour's lesson always execute their bodies (the code beneath the DO and the LOOP statements) at least one time. By putting the conditional test at the top of the loops, as part of the DO statement, you change the logic so that the body may or may not execute at least one time. If the initial values of the conditional test make the DO logic fail, the body of the loop never executes, and the program continues at the statement that follows the LOOP statement.

> Your program's requirements determine whether or not you place the conditional test at the top or bottom of a loop. For example, in Listing 10.12, the user is to enter a guess at least once, or more if the user misses on the first guess. Therefore, the following DO with the conditional at the top of the loop would not work in that particular program because the user would not be asked for the guess even once:
>
> ```
> DO WHILE (guess = compNum)
>     INPUT "What is your guess (between 1 and 100)"; guess
> LOOP
> ```

10

As you write more and more programs, you will gain a good feel for the placement of a loop's conditional test. The placement becomes almost second nature. Your program's logic, depending on whether the body of the loop should execute at least once or perhaps not at all, will determine the placement of the conditional test.

Summary

Congratulations! You can now enter data into a QBasic program and format the resulting output. You have also mastered the true power of any programming language—looping. The programs you saw in this lesson are getting to be powerful, yet you have seen that programming is easy. You have learned how the relational operators are used with the IF statement so that a QBasic program can make decisions based on the data. In addition, the looping constructs enable sections of your program to repeat as long as necessary.

The next hour shows how to store data to disk and read that data back from the disk. Disk files hold long-term data for the programs you write that process that data.

Q&A

Q Does it matter whether I select Do or For statements when I'm writing loops?

A The choice is not just between the For and Do loops, but between several formats of each loop. Generally, For loops are useful when you must count values or iterate the loop's body for a specified number of times. The Do loop is useful for iterating until or while a certain condition is met. If you are counting up or down, a For loop is easier to write and is slightly more efficient than an equivalent Do loop.

Q How does an IF loop compare to a FOR loop?

A Both the IF statement and the FOR statement, as well as the DO statements, all rely on conditional values to determine their job. Nevertheless, an IF statement is never considered to be a loop. Always keep in mind that an IF statement executes its body of code at mostly one time, and possibly never if the IF is initially false to begin with. Even if the IF conditional is true, the IF statement never executes its body more than one time, unlike the looping statements that can repeat their code bodies many times.

Workshop

The quiz questions and exercises are provided for your further understanding. See Appendix A, "Answers to End of Chapter Questions," for answers.

Quiz

1. How does a conditional operator differ from a mathematical operator?
2. What is a loop?
3. True or false: Code inside an IF statement might never execute.
4. True or false: Code inside FOR loops always execute at least once.
5. How can you abbreviate the NEXT statement?
6. What is the purpose for the EXIT FOR statement?
7. Which loop, DO or FOR...NEXT is best to use when you want to execute the loop a fixed number of times?
8. How do the DO...WHILE and DO...UNTIL loops differ?
9. How do I determine which loop, DO...WHILE or DO...UNTIL, to use?
10. How does the placement of the WHILE or UNTIL, before or after the loop's body of code, affect the loop?

Hour **11**

Managing Data and Disk Files

You are well on your way to becoming a QBasic programmer! If you were enrolled in a programming course, the material you finished in the previous lesson would take you through the first half of the course.

After you finish this lesson, you will have had tremendous exposure to QBasic and programming. The good news is that all programming languages contain the same types of statements you are learning about here. All spoken languages include verbs and nouns, and all programming languages similarly include variables, loops, and decision statements. The syntax of a statement in another language might be slightly different than in QBasic, but the types of available commands are identical. The similarity among programming languages is the primary reason that programmers often know more than one. It is very easy to learn a second or third language after you master your first one.

The highlights of this hour include:

- What an array is
- How to reserve memory for arrays
- What subscripts are
- What advantages disk files have over variables
- Why three modes of file access are available
- What the difference is between a record and a field
- How to open and close disk files
- How to write to and read from disk files

Understanding the Importance of Disk Storage and Arrays

NEW TERM This lesson teaches you some advanced ways to store your data. In the previous lessons, you learned how to work with variables. Variables are adequate for simple data, but for more advanced applications, you need to understand an advanced use of variables called an array. An *array* is nothing more than a list of variables that you can treat as a single group. You will also see some commands that store data to your disk file. Unless you can store your data long-term, your programs cannot keep track of data over time. By storing your variables and arrays to disk, you can process them whenever it is convenient.

> With disk files, you enter data once and then save it to disk. Your data will be immediately available when future programs want to use it.

Introduction to Arrays

Often, you must keep track of several data items that are the same type. For example, a teacher might need to keep track of 30 test scores, a company might need to track 150 products, or you might need to keep track of the money you've invested monthly into your retirement account. Although you could do so, it would be time-consuming to store similar data using the kind of variables you have seen. You would have to give each one a different name, so you can keep track of them.

For example, consider a teacher's test scores. If there are 30 pupils, the teacher might call the variables that contain the scores score1, score2, score3, and so on. The teacher must know which student's name goes with each score, so there would also have to be

30 separate string variables, probably called something like Sname1$, Sname2$, Sname3$, and so on. Such variable names make for tedious processing and program writing. Listing 11.1 shows you a partial listing of what is involved in such a program.

INPUT

LISTING 11.1 REQUESTING SEVERAL STUDENT NAMES AND GRADES WITHOUT USING ARRAYS CAN BECOME TEDIOUS

```
 1: ' Program that begs to have arrays instead of regular variables
 2: CLS
 3: INPUT "What is the next student's name"; Sname1$
 4: INPUT "What is the test score for that student"; score1
 5: PRINT                    ' Prints a blank line
 6: INPUT "What is the next student's name"; Sname2$
 7: INPUT "What is the test score for that student"; score2
 8: PRINT                    ' Prints a blank line
 9: INPUT "What is the next student's name"; Sname3$
10: INPUT "What is the test score for that student"; score3
11: PRINT                    ' Prints a blank line
12: INPUT "What is the next student's name"; Sname4$
13: INPUT "What is the test score for that student"; score4
14: PRINT                    ' Prints a blank line
15: INPUT "What is the next student's name"; Sname5$
16: INPUT "What is the test score for that student"; score5
17: PRINT                    ' Prints a blank line
18: ' This process continues for 25 more students
```

11

If you find yourself writing two or more sets of statements and the only differences are the variable names, you are probably not taking advantage of a better programming style. The program in Listing 11.1 begs you to use array variables. You haven't learned enough about programming to be able to use a different method of keeping all 30 variables in memory for later use (perhaps to calculate an overall class average or some such statistic).

Another drawback to using a different variable name for all 30 variables is that you cannot take advantage of the powerful loop statements you learned in the previous chapter. The goal of programming is to make your life simpler, not harder. Whenever you can put repetitive code, such as that in Listing 11.1, into a loop, you save wear and tear on your fingers by writing a single pair of INPUT statements within a FOR or DO...WHILE loop.

NEW TERM An array is a list of similar variables. Each of the like variables is called an *array element*. Instead of each individual array element having a different name, the entire array has one name. Each element in the list is distinguished by a subscript.

NEW TERM The top of Figure 11.1 shows you what five of the first 30 test score variables look like in memory. Each variable has a different name. The bottom of Figure 11.1 shows you how the same set of variables stored in an array appear. There are still five variables, and each one is separate and distinct. Unlike the differently named variables, each of the array variables has the same name. They are distinguished not by their names, but by *subscript*, which is the number inside the parentheses following the array name. Every element in each array has a subscript. This way you know which element in the list to refer to when you want to distinguish one value from another.

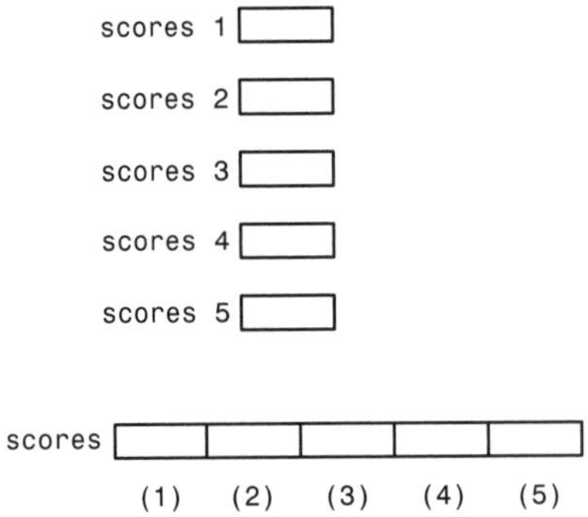

FIGURE 11.1.

Separate variables stored as an array.

Now that the teacher stores the variables in 30 array elements called scores, the teacher can use a loop to look through them. The ability to loop through array elements, either initializing or printing them, makes arrays extremely powerful and easy to program. Consider the section of code in Listing 11.2. Notice how the program asks for the student's name and score only once; that request is then repeated inside a loop.

INPUT **LISTING 11.2** YOU CAN IMPROVE THE GRADE PROGRAM WITH ARRAYS

```
1: ' Loop through the questions with array subscripts
2: CLS
3: FOR i = 1 TO 30
4:    INPUT "What is the next student's name"; Sname$(i)
5:    INPUT "What is the test score for that student"; scores(i)
6:    PRINT                    ' Prints a blank line
7: NEXT i
8: ' Rest of program follows
```

The first time through the FOR loop, i is 1. The teacher enters the value for Sname$(i) (which is really Sname$(1)) and scores(i) (which is really scores(1)), and then the loop increases the increments from i to 2. This continues until the teacher enters all 30 names and scores. The subscript runs through the data and makes the code much cleaner.

> QBasic zeroes out all the elements of numeric arrays and puts null strings in all the elements of string arrays before you use them.

Reserving Array Space

NEW TERM Often, you must tell QBasic beforehand how much array space you will need. QBasic permits only 10 array elements before requiring you to request more with a DIM statement. DIM stands for *dimension*; it is the statement that reserves array space for your program.

You have to include the appropriate DIM statement at the top of a program that uses array elements to make it work properly. The following is the statement that dimensions 30 student names and scores:

```
DIM Sname$(30), scores(30)    ' Reserve space for 30 elements each
```

ZERO SUBSCRIPTING

QBasic, unlike many of the older versions of BASIC, lets you use subscript 0. Therefore, when you dimension to 30, you are really reserving *31* elements: scores(0), scores(1), and so on through scores(30). Many QBasic programmers ignore the zero element.

You can tell QBasic that you don't want to reserve the zero element when you dimension arrays with the OPTION BASE command. Use the following command before a DIM statement:

```
OPTION BASE 1
```

QBasic starts the array elements at 1, not 0. The first array subscript you can use is scores(1) if that is the array you dimension next. Using the OPTION BASE 1 command saves you a little memory because QBasic does not reserve the zero element. The amount you save, however, is negligible.

11

Listing 11.3 shows a complete program for storing student names and scores. It dimensions array memory, asks for all the names and scores, and prints all the values to the printer. Without arrays, there isn't an easy way to duplicate this program (short of having 30 pairs of individually named student variables and inputting them with 30 different sets of statements).

```
1: ' Student name and grade listing program
2: DIM Sname$(30), scores(30)
3:
4: CLS
5: FOR i = 1 TO 30
6:    INPUT "What is the next student's name"; Sname$(i)
7:    INPUT "What is the test score for that student"; scores(i)
8:    PRINT                         ' Prints a blank line
9: NEXT i
10: ' Now that all the data is entered, print it
11: LPRINT , "** Grade Listing **"
12: LPRINT "Name", "Score"              ' Column Heading
13: FOR i = 1 TO 30
14:    LPRINT Sname$(i), scores(i)
15: NEXT i
16: END
```

To make the program in Listing 11.3 usable for any situation, you would make the program dimension all 30 elements (assuming that is the total number of students in the class), and ask the teacher how many students took the test. The FOR loop can loop for the number of students who actually took the test. If the entire class took the test, all 30 array elements are filled. If fewer took the test, the FOR loop only loops for as many students as there are test scores.

Parallel Arrays

NEW TERM   The student name and grade listing demonstrates a popular use of arrays. The Sname$() and scores() arrays are known as *parallel arrays*. That is, the arrays each have the same number of elements, and each element in one corresponds to an element in the other.

With parallel arrays, you can store arrays with any type of data. Although a single array can hold only one type of data, you can have several parallel arrays that correspond to each other on a one-to-one basis. Using parallel arrays, you can keep track of an entire set of names, addresses, phone numbers, and salaries in a payroll program.

Erasing Arrays

There is a quick way to erase the contents of any numeric or string array. The ERASE statement enables you to erase the contents of any array. This puts the array back to its initial state. If you want to reuse an array in the last part of a program for a different set of data, you will need to erase the array to prepare it for new values.

To erase two arrays named amount() and Cust$(), write the following:

ERASE amount, Cust$

The program in Listing 11.4 fills an array with the numbers from 1 to 10 and prints the array. It then erases the array and prints the new contents.

INPUT   **LISTING 11.4** THIS PROGRAM USES ERASE TO ERASE THE ELEMENTS OF AN ARRAY

```
1: ' Erases an array
2: DIM nums(10)
3:
4: FOR i = 1 TO 10
5:     nums(i) = i        ' Put 1 through 10 into each element
6: NEXT i
7:
8: CLS
9: PRINT "The array before erasing it:"
10: FOR i = 1 TO 10
11:     PRINT nums(i) ,
12: NEXT i
13:
14: ERASE nums
15: PRINT "The array after erasing it:"
16: FOR i = 1 TO 10
17:     PRINT nums(i) ,
18: NEXT i
19: END
```

11

> The numbers print across the page because of the trailing commas at the end of each PRINT.

You can see from the following output that the ERASE statement erases the array in a single statement:

```
1: The array before erasing it:
2:  1               2               3               4               5
3:  6               7               8               9               10
4: The array after erasing it:
5:  0               0               0               0               0
6:  0               0               0               0               0
```

Introduction to Disk Files

Arrays are great for storing program data, but they are stored in your computer's memory, which is erased when you turn off the computer. For long-term storage, you must store data in a disk file.

NEW TERM   Your computer acts like an electronic filing cabinet by storing files that your programs create. Disk files are *nonvolatile*; that is, they remain on the disk when you turn off the computer. Each file on the disk has a unique filename, which is similar to the files in your filing cabinet having a unique label. The filename is how you designate which file to read or write from your programs.

THE LONG AND SHORT OF FILENAMES

QBasic does not support the long filenames that first appeared with Windows 95. As you may or may not know, when a DOS application, which QBasic is, refers to a file with a long filename such as Accounting Qtr 1.DAT, DOS uses a shorthand notation for the file by taking the first 6 letters of the filename and appending ~1 like this: Accou~1.DAT. (If more than one file had this same pattern, each file would have ~2, ~3, and so on.) By converting the file to the 8.3 notation, with a maximum of eight characters before the period, DOS maintains consistency with older files while still being able to reference new files.

Therefore, when you access files with long filenames from QBasic, you must use the abbreviated version of the filename. When you create a file with QBasic, you can only create files that conform to the 8.3 pattern.

Keep all special characters, except for letters and numbers, out of a filename. Although some special characters are allowed in the name, many are not allowed. It is safest to keep special characters out of the filename. Here are some valid filenames

```
SALES.DAT      EMPLOYEE      PAYROLL.99      MYGRADE.TXT
```

Any kind of data can reside in a file. Generally, it is repetitive data that has similar patterns, such as all your employees' names and addresses, customer lists, invoice balances, and so on.

Records and Fields

NEW TERM   A disk file is divided into records. A *record* is loosely defined as a line in the file. Although records can physically span more than one line in a file, a record is a collection of related file data usually written on one line. To clarify the concept of a record, look at Table 11.1. It shows a customer file. There are five records in the table; other records continue from those, but they are not shown in the table.

TABLE 11.1 CUSTOMER DATA FILE

Customer Number	Customer Name	Customer Balance	Customer Account Code
30432	Smith, Julie	213.42	EB432
93845	Johnson, Tom	9434.34	BG895
30201	Kerry, Kim	3432.67	YT009
10392	Jensen, Judy	411.59	EW437
90323	Post, Paul	2883.45	TW326

NEW TERM Each record in a file is broken down further into fields. A *field* is a column of data. Table 11.1 contains a file that has four fields. If there were 20,000 records in the file, it would still contain four columns of data; therefore, it would contain four fields.

If the file shown in Table 11.1 contained far more data than those four fields, you might see how a single record can span more than one line in the file, yet still be considered a single record of data.

Think of a file's records as a collection of cards. Each card is a separate record of information in the card file. On each card, you have several fields of data.

11

Types of Access

Three things you can do with a data file are the following:

- Create one by writing to it
- Read from one
- Add to the end of one

That is all you do with a filing cabinet file as well. You can create a new file by filling out a file folder label and putting things into the folder, adding to an existing file by putting new items into it, or reading a file's contents.

With a filing cabinet file, you must open the proper file folder before you can read from a file. In QBasic, you must open files with the OPEN statement. The OPEN statement tells QBasic how you want to access a file.

ANALYZING THE OPEN STATEMENT

When you use the OPEN statement, QBasic does a lot behind the scenes. It searches the disk for the proper file that you want to read or append to one already opened. If you are creating a file, QBasic makes sure the filename is acceptable, and it ensures that the disk is properly prepared to hold the data. OPEN makes sure the disk is not write-protected. If you choose to write-protect a floppy disk, you will not be able to write or append to any file on that disk.

OPEN has another useful purpose: It attaches a file handle to the disk file that you are opening. A *file handle* is a number you assign to a file in the OPEN statement. After OPEN attaches a file handle to the file, the rest of your program refers to the file by its handle and not by the full filename.

NEW TERM The easiest way to learn about the OPEN statement is to look at a few examples. Suppose you want to open and read a file called SALES.DAT that resides on disk drive D. The read mode of OPEN is called *input*. The OPEN statement that you might use is

```
OPEN "D:SALES.DAT" FOR INPUT AS #1
```

The #1 is the file handle. If QBasic finds the file on drive D, it will attach the #1 file handle to the file. Subsequent disk I/O (input/output) statements will use the #1 instead of the filename. You can type the drive name and the name of the file using any combination of upper- or lowercase characters, as with any DOS filename.

If the filename resides on the *default disk drive* (the drive that was active when you first started QBasic, usually C:), you do not have to specify the drive name before the filename.

If you want to have several files open in the same program, you must assign each one a different file handle. A different file handle for each file lets QBasic know which disk file you are reading from or writing to in subsequent file I/O commands.

If you attempt to open a file for input, but the file does not exist, QBasic issues a File not found error message. You can only read from a file when it already exists.

NEW TERM The following OPEN statement opens a file for output mode. *Output mode* means that you want to write to the file. Output mode assumes the file does not exist, or if the file does exist, output mode assumes that you want to overwrite it. You must be careful about opening files in output mode because if you inadvertently open a file that exists, QBasic destroys its contents to make room for the new data. QBasic does not warn you that the file was replaced by the new one. The output mode always assumes that you want to create a brand-new file:

```
OPEN "Payroll.98" FOR OUTPUT AS #3
```

Subsequent file writing commands file handle #3 to send data to the file named Payroll.98 on the default disk drive.

NEW TERM There might be a time when you want to add to the end of a data file. You might be adding new customers, new engineering statistics, or new inventory records. Adding to the end of a file is known as *append mode*. The following is an OPEN statement that sets up a file as file handle #2 and ensures that subsequent writes to file handle #2 add to the end of the file without destroying any of the original contents:

```
OPEN "STATS.NUM" FOR APPEND AS #2
```

> If you open a file for append mode, and the file does not already exist, QBasic creates the file for you.

11

Closing Open Files

Before getting into the actual file I/O commands, you should look at the CLOSE command. You should always close every file you open in a QBasic program. (If you don't close a filing cabinet, you could hurt yourself running into it or lose important data that falls out.) Although both DOS and Windows close files for you after your QBasic program ends, it is considered sloppy if you don't specifically close every open file. Even more important, your power could go out while a file is still open. Even if you are no longer reading from the file or writing to it, there is a chance that you could lose data and possibly lose the entire file.

The CLOSE command is simple. To close the file associated with file handle #1, you can do one of the following:

```
CLOSE 1
```

or

```
CLOSE #1
```

As you can see, the pound sign is optional. You can close more than one file in a single CLOSE statement, as indicated in the following:

```
CLOSE 1, 2, 3
```

In addition, you can close *all* open files by using `CLOSE` without any options like this:

```
CLOSE
```

Creating Output Files

After you open an output file, the `WRITE #` command writes data to it. As Figure 11.2 shows, `WRITE #` is to a data file what `PRINT` is to the screen; `WRITE #` sends data to the file. The file handle must appear after `WRITE #` (the pound sign precedes the file handle).

FIGURE 11.2.

The `WRITE #` command writes data to a file.

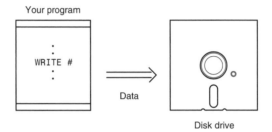

NEW TERM   The `WRITE #` writes *comma-separated* data to a disk file. Unlike `PRINT`, which prints data exactly like you type it, `WRITE #` does more for you than simply send data to a file. `WRITE #` separates each field in the data file with commas. To aid you in reading the data later (with the `INPUT #` command discussed in the next section), `WRITE #` also encloses all string data in quotation marks, instead of appending all the strings together in one long record.

To see the effects of `WRITE #`, look at the program in Listing 11.5. The first few statements assign values to variables, and the last line writes that data to disk. The program is short; only one record is written to the disk file. In reality, more records would be written in an actual application. Nevertheless, the program shows you how `WRITE #` formats the line of data. Study the program, and take a look at the data as it actually gets written to the file.

INPUT   **LISTING 11.5** USE `WRITE #` TO WRITE RECORDS TO FILES

```
1: ' First disk writing program
2: CLS
3:
4: ' Initialize some variables that will be written to the disk
```

```
 5: Cname$ = "Jim Smith"
 6: Age = 40
 7: Addr$ = "146 E. Oak"
 8: City$ = "Miami"
 9: St$ = "FL"
10: Zip$ = "34029"
11:
12: OPEN "first.dat" FOR OUTPUT AS #1    ' Open file for output
13: WRITE #1, Cname$, Age, Addr$, City$, St$, Zip$
14: CLOSE #1
15:
16: END
```

Here is what the newly created file, first.dat, looks like after this program created it:

```
"Jim Smith",40,"146 E. Oak","Miami","FL","34029"
```

Notice that QBasic put commas between each of the values and quotation marks around all the strings. The next section shows you how to read such a file.

> You can use the Windows Notepad editor to look at the data file that QBasic programs create.

11

Listing 11.6 is a more common example of how data files are created. In this program, the user controls how many records are written to the file. The program uses both arrays and the disk to keep track of the data entered. The program first collects all the data—up to 100 values—in parallel arrays. The last part of the program stores those arrays to the disk file first.dat.

INPUT   **LISTING 11.6** MORE USER INPUT HELPS WITH THE WRITING OF THE FILE

```
 1: ' Disk writing program based on user input
 2: DIM Cname$(100), Age(100), Addr$(100), City$(100), St$(100), Zip$(100)
 3:
 4: CLS
 5:
 6: PRINT , "** Data gathering program for a disk file **"
 7:
 8: ' Loop getting data that will be written to the disk
 9: FOR i = 1 TO 100
10:    PRINT
11:    INPUT "What is the customer name"; Cname$(i)
12:    INPUT "What is the customer's age"; Age(i)
```

continues

LISTING 11.6 CONTINUED

```
13:    INPUT "What is the customer's address"; Addr$(i)
14:    INPUT "What is the customer's city"; City$(i)
15:    INPUT "What is the customer's state"; St$(i)
16:    INPUT "What is the customer's zipcode"; Zip$(i)
17:    INPUT "Are there more values to get (Y/N)"; ans$
18:    IF (ans$ <> "Y") THEN
19:       EXIT FOR
20:    END IF
21: NEXT i
22:
23: OPEN "first.dat" FOR OUTPUT AS #1    ' Open file for output
24: ' At this point, variable i holds the total number
25: ' of records actually entered
26: FOR j = 1 TO i
27:    WRITE #1, Cname$(j), Age(j), Addr$(j), City$(j), St$(j), Zip$(j)
28: NEXT j
29: CLOSE #1
30:
31: END
```

The following are the contents of first.dat after the program is run and a few records are entered:

```
"Tom Wesley",32,"102 E. Lane","Miami","FL","34023"
"Joe Yard",32,"9345 West 8th","Reno","NV","54905"
"Rush Righter",38,"210 E. 5th Ave.","New York","NY","10012"
"Tina Johnson",21,"1013 Sycamore","Coweta","OK","74429"
```

STRINGS AND NUMBERS

You might wonder why the ZIP code is stored in a string variable, even though it contains only numeric digits. When programming, you should avoid using numeric variables for any data with which you are not going to do any math.

A general rule of thumb is to use numeric non-string variables only for number values with which you will calculate, and to store all other kinds of data in string variables. The digits in some numeric variables can lose accuracy because of rounding when you store their initial values. Keep ZIP codes, telephone numbers, Social Security numbers, and the like in string variables, and you will never have any trouble with them.

Reading the Disk File

Reading disk files is easy. As long as you create files with WRITE #, a corresponding INPUT # reads the data into separate variables. INPUT # is a mirror-image command from WRITE #. For instance, if you wrote values to the disk with the WRITE # command

```
WRITE #1, Cname$, Age, Addr$, City$, St$, Zip$
```

you could read those values back into variables, such as from within another program, with the following INPUT #:

```
INPUT #1, Cname$, Age, Addr$, City$, St$, Zip$
```

> You need to know the format of the data file you are reading. Every INPUT # must match, in type, the data being read. You cannot use a numeric variable as the first variable listed after the INPUT # statement if the first field in the file contains string data.

There is one additional problem with reading data files that you would not encounter when you create them. The program reading a data file might not know exactly how many records are in the file. There is a built-in function in QBasic that tells you when you have reached the end of an input file. When this routine tells you that the end of a file is reached, your program has to stop reading the data.

The end-of-file function is called EOF(); you have to put the file handle inside the parentheses. EOF() equals –1 if you just read the last record from the file. EOF() equals 0 if there are still records left to be read. Generally, you will find the DO...UNTIL to be a useful control loop for reading a file until you reach the end. Here is the general format that your programs should follow when reading files:

```
INPUT #1, variables go here
DO
    ' Process the input data here
    INPUT #1, variables go here
LOOP UNTIL ( EOF(1) = -1)
' Rest of program follows
```

The initial INPUT # reads the first data record from the file. This routine assumes there is always at least one record in the file (if there were not, OPEN would have failed because the file would probably not exist). The subsequent INPUT # statements immediately before the end-of-file check ensure that the file is read until the end of the file is reached. Then the loop terminates and the rest of the program continues.

Listing 11.7 reads the data file created in Listing 11.6. The program continues reading the file's records, printing them to the screen, until the end of the file is reached. Figure 11.3 shows you the output of this program when given the file's contents shown earlier.

INPUT

LISTING 11.7 THE EOF() FUNCTION HELPS YOU LOCATE THE END OF FILE WHEN READING DISK DATA

```
 1: ' Disk-reading program
 2: ' The program will read the data file into these arrays
 3: DIM Cname$(100), Age(100), Addr$(100), City$(100), St$(100), Zip$(100)
 4:
 5: CLS
 6:
 7: PRINT , "** Data printing program from a disk file **"
 8: PRINT
 9:
10: OPEN "first.dat" FOR INPUT AS #1
11: i = 1
12:
13: ' Loop getting data from the disk
14:    INPUT #1, Cname$(i), Age(i), Addr$(i), City$(i), St$(i), Zip$(i)
15: DO
16:    i = i + 1     ' Add 1 to subscript
17:    INPUT #1, Cname$(i), Age(i), Addr$(i), City$(i), St$(i), Zip$(i)
18: LOOP UNTIL (EOF(1) = -1)
19: CLOSE #1         ' Close file since all data has been read
20:
21: ' At this point, variable i holds the total number of records
22: FOR j = 1 TO i
23:    PRINT
24:    PRINT "Name: "; Cname$(j), "Age:"; Age(j)
25:    PRINT "Address: "; Addr$(j)
26:    PRINT "City: "; City$(j)
27:    PRINT "State: "; St$(j), "Zipcode: "; Zip$(j)
28: NEXT j
29:
30: END
```

FIGURE 11.3.

The data from the file created earlier.

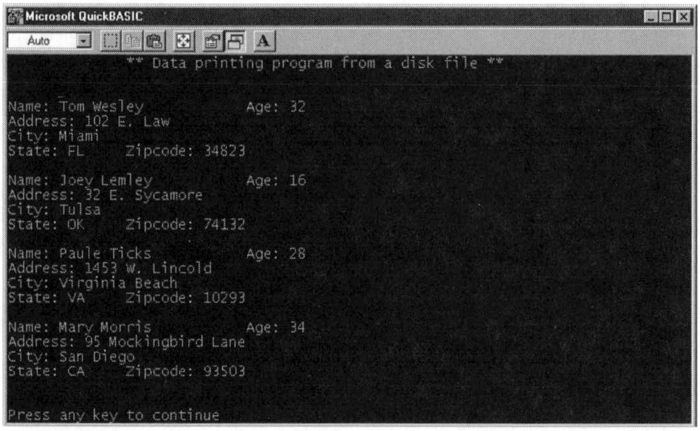

Appending to a Data File

Adding data to the end of an existing file is easy. The WRITE # command writes the data just as it would if you were creating the file. The only difference between creating a new file and appending to the end of one is the OPEN command.

> If you open a non-existing file in APPEND mode, QBasic creates the file without issuing an error. In effect, you are appending to the end of an empty file.

Listing 11.8 shows you a program that opens the data file created earlier, and then asks the user for more values.

INPUT   LISTING **11.8** YOU CAN APPEND TO THE END OF THE FILE YOU CREATED EARLIER

```
 1: ' Disk appending program
 2: CLS
 3:
 4: PRINT , "** Appending new data to the end of a file **"
 5:
 6: OPEN "first.dat" FOR APPEND AS #1    ' Open file for append mode
 7:
 8: ' Loop getting data that will be appended to the disk
 9: DO
10:    PRINT
11:    INPUT "What is the next customer name"; Cname$
12:    INPUT "What is the next customer's age"; Age
13:    INPUT "What is the next customer's address"; Addr$
14:    INPUT "What is the next customer's city"; City$
15:    INPUT "What is the next customer's state"; St$
16:    INPUT "What is the next customer's zipcode"; Zip$
17:    WRITE #1, Cname$, Age, Addr$, City$, St$, Zip$
18:
19:    INPUT "Are there more values to append (Y/N)"; ans$
20: LOOP UNTIL (ans$ = "N")
21:
22: CLOSE #1
23: END
```

11

At this point, you can run the file-reading program in Listing 11.7 to print the file as it is now written, with the new records appended to it.

Two or More Files Open

The sample programs you have seen in this chapter have been simple, yet powerful. You have seen how to store data in disk files for long-term storage. It is easy to create, read, and append to disk files using QBasic.

All the examples you have seen have had only one file open at a given time. Therefore, they used only file handle #1 for the file access. The program in Listing 11.9 opens two files at the same time. The first file (the first.dat file created in the last few program listings) is the input file, and a new file (the output file called backup.dat) is created. This program reads an entire record from first.dat and writes that same record to backup.dat until all the records have been written. The program makes an exact duplicate of the first file. This might be a useful program for backing up important data files for safekeeping.

INPUT   **LISTING 11.9** OPEN TWO FILES TO CREATE A BACKUP FILE

```
 1: ' Opens two files at once
 2: CLS
 3: PRINT "Backing up the data file..."
 4:
 5: OPEN "first.dat" FOR INPUT AS #1
 6: OPEN "backup.dat" FOR OUTPUT AS #2
 7:
 8: DO
 9:    INPUT #1, Cname$, Age, Addr$, City$, St$, Zip$
10:    WRITE #2, Cname$, Age, Addr$, City$, St$, Zip$
11: LOOP UNTIL (EOF(1) = -1)
12:
13: CLOSE #1
14: CLOSE #2
15: PRINT
16: PRINT "The file is now backed up."
17: END
```

Advanced Data Files

NEW TERM   There are some advanced ways to access files in QBasic that this lesson does not discuss. This lesson describes only *sequential file processing*, which is a fancy term for reading, writing, and appending to files. Another form of access, called *random-file access*, is helpful when you want to both read and write to the same file within the same program. Using random-file access, you can change specific file data, such as a customer's balance, without having to re-create the entire file.

Several advanced techniques exist for working with random-file access. In the past, programmers would write extraordinary routines that searched, sorted, and filtered through random-access files. When database technology gained more ground, programmers began leaving the advanced techniques of random-file access to the database system.

Although you cannot access advanced database files in QBasic, you can access many of today's most popular database systems from numerous other languages such as Visual Basic and Visual C++. Despite its advantages, random-file access is not an answer to every program's file needs, however. Many very advanced programming applications use the sequential file access techniques that you learned in this chapter.

As you become familiar with more advanced languages, you might decide to add database access to your programming toolkit of skills. When you do, you might be surprised that this hour's lesson helps you learn such file access more easily. Now that you have written programs that access files at their lowest, sequential-access level, you will understand more fully the nature of file storage. Although you won't have to write as much code to access a database file from a Visual Basic program as you would have to sequentially from Visual Basic, you will appreciate the workings of the file access that take place behind the scenes.

Summary

Beginning programmers often think arrays are difficult to learn, but you have seen that arrays are just another way to hold data for your QBasic programs to process. When you load arrays with data, you can safely tuck the data away to a disk file for later processing. Arrays offer advanced variable storage capabilities. Instead of having different names for many variables of the same kind, you can have a list of values with the same name. The list of values is called an array.

Disk files enable you to save data for long-term storage. Variables are volatile; they lose their values when your program ends or when you turn off your computer. There are three modes of access for disk files: output, input, and append. The mode you select depends on the type of file you want to access and whether or not the file already exists. You can have more than one file open simultaneously, as long as you open them with different file handles.

The next hour takes a breather from the heavy side of programming and teaches you how to create graphics and produce sound from a QBasic program.

Q&A

Q Should I begin array access with a 0 or 1 subscript?

A The OPTION BASE statement lets you begin an array with either 0 or 1 as a subscript. The default, if you do not supply an OPTION BASE statement, is to begin all array subscripts at 0. The choice is up to you. Some languages, such as C and C++, do not give you a choice and you have to begin subscripts at 0. Many QBasic programmers ignore the zero-based subscript and begin all arrays with a subscript of 1.

Q What distinguishes parallel arrays from other arrays?

A A parallel array is no different, technically, from other kinds of arrays. Parallel arrays are a concept that programmers utilize to keep track of several sets of values that are similar in form.

Workshop

The quiz questions and exercises are provided for your further understanding. See Appendix A, "Answers to End of Chapter Questions," for answers.

Quiz

1. How many names does an array with 18 elements have?
2. How does a numeric subscript help you access all the elements in an array more easily?
3. What is the difference between an array and a disk file?
4. What statement reserves space for arrays?
5. What's the easiest way to erase every element of an array?
6. True or false: The number of records in a file determines the number of fields in the file.
7. True or false: Opening a disk file for output erases any file that already resides on the disk with that name.
8. True or false: Opening a disk file for appending erases any file that already resides on the disk with that name.
9. What is the file handle for?
10. Which internal function tests for the end of file?

HOUR 12

Having Fun with QBasic

Now is the time to sit back and have some fun with QBasic. Sure, programming is fun in itself, and you know how easy and enjoyable it is writing programs with QBasic. However, there is more you can do with QBasic than write data-processing programs for business and engineering. You can also use QBasic to generate sounds and graphics.

The material you master in this chapter gives you the framework for adding pizzazz to your programs. You will get an idea of how game programmers do their job. You will learn some fundamental concepts that you need in order to write programs that capture the user's attention.

Microsoft developed Visual Basic before graphics adapters were standardized, and before Windows took control and offered a uniform graphics interface for all programs. Therefore, some of QBasic's way of doing things might seem strange today because the exact kind of graphics adapter you have is not as critical as it used to be. Nevertheless, after learning how QBasic draws graphics on the screen, you will also have a better idea of the way other languages do the same.

The highlights of this hour include:

- How to beep your computer's speaker
- What the SOUND command does
- What the term *hertz* means
- How to play music on your PC
- How to prepare your screen for graphics
- What commands turn on and off graphics dots
- How to draw lines, boxes, and circles onscreen
- How to change the location where the next PRINT appears

Beeping the Speaker

Your PC has a built-in speaker. Although the fidelity of the speaker leaves much to be desired, it can be helpful when you need to get the user's attention. Sadly, QBasic offers no way to address the sounds and sound effects of today's high-quality sound cards that produce music and speech. QBasic only produces sound that provides one tone at a time. You can still have fun with QBasic despite its limited sounds.

Perhaps the easiest way to get a sound out of your computer is with the BEEP command. Whenever QBasic encounters a BEEP in your program, it sends a signal to the speaker causing it to beep for about one-half second. Listing 12.1 shows a program that beeps the speaker.

LISTING 12.1 YOU CAN BEEP YOUR PC'S SPEAKER

```
 1: ' Program that beeps the speaker
 2: CLS
 3:
 4: BEEP
 5:
 6: PRINT "That was the speaker."
 7: PRINT
 8: INPUT "Want to hear it again"; ans$
 9: BEEP
10: END
```

Using the SOUND Command

The SOUND command gives you much more control over your computer's speaker than the BEEP command does. With SOUND, you can control both what note is sent to the speaker and how long it plays. It is helpful to have some familiarity with a musical keyboard or musical theory before using SOUND. Here is a sample SOUND command:

```
SOUND 880, 36.4     ' Sound a tone on the PC speaker
```

NEW TERM The SOUND command generates a tone from 37 hertz to 32,767 hertz. *Hertz* (Hz) is the number of cycles per second at which a note vibrates. The first of the two values after SOUND is the value of hertz you are sounding. If the hertz is higher in value, the note's pitch will sound higher. To give you an idea of the range of hertz, the A below middle C on a piano is 440 Hz, which is a frequency commonly used for tuning musical instruments. If you halve the value of 440 Hz to 220 Hz, you get the next lowest A on the piano. Halving 220 Hz to 110 Hz produces another A an octave lower.

In the opposite direction, doubling 440 Hz to 880 Hz gives you the A above middle C. Table 12.1 shows you where the A notes fall in the range of possible SOUND hertz. To make other notes in between, use hertz values between the hertz values of two A notes.

TABLE 12.1 SOUND FREQUENCY VALUES FOR DIFFERENT HERTZ VALUES

Hertz	Note Sounded
55	Fourth A below middle C
110	Third A below middle C
220	Second A below middle C
440	First A below middle C
880	First A above middle C
1760	Second A above middle C
3520	Third A above middle C
7040	Fourth A above middle C

12

NEW TERM The second value in the SOUND command is the *duration* of the note you want to play. Similar to the hertz value, the duration value can be confusing at first. The duration is the number of CPU clock ticks during which the sound persists. There are a total of 18.2 CPU clock ticks per second. (Your CPU includes a clock to keep everything timed properly inside the computer.) If you want to sound a tone for one second, use 18.2 as the second value of SOUND. To sound a tone for 2 seconds, use 36.4 for the duration value, and so forth.

The program in Listing 12.2 uses the SOUND command to generate every tone possible on the PC for a fraction of time. (Because a duration of 2 is only about one-tenth of a second, each note sounds for only a short time.)

> The program takes a while to circulate through all possible notes, even though each note is sounded for just a fraction of a second. With a hertz range from 37 to 32,767, there are a lot of notes to cycle through.

LISTING 12.2   USE SOUND TO PRODUCE EVERY NOTE POSSIBLE ON A PC

```
 1: ' Program that produces all notes with SOUND
 2: CLS
 3:
 4: PRINT "Get your ears ready..."
 5:
 6: FOR Note = 37 TO 32767
 7:     SOUND Note, 2
 8: NEXT Note
 9:
10: PRINT "Things are sounding uppity around here!"
11: END
```

You can cycle through the sounds faster by adding a step value to the FOR loop. The program in Listing 12.3 takes the sounds up and down again with a couple of FOR loops.

LISTING 12.3   USE SOUND TO PRODUCE A RISING AND FALLING SIREN

```
 1: ' Program that steps up and down through notes
 2: CLS
 3:
 4: PRINT "Here's a siren..."
 5:
 6: FOR Note = 450 TO 750 STEP 5    ' The siren goes up
 7:     SOUND Note, 2
 8: NEXT Note
 9:
10: FOR Note = 750 TO 450 STEP -5  ' The siren goes down
11:     SOUND Note, 2
12: NEXT Note
13: END
```

By changing a few values and adding SOUND commands, you can create some interesting effects. The program in Listing 12.4 produces an effect as though your computer has two speakers inside, each doing its own thing.

LISTING 12.4   THE SOUND COMMAND CAN PRODUCE STRANGE SOUNDS

```
 1: ' Program that produces really weird sounds
 2: CLS
 3:
 4: PRINT "Hold your ears..."
 5:
 6: FOR Note = 450 TO 750 STEP 5    ' The siren goes up
 7:     SOUND Note, 1
 8:     SOUND 800 - Note, 1
 9: NEXT Note
10:
11: FOR Note = 750 TO 450 STEP -5  ' The siren goes down
12:     SOUND Note, 1
13:     SOUND 750 + Note, 1
14: NEXT Note
15:
16: END
```

Using the PLAY Command

QBasic contains an additional command, called PLAY, which offers a more advanced method for generating sounds and music from the single-tone speaker inside your PC. Obviously, you cannot generate multipart harmony with PLAY, but you can generate a chorus line from virtually any piece of music.

The PLAY command requires that you master a minilanguage within QBasic, the PLAY language. PLAY is a command that requires a string after it. Here is a sample of a PLAY command:

```
PLAY "L4 C2 E G < B. > L16 C D L2 C"
```

The data inside the string after PLAY looks cryptic. The PLAY string, called a *command string*, contains a QBasic musical representation. The L4 (for Length of 4) tells the computer how long to play the notes that follow—until another L command changes it. A 4 designates a quarter note, 3 a half note, 2 a dotted half note, and 1 a whole note. The letters following each L command are notes on the musical scale. Whenever a number follows a note, that number overrides the L value currently in effect, but just for that particular note.

When you want to raise or lower an octave, you must include a greater than (>) symbol to raise the notes that follow an octave, or a less than (<) symbol to lower those notes an octave. A period after a note "dots" it, which extends the note for another one-half of its original duration.

12

There are many more commands possible inside the PLAY command string. If you are familiar with music, you probably understood the last few paragraphs and want more information. Otherwise, it might be best to type the PLAY command shown earlier and sit back and enjoy it. If you want more information about PLAY, you can check out QBasic's online help system for more options.

Although it is possible to add a sound card to your computer so you can generate multiple note and instrument sounds, programming those sound cards takes a lot more work than QBasic can accomplish.

Introduction to Graphics

NEW TERM   Your graphics screen is made up of many columns and rows. A measurement known as *resolution* determines how detailed your screen's graphics can be. If the resolution is higher, your graphics will look better. Similarly, a lower resolution will make your graphics look worse. In its highest graphics resolution mode, a standard VGA screen can display 640 columns and 480 rows of dots, as Figure 12.1 illustrates. Where every column and row intersect there is a graphics dot on the screen. The dot is called a *picture element*, or *pixel* for short. Because 640 times 480 equals 307,200, there are a total of 307,200 pixels on a generic VGA screen that you can turn on and off.

FIGURE **12.1.**

The resolution on a standard VGA computer screen.

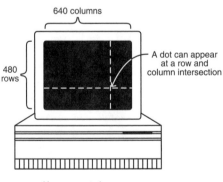

Your computer's screen

The column and row numbers begin at 0. Therefore, the 640 columns are numbered from 0 to 639, and the rows are numbered from 0 to 479.

QBASIC'S GRAPHICS SUPPORT IS LACKING

Virtually every PC that runs Windows these days conforms at a *minimum* to the VGA standard, and most of the time produces much higher resolution than the 640 by 480 resolution described here. Probably, no programmer will ever write a program that produces graphics that are no higher in resolution than the most generic VGA resolution. Yet, much of this section explains how to achieve only a generic VGA resolution and never higher.

Sadly, QBasic was written back in the pre-Windows days when DOS ruled and when the VGA graphics adapter card was not the most common card in people's systems. Therefore, the QBasic language is more centered around the lowest-level VGA resolution than it would have to be today and Microsoft never updated the language to bring it into the Windows way of doing things.

Although this chapter only shows you how to turn on white pixels over a black background, many colors are possible. QBasic supports a wide range of colors. After you master black-and-white graphics, you might want to try your hand at adding color.

Using the SCREEN Command

Before you can turn on a graphics pixel, you must tell QBasic to exit its normal text display mode and generate a graphics screen image. The SCREEN command does this for you. There are several possible SCREEN values. The one used throughout this lesson is 12, which is the highest VGA black-and-white resolution value. The following SCREEN command sets up your VGA screen in a high-resolution black-and-white graphics mode:

```
SCREEN 12      ' Places the screen in high-res graphics mode
```

The number after SCREEN can be any number from 0 to 13. Each number represents a different type of display adapter and monitor.

12

SCREEN automatically clears the screen. You do not need to issue a CLS command before producing graphics.

If your program sets the video screen to one of the graphics modes, and you are writing a program for general use, be sure to reset the screen to text mode when you are done. You can do so with this command:

```
SCREEN 0          ' Resets the screen back to text mode
```

When your program finishes, the text mode is reset to its normal state. If you fail to reset the screen to text, QBasic does it for you. However, there are advanced ways to execute a QBasic program, either from the DOS prompt or from Windows, and then automatically proceed to another program. Therefore, resetting the adapter back to text mode is a good habit to develop.

Turning Pixels On and Off

The PSET command turns pixels on, and PRESET turns them off. After each of these commands, you must give an *x coordinate* and a *y coordinate,* which are nothing more than the column and row numbers that intersect the pixel you want turned on. For example, if you want to turn on the pixel at the intersection of column 100 and row 150 (and provided that, earlier in the program, you set the screen to a graphics mode), you would do this:

```
PSET (100, 150)   ' Turns on a pixel
```

If you want to turn off the pixel at the intersection of column 50 and row 45, you would do this:

```
PRESET (50, 45)    ' Turns off a pixel
```

You can add a handy option to PSET and PRESET that turns pixels on and off at a *relative location* from where you last turned one on or off. The STEP option, placed before the x and y coordinates of a PSET or PRESET command, indicates that you want the computer to turn a pixel on or off that is a given number of pixels away from the previous one. In other words, the command

```
PSET STEP (50, 75)
```

does *not* turn on the pixel at column 50 and row 75. Instead, it turns on the pixel 50 columns and 75 rows away from where the last PSET turned on a pixel.

The program in Listing 12.5 produces a graphics output you can study to learn how PSET and PRESET work. The program turns on pixels at various locations on the screen; it then uses two FOR loops to draw some lines. (The FOR loops enable you to trace across several columns or rows easily.)

LISTING 12.5   TURN ON GRAPHICS PIXELS WITH PSET

```
 1: ' Produces dots on the screen and some lines
 2: CLS
 3: SCREEN 12
 4:
 5: PSET (10, 10)
 6: PSET (20, 20)
 7: PSET (30, 30)
 8: PSET (40, 40)
 9: PSET (50, 50)
10: PSET (100, 200)
11: PSET (101, 202)
12: PSET (105, 210)
13: PSET (200, 33)
14: PSET (220, 30)
15: PSET (400, 400)
16: PSET (300, 25)
17: PSET (301, 27)
18: PSET (303, 30)
19:
20: FOR row = 275 TO 375
21:     PSET (400, row)
22: NEXT row
23:
24: FOR col = 100 TO 500
25:     PSET (col, 50)
26: NEXT col
27: END
```

Figure 12.2 shows you the output from this pixel-setting program. The VGA's resolution is so high that some of the dots are very small. The lines drawn via the FOR loops are easy to spot.

FIGURE 12.2.

Setting pixels on the screen.

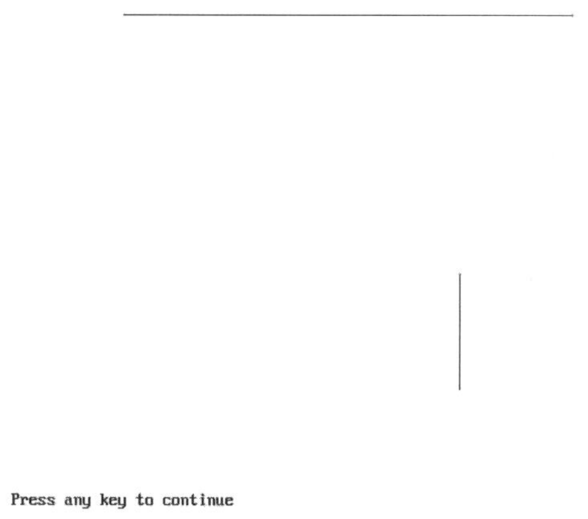

The program in Listing 12.6 is an extension of the one in Listing 12.5. First, it turns on all the pixels that Listing 12.5 did, and then it turns them off with PRESET. Watch carefully; the pixels are erased fairly quickly.

LISTING 12.6   YOU CAN ALSO TURN OFF SOME PIXELS

```
 1: ' Produces dots on the screen and some lines
 2: ' then erases them
 3: CLS
 4: SCREEN 12
 5:
 6: PSET (10, 10)
 7: PSET (20, 20)
 8: PSET (30, 30)
 9: PSET (40, 40)
10: PSET (50, 50)
11: PSET (100, 200)
12: PSET (101, 202)
13: PSET (105, 210)
14: PSET (200, 33)
15: PSET (220, 30)
16: PSET (400, 400)
17: PSET (300, 25)
18: PSET (301, 27)
19: PSET (303, 30)
20:
21: FOR row = 275 TO 375
22:     PSET (400, row)
23: NEXT row
24:
25: FOR col = 100 TO 500
26:     PSET (col, 50)
27: NEXT col
28:
29: PRESET (10, 10)
30: PRESET (20, 20)
31: PRESET (30, 30)
32: PRESET (40, 40)
33: PRESET (50, 50)
34: PRESET (100, 200)
35: PRESET (101, 202)
36: PRESET (105, 210)
37: PRESET (200, 33)
38: PRESET (220, 30)
39: PRESET (400, 400)
40: PRESET (300, 25)
41: PRESET (301, 27)
42: PRESET (303, 30)
43:
```

```
44: FOR row = 275 TO 375
45:    PRESET (400, row)
46: NEXT row
47:
48: FOR col = 100 TO 500
49:    PRESET (col, 50)
50: NEXT col
51: END
```

NEW TERM The program in Listing 12.7 uses FOR loops to turn on pixels and shows you how to nest loops. *Nesting* loops is the process of putting one loop inside another loop. The number of times that the inner loop executes is multiplied by the outer loop's controlling variable.

The program in Listing 12.7 is not very long, yet it fills up almost the entire screen by turning on many pixels.

LISTING 12.7 NESTED LOOPS CAN ENABLE YOU TO WRITE A PROGRAM THAT TURNS ON MANY PIXELS

```
 1: ' Paints the screen with pixels
 2: CLS
 3: SCREEN 12
 4:
 5: FOR col = 0 TO 639 STEP 3
 6:    FOR row = 0 TO 479 STEP 2
 7:       PSET (col, row)
 8:    NEXT row
 9: NEXT col
10: END
```

12

Figure 12.3 shows you the output of the program from Listing 12.7 after the screen is completely painted by the PSET commands.

> Removing both STEP values from the two FOR loops in Listing 12.7 would paint the entire screen solid white instead of creating a plaid effect. If you run a program without the STEP values, have patience; painting an entire VGA screen takes a few seconds.

Figure 12.3.

*Painting the screen
with pixels.*

```
Press any key to continue
```

Drawing Lines and Boxes

The PSET is too slow for drawing lines and boxes. QBasic supplies the LINE statement to help make your line drawing easier and faster. Instead of collecting a group of PSET statements to draw a line or box, the LINE statement does all the work at once. Depending on the format you use, LINE draws either a line or a box. The simplest format of LINE draws a line from one x,y coordinate to another.

> LINE is faster and easier to use than drawing a straight line of pixels with PSET.

A line is determined by its two end points. To draw a line, you have to know only the x and y coordinates of both end points. QBasic does the rest. For example, if you want to draw a line from the pixel at column 100 and row 100 to the pixel at column 200 and row 200, you would specify this LINE command:

```
LINE (100, 100) - (200, 200)
```

As with PSET and PRESET, the LINE command's STEP option draws the line relative to the starting location—the last pixel drawn or turned off. You don't have to include the starting coordinate pair because STEP knows where to begin. Therefore, by using STEP, some of the coordinates might be negative, such as the following:

```
LINE STEP (-12, 0) - (10, 1)
```

Translated, this statement means: Draw a line, one of whose end points is 12 pixels to the left of (and zero rows up or down from) the last pixel turned on, and whose other endpoint is 10 pixels to the right of and down one row from the other endpoint. If you have not already drawn anything, STEP draws pixels from your screen's center point.

 You can draw lines up, down, left, and right. QBasic doesn't care what direction the line travels as long as you specify two end points with the pairs of screen coordinates.

Listing 12.8 shows a program that draws several lines on the screen. Run the program and see how much faster you can draw lines with LINE than by setting individual pixels.

LISTING 12.8 USE LINE TO DRAW LINES ONSCREEN

```
 1: ' Drawing lines on the screen
 2: CLS
 3: SCREEN 12
 4:
 5: LINE (100, 100)-(200, 200)
 6: LINE (400, 20)-(620, 400)
 7: LINE (20, 450)-(5, 30)
 8: LINE (300, 200)-(200, 400)
 9: LINE (100, 20)-(600, 450)
10: END
```

Figure 12.4 shows you what these lines look like onscreen.

You can add an option to use LINE to draw a box or a rectangle—they are the same thing in QBasic. The LINE statement's B option draws boxes. As with a line, a box is determined by two points, its upper-left and lower-right corners. Here is a LINE command that draws a box onscreen:

```
LINE (40, 50) - (200, 200), , B     ' Draws a box
```

The upper-left corner of the box is at column 40 and row 50, and its lower-right corner is at column 200 and row 200. The B indicates that you want a box and not a line. The two commas before the B are placeholders for an optional color attribute. You must use the two commas if you want to draw a box.

The program in Listing 12.9 draws several boxes onscreen, with some overlapping the others.

12

FIGURE 12.4.

After drawing some lines on the screen.

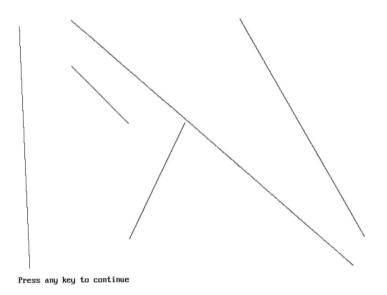

Press any key to continue

LISTING 12.9   YOU CAN USE LINE TO DRAW BOXES ONSCREEN

```
 1: ' Drawing several boxes
 2: CLS
 3: SCREEN 12
 4:
 5: LINE (100, 100)-(200, 200), , B
 6: LINE (400, 20)-(620, 400), , B
 7: LINE (20, 450)-(5, 30), , B
 8: LINE (300, 200)-(195, 405), , B
 9: LINE (110, 25)-(600, 450), , B
10:
11: END
```

Figure 12.5 shows you the result of running the box-drawing program shown in Listing 12.9.

Drawing Circles

You can draw circles and ellipses onscreen with the CIRCLE command. You will probably have to practice a bit to get circles that are exactly round. Because there are fewer rows than columns, QBasic often draws elongated circles that you must correct. This section shows you the basics of circle-drawing so you can have some fun with them.

FIGURE 12.5.

After drawing some boxes onscreen.

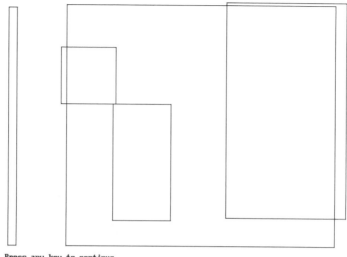

Press any key to continue

To draw a circle, you must specify the radius in numbers of pixels. The radius of a circle is the distance from its center point to the edge. The following CIRCLE command draws a circle with a center point at column 300 and row 150, and a radius of 125 pixels:

```
CIRCLE (300, 150), 125
```

The program in Listing 12.10 draws several circles on the screen. It uses a FOR loop to move the drawing to the right a few pixels for each circle.

LISTING 12.10   USE CIRCLE TO DRAW CIRCLES

```
1: ' Draws circles across the center of the screen
2:
3: SCREEN 12
4:
5: FOR col = 100 TO 520 STEP 50
6:    CIRCLE (col, 225), 100
7: NEXT col
8: END
```

Figure 12.6 shows you the result of running the circle-drawing program.

12

FIGURE 12.6.

*After drawing some
circles across the
screen.*

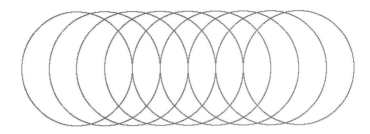

Textual Graphs

Not all graphics require a graphics card, although those with the best resolution do. With
a little imagination, you can chart some graphs without leaving the text mode. The program in Listing 12.11 gives you an idea of what is possible. It draws a graph based on
the values of children's ages. Instead of using pixels, it prints asterisks on the screen to
show which age is the highest (the one farthest to the right).

LISTING 12.11 YOU CAN PRODUCE A TEXT GRAPH WITHOUT GRAPHICS

```
 1: ' Draws a textual graph based on children's ages
 2:
 3: OPTION BASE 1
 4: DIM ages(8)
 5:
 6: ages(1) = 8        ' Fill the 8 array elements with various ages
 7: ages(2) = 9
 8: ages(3) = 5
 9: ages(4) = 6
10: ages(5) = 10
11: ages(6) = 6
12: ages(7) = 6
13: ages(8) = 9
14:
15: CLS
16: PRINT "Here is a graph of the children's ages:"
17: PRINT
18:
19: FOR child = 1 TO 8
20:    PRINT "Child #"; child;
21:    FOR stars = 1 TO ages(child)
22:       PRINT "*";       ' The semicolon keeps the cursor on this line
23:    NEXT stars
24:    PRINT                 ' Moves cursor down for the next child
25: NEXT child
26: END
```

The program effectively uses the trailing semicolon after the PRINT statement. The semicolon keeps the cursor on the line that is printing until as many asterisks print as the age of the child. A blank PRINT then moves the cursor down to the next line ready for the next child's age. Figure 12.7 shows the result of running the program.

FIGURE 12.7.

Displaying a text-based graph.

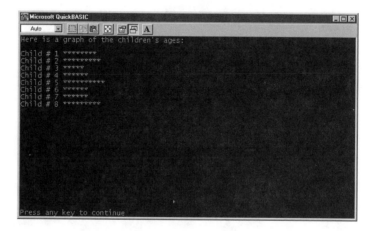

As you can see from Figure 12.7, you don't always need a graphics adapter to produce visual program output.

Changing the PRINT Location

QBasic has a way to print text on various parts of the computer screen. The PRINT statement prints your text at the cursor's current position. Using the LOCATE command, you can move the cursor to another place on the screen. By doing so, you can print anything you want anywhere on the screen while in text mode.

The LOCATE command works like the graphics commands in that it requires a column and row position. Unlike the graphics commands, however, LOCATE works on a maximum of 80 columns and 25 rows (the default limits on most PC text screens). The program in Listing 12.12 uses LOCATE to print the word QBasic at four different places on the screen.

Without the LOCATE command, all four occurrences of QBasic would print one after another.

12

LISTING 12.12 USE LOCATE TO PRINT A WORD AT DIFFERENT LOCATIONS ONSCREEN

```
 1: ' Print QBasic all over the screen
 2:
 3: CLS
 4: LOCATE 22, 60
 5: PRINT "QBasic"
 6:
 7: LOCATE 2, 5
 8: PRINT "QBasic"
 9:
10: LOCATE 17, 25
11: PRINT "QBasic"
12:
13: LOCATE 3, 40
14: PRINT "QBasic"
15: END
```

Figure 12.8 shows the various placements of QBasic onscreen.

FIGURE 12.8.

Displaying another text-based graph.

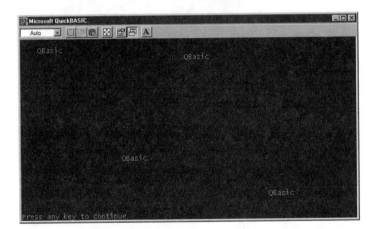

Summary

As you saw here, QBasic programming is far from boring. By drawing graphics and editing sounds, you can spruce up your programs and really get the user's attention. The BEEP is one of the easiest ways to put sound on your computer. Unlike BEEP, however, the SOUND command can control the duration as well as the tone that your program generates. For the musically inclined, PLAY is a command that includes its own programming language that uses musical elements to produce a chorus.

Graphics are important in today's visual computing environments. Although QBasic's graphics capabilities are limited, you will learn much about how graphics are reproduced in other languages and environments by learning QBasic's way. For example, Visual Basic uses an almost identical set of PSET, PRESET, LINE, and CIRCLE commands.

The next hour begins a new part of the book that takes you out of the QBasic environment and describes the nature of Windows programming as well as how other languages work. You will appreciate QBasic because the concepts you learned in this part of the book will carry over into subsequent languages that you learn.

Q&A

Q Can I create animated graphics in QBasic?

A Certainly. Such graphics, however, are tedious to implement. You literally must draw, erase, and then draw again at a position slightly askew from the previously drawn image. One of the troubles with animating very many graphics at once, even with a fast machine, is that QBasic is an interpreted language that runs in a DOS window and such resources are not the most efficient. Therefore, the constant drawing, erasing, moving, and drawing again in QBasic often results in a sluggish picture that doesn't really seem to move.

Q Even the old-fashioned PC speakers that were popular when QBasic first appeared can produce multiple sounds, such as a recorded song, when hooked to a stereo output. Why can't the PC generate multiple sounds without the use of a sound card?

A The PC speaker can indeed produce multiple notes at once, but the speaker is not the problem. As a matter of fact, about a year before sound cards dropped in price so that most PC owners could afford them, a technology called RealSound came out for PCs that, through software, could produce voices and music from the tiny speaker. The hardware is willing, but the software is a different story! QBasic simply does not provide the commands to produce such sound. The SOUND and PLAY commands inherently produce only one sound at a time no matter how you program them. Therefore, as a QBasic programmer, you are limited. Nevertheless, and despite the fact that most programmers consider DOS to be dead, QBasic is still arguably the best environment in which to learn to program. In five short chapters, you learned about variables, control statements, operators, I/O, and even sound and graphics. QBasic's simplicity and limitations produce a great way to learn to program.

12

Workshop

The quiz questions are provided for your further understanding. See Appendix A, "Answers to End of Chapter Questions," for answers.

Quiz

1. What's the easiest way to produce a tone on your PC's speaker?

2. How does SOUND command use hertz values?

3. How does the PLAY command differ from the SOUND command?

4. What is another name for *picture element*?

5. How many pixels across and down can QBasic address on a standard VGA screen?

6. True or false: You must place your QBasic screen in a graphics mode before you can draw graphics pixels.

7. True or false: You can draw lines, boxes, and circles with the PSET command.

8. How many points define a line?

9. How many points define a box?

10. What command determines the next location where PRINT will print?

Hour **13**

Windows Programming Considerations

Throughout the previous chapters, you have learned the fundamentals of computer programming. QBasic makes an excellent learning tool for the newcomer to programming because of its simple program statements and its text-mode environment. Nevertheless, most computing environments today such as Windows are *not* text-based but are visual.

Visual environments offer many challenges for the programmer that the text-based environments did not. Not only must the programmer be concerned with program logic, but the programmer must also make programs aware of the constant possibilities that can happen in a multitasked, visual environment such as Windows.

The highlights of this hour include:

- What makes a GUI
- What makes an event so important
- How events give the user control over an application

- What controls do
- Why you must set property values for the application's controls
- How to respond to events
- Which two approaches for event-checking are the most popular

Visual Programming Issues

NEW TERM Visual environments such as Windows offer a graphics-based user interface called a *graphical user interface* (*GUI*). The GUI provides many unique programming requirements that do not exist in a text-based environment. With a text-based environment, the program generally controls the user. In a GUI, the user more often controls what happens next.

Consider the menu shown in Figure 13.1. Such menus were popular in text-based programs because the user had a fixed choice of options from which to choose. The program allowed for some user freedom in that the user could select an option from the menu, but the user's selections were limited *only* to the menus. The user could not decide to take a course of action that the menus did not provide (except, perhaps, to turn off the computer).

FIGURE 13.1.

Menus controlled the user's choice of actions.

In a graphical environment, the user can do many things that aren't necessarily related to the menu that appears onscreen. Think of a Windows program that you use often, such as an Internet browser or a word processor. Although a menu appears at the top of the screen, you often do many things with the program without the menu. For example, you might click a command button, scroll the window, select from a pull-down list, start a completely different program and run both at the same time, highlight text, paste from the Windows Clipboard, or draw an illustration with the mouse. One of the tasks you might rarely perform might be to select from the menu. That's a large collection of actions you can perform and you, the user, have complete freedom, within some constraints of the program and environment, to do what you want.

All the graphical elements of a visual application lend themselves to this wide selection. Consider Figure 13.2; it shows a menu at the top of the screen but there are also other objects the user can select from. As you look at the figure, ask yourself this: What is the next action that the user of this program will perform? You cannot accurately answer the question. In Figure 13.1, you knew beyond a shadow of a doubt that the user would choose one of the menu options but with a Windows program, the user might do any of the following:

- Select from a menu option.
- Click either mouse button over an object.
- Double-click a mouse button over an object.
- Start a new Windows program.
- Use the keyboard to activate a control such as a command button.
- Select from the Windows control menu that appears in the upper-left corner of every Windows program.
- Resize, close, or move the program's window.

FIGURE 13.2.

In a GUI, nobody can guess what the user will do next.

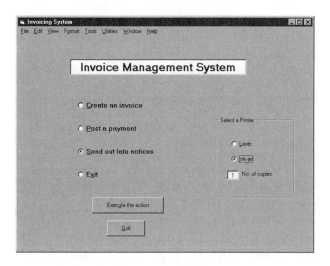

13

As you can see, a Windows application must be ready to respond to an extremely large number of possibilities at all times during the execution of the running application.

The term *application* is often used interchangeably with the term *program*. Throughout the history of programming, programmers and analysts have called programs either programs or applications. The term application was most frequently used in the past for end-user programs and not for dedicated system programs such as an operating system utility that manages memory, but even operating system programs could be viewed as applications by the programmers who wrote them. The term *program*, however, does seem to lack something when one describes a Windows program. Windows programs are rarely composed of a single file as a QBasic program almost always is. A Windows program is more often a collection of files that work together and provide resources for each other. Therefore, the term *application* is more often used today for a Windows program than just *program*. Don't worry too much about the distinction, however; calling a Windows-based application either a program or an application is acceptable.

Was QBasic a Waste of Time?

Virtually all of your programming future lies in a graphically based environment. You will probably never have to write a program again that runs within anything but a visual environment. For the next several years, the Windows operating system will be the platform for which most programs will be written. Given that future, why would this 24-hour tutorial spend the time walking you through several hours' worth of QBasic lessons? Why not jump right in and master GUI programming?

The time you spent learning QBasic was *not* a waste of time. In the text-based environment of QBasic, you did not have the visual elements getting in your way as they would if you began learning to program under a visual language such as Visual Basic. Not only would you have to master loops and variables, but you would also have to master icons, controls (such as scroll bars and command buttons), Windows-based menu selection, window management (such as the sizing and placement of a program's windows), and the multitasking nature of Windows that enables multiple programs to run in memory at the same time. Because you took the time to master the art of programming using the pure language approach without letting the visual elements get in your way, you are now better equipped to handle visual programming. You now understand what variables and loops are and you can see how such programming instructions work within a visual environment.

Controls Offer User Interaction

Before proceeding with the discussion about how Windows applications respond to various actions, take a moment to consider what comprises a Windows application's visual interface. The visual interface is not just a bunch of lines and circles, but rather a collection of specific *controls* with which the user interacts. These controls, also called objects (although the term object is thrown around perhaps too loosely at times given its specific application to object-oriented programming that you'll learn about in Hour 16's lesson), provide a way for the user to give controlling instructions to the program.

Figure 13.3 shows a window from Microsoft Word that contains several controls. These controls compose the user interface for the window shown.

FIGURE 13.3.

The user provides program instructions by interacting with controls.

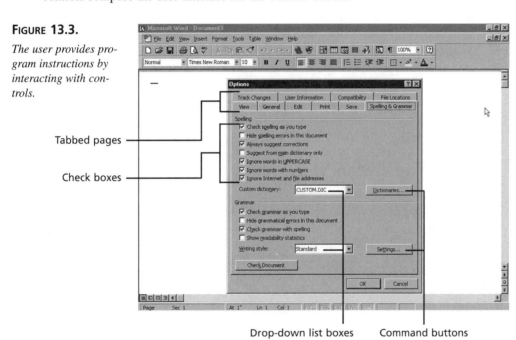

Tabbed pages

Check boxes

Drop-down list boxes   Command buttons

Perhaps the most significant reason controls are important is because they take on the job of user interaction and they free your program from the drudgery of user I/O. You no longer need to write programs that use an Input or Print statement to get input or display output. You can concentrate on the data-processing aspects of your program and not worry as much about I/O specifics.

The controls take over the tedium of I/O. For example, after you place a text box on a window, you never have to write one statement that makes the text box work. The text box sits in the window and receives input when the user types text into the text box. The user will be able to edit text already entered in the text box by clicking on the text and using the arrow keys and the Insert and Delete keys to change the text that appears there. The text box control works independently of your code and handles the user's input as well as the editing.

13

Application windows are often called forms. A *form* is the background of a user's application where the objects that the user interacts with appear.

Controls make your programming work easier, as you'll learn in the next section, but controls don't exist just for the programmer. Users appreciate controls. In spite of the fact that Windows offers a more complex environment than text-based environments, after a user learns how to use one Windows application, that user already knows much about other Windows applications. The menus, command buttons, and other controls generally work the same way and the user interacts with these standard controls the same way from program to program. If you provide controls that the user is already familiar with, your user is much more likely to adapt to your program, use it, and have fewer problems. Your customer support calls, therefore, will decrease and the chance of your users upgrading to the next version of the application are greater.

Controls Lighten Your Job

The same automation works for all the controls. After you place a command button on a form, you don't have to write code that depresses the command button when the user clicks the command button. The command button itself performs the visual clicking action when the user clicks the button. The only thing your program must do is respond to the click.

When you write your own I/O routines using text-mode environments, you must control exactly what happens if the user enters text. When you use a control that knows how to respond to the user already, you can leave the details, such as moving the cursor properly and checking for some errors, to the control itself.

Here are just a few of the standard controls you'll be able to place on your applications' windows from most programming languages:

- Command button—Enables the user to indicate a readiness to perform an action such as the termination of a program or the printing of a report
- Label—Holds text, such as titles and prompts
- Text box—Enables the user to enter and edit text or accept default text
- Check box—Provides a way for your user to select one or more options

- Option button—Enables the user to select one option from a list of mutually exclusive options

- List box—Provides a list of items from which the user can select

- Combo box—Offers several alternative list box styles, such as a drop-down list box that remains closed to save screen space until the user clicks to open the list box

- Picture box—Holds graphics images from files

- Scroll bars—Available in horizontal and vertical styles so that your users can select from a wide range of choices

> Although the controls listed here are representative of common controls, most programming languages offer a huge assortment of controls that go beyond this standard set. In addition, you can add controls that you purchase from third-party vendors, download from the Internet, and write yourself. Today's most popular programming languages, such as Visual Basic and Visual C++, support *ActiveX technology,* which assures that ActiveX-based controls that you obtain for one language will work in other ActiveX-compatible languages.

Some controls can be very fancy indeed. For example, Visual Basic comes with Internet-ready controls that enable you to drop an Internet browser into your application without requiring that you understand all the in-depth programming requirements of online computing that you would otherwise have to master if you did not have access to the controls.

Controls exist to make your life easier as a programmer. You don't have to concentrate on the exact details of how a control works but, rather, you can concentrate on your application's overall goals and data-processing requirements. Just as you can drop expansion cards into your PC to add to its functionality, you can add controls to an application to add to the application's functionality.

Placing Controls

The first step in creating a Windows application is to place the controls on the application's form (or forms if the application requires several form windows). You'll place controls before you ever write code in most instances. The code will process data and handle the I/O provided by the controls.

NEW TERM   Although the earliest Windows programming languages did not provide a simple way to place controls on a window during application development, all of today's common Windows languages usually provide a *Toolbox window,* such as the one in

13

Figure 13.4 from Visual Basic, that contains controls you can place on your application's windows.

FIGURE 13.4.

Toolbox windows contain the controls you can place on your application's windows.

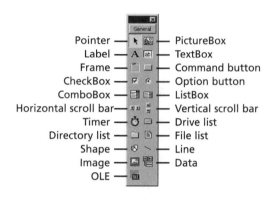

Pointer — PictureBox
Label — TextBox
Frame — Command button
CheckBox — Option button
ComboBox — ListBox
Horizontal scroll bar — Vertical scroll bar
Timer — Drive list
Directory list — File list
Shape — Line
Image — Data
OLE —

Properties Differentiate Controls

Different controls perform different tasks:

- A command button determines whether the user is ready for a task such as the printing of a report.
- A text box is useful for obtaining text input from a user.
- A list box displays several choices for the user in a list and lets the user select from the list.

The same control, however, may appear on a form several times. For example, a window might require both a name and an account number from the user so the window will have two text boxes where the user enters the two values. Of course, the user may or may not enter both values and your code must ensure that all the information is there when needed and, if not, your program will have to let the user know that both values are required.

NEW TERM   The way that a program distinguishes one control from another is that each control on a form window has its own set of *properties*. A property is a description of a control's behavior or appearance. Each kind of control supports several different kinds of properties.

A command button, for example, supports the following kinds of properties as well as many others not listed here:

- `BackColor`—The command button's background color
- `Caption`—The text that appears on the command button

- Height—The height in twips (a *twip* is the smallest addressable dot on the screen, measuring 1/1440th of an inch)
- Font—The various font-descriptor information, such as the name, style, and size, that appears as the command button's Caption
- Left—The location of the command button, measured in the number of twips from the left edge of the form window
- Name—Used internally in the application to access a specific command button
- Width—The width, in twips, of the command button

Many of these same command button properties exist for other controls. For example, all controls have a Name property so that your application can access a specific control; most controls have a Width property that determines how wide the control appears on the form; and most controls have a Left property that determines where the control appears on the form.

Figure 13.5 illustrates the difference between property values very well. Although the figure shows a window with six command buttons, each command button is different because its property values differ.

FIGURE 13.5.

Each of these command buttons has different property values.

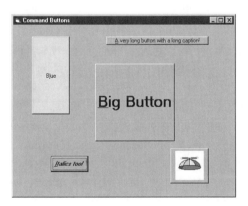

NEW TERM When you create an application, you don't have to write code that specifies and initializes control property values such as the size, color, and caption. Although you can, and will at times, set many properties from code, you'll more likely assign property values to a control when you first place the control on a form. Most of today's Windows programming languages provide a special *Properties window*, such as the one you see in Figure 13.6, that provides a table in which you can specify and select control

13

property values after you place a control on a form. The control will initially appear with a set of default properties, such as a standard size and color, and then you can make that control unique by changing specific properties.

FIGURE 13.6.

The Properties window provides a simple way to set property values for controls on the form.

If you need to change the appearance of a control during a program's execution, you can. For example, you may have to change the Caption property of a command button depending on the user's actions or you might change the color of a command button when the command button enables the user to perform a critical task such as the deletion of a file.

One of the most important properties is the Name property because this is how your program accesses the control. When you first place a control on the form, the programming language assigns a default name to the control, such as Command1, Text1 (the numbers increment as the number of those controls increase so the second command button is automatically named Command2, the third Command3, and so on).

These default names don't indicate the reason for the control so programmers will almost always rename any control that the code in the program references. First, programmers often assign three-letter prefixes when assigning names so that a command button's name might begin with the letters cmd and a list box's name might begin with lst. A command button used for exiting the program might, therefore, have the name cmdExit. Such a name not only indicates the type of control being referenced but also indicates the use for that control. By assigning helpful names, you will write more legible code that is easier to maintain later if needed.

Control property values are almost always changeable and readable. Therefore, you can assign a new property value at runtime such as the following assignment statement:

```
cmdExit.Width = 1500        ' Change the width
```

Notice the dot separates the control name and property value. You can also read the value of a control. A text box value, entered by the user, is stored in a property named Text and you could store that value in a string variable (assuming you are using a BASIC-like Windows programming language such as Visual Basic) like this:

```
strTitle = txtCompName.Text      ' Store the text box's value
```

Capturing the Focus

NEW TERM The *focus* determines which control is currently active. When multiple controls appear on a window, only one control is active and is said to have the focus. The focus is indicated usually by a darkened caption or a dashed line around the control, or a highlight of some kind. Figure 13.7 shows a window with three command buttons and four options. The second option has the focus as indicated by its outline.

FIGURE 13.7.

Focus determines which control is currently active.

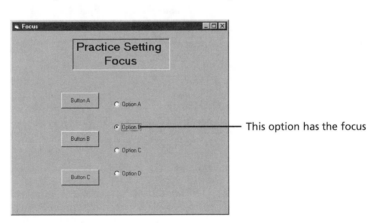

This option has the focus

13

The focus is important because that is the currently active control that receives the user's keyboard input. The user can move the focus from control to control. For example, in Figure 13.7, the user can press Tab or Shift+Tab to move the focus forward or backward throughout the window. Whenever a control has the focus, the next Enter or other keystroke will apply to that control. In other words, if the user presses Enter, the Enter will apply to the control with the focus.

The focus is available for any control that is currently enabled on the window. The user can move the focus to a different control by pressing Tab or Shift+Tab as just explained, but the user can also click any control on the form to send the focus instantly to that control even if the control is not next in line to receive the focus.

> Whenever more than one control appears on a form, a *focus order* determines the order of the controls that receive the focus as the user presses Tab to move the focus from control to control. The focus order is under programmer control and you can change the order of controls that will receive the focus.

NEW TERM If a control contains a *hotkey*, as indicated by a caption that has an underlined letter, the user will be able to activate that control by pressing the hotkey even if another control has the focus. Figure 13.8 shows a window with two command buttons and the user can send the focus directly to the Exit command button and trigger the command button's click in the same step by pressing Alt+X, the hotkey for the command button.

FIGURE 13.8.

If a control has a hotkey designation, the user can change the focus to that key instantly.

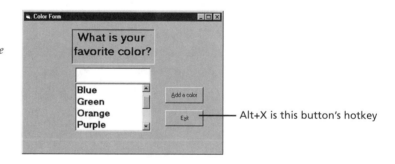

Alt+X is this button's hotkey

> If a command button or other control that is activated by Enter has the focus, that control will be activated as soon as the user presses Enter. Therefore, the user can press Tab until a certain command button gets the focus and press Enter to trigger the command button.

The Caption property is the property that usually determines the hotkey for a control; if the Caption property for a command button reads Exit, that command button's hotkey is Alt+X. To designate the hotkey, precede the letter that is to represent the hotkey with an ampersand, &. A command button that is to display Exit with Alt+X as its hotkey will have a `Caption` value of `E&xit`. The programming language will then make the letter that follows the ampersand the hotkey.

Event-Driven Programs

Given the wide assortment of activities a Windows program's user can perform, how can a program handle all the possibilities? It turns out that a program doesn't have to handle every possibility because Windows will take care of some initial user interaction and, if needed, pass only those actions your program needs to know to your program.

For example, what if a user runs two programs—a word processor and a spreadsheet program—and begins typing in the word processor. The user then switches to the spreadsheet program and clicks the mouse. The word processing program is still in memory and running even though its program window is not active. Therefore, the word processor's program looks for keystrokes or mouse clicks that the user might perform. What happens if the user clicks a command button inside the spreadsheet window? Windows takes care of keeping the mouse click from the word processor by recognizing that the click belongs to the spreadsheet program. Windows, therefore, is the traffic cop through which all Windows user activities pass.

Windows observes all user actions. When an action occurs, Windows must analyze the action and decide what to do with that action. If the action is an operating system command of some kind, such as the execution of another Windows program or the opening of a program window that's been minimized down to the taskbar, Windows responds accordingly. If the action belongs to one of the running programs, however, such as a mouse click over a command button, Windows sends *that* program the mouse-click action. It is then up to the program to respond to that action. If the program ignores the action, nothing takes place. If the program is set up to respond to that particular action in some way, however, the program takes charge and responds.

These various Windows actions are called *events*. An event is just about anything the user can do in a Windows program, such as click the mouse, double-click the mouse, right-click the mouse, or press a key. When you write a program that responds to events sent to the program by Windows, you are writing what is known as an *event-driven* program. Therefore, much of a Windows application consists of writing the event-driven features of the program that respond to the user. Figure 13.9 illustrates the use of Windows as the go-between that takes the user's events and routes those events to the appropriate location.

13

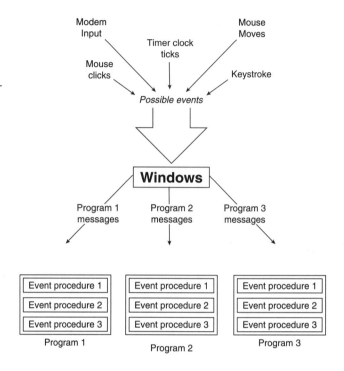

FIGURE 13.9.

Windows is the traffic cop that manages events and sends them to their proper destination.

An event may not be a result of the user's action. Some events are system generated, such as an application close event that the system sends to all running applications when the user shuts down Windows before closing the applications that are still running. Others occur from outside the PC, such as an event that can occur when a printer runs out of paper during the printing of a report. Another kind of event is a timer event that can take place every few milliseconds depending on how that event is created and made to act.

Many events are possible and each event has a name. For example, clicking a mouse button triggers a `Click` event, a keystroke triggers a `KeyDown` event, and the resizing of a window triggers a `Resize` event. When Windows passes an event to an application, it passes that event's type by name, such as `Click` or `DblClick`, so that the application can respond.

Here are just a few of the events that are possible for various controls (many events, such as `Click`, are available for more than one kind of control):

- Change—Occurs when the user changes the value of a control, as can happen with a text box's text or when the user changes the position of a scroll bar
- Click—Occurs when the user clicks the mouse over a control
- DblClick—Occurs when the user double-clicks the mouse button over a control
- DragDrop—Occurs when the user drags and drops a control on top of another control
- KeyDown—Occurs when the user presses a key
- KeyUp—Occurs when the user releases a key
- Load—Occurs when a form first loads into memory and is often used to initialize data
- MouseDown—Occurs when the user clicks over a control (this also may trigger a Click or a DblClick event depending on how long the user keeps the mouse button down)
- MouseUp—Occurs when the user releases a mouse button (other mouse-related events can also occur)
- Resize—Occurs when the user resizes a control
- UnLoad—Occurs when the form window goes away (closes), perhaps as the result of the user terminating the application or by the application freeing the window so that another can load in its place

The user can trigger many of the events in different ways. For example, a Click event takes place when the user clicks a command button, presses Enter when the command button has the focus, or when the user triggers the hotkey combination such as Alt+X to simulate the click of the command button. Some events are very specific to certain kinds of controls, such as the Change event that occurs when the user changes the value of a scroll bar. Other kinds of events can occur to almost any kind of control, such as the Click event.

Windows passes more than just the event, however. All events apply to specific objects. Your application will not just respond to an event, but to a combination of an event attached to a control. Suppose you wrote an application that included a window with three command buttons that trigger these tasks:

- Computes month-end accounting summaries
- Prints a report
- Exits the program

These three command buttons might have the names cmdMonth, cmdReport, and cmdExit. When the user clicks one of the command buttons, if Windows passed only a Click

13

event to your application, your application would have no idea which command button the user clicked. The exact message that your application receives when Windows sends an event to the application takes on this format:

controlName_eventName

If the user clicked the command button to print the report, Windows would pass a message to your application that reads as follows: cmdReport_Click. It is then up to your application to respond to that command button's event in the way that you've programmed the application to respond. The code that you write to handle an event is called an *event handler*.

 You won't write event handlers for all possible events for all controls in the application, but only for the events you want to handle. For example, if you don't want anything special to occur when the user double-clicks a label, you won't add DblClick event code for that label.

Events can apply not only to controls but also to forms. Therefore, you can write applications that respond both to a click or double-click on a form or a control.

Event-Handling Methods

Different programming languages respond to events in different ways. Visual Basic's approach to event handling is perhaps the simplest. As you'll learn in the next hour, "Programming with Visual Basic," a Visual Basic program is not just one long list of instructions as a QBasic program is. Instead, a Visual Basic program's code is comprised of several small routines, called *procedures*. These procedures all work together to form one big program.

You can write a procedure for each control's event that you want to respond to. For example, if you want your application to do something special when the user double-clicks a label, you can write a Visual Basic procedure that responds to that particular label's DblClick event. Then, when Windows passes that event to your Visual Basic application, Visual Basic makes sure that the event-handling procedure takes over. In other words, the procedure lies dormant until its event occurs. A certain procedure may never execute if the user never triggers the event for that procedure. In other situations, the user might trigger that procedure's event several times in one session, which means that the procedure's code will execute several times.

Originally, all Windows applications were written in the C language, although many are now written in C++. C handled events differently from Visual Basic's approach. Such a

C program would consist of a large Case statement. In C, a Case statement works a lot like QBasic's Select Case statement. In other words, the C programmer would write a separate Case-like set of statements that would loop through all possibilities of events that might take place. If and when an event did occur, the next time through the Case cycle that event would align with a particular Case and the code assigned to that Case would then execute.

In a way, C's approach to handling events was more of a brute-force method for dealing with events. A Visual Basic programmer never has to look for possibilities of an event in a big Select Case block as do C programmers. When an event takes place for which a Visual Basic programmer has written an event handler, Visual Basic's runtime system automatically makes that event procedure execute.

Summary

Perhaps you never guessed that a Windows application could differ so much from a text-based program such as the ones you write in QBasic. Even though you've yet to see one statement from a Windows programming language, you understand the fundamentals needed to master Windows programming in any language. The controls that appear on a Windows application window comprise that application's interface to the users who use the program. The controls not only lighten the programmer's load, but they also provide uniform access to standard Windows applications. After the user masters the controls in one application, for example, the user will understand how to use the control in other Windows applications.

Writing Windows applications requires that you understand controls, properties, and events. Unlike a text-based program, a Windows program contains very little code that manages the way that the user interacts with the application because the controls automatically respond to the user when needed. Your program must be able to handle events that occur to the controls, and your program must process the data properly, but your program doesn't need to spend as much time tediously managing the input and output of data for the user as you had to do before Windows controls came on the scene.

The next hour takes you to the next step by showing you the specifics of one of the most popular Windows programming languages in use today, Visual Basic.

13

Q&A

Q What is the difference between a property and an event?

A A *property* determines how a control looks or behaves. For example, a property might be a control's color, its font style, or its size. An *event* is an action that occurs as a result of the user or an operating system function. Most of the time, you'll set property values for all your application's controls when you write the Windows program. Some of the program's code may also change one or more of a control's properties depending on the nature of the program. The events, however, are usually triggered from outside your application. Events are actions that apply to objects such as controls and the forms in your application.

Q How does my Windows application know that an event occurred for one of its controls?

A Windows is smart and makes sure that applications receive event information only on a need-to-know basis. Windows passes events to your application only if your application is responsible for handling that event. If the user is running several Windows programs and clicks the mouse in one of them, Windows sends that mouse click (and the related control name) to that application and the other running applications have no idea that a Click event occurred.

Workshop

The quiz questions are provided for your further understanding. See Appendix A, "Answers to End of Chapter Questions," for answers.

Quiz

1. What is a control?
2. What is a property?
3. What is an event?
4. Why is a Windows program often called an *application*?
5. Why do controls all have their own set of property values?
6. What is a hotkey?
7. What is meant by *focus*?
8. What are two ways that a control can receive the focus?
9. How does a program know which control an event belongs to?
10. Many events take place as you run Windows. How does your application know which events belong to it?

Hour 14

Programming with Visual Basic

You now have two advantages that most newcomers to Visual Basic don't have: You understand QBasic, the precursor language to the Visual Basic language; and you understand how controls, properties, and events work within the Windows environment. Therefore, even in this one-hour lesson, you can learn and understand quite a lot about programming with Visual Basic.

Unlike QBasic, much of the work of a Visual Basic programmer doesn't lie in code but in the design of the application's visual elements, such as the controls that the programmer places on forms at design time. These controls provide the interaction to and from the user. The code that the programmer places behind the controls handles the events as well as data calculations and manipulations that produce the information required by the program.

The highlights of this hour include:

- When to use the Application Wizard to create an application's shell
- What the programmer must do to make the wizard's generated application a more specific application

- How to set control property values

- How to embed code within a Visual Basic application

- How to place and size controls so they look correct on the form

- What kind of code appears in a Visual Basic application

Reviewing the Visual Basic Screen

Unlike most programming languages, Visual Basic is and always has been a Windows programming language. You learn not only the language but also its environment when you learn to write programs with Visual Basic. Before you can do anything in Visual Basic you must understand the Visual Basic screen.

Figure 14.1 shows the Visual Basic screen with its most important screen elements called out. After last hour's lesson, you already know what the Toolbox and Properties windows are for. The toolbox contains a list of available controls that you can add to the application's Form window. You can add new controls to the toolbox. The Form window works as your application's background, holding the various controls that you place on the application. If the application contains only a single window, you'll only design and create one Form window and that window becomes the program window when the user eventually runs the program.

A Windows application is often comprised of several files, including the following:

- Form files that contain the form and its description, controls, and related event procedure code

- Code modules that hold general-purpose code

- Other files that contain elements needed by the application

The Project window keeps track of all items within an application.

New Term   The term *project* is used to describe the collection of all files that compose a single Windows application. (The Project window is often called the Project Explorer window because of its tree-structured nature that mimics the Windows Explorer program.) The Form Layout window lets you determine, by dragging with your mouse, the location of the current form on the user's screen when the user runs the program.

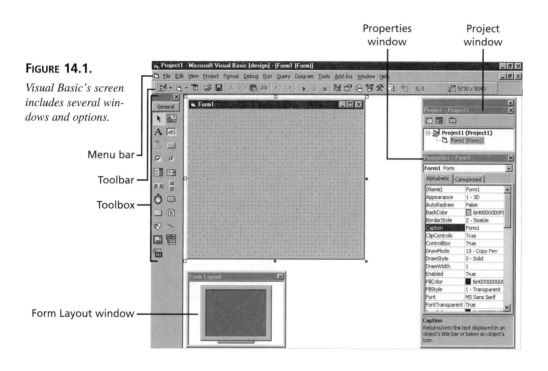

FIGURE 14.1.

Visual Basic's screen includes several windows and options.

Properties window

Project window

Menu bar

Toolbar

Toolbox

Form Layout window

If you have access to a copy of Visual Basic, you will not see the same screen as Figure 14.1 shows when you first start Visual Basic. Instead, a dialog box appears that offers several options. The next section explains how to use this dialog box and make a selection from it.

The latest versions of Visual Basic include tools that go far beyond those found in most other languages. However, creating a Visual Basic application from scratch involves little more than these steps:

1. Design the application by stating its goals and detailing its requirements.

2. Place graphics controls on the application's Form window (this is the output definition design stage). As you place the controls, you'll assign many of the initial properties to the controls.

3. Add event procedures that handle control events.

4. Add any other code needed to tie the controls together and process data as required by the application.

5. Test and distribute the application to users.

14

Visual Basic can greatly help reduce the time it takes between steps 1 and 5 as you'll see in the next section.

Visual Basic Programming Wizard

NEW TERM   If you are familiar with other Windows products such as Microsoft Publisher, you've see wizards that work with you, helping you create the documents you require. A *wizard* presents step-by-step questions and prompts that you respond to. As you respond, the wizard generates an application that matches the criteria you specify. Visual Basic offers several wizards, but the one you'll use most frequently with Visual Basic is called the *Application Wizard*. When you write a Visual Basic program, you have a choice to create an application from scratch or use a wizard to create an application's shell or general structure. After the wizard creates the application's shell, you can fill in the details.

This hour will not walk you through the step-by-step process that you'll go through when you use the Application Wizard because the goal of this hour is to give you insight into the requirements of Visual Basic programming. Nevertheless, knowing something about the Application Wizard is vital to understanding the nature of Visual Basic.

> If you have access to a copy of Visual Basic, you will not see the same screen as Figure 14.1 shows when you first start Visual Basic. Instead, a dialog box appears that offers several options. The next section explains how to use this dialog box and make a selection from it.

Introducing the Application Wizard

Although the resulting application that the wizard creates will not do much (the application is only a program outline, after all), you will see how much Visual Basic can automatically create when you use the Application Wizard. As soon as you start Visual Basic, the Application Wizard is there to help. The New Project dialog box, shown in Figure 14.2, appears when you start Visual Basic from the Windows Start menu. The tabs on the New Project dialog box offer these choices:

- New lets you create new applications by using various wizards or starting from scratch.
- Existing lets you select and open an existing Visual Basic project.
- Recent displays a list of Visual Basic projects you've recently opened or created.

FIGURE 14.2.

You can select the Application Wizard from the New Project dialog box.

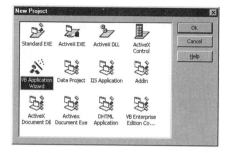

Even if you don't have Visual Basic, you can still get an idea of the wizard's power by studying some of these options that the wizard can add to the application. Your only job as the programmer is to answer a few of the wizard's prompts:

- Application style—Creates an application that produces *single document interface (SDI)*–style where only one data file window can be open at once, a *multiple document interface (MDI)* where more than one data file window can be open at once, and *Explorer-style* that produces a tree-structured view of data with a data summary window pane at the right of the screen and the detailed data in the right window pane.

- Menu options—As Figure 14.3 shows, you can select from a series of menu bar options and pull-down menu options that appear in the created application.

FIGURE 14.3.

You can select from a comprehensive list of menu options to add to your application.

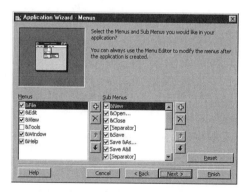

- Toolbar selection—Select from a list of toolbar buttons that you want the created application to include.

- Internet connectivity—Specify whether the application is to have Internet access by providing an embedded browser (available from a menu option in the application) that points to an initial start page when the user activates the browser.

14

- Special screens—As Figure 14.4 shows, you can add one or more special windows to the application such as an About dialog box that appears in most standard Windows applications when the user selects Help, About.

FIGURE 14.4.

Add one or more special windows to your application.

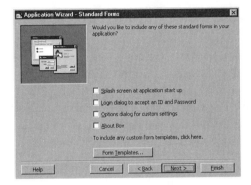

- Database access—Request embedded database technology so that the application created by the wizard has access to special database files you've created or that you use from other sources.

Along the way, you can terminate the Application Wizard early if you want to quit running the wizard. Click Cancel to stop the wizard and discard the application built to that point. You can rerun the Application Wizard again later to create the program once more.

After running the wizard, you will have created your first Visual Basic application even if you knew nothing about Visual Basic and without knowing *any* of the Visual Basic programming language! After a few gyrations on the screen, Visual Basic completes the application and you can run the application—just as you run any Visual Basic application that you create—by pressing the F5 key, by clicking the Run toolbar button, or by selecting Run, Start from the menu.

You can run a Visual Basic application from Visual Basic's own environment or from Windows itself. Hour 23, "Distributing Your Applications," explains more about how you can distribute applications and connect the applications to the Windows interface such as the Start menu.

After the Wizard Completes

After running the Application Wizard, you will have created a fully working program just by answering the wizard's screen prompts. Depending on your responses to the wizard, you quickly create a working Visual Basic application that produces the following:

- A standard program window appears that the user can resize and move. The name of the project appears in the window's toolbar.

- A status bar that displays the date and time at the bottom of the program window.

- A working menu appears with several options. Only the Help, About menu option works (it produces the About dialog box), but the usual menu options, such as File, Open and Edit, Cut, are all there ready for you to insert active code behind them.

- An Internet browser appears from which the user can sign onto and browse the Internet.

- A standard toolbar appears that you can add functionality to and turn on and off from the View menu.

The application doesn't do much yet, but it's ready for you, the programmer, to complete. You can easily change and add to the application, its menus, and its windows. You'll find in tomorrow's lesson that you can create working projects quite easily, but the Application Wizard adds functionality that applications often require.

 If you happen to have Visual Basic and want to create an application with the Application Wizard, you can stop running the application by clicking the Close window button in the application's upper-right corner.

Creating a Simple Application from Scratch

Now that you've seen how easy the Application Wizard is to use, you are ready to take the plunge into the creation of a program from scratch. Again, if you don't have access to a Visual Basic programming environment, you can read through the following task list to get an idea of what Visual Basic requires when you create applications.

This first application displays a picture and a command button. The program will change the picture when you click the command button. You would follow these steps to create this simple application:

1. After starting Visual Basic, select File, New Project to display the New Project dialog box.

2. Select the Standard EXE icon. Your Visual Basic environment will hold only a single form named Form1 (as the title bar shows). The form appears on the background of the Form window editing area, which is white. By selecting the Standard EXE icon, you forgo the use of the Application Wizard to create an application shell.

14

3. Click the Maximize window button to expand the Form window editing area (the white background, *not* the gray form itself) to its maximum size. This action gives you room to expand the form.

> Sizing handles appear around the form because the form is the only object inside the Form window editing area. Notice that the Properties window displays properties about the form.

4. Drag the form's lower-right sizing handle down and to the right. As you drag the form, notice the width and height measurements at the right of the toolbar as they change. Size the form so that it measures about 7,400 by 5,200 twips. This step produces a sized background for your program. Figure 14.5 shows your screen. (Your Form Layout window may appear beneath your Properties window.)

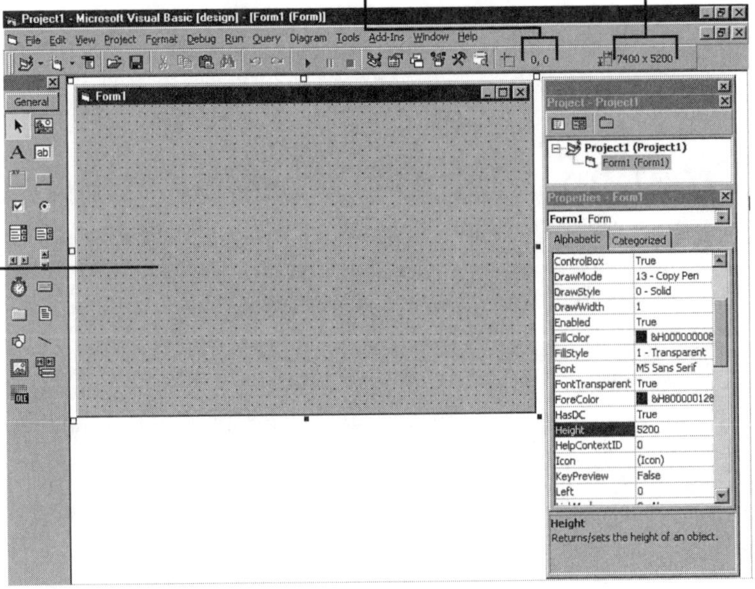

Form-location coordinates   Size coordinates

FIGURE 14.5.

When you resize the Form window, you are resizing your application's program window.

Form window

> As you locate and size form windows, pay attention to the form-location coordinates and the size coordinates at the right of the toolbar. These values always appear in pairs. The first value in the form-location pair

represents the number of twips from the left edge of the screen where the window begins. The second value represents the number of twips from the top edge of the screen where the window will appear. The second pair of values, the size coordinates, represents the number of twips wide and high that the window consumes. The form properties for the form-location coordinates are named Left and Top to represent the number of twips from the left and top of the screen. The form properties for the size coordinates are named Width and Height and represent the width and height of the Form window. Visual Basic automatically updates these values in the Properties window when you move and resize the form in the Form window editing area.

5. Center the thumbnail screen inside the Form Layout window so that your application window will be centered on the screen when the program starts.

6. Close the Form Layout window to give you more room for the other windows.

The dots that appear inside the Form window make up the *grid*. You can turn on and off the grid by selecting Tools, Options, clicking the General page, and checking or unchecking the Show Grid option. The grid won't appear when you run the application; it appears solely to help you place and size controls on the form.

7. Assign a better name than Form1 to the form. To do so, you'll see how to work with the Properties window. A property called (Name) (enclosed in parentheses to keep the name at the top of the alphabetical property list) holds the selected form's name. (In the future, this tutorial will omit the parentheses from around the Name property.) Scroll up the Properties window if necessary until you see the Name value, and notice that the Name value is currently assigned Form1.

8. Click the form's Name property and type frmMyFirst for the form name. As you type, the name appears to the right of the property called Name as well as Visual Basic's title bar.

You'll change and assign all properties inside the Properties window the same way you just changed the form's name. Scroll to the property, click the property, and enter (or select for those properties with drop-down list boxes) a new property value.

14

9. Change the form's title bar from its original value to Happy Application by select-ing the `Caption` property and typing `Hat Picture Application`. The `Caption` property determines what appears in the form's title bar when the user runs the program. The new name appears in both the Properties window and the form's title bar.

10. Save the form to disk for safety. Select File, Save Project. The Save Project option saves every file inside your project (your project currently holds only a single form file) as well as a project description file with the filename extension .VBP. Visual Basic asks first for the filename you want to assign to your form. Visual Basic uses the form's `Name` property as the default filename. If you accept that default name, as you should now do, Visual Basic also adds the extension .FRM to the form's filename. (If your project contained more forms or modules or other objects stored in files, Visual Basic would ask you to name the remaining items as well.) Visual Basic then asks for a project name for the project description file. Name the project `HatApp` before saving the project. Answer No if Visual Basic asks to add the project to the SourceSafe library.

Now that the application's background is complete, you are ready to add the details by putting controls on the form.

Adding the Details

Adding controls to a form typically involves one or more of these steps:

1. Select the control from the toolbox.
2. Place the control in its proper location.
3. Size the control.
4. Set the control's properties.
5. Activate the control with Visual Basic code if needed.

In the steps that follow, you'll quickly learn how to select controls from the toolbox and place those controls on the form. Generally, you'll perform these steps in one of two ways:

• Double-click the control's icon on the toolbox. Visual Basic then places that con-trol in the center of the form. You then can drag the control to its proper location and size the control by dragging the control's sizing handles in or out.

• Click the control's icon on the toolbox and move the resulting crosshair mouse cur-sor to the form where the control is to go. Click and hold your mouse button where the control is to go. As you drag the mouse, Visual Basic draws the control's outline on your form. When you've drawn the control at its proper location and size, release the mouse button to place the control in its proper location.

The following steps spruce up the application you began in the previous section:

1. Double-click the Label control so that Visual Basic places the label in the center of your form. The Label control contains the letter *A*. (Remember that ToolTips pop up to let you know what a toolbox icon is for.) The label is now the selected tool on your Form window editing area so the sizing handles appear around the label. In addition, the Properties window changes to show the label's properties, and the toolbar's location and size coordinate pairs now reflect the label's measurements. A label displays text on a form. This new label will hold a title banner for your application.

2. Drag the label up the form until it rests approximately 1,320 twips from the left edge of the form window and 120 twips from the top of the form. The toolbar's location coordinates will let you know the location.

3. Double-click the toolbox's Command Button control to place a command button in the center of your form.

4. Locate the toolbox's Image control and click the control's icon once instead of double-clicking to place the control as you did with the label. Move your mouse to the Form window and draw the Image control, trying to first anchor the image at 2,520 twips from the form's left edge and 2,880 from the form's top edge. Size the image at approximately 2,175 twips wide and 1,825 twips high. As you size the image, drag the image's sizing handles slowly so that Visual Basic's ScreenTips pop up showing you the coordinates of the image. When the coordinates appear at their proper size, release your mouse button to place the image at that size. Figure 14.6 shows your screen at this point. The Image control displays a graphics image when you run the program.

You can match the location and size twip measurements exactly by filling in the following properties with the measurement values described in the previous step: Left: 2520, Top: 2880, Width: 2175, and Height: 1825.

Location twip coordinates and size twip coordinates are always specified in pairs. Often, you'll see such coordinate pairs specified inside parentheses, as in a location value of (2520, 2880). For the coordinates, such a pair of values would signify that the width is 2,520 twips and the height is 2,880 twips.

14

FIGURE **14.6.**

Your application is
taking shape.

Label control ——

Command button ——

Image control ——

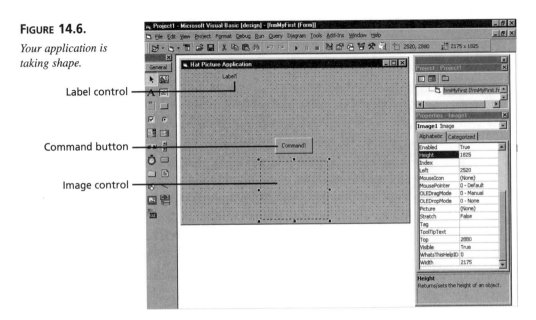

5. Now that you're more familiar with setting property values for controls, even though you may not understand many of the properties yet, you are now equipped to set additional properties for the form and controls to finalize the look of the application. After you set appropriate property values, you will then add code to connect the controls and make them work together.

   Table 14.1 contains a list of properties that you now need to set for the form and the three controls. Remember that you must select the form or specific control before you can change property values for that form or control. To select the form, click anywhere inside the form or title bar but not over any of the controls. The Properties window will change to display the form's properties. Click either the label, command button, or image to select the control, and then you can change one of that control's properties by clicking the property name and typing the new value.

At first, setting a control's font information is confusing. When you select the Font property for a control, an ellipsis appears after the property value. The ellipsis indicates that you can set more than one value for the Font property, and clicking the ellipsis displays a Font dialog box. After setting the Font dialog box values and clicking OK, several property values related to the font used on the control's caption will change to reflect your new values.

TABLE 14.1 PROPERTY VALUES TO SET FOR THE APPLICATION'S FORM AND CONTROLS

Control	Property	Property Value
Form	Max Button	False (open the drop-down list box to see values)
Label	Alignment	Center (open the drop-down list box to see values)
Label	Name	lblHat
Label	Caption	Thinking Caps On!
Label	Font	Courier New
Label	Font style	Bold
Label	Size	36
Label	Left	1320
Label	Height	1695
Label	Top	120
Label	Width	4695
Image	Name	imgHat
Image	Stretch	True
Command Button	Name	cmdHat
Command Button	Caption	Click Here

Finalizing with Code

Adding Visual Basic programming statements will turn your creation into a working, although simple, application. The following process may seem like magic because you'll be adding code that looks somewhat cryptic in a Code window that will pop up unexpectedly. Follow the next few steps to add the code to the application:

1. Double-click the command button to open the Code window. A set of beginning and ending statements will appear for a new procedure related to the command button that look like this:

```
Private Sub cmdHat_Click()

End Sub
```

These lines are two of the three lines needed for code required by the command button. The Code window works like a miniature word processor in which you can add, delete, and change statements that appear in your program code.

14

All code appears in procedures and all procedures require beginning and ending lines of code that define the procedure's start and stop locations. Visual Basic automatically adds the first and final line of many procedures.

2. Press the spacebar three times and type the following line between the two that are there:

```
imgHat.Picture = LoadPicture("\Program Files\Microsoft
Visual Studio\Common\Graphics\Bitmaps\Assorted\Beany.bmp")
```

As soon as you type the LoadPicture's opening parenthesis, Visual Basic offers pop-up help with the statement's format. Some Visual Basic statements, especially those with parentheses such as the ones you see in this statement, require that you type one or more values. Visual Basic pops up the format of these required values, so you'll know how many to enter. You'll learn more about why these values are required if you decide to pursue a mastery of the language in more depth. Visual Basic is a large language, so this help from Visual Basic comes in handy. By the way, depending on the location where you installed Visual Basic, your pathname to the graphics file may differ from the pathname specified here. You may have to use the Windows Start menu's Find option to locate the Beany.bmp file on your hard disk or on the Visual Basic installation CD-ROM and then change the path accordingly.

3. Run your program and click the command button. A figure appears as shown in Figure 14.7. You have successfully completed your new application without resorting to the Application Wizard. You've created an application that displays a picture when you click the command button. The application contains code, and its controls all have property values that you've set.

4. Click the Close window button to terminate the program. Be sure to save your project before you exit Visual Basic.

FIGURE 14.7.

Your application produces a graphics image from the click of your mouse.

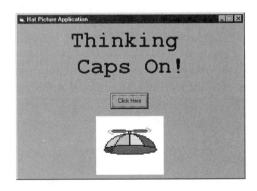

Other Visual Basic Programming Considerations

This hour approaches the Visual Basic language differently from most other languages discussed in these 24 hours. Instead of walking you through specific programming language commands, this hour walked you through the steps required to create a sample application from start to finish. If you look back through the previous sections, you'll notice that very little of the discussion included actual programming language statements. Visual Basic does so much just from its visual environment that adding code sometimes seems like an afterthought.

NEW TERM Even adding menus to the Visual Basic applications that you create from scratch is relatively simple because of another tool called the Menu Editor (see Figure 14.8). The *Menu Editor* lets you build a menu bar and the pull-down options from that menu bar by selecting and specifying options inside the Menu Editor. No code is required as you add the menu options to your application but once you do use the Menu Editor to add the options, you'll have to specify event code procedures for each menu option. When the user selects a menu option, a `Click` event for that menu option occurs and each event procedure that you write will tell Visual Basic how to respond to that event.

FIGURE 14.8.

Use the Menu Editor to add menu options to your Visual Basic application.

Understanding Procedures

Consider the following event procedure for the File, Exit menu option:

```
Private Sub mnuFileExit_Click()
   ' Terminate the application
   End
End Sub
```

14

By studying this simple procedure, you can learn quite a bit about all event procedures. The `Private` keyword indicates that the procedure is *local* to the current form and cannot be called by other form modules. Therefore, if several forms exist in the current Windows application, selecting File, Exit from this form will execute this specific event procedure and not one outside the scope of this form. The opposite of `Private` is `Public` and public procedures are available to any code in the entire application. Such public procedures are known as *global* procedures because any procedure in the application can call them.

The keyword `Sub` or `Function` always follows the `Private` (or `Public`) keyword and indicates the type of the procedure. A subroutine is a procedure that always performs work and then returns control to whatever code was executing before the event takes place. A function is a procedure that always performs its job when the event takes place and then returns a value to another place in the program that might need that value. Hour 17, "Program Algorithms," explains more about the use of subroutines.

The name of the event procedure specifies exactly which control and event this procedure responds to. The body of the procedure may consist of several lines but this one happens to include only two lines, a remark and the `End` statement that stops the running program. All procedures end with an `End Sub` or `End Function` statement. The parentheses that follow the procedure name indicate that the code begins a new procedure; sometimes, when one procedure must pass data values to another, you'll list one or more values separated by commas inside the parentheses. Even if you don't pass data, you must type the parentheses after every procedure declaration.

Some applications include many event procedures, when something is to happen in response to an event. Figure 14.9 shows a Code window with several event procedures inside. Visual Basic automatically adds the separating lines between event procedures so you can locate a specific procedure quickly. In addition, the two drop-down list boxes at the top of the Code window enable you to locate specific event procedures related to specific controls by selecting from the lists.

Understanding the Language Behind Visual Basic

The language behind Visual Basic is virtually identical to QBasic, with the exception of some format differences and differences related to the separation of event procedures I just discussed. Visual Basic includes several statements that are unique to the Windows environment, but for the most part, the languages are the same.

FIGURE 14.9.

Visual Basic organizes your application's event procedures in the Code window.

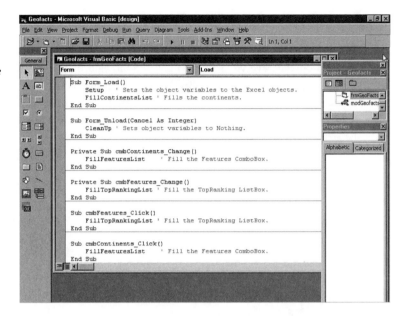

One of the ways that Visual Basic is unique, however, is in its distribution of procedures across different areas of an application. You now know that several small event procedures reside in a form's Code window to handle any events that occur on that form. Other forms can exist as well and code appears in them to handle events that occur there. In addition, other files might be a part of a complex application. A *code module* is a file, separate from any form and the form's associated code, which holds code that you might use in more than one application. Suppose that you write a procedure that prints your company logo at the top of a page. Such a logo would appear before any report that you produce, before any accounting statement, and before anything you ever print. Therefore, you'll use this procedure in many different applications.

Instead of typing the procedure in every application that needs it, you can put the code in a general-purpose code module that you then can copy into a new code module for all applications that need to produce the logo. You can, from anywhere else in the application, call a `Public` general procedure with a `Call` statement such as this:

```
Call logoPrint   ' Detour to the procedure
```

When the `Call` finishes, execution returns to the statement that follows the `Call`.

14

Your Next Step

This hour offered only a walkthrough of the steps that you take to create a Visual Basic application and gave you some insight into the nature of Visual Basic programming. Although Visual Basic is probably the easiest programming tool available for creating Windows applications, Visual Basic is vast compared to a simple, text-based language such as QBasic. Therefore, an hour's lesson could not hope to cover more than you saw here. Nevertheless, you now have a firm grasp of what it takes to write Windows applications in Visual Basic.

If you want more in-depth Visual Basic programming coverage, pick up a copy of *Sams Teach Yourself Visual Basic 6 in 21 Days*, from Sams Publishing, a tutorial that explores Visual Basic programming and takes the beginning Visual Basic programmer to advanced levels in 21 daily lessons.

Summary

Visual Basic is more than a language; it is a complete programming environment, and one of the first that is still greatly in use today. When you create a Visual Basic application, you first create the visual elements of the program by placing the controls from the Toolbox window onto the form. As you place the controls, you set the properties and then write event procedure code to activate the controls when certain events take place.

Of course, you can forego the initial application creation and let Visual Basic create the initial application shell for you. The Visual Basic Application Wizard creates an application that contains menu options, a toolbar, Internet access, and database access. After the wizard creates the application shell, you then can fill in the details and add controls to complete the form and code to process data properly.

The next hour describes the C programming languages. Next to Visual Basic, C is one of the newest languages in wide use today. Although C's successor, C++, has taken the lead in the C/C++ race, a fundamental understanding of C is necessary for a mastery of C++.

Q&A

Q Can the Application Wizard write my program's code for me?

A The Application Wizard cannot write code for specific data processing requirements such as payroll calculations or the printing of accounting statements. The wizard is far too general to generate code that does anything more than support the wizard's options such as the About box, the Internet browser, and the database access. The code that the Application Wizard generates ensures that these features work in a general way, but you must add your own code to the application after the wizard generates the program to make the program perform specific work.

Q Do all Visual Basic applications contain code in addition to event procedures?

A Some Visual Basic applications contain code that forms event procedures only but most other Visual Basic applications contain other kinds of code. More goes on in most applications than events. Data must be processed, calculations must be performed, reports must be printed, and files must be read and written. The code behind these specific tasks often appears in a code module separate from the form module.

Workshop

The quiz questions and exercises are provided for your further understanding. See Appendix A, "Answers to End of Chapter Questions," for answers.

Quiz

1. How much code do you have to write to add Internet access to a Visual Basic application?

2. True or false: The programmer's job is only just beginning when the Application Wizard completes its work.

3. Why is it a good practice to change the names of controls from their default names that Visual Basic assigns?

4. What happens when you double-click a Toolbox control?

5. What tool do you use to help you create menus for Visual Basic applications?

6. How does Visual Basic determine which control properties appear in the Properties window?

7. Name one advantage to running a Visual Basic application inside of Visual Basic's environment as opposed to running a compiled application from Windows.

8. Which runs faster: a Visual Basic application running inside Visual Basic's environment or a compiled Visual Basic application running outside Visual Basic's environment?

9. What information can you gather from the following Visual Basic procedure's declaration line?

```
Private Sub scrMeter_Change()
```

10. True or false: All Visual Basic procedures reside in the application's form module.

14

HOUR 15

Programming with C

C is one of those programming languages that most programmers never predicted would take off. Designed as a highly efficient, somewhat cryptic language used to write an operating system named *UNIX*, C is a language designed by systems programmers. C was never intended to be used by the application programming community.

Today, virtually every program you see on the store shelves is written in C (or its evolutionary offshoot, C++). A C-based compiler is on a high percentage of programmers' computers. C quickly replaced the popular Pascal language in the 1980s and only Visual Basic has made a dent in C's massive usage ever since. As you can see, C's importance to the programmer cannot be stressed enough. For the next hour, you will get a tour of this unusual language.

The highlights of this hour include:

- Why C is so efficient
- Which commands and operators C recognizes
- How to use C's `printf()` function

- What control characters can do
- How to use C's scanf() function
- How to format C programs
- Which statements C uses to control program flow

Introducing C

C is highly efficient and C's developers required that efficiency because, until C, programmers used assembly language to write operating systems. Only assembly language had the efficiency needed for systems programs. C brought the advantage of a higher-level language to the table when developers used C for operating systems. Along with the efficiency of a low-level language, C was more maintainable and programmers were more easily able to update the operating system and produce accurate code. Assembly language doesn't lend itself very well to proper program maintenance that the higher-level languages offer.

To achieve its efficiency, C did have one drawback that other high-level languages didn't require: C is more cryptic than most other programming languages. Its cryptic nature comes in the form of a huge collection of operators and a small number of keywords. Table 15.1 lists C's keywords. In the standard C language, C has only 32 keywords, an extremely small number compared to other languages such as Visual Basic, QBasic, and COBOL.

TABLE 15.1 32 SUPPORTED C COMMAND KEYWORDS

auto	double	int	struct
break	else	long	switch
case	enum	register	typedef
char	extern	return	union
const	float	short	unsigned
continue	for	signed	void
default	goto	sizeof	volatile
do	if	static	while

Notice that C's keywords all appear in lowercase, quite a change from QBasic. C's built-in functions also require lowercase names. C is *case sensitive* so if you use an uppercase letter anywhere inside a keyword or function, your program will not compile properly.

Notice that many of C's keywords match QBasic's. The case, do, else, for, goto, if, return, and while keywords work much like their QBasic (and Visual Basic) counterparts. Therefore, you already know how eight commands work—you know one-fourth of the C language already.

C has more operators than any other programming language with the exception of the scientific APL language described in Hour 6, "Programming Languages: The Early Years." As you know from QBasic and Visual Basic, an operator is usually a special character that performs some operation on data. Not all operators are mathematical, but the primary math operators are the most obvious way to learn about operators because you are already used to them. In the expression 5 + 6, the plus sign (+) is an operator. As with QBasic and others, most programming languages use the same four operators that C uses (see Table 15.2).

TABLE 15.2 C's PRIMARY MATH OPERATORS

Operator	Example	Description
+	5 + 6	Performs addition
-	10 - 4	Performs subtraction
*	4 * 7	Performs multiplication
/	27 / 9	Performs division

Unlike most languages, learning how C's operators work is of utmost importance. Most of your time learning C will be spent working with C's operators. It is the large number of operators that make people think C is a cryptic or mathematical language. Actually, C's operators (a complete list is shown in Table 15.3) are not all mathematical. Many of them take the place of commands used by other languages. It is the abundant use of operators in C that make it very efficient and succinct.

TABLE 15.3 COMPLETE LIST OF C's OPERATORS

++	—	()	[]	->	.
!	~	.	+	(type)	*
&	sizeof	/	%	<<	>>
<	<=	>	>=	==	!=
^	|	&&	||	?:	=
+=	-=	*=	/=	%=	>>=
>>=	&=	^=	!=	,	

Two of the operators, (type) and sizeof, appear to be command names, but the C compiler treats them as if they were operators.

Many extensions to C exist, but the standard language supports only the commands and operators shown in Tables 15.1 and 15.3.

What You Need

To program in C, you need a C compiler. Today, when you obtain a C compiler, you almost always get a C++ compiler as well. Therefore, you get two languages for one, although C++ is really just an extension of the C language. The next hour's lesson, "Programming with C++," explains how C++ compares to C.

One of the most popular C compilers sold today is the Windows-based Visual C++. Fortunately, Visual C++'s interface is virtually identical to that of Visual Basic's interface so you'll feel at home using the Visual C++ environment.

Creating a Windows application in C (or C++) is not as simple as creating one in Visual Basic. Remember that developers created Visual Basic from the beginning to be a Windows programming system. C, on the other hand, began in the world of text-based computers. Therefore, nothing is embedded in the C programming language to support a graphical interface.

To learn C, you don't need to know anything about Windows applications. You can, and should, learn C in a text-based mode so that you learn the language without the visual elements getting in the way. (Remember that when you first learned Visual Basic, you learned its visual interface *before* you saw any programming code.) The rest of this hour teaches you the basics of the C language. Although this hour quickly surveys C without getting into the depth that the language deserves, you will have a good understanding of C's nature after you complete this lesson.

Looking at C

Listing 15.1 contains a short but complete C program.

LISTING 15.1 C IS CRYPTIC AND REQUIRES SEVERAL ELEMENTS THAT OTHER
INPUT LANGUAGES DO NOT

```
1: /* Prints a message on the screen */
2: #include <stdio.h>
```

15

```
3: main()
4: {
5:     printf("C is efficient.\n");
6:     return 0;
7: }
```

If you were to enter the program in Listing 15.1 in your C compiler's editor, compile the program, and run it, you would see this message on the screen:

```
C is efficient.
```

You can test this program using Visual C++ or any of the many shareware C and C++ compilers available on the market or from the Internet. You may still find a copy of Turbo C or Turbo C++ at a school or business that makes entering and learning C simple.

The program required seven lines to output one simple sentence. QBasic could have done it in *one* statement using PRINT, and they say C is more efficient! Actually, C is *vastly* more efficient than QBasic, but the C programmer's job is greater. Remember that QBasic was developed as an interpreted language for beginners. C requires more effort and C was written by programmers for programmers. With C's compiled efficiency and power comes the responsibility to master the language and all its nuances.

Listing 15.1 contains three sets of grouping symbols: angled brackets, <>, braces, {}, and parentheses, (). Be extremely careful when typing a C program because the correct and exact symbol is important. C doesn't handle ambiguity very well so if you type the wrong symbol, C won't work properly.

> C's error checking is much more liberal than QBasic, so if you misspell a keyword, C won't always issue an error and you will only know that a problem exists when you (or worse, when a user) find a mistake in the output. Be extremely careful when entering a C program because C often allows what other languages would not.

Using the `main()` Function's Format

The cornerstone of every C program is the main() function. Because main() is a function and not a command, the parentheses after are required. A C function, just like a Visual Basic procedure, is a section of code that does something. main() is required because execution of a C program always begins in its main() function. Programmers use main() to control the rest of the program. main() often includes a series of procedure calls. (All procedures in C are function procedures and you'll learn more about C functions in the section "C Functions," later in this chapter.)

The actual code for main(), as with all C functions (except the built-in functions whose code you never see), begins after the opening brace, {, and main() continues until the closing brace, }, where main() terminates and other functions often begin. Other sets of braces, always in pairs, may appear within a function such as main() as well.

Notice in Listing 15.1 that many of the statements end with a semicolon (;). The more you work with C, the better you'll learn which statements require the semicolon and which don't. Full statements require the semicolon. For example, assignment statements and lines that perform I/O require the semicolon but formatting and grouping statements don't. In Listing 15.1, the line with main() doesn't require a semicolon because main() doesn't terminate until the final closing brace in the last line. The brace requires no semicolon because it is a grouping character and does nothing on its own.

Using the #include Statement

NEW TERM   Surprisingly, you'll never see #include in a list of C commands because #include is *not* a C command. Statements in a C program that begin with the pound sign are called *pre-processor directives*. The compiler analyzes the directive and, instead of compiling the statement, acts upon the statement immediately during compilation.

The #include pre-processor directive tells the compiler to insert another file that resides in source code form at the location in the program where the directive resides. Therefore, before the program is actually compiled, more code is inserted, at the programmer's request, at the place where #include occurs. That code is compiled along with the programmer's code.

NEW TERM   The stdio.h file is a source code auxiliary file that helps a C program perform I/O properly. C files that end with the .H extension are called *header files* as opposed to C program source code files that end with the .C filename extension. All C programs perform some kind of I/O, and the most common header file used to help C with its I/O is stdio.h. As you learn more about C, you'll learn additional header files that can be helpful, such as the time.h header file that includes definitions that help with time and date conversions.

C Data

C supports data formats that work much like QBasic's data formats. For example, C supports the following kinds of data:

- Character
- Integers
- Floating-points (decimal numbers)

15

C supports several types of integers and floating-point data such as long and short integers as well as single-precision and double-precision floating-point decimal data.

Unlike QBasic, C does *not* support a string data type. Although C has some built-in functionality to handle strings in some situations, generally the C language leaves it to the programmer and functions to handle strings. C doesn't support an intrinsic string data type. Therefore, the only text-based data type that C supports is a single character.

> The fact that C doesn't include support for a built-in string data type isn't a huge problem because ample built-in functions are available in the language to work with string data. Also, C does allow for string *literals*, such as strings that you type directly in the code, just not string variables. Unlike QBasic, however, string data is not inherently supported in the fundamental language, though, which sometimes makes for some interesting programming.

All of C's character literals must be enclosed in apostrophes, ', often called single quotation marks. The single quote differentiates character data from other kinds of data such as numbers and symbols. All of the following are character literals:

`'Q'      '8'      '*'      ' '      'a'`

None of the following are character literals because none of them appear inside single quotes:

`Q      8      *      a`

Listing 15.1 contains a special character, \n. At first, \n doesn't look like a character but it is one of the few two-character combinations that C treats as a single character. \n tells C to drop the cursor down to the next line. Listing 15.1 didn't use \n as a single character but \n is always considered a single character as well as most occurrences of a letter that follows a backslash.

Listing 15.1 included a string literal as well. String literals (remember there is no string variable) are always enclosed in quotation marks. Therefore, the following are string literals:

`"C is efficient.\n"`

`"3"`

`"443-55-9999"`

C Comments

NEW TERM A C *comment* is the same as a QBasic remark. Comments document the code. A comment begins with /* and ends with a closing */, even if the comment spans several lines of code. C comments can go anywhere in a program, including the end of lines.

> Given the cryptic nature of C, you should add comments to your code as much as possible. You will need the comments when you later make changes to the program.

What does the following C statement do?

```
return ((s1 < s2) ? s1 : s2);
```

How could anyone expect to know what that statement does? Even an advanced C programmer will have to analyze the statement for a while to understand it. Yet, a simple comment makes everything much easier as the following statement shows:

```
return ((s1 < s2) ? s1 : s2); /* Finds the smaller of 2 values */
```

From the comment, you know that the statement locates the smaller of the two values stored in s1 or s2 (s1 and s2 are variables).

Declaring Variables

Keeping in mind that no string variables exist in C, declaring variables in C is about as simple as declaring them in QBasic or Visual Basic. Consider the following section of a main() function:

```
main()
{
   char initial;
   int age;
   float amount;
```

This code declares three variables, initial, age, and amount. They hold three different types of data: a character, an integer, and a floating-point value. These variables are local to the function and cannot be used outside main(). (You can declare variables before main() and those variables would be global to the whole program, but global variables are not recommended, as you already know.)

The assignment statement works just as it does in Visual Basic. You can initialize variables like this:

```
initial = 'G';
age = 21;
amount = 6.75;
```

C doesn't initialize any variables to zero unlike QBasic.

C Functions

C is built on a foundation of functions—both those functions that you write and the functions supplied by C. The next two sections should help you understand the nature of C functions.

Using Built-In Functions

Unlike just about every other programming language in the world, C has *no* input or output statements. Look through Table 15.1 once more. You don't see a print statement or anything else that might be considered an I/O statement.

NEW TERM C performs all its I/O through functions that your C compiler provides. By letting the compiler makers implement I/O in functions, the C language is highly *portable*, meaning that a C program that runs on one kind of computer should run on any other computer than is capable of running C programs. A C program written for a Macintosh will work on a PC without change, assuming that you compile the program using each computer's own C compiler.

The printf() Output Function

The most common I/O function is the printf() function. printf() outputs data to the screen in most cases (although the programmer can route the output to other devices if needed through operating system options). Here is the format for printf():

```
printf(controlString [, data]);
```

The *controlString* determines how the output will look. The *controlString* will format any data values that you specify (separated by commas if more than one value is output) in the *data* area. Consider the following printf():

```
printf("Read a lot");
```

This `printf()` doesn't include a *data* list of any kind. The *controlString* is the only argument to this `printf()`. When you use a string of text for the *controlString* value, C outputs the text directly to the screen. Therefore, the `printf()` produces this onscreen when the user runs the program:

```
Read a lot
```

> Remember to use the \n character if you want output to force the cursor to the next line. If the previous `printf()` was followed by this `printf()`:
>
> `printf("Keep learning");`
>
> the output would look like this:
>
> `Read a lotKeep learning`
>
> Obviously, the first `printf()` should have used the \n character like this:
>
> `printf("Keep learning\n");`
>
> With \n, subsequent `printf()` output would appear on the next line.

NEW TERM When you print numbers and characters, you must tell C exactly how to print them. You indicate the format of numbers with *conversion characters* that format data. The conversion characters format data in functions such as `printf()` (see Table 15.4).

TABLE 15.4 C's MOST-USED CONVERSION CHARACTERS

Control Character	Description
%d	Integer
%f	Floating-point
%c	Character
%s	String

When you want to print a value inside a string, insert the appropriate conversion characters in the *controlString*. Then, to the right of the *controlString*, list the value you want printed. Figure 15.1 shows how a `printf()` can print three numbers—an integer, a floating-point value, and another integer.

Strings and characters have their own conversion characters as well. You don't need %s to print strings by themselves because strings included inside the *controlString* that don't have the formatting percent sign before them print exactly as you type them. Nevertheless, you might need to use %s when combining strings with other data.

FIGURE 15.1.

The conversion characters determine how and where the output appears.

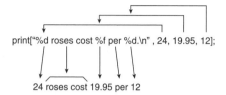

```
print["%d roses cost %f per %d.\n" , 24, 19.95, 12];
```

24 roses cost 19.95 per 12

The next `printf()` prints a different type of data value using each of the conversion characters from Table 15.4:

```
printf("%s %d %f %c\n", "Sam", 14, -8.76, 'X');
```

This `printf()` produces this:

```
Sam 14 -8.760000 X
```

The string `Sam` needs quotation marks, as do all string literals, and the character `X` needs single quote marks, as do all characters. C formats the floating-point numbers with full precision, hence the four zeros at the end of the value. You can limit the number of places printed by using format specifiers. If the `printf()`'s conversion characters for the floating-point number had been `%5.2`, the `-8.76` would have been output in five spaces, with two of those five spaces used for the decimal portion.

WORKING WITH STRINGS

Although C doesn't support string variables, there is a way to store strings. C represents all strings with a *null zero* character at the end of the string. This null zero has an ASCII value of zero. When C encounters the null zero, the end of the string is reached. You never see this null zero on a string, but it is there, internally, at the closing quotation mark. You never do anything to add the null zero because C adds it.

If a string includes a `0` as part of its text, such as the following address: `"190 S. Oak Road"`, the embedded zero is not the null zero because the embedded zero is a regular ASCII character for zero (ASCII number 48).

Figure 15.2 shows how the string `"Sams"` is stored in memory as a string. The `\0` character is C's representation for the null string. The length of a string includes the characters within the string but never includes the null zero.

C uses a character array to hold strings, including the string's null zero. All of C's data types can appear in their own arrays, but when a character array appears and a null zero is included at the end of the data, C treats that character array just like a string. C uses brackets instead of parentheses for array subscripts. To define a character array that will hold a ten-character string, you could declare the following array:

```
char month[10];   /* Defines a character array */
```

The month array can hold ten individual characters or a string if the string includes the null zero. Always leave room for the null zero in the array. C uses zero-based arrays, so month can hold a ten-character string in elements 0 through 9 and the null zero in element 10. You can initialize a string when you define the array like this:

```
char month[10] = "September"; /* Declare and initialize the string */
```

You can also assign the array at runtime using a special strcpy() function like this:

```
strcpy(month, "September");  /* Assigns September to the month array */
```

To use strcpy(), you must include the header file named string.h in the same area of the program where you include stdio.h.

FIGURE 15.2.

Strings always termi-nate with a null zero character.

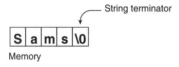
String terminator

Memory

The only data printf() doesn't format is string data. Therefore, if you use printf() to print anything other than a single string, you must supply a conversion code.

This hour is more than half over and you're still learning about the output of data! What about the control statements and operators? You'll see a quick review of those in the last sections of this lesson. For a newcomer to C, understanding the data types and functions is the most critical way to spend your time.

The scanf() Input Function

Getting keyboard input is much more difficult than producing output on the screen. Use scanf() to accept keyboard input. scanf() is fairly simple now that you understand printf() but scanf() does act funny at times. Here is the format for scanf():

```
scanf(controlString [, data]);
```

Understand the following rule and scanf() should work for you every time:

Prefix each variable inside the scanf() with an ampersand unless that variable is an array.

Therefore, the following scanf() gets an age value entered by the user:

```
scanf(" %d", &Age);
```

 Do you see the blank before the %d in scanf()'s *controlString*? Always include the blank because sometimes input of values works better with the blank. (A reason does exist for this, but it's technical and not important here.)

The following scanf() gets the user's first name into a character array as a result of the user following the prompting printf():

```
printf("What is your first name? ");
scanf(" %s", name);   /* Get the name */
```

scanf() is a mirror-image function to printf(). Often, you will write programs that ask the user for values with a printf() and get those values with scanf(). When your program gets to scanf(), C stops and waits for the user to type values. The variables listed inside scanf() (following the *controlString* argument) will accept whatever the user types and scanf() quits receiving input when the user presses Enter.

scanf() also stops getting input when the user types a space! Therefore, scanf() is good for getting only one word at a time in a string.

Despite its problems, scanf() is useful to learn early in your C tutorial so you can practice getting user input. There are many other ways to get user input in C, and often they work better than scanf(), but scanf()'s similarity to the simpler printf() makes scanf() an acceptable keyboard-input function for beginners.

The program in Listing 15.2 shows a complete program that prompts for user input and gets output. You can study the program to gain a better understanding on the material you've covered so far in this lesson.

INPUT   **LISTING 15.2** USE scanf() AND printf() FOR INPUT AND OUTPUT

```
1: #include <stdio.h>
2: main()
3: {
4:   int age;
5:   float weight;
```

continues

LISTING 15.2 CONTINUED

```
 6:    char first[15], last[15];  /* 2 char arrays */
 7:
 8:    printf("\nWhat is your first name? ");
 9:    scanf(" %s", first);  /* No ampersand on char arrays */
10:    printf("What is your last name? ");
11:    scanf(" %s", last);
12:
13:    printf("How old are you? ");
14:    scanf(" %d", &age);     /* Ampersand required */
15:    printf("How much do you weigh? ");
16:    scanf(" %f", &weight); /* Ampersand required */
17:
18:    printf("\nHere is the information you entered:\n");
19:    printf("Name: %s %s\n", first, last);
20:    printf("Weight: %3.0f\n", weight);
21:    printf("Age: %d", age);
22:    return 0;  /* Always best to do this */
23: }
```

Here is a sample execution of Listing 15.2:

```
What is your first name? Joe
What is your last name? Harrison
How old are you? 41
How much do you weigh? 205

Here is the information you entered:
Name: Joe Harrison
Weight: 205
Age: 41
```

Writing General Program Functions

As with a Visual Basic program's collection of event procedures, C programs are modular and are comprised of many functions. Although you *can* put all of a C program's code in the main() function, main() was intended to be used as a controlling function for the rest of the program. Listing 15.3 illustrates the outline of a C program that has proper form.

INPUT   **LISTING 15.3** USE main() TO CONTROL THE REST OF THE PROGRAM

```
1: #include <stdio.h>
2: main()
3: {
4:   getNums();   /* Get a list of numbers */
5:   sortNums();  /* Sort the numbers */
```

```
 6:   printNums(); /* Print the list */
 7:   return 0;    /* End the program */
 8: }
 9: getNums()
10: {
11:   /* Body of function goes here
12:        that gets a list of values
13:        from the user */
14: }
15: sortNums()
16: {
17:   /* Body of function goes here
18:        that sorts the values */
19: }
20: printNums()
21: {
22:   /* Body of function goes here
23:        that prints the values */
24: }
```

> You (and C) can distinguish between a function's declaration and a function's call by the trailing semicolon. A semicolon always follows a function call (such as the lines in main()) and a semicolon never follows the first line of a function (called the *function declaration*).

One of the first aspects of Listing 15.3 that you'll notice is that main() doesn't use a Call statement to call other procedures. Instead, C calls a function procedure when C encounters the function's name. Therefore, main() is comprised of a series of function calls to three separate procedures. (The code bodies of the procedures are not included in this example.)

main(), and hence the entire running program, terminates when the return 0; statement is reached. The return often appears at the end of a function when the function is returning a value to the calling function. main() is returning a 0 to the operating system. Zero is a standard return value that the operating system can check. (If you perform error-checking, you could return a different value to the operating system if an error occurs and then program the operating system to do something in response to a non-zero value.)

One problem with C, as with all languages, is that its local data is known only to function procedures that declare that data. In other words, if no global variables exist in Listing 15.3, the local array holding the user's values will be known only to the GetNums() function. To pass this data to the other functions for sorting and printing, you would write the program in such a way as to pass the list from function to function, or perhaps declare the list locally in main() and then main() can pass the list between the called functions. The parentheses after a function name is where that passing takes place.

A discussion of the ways that C programmers pass data would take several chapters in itself. For now, you already understand much of the structure of a C program even though this one-hour lesson is not yet over.

C Operators

Many of C's operators, such as the plus sign, work exactly like those in other languages. Nevertheless, C's rich collection of operators requires some review, even at a high level, so you can grasp what C is all about. This section will provide a quick overview of some of C's more interesting operators.

C supports *increment* and *decrement* operators. You'll learn in Hour 17, "Program Algorithms," about the concept of adding or subtracting one to or from a variable to keep track of a count. C's ++ and -- operators add and subtract one from whatever variable you apply them to. The following statements each add one to the variables a, b, and c:

```
a++;
b++;
c++;
```

The following statements decrease a, b, and c by one:

```
a--;
b--;
c--;
```

C follows an operator precedence (order of operation), such as performing multiplication and division before subtraction and addition if multiple kinds of operators appear together in expressions. You can break the precedence rules by putting parentheses around the expressions you want calculated first.

NEW TERM C also supports the following operators that update the values of variables: +=, -=, *=, and /=. These operators, called *compound assignments*, update variable values. The following statement

```
a += 25;    /* Add 25 to a */
```

is identical to this statement:

```
a = a + 25;   /* Add 25 to a */
```

The succinct operator helps speed the programmer's job as well as making the compilation of the program more efficient. The shortcut operators, however, do make for more cryptic code at times.

C Control Statements

C supports an `if...else` statement that works a lot like Visual Basic and QBasic's `IF...ELSE` statement. Table 15.5 lists the relational operators with which you can compare data.

TABLE 15.5 C SUPPORTED RELATIONAL OPERATORS

Relational Operator	Description
==	Integer
>	Greater than
<	Less than
>=	Greater than or equal to
<=	Less than or equal to
!=	Not equal to

Use braces to group the body of the `if` statement as shown in the following statement:

```
if (age < 18)
  { printf("You cannot vote yet\n");
    yrs = 18 - age;
    printf("You can vote in %d years.\n", yrs);
  }
else
  {
    printf("You can vote.\n");
  }
```

The individual statements in the `if` statement end with semicolons but not the `if`. The `if...else` spans several lines so you don't put semicolons after the first line of the `if` statement.

C also supports several kinds of looping statements that use the relational operators. For example, the following code shows a `while` loop that continues as long as the relational expression evaluates to `true`:

```
while (amount < 25)
  {
    printf("Amount is too small.\n");
    wrongVal++;    /* Keep track of number of problems */
    printf("Try again... What is the new amount? ");
    scanf(" %d", &amount);
  }
```

C's for looping statement is much more succinct than QBasic's. In QBasic, the following set of statements prints the numbers from 1 to 10:

```
FOR ctr = 1 TO 10
  PRINT ctr
NEXT ctr
```

In C, the same code looks like this:

```
for (ctr=1; ctr<=10; ctr++)
  {
    printf(" %d\n", ctr);
  }
```

Several other control statements also work not unlike those in Visual Basic and QBasic, such as C's switch statement that produces virtually the same relational testing control that QBasic's SELECT CASE statement provides.

For more practice with the C language, check out *Absolute Beginner's Guide to C, 2nd Edition* and *Sams Teach Yourself C in 21 Days*. Both books provide excellent tutorials for C.

Summary

Are you a C expert after one hour's lesson? No way. Do you understand the fundamentals of C? You'd be surprised at how well you now already understand the language. With your QBasic background, you understand the nature of many of C's controlling statements. C's syntax and operators certainly take some time to master, but you will have little trouble progressing from here.

The next hour describes C's successor, C++. Many times, C++ code is identical to that of C. Instead of focusing on specific language statements, an introduction to C++ focuses more on the object-oriented programming aspects of C++.

Q&A

Q Why does the `scanf()` function require the ampersand symbols?

A The problem resides in the way that `scanf()` passes data to the internal code that handles the input. Without the ampersands, the values that the user types will not make it into `scanf()`'s variables.

Q Why is `#include` not a C command?

A `#include` is a pre-processor directive and is not part of the C language. `#include`, and all other lines that begin with `#` such as `#define`, control how C compiles a program instead of controlling the way that the C program executes.

Workshop

The quiz questions and exercises are provided for your further understanding. See Appendix A, "Answers to End of Chapter Questions," for answers.

Quiz

1. How is C more efficient than QBasic?
2. What is a header file?
3. What function do all C programs begin with?
4. Which of the following variable data types does C *not* support: `char`, `string`, `int`, or `float`?
5. True or false: C supports string literals.
6. How can you make C store string data?
7. What is wrong with the following statement?

   ```
   if (sales < 2500.00);
     {
       printf("You need to work harder.\n");
     }
   ```

8. How does C support shortcut operators?
9. What are braces used for in C?
10. How many characters of memory does the following consume: `\n`?

HOUR 16

Programming with C++

The language competing with Visual Basic for the top programming language in use today is C++. Whereas C was the original Windows programming language, C++ is the Windows programming language of choice today for those who don't want to use Visual Basic, or for those who want to use C++ as well as Visual Basic.

C++ is considered a better language than C. C++ offers full support for object-oriented programming (OOP). Whereas you work with objects in Visual Basic, the Visual Basic language is not a true OOP language. You'll learn in this hour how and why C++ provides strong OOP support and how the mechanics of C++ provide for more flexible, maintainable, and efficient programming than its predecessor, C.

The highlights of this hour include:

- How C++ offers improvements over C
- When OOP increases your productivity
- Which new terms you must know to master OOP with C++
- Why classes are important
- How to define objects from classes

- Why object reuse improves programming productivity
- How C++ object libraries extend your programming skills
- How you can use inheritance to decrease programming time

Learning C++

In the previous hour, you learned about C's increment operator, ++. The increment operator increases a variable's value by one. C++ is an incremental improvement over C, hence its name. Much of a C++ program looks like pure C code, which it is. The C++ language introduces some new language elements, but the keywords and structure are similar to C.

Most of C++'s change over C is a result of injecting OOP technology into C. The primary differences between C and C++ don't lie in commands and keyword differences but rather in how the language supports the use of objects.

Scholars debate whether one should learn C before C++. One side argues that learning C without dealing with the OOP issues makes it easier to learn C's mechanics; then one can learn the OOP additions to the language. Others argue that object-oriented programming is simpler than programming without objects so that one learns bad habits when the OOP structure is not present. They say that C++ should be learned first and that one should not take the time to deal with C. Given that the huge majority of C++ programmers first began with C, learning C obviously doesn't seem to slow down C++ programmers too much.

Virtually every C program in use use today is actually compiled by a C++ compiler. C++ compilers support C as well as the OOP additions that C++ provides. Therefore, if you obtain a C compiler distributed in the last few years, chances are that it also compiles C++ applications. The compiler distinguishes between C and C++ programs by the source code's extension; C programs use .C and C++ use the .CPP filename extension. Not all C++ compilers support programming in the Windows environment, but most PC-based C++ compilers sold today do provide full Windows programming support, including the support for a visual interface such as a toolbox with controls, just like Visual Basic provides.

Object Terminology

OOP is laden with terminology that seems daunting at first. The actual implementation of OOP is fairly easy to understand, but to prepare you for the terms ahead, take a moment to study the following OOP-related characteristics:

- Abstraction—The internals of an object do not always have to be known by the programmer to use an object.

- Class—The definition of a related group of objects.

- Inheritance—The ability to create a new class of objects from an existing class. By inheriting a new class of objects, you can create new objects with new behaviors and characteristics based on existing objects and classes.

- Message—A command that acts on specific objects as opposed to the other language commands that are not tied to specific objects.

- Object—A collection of characteristics and behaviors, perhaps even two or more variables treated as a single unit, that appears in OOP programs.

- Polymorphism—A name given to the ability of different objects to respond differently to the same commands (called *messages*).

- Reuse—The ability of the language to utilize objects defined in other programs.

 All OOP languages, not just C++, support these same characteristics.

Fortunately, once you begin learning C++, many of these terms are simple to grasp. Unfortunately, one hour is not enough time to learn C++. Nevertheless, by the time you finish this hour's lesson, you will know the foundation of C++ and understand exactly what's in store for you if you become a C++ programmer.

Fundamental Differences Between C and C++

Some of the new language features that C++ provides over C have nothing directly to do with OOP. The following sections preview some of the non-OOP language differences that you'll find between C and C++.

Comments

One of the differences is the way that C++ enables you to place comments in your C++ programs. Any text that follows a double slash, //, is considered a comment by C++. Therefore, you don't need a closing comment symbol, such as */, as you need in C. The following shows the same comment in C++ and then in C:

```
intCust++;  // Add to customer count

intCust++;  /* Add to customer count */
```

The C++ format is often simpler to code because the programmer doesn't have to terminate the comment. In addition, fewer bugs appear; if a programmer fails to terminate a C comment, code that should not be included in the comment is included until the next closing comment symbol.

> C++ recognizes C's /* and */ comments. Many of today's C compilers also recognize the C++ // comment.

Name Differences

Some differences between C and C++ are simple changes. For example, instead of C's `#include <stdio.h>` directive, C++ programs almost always include this directive:

```
#include <iostream.h>
```

As with the C header files, C++ programmers will include many other header files in addition to `iostream.h`, but `iostream.h` is the most commonly included file. `iostream.h` is the header file that defines basic input and output.

I/O Differences

NEW TERM C++ includes several new operators. The two most common C++ > (the *extraction* operator). These operators are usually combined with the two *stream objects* `cout` and `cin`. A stream object is nothing more than a series of data that is being input or output.

A few examples will quickly show you how to combine the insertion and the extraction operators with stream objects. The following statement sends a string and a number to the screen (typically the output stream goes to the screen although you can change that destination to a different device):

```
cout << "Here is the total: " << 1000.00;
```

If you want to write several lines of output, you can by embedding the newline character in the output stream. The following line

```
cout << "Line 1" << '\n' << "Line 2" << '\n' << "Line 3" << '\n';
```

produces this output:

OUTPUT
```
Line 1
Line 2
Line 3
```

Generally, C++ programmers don't use the newline character, \n, at the end of a statement with cout but they use a special object called endl. endl is an object that not only produces a newline character but also empties the output buffer if you send data to a device that buffers output, such as a printer. Therefore, the following statement would be more likely than the one shown before this tip:

```
cout << "Line 1" << '\n' << "Line 2" << '\n' << "Line 3" << endl;
```

16

C++ combines the cin input stream with the >> extraction object to support keyboard input. As with scanf(), keyboard-based input with C++ is fairly simple to understand and implement, but C++'s input capabilities are limited when you use cin > just to start the student with a way to get keyboard input quickly, but keep in mind that more advanced and better input methods exist that you will master if you pursue the C++ language.

To get a keyboard value into an integer variable named intAge, you could do this:

```
cin >> intAge;
```

Of course, you would probably prompt the user first with a cout so the I/O would more likely look like this:

```
cout << "How old are you? ";
cin >> intAge;    // Get the age
```

Introducing Objects

You've already seen examples of objects. All data values are potential objects in the C++ language. Variables are objects. Although objects can become much more complex than simple variables, a variable is a valid object. In addition, you've now been introduced to the objects cin and cout. Although cin and cout are predefined language objects, and not objects that you define like many other objects in programs, they do work in the same way that all other objects work. You'll learn a little about how objects work in the rest of this lesson.

An object is like a package that exists inside a C++ program. All objects have behaviors and properties. Consider the following object definition:

```
int intObj = 17;   // Defines an integer object
```

The integer variable intObj has properties; the object can hold non-decimal, whole number values that can be either negative, zero, or positive. In addition, the object has behavior; when you output the object, an integer appears. When you assign a decimal value such as 12.34 to intObj, the object throws out the fractional portion and receives only the 12.

Obviously, the idea of OOP-based objects goes far beyond single variables. Objects can be as simple as variables, but often an object represents a non-language item such as a database table, a printer, or a keyboard. After developing a collection of several object classes, you will be able to, through code, manage an object such as a color printer as easily as you manage a variable. Of course, that's the goal of OOP; in reality, abstracting real-world objects to programming-language equivalents is not so easy, but the goal of OOP is to make programming as simple as using objects that you define.

The cornerstone of objects in C++ (as well as any other OOP-based language, such as SmallTalk) is object reuse. After you develop an object, you can easily port that object to other programs. Even objects that others write are available to your program. Therefore, if someone in your company develops a collection of objects that represent company data, such as a company personnel record, your program can also use the object. The details of how the object is formed is unimportant; your program can access the object without knowing everything about the object. In other words, you can reuse an object declared elsewhere without even knowing all the details of the object but knowing only enough to use the object in your code.

Everything electronic today is composed of modules. Your television set is a collection of electronic modules; if something goes wrong with your TV, the repair center will probably replace a whole circuit board even if only a small part on the board is the problem. Your stereo might be made up of a collection of components that you can add, remove, and interchange with others. This kind of object reuse is the lofty goal of OOP. When someone develops an object, others can use that object in their own programs without having to design and declare the object all over again and without having to know all about the object's internals. With this object reuse, the backlog of programming projects, in theory, should be reduced. The problem is that the backlog is *not* reduced because of the demand of programs in today's computing world. Without OOP, however, that backlog might even be greater than it already is.

OBJECTS BUILD UP THE LANGUAGE

The input and output streams provide the fundamental I/O capabilities of C++ but, through classes, you can increase the ability of these streams to input and output more than single characters. Through OOP-related techniques such as inheritance and abstraction, you can route *any* kind of data to *any* kind of object. For example, a C++ program might even send the contents of a database record to a series of text boxes with the following simple statement:

```
txtSet << dtaRecord;  // Write record to text boxes
```

Now to get to this point where you could output consolidated records to a set of text boxes requires quite a bit of programming. Nevertheless, C++ makes that intermediate programming simpler than would otherwise be the case because of the OOP foundation of C++. After you build these special and powerful I/O streams, your programs become much easier to manage and maintain. In another language, writing a database record to a set of text boxes on the screen would take many statements.

16

Defining Classes

In general, to declare a C++ object, you must declare a class. A class is not an object but rather a description of an object. The C++ language includes a new keyword called `class` that you use to define a class.

Consider the following class declaration:

```
class Person {
  char strLastName[25];
  int  intAge;
  float flSalary;
};
```

NEW TERM The class name is `Person`. The class is said to have three *members*. The member names are `strLastName`, `intAge`, and `flSalary`. This class, therefore, describes objects that contain three members. Individually, each member could be considered a separate variable, but taken together (and C++ will *always* consider the members to be part of the class) the members form the class. The members are not objects but parts of objects that you can define with this class.

Remember, a class is a description of an object but not the object itself. In a way, `int` is a keyword that defines a class. `int` is a data type that describes a type of numeric value or variable. Only after you define integer variables do you have an integer object. In the same way, only after declaring variables from a class does an instance of that class, or more accurately, an object of that class exist in code.

Declaring Object Variables

Consider the following statement that declares a simple C++ integer variable:

```
int intCount;
```

You don't have to tell C++ what an integer is because C++ already understands the integer class. The integer class is internal to the language. Therefore, intCount will be an integer variable that takes on all the characteristics of all integer variables.

C++, without your help, would have no idea what the Person class would be because Person is not some internal class native to C++. Therefore, the multilined class statement shown earlier tells C++ exactly what the class's characteristics are like. After you define the class, you then can declare variables, or more accurately, objects of the class. The following statement declares a Person object called Mike:

```
Person Mike;    // Declares an instance of the Person class
```

Figure 16.1 shows what the object (or variable or instance of the class) looks like. The object named Mike is a three-part object. The characteristics are as follows: Mike is an object that begins with a 25-character array, followed by an integer, followed by a floating-point value.

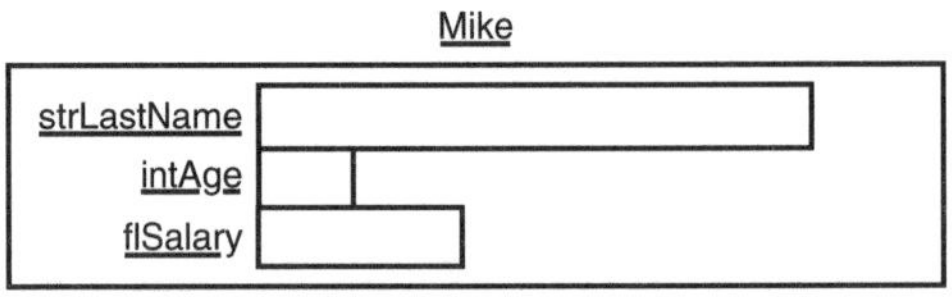

FIGURE 16.1.

The object named Mike
internally contains
three members.

Mike

strLastName	
intAge	
flSalary	

All Person objects that you declare from the Person class will look like Mike, but they will have different names just as integer variables in a program have different names. In addition, the objects will have local or global scope depending on where you declare them.

Generally, programmers place the class definition globally, or even stored in a header file that they include in subsequent programs. After the class definition appears globally (such as before the main() procedure), any place in the rest of the program can declare object variables from the class. The variables might be global, but they will probably be local if the programmer follows the suggested standards and maintains only local variables to a procedure. As with any variables, you can pass object variables between procedures as needed.

Any place in the program can declare additional object variables. The following statement would declare three additional objects that take on the characteristics of the Person class:

```
Person Judy, Paul, Terry;
```

Accessing Members

You'll use the dot operator (a period) to access members in an object. For example, the following assignment stores a value in the Mike object's intAge member:

```
Mike.intAge = 32;  // Initialize the member named age
```

As long as you qualify the member name with the object name, C++ knows which object to assign to. Therefore, if several Person objects are declared in the program, the object name before the member informs the program exactly which object member you want to initialize. Anywhere you can use a variable, you can use a member name as long as you qualify the name with the object. For example, you cannot directly assign a string literal to a character array in C++ (or in C), but you can use the strcpy() function like this:

```
strcpy(Mike.strLastName, "Johnson");  // Assign the name
```

You could print one of the members like this:

```
cout << Mike.intAge;  // Display the age
```

If you wanted to print the three members, you might do so like this:

```
cout << Mike.strLastName << ", " << Mike.intAge << ", " << Mike.flSalary
<< endl;
```

If you've ever seen C's struct statement, you will recognize that class is identical in every respect, until you begin to learn how to add characteristics to the class as you'll learn in the next section.

Adding Behavior to Objects

Until now, you've only seen how to add characteristics to a class by defining the class members. You can also define the class behaviors. The behaviors describe what objects in the class can do. Adding behaviors to a class requires much more time to cover than the rest of this hour will allow. Nevertheless, by seeing an example or two of a class with defined behavior, you will begin to see how objects begin to take on a life of their own that simple variables cannot do.

NEW TERM   The following `Person` class definition is more complete than the previous one because it defines not only the characteristics (the members and their data types) but also the behaviors (called *member functions*):

```
class Person {
  char strLastName[25];
  int  intAge;
  float flSalary;
  // Member functions appear next
  void dispName( void )
    { cout << "The last name is ";
      cout << strLastName << endl;
    }
  void compTaxes(float taxRate)
    { float taxes;
      taxes = taxRate * flSalary;
      cout << "The taxes are ";
      cout << taxes << endl;
    }
  char [] getName( void )
    { return strLastName; }
  int getAge ( void )
    { return intAge; }
  float getSalary ( void )
    { return flSalary; }
};
```

Just as a member can be an instance of a variable, a member can also be a function. The embedded function, the member function, applies only to objects declared from this class. In other words, only `Person` objects behave exactly this way but those `Person` objects can perform the operations defined by the member functions. In a way, the objects are smart; they know how to behave and the more member functions you supply, the more the objects know how to do.

NEW TERM   Many programmers elect to use function declarations (the declaration, or first line of a function, is called the function's *prototype*) in the `class` statement but then define the actual function code later. By placing function prototypes after the `class` itself, you keep the class cleaner like this:

```
class Person {
  char strLastName[25];
  int  intAge;
  float flSalary;
  // Member functions appear next
  void dispName( void );
  void compTaxes(float taxRate);
  char [] getName( void );
  int getAge ( void );
  float getSalary ( void );
```

```
};
void Person::dispName( void )
  { cout << "The last name is ";
    cout << strLastName << endl;
  }
void Person::compTaxes(float taxRate)
  {   float taxes;
      taxes = taxRate * flSalary;
      cout << "The taxes are ";
      cout << taxes << endl;
  }
char [] Person::getName( void )
  { return strLastName; }
int Person::getAge ( void )
  { return intAge; }
float Person::getSalary ( void )
  { return flSalary; }
```

The class statement is more compact because only prototypes appear in the definition
and not member function code. The member function code could appear elsewhere in the
program or, more likely, would be included from a library file of member functions.
Notice that if you place the function's definition later in the program, you must preface
the definition with the class name followed by the :: operator. The class name qualifies
the function because different classes may have member functions with the same name
as other classes in the program.

| NEW TERM | You can define special member functions, with names such as *constructor* and *destructor*, that perform specialized operations on the objects in a class. For example, a constructor automatically declares and initializes an object when you first declare the object and a destructor completely frees memory used by the object when you no longer need the object. |

Before explaining how to apply the member functions to objects, you need to understand
how scope affects objects and their member functions.

Working with Class Scope

The class statement defines a class and its members and member functions, as you
know. However, special consideration must be given to the scope of individual data and
function members. In the previous class definition, all members were known to be private, which makes the class virtually unusable. By adding special public and private
qualifiers, you make the class available to code.

Consider this modified `Person` class definition (the member function code is omitted for brevity):

```
class Person {
  char strLastName[25];
  int  intAge;
  float flSalary;
  // Member functions appear next
public:
  void dispName( void );
  void compTaxes(float taxRate);
  char [] getName( void );
  int getAge ( void );
  float getSalary ( void );
};
```

All members are considered to be private unless you precede them with the `public` keyword. All members before `public` are private but you can optionally place `private:` before the first member so other programmers know your intention is that the class members up to the next `public` keyword remain private. All members (both data members and function members) that follow `public:` are public.

Being private means that any program that uses the class can *never access private members*. This is critical for data protection that the class provides. Earlier in this lesson, you saw the following statement:

```
cout << Mike.intAge;  // Display the age
```

Actually, this statement will not work in the program because the program does *not* have access to the `intAge` data member. `intAge` is a private member so no code outside the class can access `intAge`. By protecting the data members, you keep the object intact and ensure that only predefined functions available in the class can access the age. That's why you often see member functions that begin with `get` as in the `getAge()` function shown previously. Due to the fact that `getAge()` is in the public section of the class, any program that defines `Person` objects *can* use the `getAge()` function. Therefore, you cannot display `intAge` directly, but you can call the `getAge()` function like this:

```
cout << Mike.getAge();  // Display the age
```

Notice that when you apply the member function to the object, you use the dot operator just as you do for data members. Other class objects may be defined and also have functions named `getAge()`, so you must qualify the member function by letting the program know you want the `getAge()` function applied to one specific object variable in the program named `Mike`.

Actually, when you see a member function combined with an object, you are sending a message to the object. The object, by containing the getAge() member function, knows how to return its age value when properly requested with the getAge() member function. Therefore, the code Mike.getAge() is known to be sending a message to the object named Mike telling Mike to return its intAge value. One behavior of Mike is that when a getAge() message is applied to Mike, Mike returns the age due to the member function.

Keep in mind that complete college courses and huge texts exist that teach object-oriented programming in C++. You're getting only an overview here, although the overview is actually rather complete. After mastering this introductory hour, you should be able to understand the early portions of a course or text on C++ much more easily.

Things to Come

Given the introduction to C++ that you've now had, you can better understand the advantages that C++ provides over more traditional, non-OOP languages. One of the benefits of OOP is that you can create your own operators. More accurately, you can change the way an operator works when the program uses that operator with one of your objects.

NEW TERM By writing special *operator overloading* member functions, you can make any C++ operator work on your own objects. For example, a plus sign is the addition operator that automatically works on all numeric values. The plus sign, however, cannot work on a Person object such as Mike. Therefore, if you wanted to add two Person objects together to get a total of the salaries, you could write a function that added the salaries of two or more flSalary data members. When you apply the totaling function members to objects, you can produce the total of the salaries, but you can also overload the plus sign operator so that plus works not only for two numbers but also for two Person objects.

After you overload the operator, the code Mike + Terry works just fine, whereas you could never ordinarily use a plus sign between two Person objects that contain three data members of different data types. Such operator overloading means that you can simplify a program's code. Instead of using a function to simulate a common operation, you can actually use the operator itself applied to your own objects. The member function that describes the operator overloading determines exactly which data members are affected and used by the operation.

The overloading of operators is how you can use the << and >> to input and output complete classes of objects with multiple members and even use Windows-based controls such as text boxes to receive or initiate the special I/O.

The concept of polymorphism makes the overloading of operators possible. For example, the same operator applied to an integer variable behaves much differently if you apply that operator to a class object that you define.

In addition to overloading operators, you can create your own data types. Keep in mind, a class simply defines a collection of data that is composed of data members that conform to an ordinary data type. You could, for example, create a String class whose only data member is a character array. By overloading the appropriate operators, you can make C++ behave like QBasic and support string-like variables.

The String class is just one example of the many classes you and others can write to support object reuse later down the road. Over time, you will build a large library of classes that you can use for future programs. As you build classes, the amount of code that you have to write should lessen and you should complete applications more quickly. In addition, as you build and debug object class libraries, your programs should become more maintainable. Using operator overloading and other OOP advantages means that your code will be less bulky. When you need an object, you will simply create one from one of your class libraries just as you add new stereo components when you want to expand your music system.

One of C++'s most productive features is inheritance. When you or someone else writes a class that you use, you are not limited to objects of that class. The C++ language supports inheritance so that you can derive new classes and create new objects that have all the benefits and features of their parent classes but with additional features as well.

Summary

You can't master OOP with C++ in one hour, but you've already learned the fundamentals of how C++ works. At its most basic level, the C++ language offers language improvements over C even if you don't use OOP. Nevertheless, when you begin to use OOP, you will learn to create classes that define objects that seem to take on a life of their own. The objects understand how to perform some duties based on their member functions and you can extend the objects through inheritance to derive new classes that you can use later.

The next hour explains some fundamental algorithms that you can use in any programming language. Instead of learning new language commands, you will learn how a programmer can use any language to manipulate data.

Q&A

Q How do other programs recognize and use classes defined in C++ programs?

A Many C++ programmers store all their class definitions in a header file, or perhaps in libraries of header files that each contain class code. The code itself for the class's member functions is compiled but the class header with all the data members and the member function prototypes exist in source code form in the header file. The programmer who wants to use the class simply has to link the compiled library into her own compiled program (C++ compilers have full support for this process) and use the `#insert` preprocessor directive to load the class definition at the top of the program.

The programmer will be able to access any and all public data members and member functions in the program. The programmer doesn't need to understand the private members in the class (other than, perhaps, the data member data types which are obvious from the class definition) and the programmer has no need to see the source code of the member functions. The programmer only has to define new objects of the class and all those objects automatically have the functionality given to them in the class.

Q Can the programmer extend the class by adding functionality if a class does not quite contain enough power?

A Certainly. That's where the power of class inheritance comes into play. The programmer can include the class and then inherit a new class from the existing class. The inherited class contains all the data members and member functions of the parent class without the programmer doing anything special. Then, the programmer can add additional data members and member functions (both private and public) to the class to make the class operate as needed. Such inheritance makes the reuse and extension of objects extremely easy and should improve the efficiency of programmers as more object libraries are written and distributed.

Workshop

The quiz questions are provided for your further understanding. See Appendix A, "Answers to End of Chapter Questions," for answers.

16

Quiz

1. True or false: C++ compilers usually recognize and compile C programs.

2. Given the following multiline C statement:

```
/* Perform a data check
  if (a < 50)
    { flag = 0; }   /* False */
  else
    { flag = 1; }   /* True */
```

   a. Does a bug exist in the statement?

   b. How would you write this multiline statement in C++?

3. What is the purpose for a class?

4. What included header file defines I/O in most C++ programs?

5. Where do you define an object's data members and member functions?

6. Which parts of a program have access to private data members?

7. What is the difference between a class, a data member, and an object?

8. What two operators and system objects do C++ programmers often use for input and output?

9. What OOP term allows for operator overloading?

10. How does inheritance improve a C++ programmer's efficiency?

HOUR 17

Programming Algorithms

NEW TERM This hour's lesson is more theory-oriented than the previous lessons. You'll learn about programming algorithms that are common across all programming languages. An *algorithm* is a common procedure or methodology for performing a certain task. To keep things simple, you'll see the algorithms in QBasic but the concepts you learn here are important no matter which programming language you use.

You will learn how to use your programs to count data values and accumulate totals. The computer is a perfect tool for counting values such as the number of customers in a day, month, or year, or the number of inventory items in a department's warehouse. Your computer also is capable of lightning-fast accumulations of totals. You can determine the total amount of a weekly payroll or the total amount of your tax liability this year.

Computers are masterful at sorting and searching for data. When you sort data, you put it in alphabetical or numerical order. There are different methods for doing this, and this chapter presents the most common one. There are also many ways to search a list of data for a specific value. You might give the computer a customer number, have it search a customer list, and then have it return the full name and account balance for that customer. Although computers are fast, it takes time to sift through thousands of data items, especially when searching through disk files (your disk is much slower than memory). Therefore, it behooves you to gain some insight into some efficient means of performing a search.

After you master the sorting and searching techniques, this chapter finishes by introducing you to the most important programming tool at your disposal in any programming language: the subroutine.

The highlights of this hour include:

- What counter variables are
- When to use accumulator variables
- How to swap the values of two variables
- What ascending and descending sorts are
- What a bubble sort does
- How to search for values in unsorted lists
- How a binary search works
- How subroutines work
- How the nesting of loops improves a program's effectiveness

Counters and Accumulators

When you see a statement such as the following, what do you think?

```
number = number + 1
```

Your first impression might be that the statement isn't possible. After all, nothing can be equal to itself plus one. Take a second glance, however, and you will see that in a programming language such as QBasic, the equal sign acts like a left-pointing arrow. The assignment statement, in effect, says "take whatever is on the right side of the equal sign, evaluate it, and put it in the variable to the left of the equal sign." (All the other programming languages you've learned about also use assignment statements that work like the QBasic assignment.) Hour 15, "Programming with C," explains how special C operators can shortcut this section's calculations.

When QBasic reaches the statement just shown, it adds 1 to the variable named number. If number has a 7 to begin with, it now holds an 8. After it adds the 1 and gets 8, it then stores 8 in number, replacing the 7 that was originally there. The final result is one more than the initial value.

NEW TERM When you see a variable on both sides of an equal sign, and you are adding 1 to the variable, you are *incrementing* that variable. You might wonder how adding 1 to a variable is useful. It turns out to be extremely useful. Many programmers put such an assignment statement inside a loop to count items. The variable used is called a *counter*. Every time the loop repeats, 1 is added to the counter variable, incrementing it. When the loop finishes, the counter variable has the total of the loop.

The program in Listing 17.1 uses such a counter. It is an improved version of a number-guessing game you first saw in Hour 10, "Data Processing with QBasic." This program gives the user a hint as to whether the guess was too low or too high. The program counts the number of guesses. The `Tries` variable holds the count.

INPUT **LISTING 17.1** A NUMBER-GUESSING GAME CAN USE A COUNTER VARIABLE

17

```
 1: ' Number-guessing game
 2: CLS
 3:
 4: compNum = 47    ' The computer's number
 5:
 6: PRINT "I am thinking of a number..."
 7: PRINT "Try to guess it."
 8:
 9: Tries = 0
10:
11: DO
12:     PRINT
13:     INPUT "What is your guess (between 1 and 100)"; guess
14:     IF (guess < compNum) THEN
15:         PRINT "Your guess was too low, try again."
16:     ELSEIF (guess > compNum) THEN
17:         PRINT "Your guess was too high, try again."
18:     END IF
19:     Tries = Tries + 1      ' Add one to the counter
20: LOOP UNTIL (guess = compNum)
21: PRINT "You got it in only"; Tries; "tries!"
22: END
```

Figure 17.1 shows a sample run of this program. Without the counter, the program cannot tell the user how many guesses were tried.

NEW TERM An *accumulator* is similar to a counter in that the same variable name appears on both sides of the equal sign. Unlike counter variables, accumulators usually add something other than 1 to the variable. Use accumulators for totaling dollar amounts, people's sales figures, and so forth.

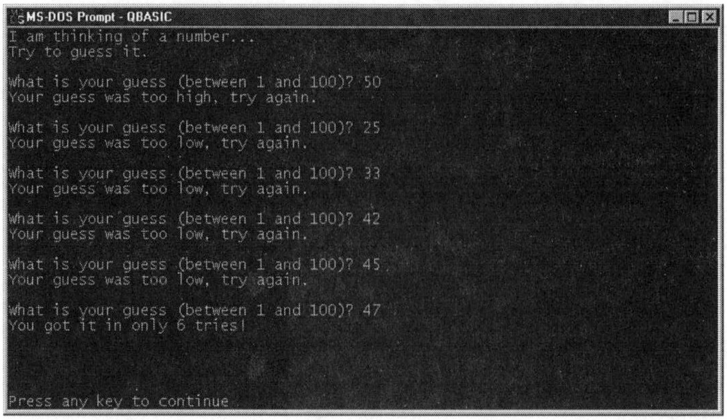

FIGURE 17.1.

The number-guessing game's counter keeps track of the number of tries.

In Hour 11, "Managing Data and Disk Files," you saw a teacher's grade-printing program that stored a teacher's input in arrays and then printed a report on the printer that showed each student's name and score. You can use a total to expand on that listing and produce a class average for the bottom of the report.

To compute an average, you must accumulate the test scores, adding one at a time to an accumulator (the totaling variable). Because an average is based on the total number entered, you must also count the number of scores entered. After all the scores are entered, the program must divide the total amount of the scores by the total tests taken. This produces an average. The program in Listing 17.2 shows you how to do this. The counting and accumulating processes shown in this program are used frequently in data processing, no matter what programming language you use.

INPUT

LISTING 17.2 A GRADE-REPORTING AND AVERAGING PROGRAM CAN USE AN ACCUMULATOR FOR SCORE TOTALS

```
 1: ' Student name and grade listing program
 2: ' Print an average at the end of the report
 3: DIM Sname$(30), score(30)   ' Assumes no MORE than 30 students
 4: numStds = 0   ' Initialize counter
 5: Total = 0      ' and accumulator
 6:
 7: CLS
 8: DO
 9:    numStds = numStds + 1   ' Increment for number entered
10:    INPUT "What is the next student's name"; Sname$(numStds)
11:    INPUT "What is the test score for that student"; score(numStds)
12:    Total = Total + score(numStds)   ' Must add the latest score
13:    INPUT "Another student (Y/N)"; ans$
14:    PRINT                      ' Prints a blank line
15: LOOP UNTIL (ans$ = "N")
```

```
16:
17: ' Now that all the data is entered, print it
18: LPRINT , "** Grade Listing **"
19: LPRINT "Name", score              ' Column Heading
20: FOR i = 1 TO numStds
21:    LPRINT Sname$(i), score(i)
22: NEXT i
23: LPRINT
24: LPRINT "The average is"; (Total / numStds)
25: END
```

Here is the output from this program:

```
** Grade Listing **
Name            Score
Tim Jones       98
Jane Wells      45
Heath Majors    100
Chris Reed      78

The average is 80.25
```

17

Swapping Values

The cornerstone of any sorting algorithm is data swapping. As you sort data, you have to rearrange it, swapping higher values for lower values. As Figure 17.2 shows, swapping values simply means replacing one variable's contents with another's and vice versa.

FIGURE 17.2.

Swapping the values of two variables.

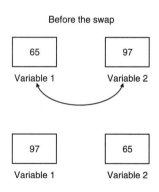

Suppose you assigned two variables named variable1 and variable2 with the following statements:

```
variable1 = 65
variable2 = 97
```

The concept of swapping them is simple. How would you do it? If you said the following, you would not quite be correct:

```
variable1 = variable2
variable2 = variable1
```

Can you see why these two assignment statements don't swap the values in the two variables? The first statement assigns `variable2` to `variable1`, which wipes out `variable1`'s original value. The second statement is then redundant because both variables already hold the same value after the first statement.

> QBasic and Visual Basic both have a `Swap` command that performs a swap of two variables, but many programming languages don't, such as C++. If you want to write programs that are easily ported to other languages, you should use the procedure shown here.

 NEW TERM An accurate approach to swapping variables is to use a third variable, often called a *temporary variable*, because you don't use its value once you swap the original variables. Here is the code to perform the swapping accurately:

```
temp = variable1
variable1 = variable2
variable2 = temp
```

Sorting

The following list of numbers isn't sorted:

10

54

34

21

23

NEW TERM Here is the list sorted in *ascending order* (from lowest to highest):

10

21

23

34

54

NEW TERM Here is the list sorted in *descending order* (from highest to lowest):

54

34

23

21

10

You can also sort character string data, such as a list of names. Here is a list of five sorted names (unless otherwise specified, an ascending sort is always used):

Adams, Jim

Fowler, Lisa

Kingston, William

Stephenson, Mike

Williams, Pete

> When sorting a list of string data, your computer uses the ASCII table to compare characters. (Hour 6, "Programming Languages: The Early Years,") explained the ASCII table.) If a character comes before another in the ASCII table, it is considered to be lower in a sorted list than the other.

Using the Bubble Sort

NEW TERM There are several ways to sort lists of data. The most popular one for beginning programmers is called the *bubble sort*. The bubble sort isn't the most efficient sorting algorithm. As a matter of fact, it is one of the slowest. However, the bubble sort, unlike other sorting algorithms (such as the heap sort and the quicksort) is easy to understand and to program.

17

The data that you want to sort is typically stored in an array. Using the array subscripts, you can rearrange the array elements, swapping values until the array is sorted in the order you want.

In the bubble sort, the elements of an array are compared and swapped two at a time. Your program must perform several passes through the array before the list is sorted. During each pass through the array, the bubble sort places the lowest value in the first element of the array. In effect, the smaller values "bubble" their way up the list, hence the name bubble sort.

After the first pass of the bubble sort (controlled by an outer loop in a nested FOR loop, as you will see in the following program), the lowest value of 10 is still at the top of the array (it happened to be there already). In the second pass, the 21 is placed right after the 10, and so on until no more swaps take place. The program in Listing 17.3 shows the bubble sort being used on the five values shown earlier.

INPUT   LISTING **17.3** YOU CAN SORT A LIST OF VALUES WITH THE BUBBLE SORT

```
 1: ' Bubble sorting algorithm
 2: DIM Values(5)
 3:
 4: ' Fill the array with an unsorted list of numbers
 5: Values(1) = 10
 6: Values(2) = 54
 7: Values(3) = 34
 8: Values(4) = 21
 9: Values(5) = 23
10:
11: ' Sort the array
12: FOR pass = 1 TO 5        ' Outer loop
13:     FOR ctr = 1 TO 4     ' Inner loop to form the comparisons each
   ➥pass
14:         IF (Values(ctr) > Values(ctr + 1)) THEN
15:             t = Values(ctr) ' Swap the pair currently being looked at
16:             Values(ctr) = Values(ctr + 1)
17:             Values(ctr + 1) = t
18:         END IF
19:     NEXT ctr
20: NEXT pass
21:
22: ' Print the array to show it is sorted
23: PRINT "Here is the array after being sorted:"
24: FOR i = 1 TO 5
25:     PRINT Values(i)
26: NEXT i
27: END
```

Here is the output from the program in Listing 17.3:

```
Here is the array after being sorted:
10
21
23
34
54
```

Analyzing the Bubble Sort

To give you a better understanding of the bubble sort routine used in this program, Figure 17.3 shows you a flowchart of the bubble sort process. By using the flowchart and by following the program, you should be able to trace through the bubble sort and better understand how it works. At the heart of any sorting algorithm is a swapping routine, and you can see one in the body of the bubble sort's FOR loops.

17

FIGURE 17.3.

The flowchart of the bubble sort routine shows the swapping of values.

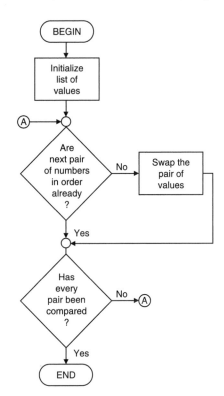

If you want a descending sort, you only have to change one statement in Listing 17.3's program—the first statement inside the FOR loops. Instead of swapping the values if the second item of the pair is lower, swap them if the second item of the pair is higher. The new line looks like this:

```
IF (Values(ctr) < Values(ctr + 1)) THEN
```

If you want to sort names and addresses by zip code and store them in several parallel arrays (the names would be in one array, the address lines in another, the cities in another, the state in another, and the zip codes in another, each array having the same number of elements), perform the comparison on the zip code array. Once you find a pair of zip codes that you have to swap, swap them and the corresponding elements in each of the other arrays as well. Figure 17.4 shows you how such parallel arrays might be organized.

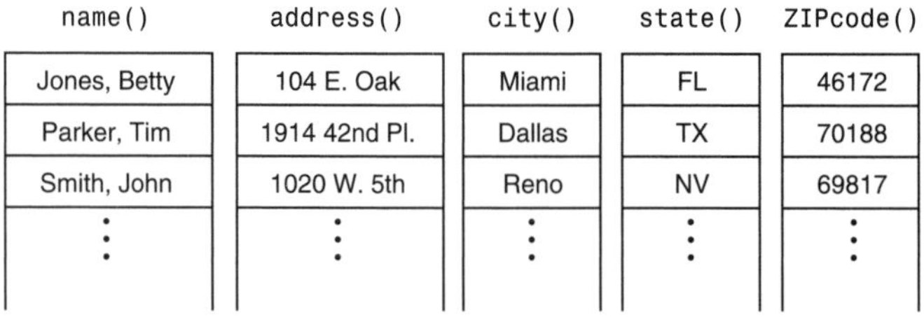

FIGURE 17.4.

Sort with parallel arrays when you must order names and addresses.

name()	address()	city()	state()	ZIPcode()
Jones, Betty	104 E. Oak	Miami	FL	46172
Parker, Tim	1914 42nd Pl.	Dallas	TX	70188
Smith, John	1020 W. 5th	Reno	NV	69817
⋮	⋮	⋮	⋮	⋮

Just to show you that a bubble sort works with character string data as easily as with numbers, the program in Listing 17.4 uses the same algorithm as you saw earlier to sort an array of names.

INPUT   **LISTING 17.4** SORTING NAMES IS AS EASY AS SORTING NUMBERS IN QBASIC

```
1:  ' Bubble sorting algorithm for strings
2:  DIM Names$(5)
3:
4:  ' Fill the array with an unsorted list of numbers
5:  Names$(1) = "Breckenridge, Peter"
6:  Names$(2) = "Sands, Tracy"
7:  Names$(3) = "Quincy, Ed"
8:  Names$(4) = "Moore, Diane"
9:  Names$(5) = "Harris, Larry"
10:
11: ' Sort the array
12: FOR pass = 1 TO 5      ' Outer loop
13:    FOR ctr = 1 TO 4    ' Inner loop to form the comparisons each pass
14:       IF (Names$(ctr) > Names$(ctr + 1)) THEN
```

```
15:              t$ = Names$(ctr) ' Swap the pair currently being looked at
16:              Names$(ctr) = Names$(ctr + 1)
17:              Names$(ctr + 1) = t$
18:          END IF
19:      NEXT ctr
20: NEXT pass
21:
22: ' Print the array to show it is sorted
23: PRINT "Here is the array after being sorted:"
24: FOR i = 1 TO 5
25:     PRINT Names$(i)
26: NEXT i
27: END
```

The output from Listing 17.4 looks like this:

```
Here is the array after being sorted:
Breckenridge, Peter
Harris, Larry
Moore, Diane
Quincy, Ed
Sands, Tracy
```

17

Searching Arrays

There are many methods for searching arrays for a specific value. Suppose you have several parallel arrays with inventory data. The first array, PartNo$(), holds all your inventory item part numbers. The second array, Desc$(), holds the description of each of those parts. The third array, Price(), contains the price of each corresponding part. You might keep all the inventory data on the disk and then read that data into the parallel arrays when it is time to work with the data.

One use for an inventory program that uses parallel arrays is a look-up routine. A user could type a part number, and the computer program would search the PartNo$() array for a match. When it finds one (for example, at element subscript number 246), you could then print the 246th element in the Desc$() and Price() arrays, which shows the user the description and price of the part number just entered.

You often have more disk space than internal memory. Computers have 25 or more times the disk space size than internal memory. Because your disk drives hold data more often than memory does, you frequently cannot fit a disk file into memory arrays all at once. (QBasic imposes the additional restriction that no array in your program can take more than 64K of memory.) When you begin writing programs with data that needs more memory than your computer has, you will begin using an advanced programming technique (mentioned at the end of Hour 11, although it is beyond the scope of this book) called *random-access control*. Random-access files enable you to treat your disk file as if it was a huge array.

New Term There are several ways to search an array for values. The various searching methods each have their own advantages. One of the easiest to program and understand, the *sequential search*, is also one of the least efficient. The search method you decide on depends on how much data you expect to search through and how skilled you are at understanding and writing advanced searching programs. The next few sections walk you through some introductory searching algorithms that you might use someday in the programs you write.

Performing the Sequential Search

The sequential search technique is easy, but inefficient. With it, you start at the beginning of the array and look at each value, in sequence, until you find a value in the array that matches the value for which you are searching. (You then can use the subscript of the matching element to look in corresponding parallel arrays for related data.)

The array being searched doesn't have to be sorted for the sequential search to work. The fact that sequential searches work on unsorted arrays makes them more useful than if they required sorted arrays because you don't have to take the processing time (or programming time) to sort the array before each search.

Figure 17.5 shows a flowchart of the sequential search routine (as with most flowcharts in this chapter, only the sequential search routine is described, not the now-trivial task of filling the array with data through disk I/O or user input). Study the flowchart and see if you can think of ways to improve the searching technique being used.

The program in Listing 17.5 shows you the sequential search algorithm coded in QBasic. The inventory arrays described earlier are used in the program. The program asks the user for the part number, and then the sequential search routine finds the matching description and price in the other two arrays. After you study the program, you should find that the sequential search is very easy to understand.

FIGURE 17.5.

*Flowcharting the
sequential search
technique.*

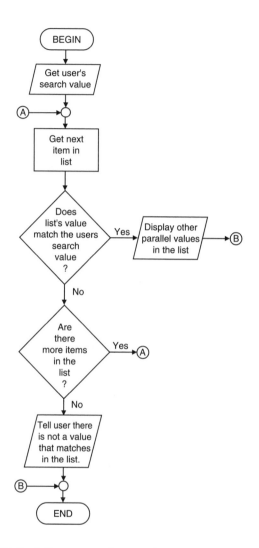

17

LISTING 17.5 A SEQUENTIAL SEARCH CAN HELP AN INVENTORY APPLICATION

```
1: ' Sequential search for an item's description and price.
2: ' (This assumes the arrays have been filled elsewhere.)
3: '
4: ' This code would be part of a larger inventory program.
5:
6: ' ** This program assumes that the variable named TotalNumber
7: '    contains the total number of items in the inventory,
8: '    and therefore, in the arrays as well.
9:
```

continues

LISTING **17.5** CONTINUED

```
10: CLS
11: ' First, get the part number the user wants to look up
12: INPUT "What is the number of the part you want to see"; searchPart$
13:
14: FOR i = 1 TO TotalNumber     ' Look through all inventory items
15:    IF (PartNo$(i) = searchPart$) THEN
16:        PRINT "Part Number "; searchPart$; "'s description is"
17:        PRINT Desc$(i)
18:        PRINT USING "With a price of ####,.##"; Price(i)
19:        END   ' Quit the program early once it is found
20:    END IF
21: NEXT i      ' Get the next item since it did not match
22:
23: ' If the program flow gets here (and did not END in the loop),
24: ' the searched part number must not be in the inventory arrays.
25: BEEP    ' Sound an error beep
26: PRINT
27: PRINT "** Sorry, but that part number is not in the inventory."
28: END
```

Improving the Sequential Search

There is one way to improve upon the sequential search. If you are searching an array
that is already sorted, you don't always have to search the entire array if the element
doesn't exist (as has to be done with unsorted arrays). If the array you are searching is
already sorted, you will know that the search data isn't in the array if you find an item
that is higher (in sorted order) than the one for which you are looking.

For example, consider the following list of part numbers (notice that the list is sorted in
ascending order):

    32345

    43495

    67545

    68878

    88983

    99000

If you are looking for part number 67994, you don't have to search all six values. As
soon as the search takes you to 68878, you know that 67994 isn't in the list. Therefore, a
simple additional check to the sequential search routine shown earlier implements this

change, as Listing 17.6 shows. Remember that this revised sequential search is only advantageous when the item you are looking for isn't in the list. If the item you are searching for is in the list, the program in Listing 17.6 is no more efficient than the last. (In reality, Listing 17.6's program is slightly less efficient if the search value is found due to the extra checking involved inside the loop. However, the extra time needed for the check is minimal.)

INPUT **LISTING 17.6** IMPROVE THE SEQUENTIAL SEARCH TO TEST FOR NO MATCH

```
 1: ' Improved sequential search for an item's description and price.
 2: ' (This assumes the arrays have been filled
 3: '  and SORTED in PartNum$ order elsewhere.)
 4: '
 5: ' This code would be part of a larger inventory program.
 6:
 7: ' ** This program assumes that the variable named TotalNumber
 8: '    contains the total number of items in the inventory,
 9: '    and therefore, in the arrays as well.
10:
11: CLS
12: ' First, get the part number the user wants to look up
13: INPUT "What is the number of the part you want to see"; searchPart$
14:
15: FOR i = 1 TO TotalNumber      ' Look through all inventory items
16:    IF (PartNo$(i) = searchPart$) THEN
17:       PRINT "Part Number "; searchPart$; "'s description is"
18:       PRINT Desc$(i)
19:       PRINT USING "With a price of ####,.##"; Price(i)
20:       END       ' Quit the program early once it is found
21:    ELSEIF (PartNo$(i) > searchPart$) THEN       ' Gone too far
22:       BEEP   ' Sound an error beep
23:       PRINT
24:       PRINT "** Sorry, but that part number is not in the inventory."
25:       END     ' Quit the program
26:    END IF
27: NEXT i      ' Get the next item since it did not match or fail
28:
29: ' The searched part was neither found, nor bypassed, if the code
30: ' gets to this point (one of the two END statements above would
31: ' have been triggered otherwise).  Therefore, the last item in
32: ' the array is not larger than the searched value, and the searched
33: ' value was never found.  The "not found" message must be repeated
➥here.
34: BEEP    ' Sound an error beep
35: PRINT
36: PRINT "** Sorry, but that part number is not in the inventory."
37: END
```

The biggest drawback to this "improved" sequential search method is that you must sort the array before it works. If you don't sort the array, you must search the entire list. When the list is thousands of elements long, efficiency can be critical. However, the time it takes to sort the list before each search negates the advantage. Figure 17.6 shows you a flowchart of the improved sequential search technique.

FIGURE 17.6.

Flowcharting the improved sequential search.

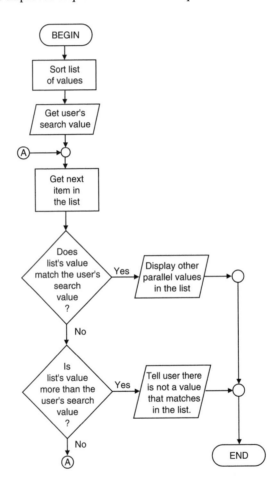

The improved sequential search is useful for data that you must sort for reasons other than the search itself. For instance, if you are keeping a name and address list in your computer and want to take advantage of bulk mailings, you always want to sort your data in ZIP code order. Because you must sort the data every time you add a new name and address, you might as well use the improved sequential search techniques shown in this section. Sorting just for the sake of searching, however, isn't worth the improved search time.

Performing the Binary Search

NEW TERM If your array is already sorted, there is another technique that offers tremendous searching speed advantages over either of the sequential searches shown in the previous sections. This technique is known as the *binary search*. The binary search is more complex to understand and program than the sequential search, but, as with most things in the programming world, it is worth the effort in many cases.

The binary search technique uses a divide-and-conquer approach to searching. One of the primary advantages of the binary search is that with every comparison you make, you can rule out one-half of the remaining array if a match isn't found. In other words, if you are searching for a value in a 100-element array, and the first comparison you make fails to match, you only have at most 50 elements left to search (with the sequential search, you would still have a possible 99 elements left to search). On the second search, assuming there is no match, you rule out one-half of the remaining list, meaning that there are only 25 more items to search through.

The multiplicative advantages of a binary search will surprise you. If you have a friend write down a number from 1 to 1,000 and then use the binary search technique to make your guesses (your friend will only have to tell you if you are "too low" or "too high" with each guess), you can often zero-in on the number in 5 to 15 tries. This is an amazing feat when there is a pool of 1,000 numbers to choose from!

The binary search technique is simple. Your first guess (or the computer's first try at matching a search value to one in the list) should be exactly in the middle of the sorted list. If you guess incorrectly, you only need to know if you were too high or low. If you were too high, your next guess should split the lower half of the list. If you were too low, you should split the higher half of the list. Your new list (one-half the size of the original one) is now the list you split in the middle. Repeat the process until you guess the value.

Suppose your friend thinks of the number 390. Your first guess would be 500 (half of 1,000). When your friend says "too high," you would immediately know that your next guess should be between 1 and 499. Splitting that range takes you to your second guess of 250. "Too low," replies your friend, so you know the number is between 251 and 499. Splitting that gives you 375. "Too low" means the number is between 376 and 499. Your next guess might be 430, then 400, then 390 and you've guessed it. One out of 1,000 numbers, and it only took six guesses.

Listing 17.7 uses the binary search technique to find the correct inventory value. As you can see from the code, a binary search technique doesn't require a very long program. However, when you first learn the binary search, it takes some getting used to. Therefore, the flowchart in Figure 17.7 will help you understand the binary search technique a little better.

17

INPUT LISTING **17.7** A BINARY SEARCH CAN SPEED SEARCHING TREMENDOUSLY

```
 1: ' Binary search for an item's description and price.
 2: ' (This assumes the arrays have been filled
 3: '   and SORTED in PartNum$ order elsewhere.)
 4: '
 5: ' This code would be part of a larger inventory program.
 6:
 7: ' ** This program assumes that the variable named TotalNumber
 8: '    contains the total number of items in the inventory,
 9: '    and therefore, in the arrays as well.
10: CLS
11: ' First, get the part number the user wants to look up
12: INPUT "What is the number of the part you want to see"; searchPart$
13:
14: first = 1    ' Must begin the lower-bound of the search at 1
15: last = TotalNumber   ' The upper-bound of the search
16:
17: DO
18:    mid = (first + last) \ 2   ' Note the backslash for integer
  ➥division
19:    IF (searchPart$ = PartNo$(mid)) THEN
20:       PRINT "Part number "; searchPart$; "'s description is"
21:       PRINT Desc$(mid)
22:       PRINT USING "With a price of ####,.##"; Price(mid)
23:       END
24:    ELSEIF (searchPart$ < PartNo$(mid)) THEN     ' Must half array
25:       last = mid - 1
26:    ELSE
27:        first = mid + 1
28:    END IF
29: LOOP WHILE (first <= last)
30:
31: ' The searched part was not found if the code gets here (the END
32: ' statement above would have been triggered otherwise).
33: BEEP    ' Sound an error beep
34: PRINT
35: PRINT "** Sorry, but that part number is not in the inventory."
36: END
```

Remember that a binary search always requires that you sort the array before you begin the search.

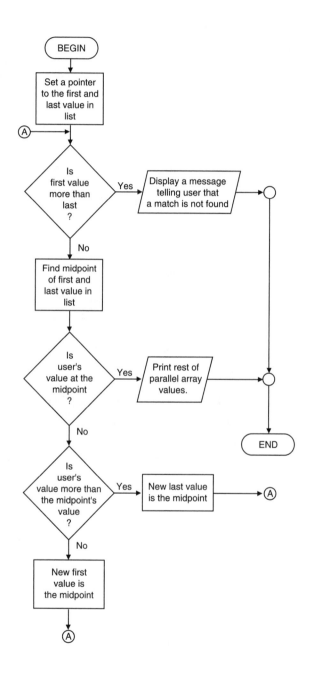

Figure 17.7.

Flowcharting the binary search.

Subroutines

NEW TERM No text on programming languages would be complete without talking a little about subroutines. A *subroutine* is a set of code inside a program that you execute from another part of a program. A subroutine is like a detour; it is a side trip your program makes for a few statements, and then it gets back on the path it was executing and continues from there.

In Hour 14, "Programming with Visual Basic," you saw how to write a Sub procedure in Visual Basic. The subroutine is a set of code that works as a unit, as a procedure works. Subroutines are available for all languages, however, not just for Visual Basic. Subroutines aren't difficult to understand. The algorithms presented in this hour make perfect candidates for subroutines. A subroutine turns your program into a collection of modules that you can integrate together. Instead of one long program, your program becomes lots of little sets (subroutines) of code.

To call subroutines from QBasic, use the GOSUB statement. Use RETURN to end the subroutine. (QBasic also supports the same kind of CALL statement used by Visual Basic subroutine procedures.) When you call a subroutine in C or C++, you only need to specify the subroutine's name and the subroutine returns to the calling code when the subroutine finishes its final statement.

Understanding the Need for Subroutines

Suppose you're writing a program that prints your name and address on the printer several times. Without having subroutines, you would write a program similar to the outline shown in Listing 17.8. The program repeats the same printing code, over and over.

INPUT

LISTING 17.8 A PROGRAM OUTLINE THAT DOESN'T USE SUBROUTINES CAN BE HARD TO MAINTAIN

```
 1: ' Long program that prints name and address throughout
 2: ' (The rest of the code is not shown.)
 3: '
 4: '      :
 5: '   Program statements go here
 6: '   :
 7: LPRINT "Sally Delaney"
 8: LPRINT "304 West Sycamore"
 9: LPRINT "St. Louis, MO  63443"
10: '   :
11: '   More program statements go here
12: '   :
13: LPRINT "Sally Delaney"
```

```
14: LPRINT "304 West Sycamore"
15: LPRINT "St. Louis, MO  63443"
16: '    :
17: '  More program statements go here
18: '    :
19: LPRINT "Sally Delaney"
20: LPRINT "304 West Sycamore"
21: LPRINT "St. Louis, MO  63443"
22: '    :
23: '  More program statements go here
24: '    :
25: LPRINT "Sally Delaney"
26: LPRINT "304 West Sycamore"
27: LPRINT "St. Louis, MO  63443"
28: '    :
29: '  Rest of program finishes up here
30: '    :
```

17

> Not only is repeating the same code tedious, but by requiring more typing, it lends itself to errors. If you only have to type in the code once, but can still execute that code repeatedly whenever you want (as in a subroutine), your chances of typing errors decrease. Also, if your address ever changes, you only have to change it in one place (inside the subroutine), not everywhere it appears in the program.

NEW TERM If you could put the LPRINT statements in a subroutine, you could save yourself some typing. When you're ready to execute the subroutine, issue a GOSUB (for *go subroutine*) statement that tells QBasic exactly which subroutine to execute. You have to label the subroutine and put that label in the GOSUB statement because you can have more than one subroutine in any program. QBasic has to know which one you want to execute.

Listing 17.9 is an improved version of the previous program outline. Notice that the subroutine's name and address printing code is preceded by a statement that begins PrNmAddr:. This strange-looking message isn't a QBasic command, but simply a label that you make up which names the subroutine's location.

> The colon is required at the end of all label names in the code. When you use a label in a GOSUB, however, you don't type the colon.

INPUT   **LISTING 17.9** A PROGRAM OUTLINE THAT USES SUBROUTINES IS SIMPLE

```
 1: ' Long program that prints name and address throughout
 2: ' (The rest of the code is not shown.)
 3: '
 4: '    :
 5: '  Program statements go here
 6: '    :
 7: GOSUB PrNmAddr            ' Executes the subroutine
 8: '    :
 9: '  More program statements go here
10: '    :
11: GOSUB PrNmAddr            ' Executes the subroutine
12: '    :
13: '  More program statements go here
14: '    :
15: GOSUB PrNmAddr            ' Executes the subroutine
16: '    :
17: '  More program statements go here
18: '    :
19: END             ' Required so subroutine doesn't execute on its
20:                 ' own by the program falling through to it
21:
22: PrNmAddr:
23:   LPRINT "Sally Delaney"
24:   LPRINT "304 West Sycamore"
25:   LPRINT "St. Louis, MO  63443"
26:   RETURN
```

The END is put before the subroutine so the program doesn't continue through to the subroutine and attempt to execute it one last time before quitting.

At the end of the subroutine is the RETURN statement. RETURN informs QBasic that you want the program's code that called the subroutine to continue from where it left off. GOSUB doesn't create spaghetti code like a branching statement such as GOTO. GOSUB ensures that execution always returns to the original GOSUB statement that called the subroutine. Execution then proceeds with the original sequence.

You may not see a tremendous advantage in using subroutines when the subroutine is only three lines long, as in this example. However, you can place the searching and sorting algorithms in subroutines and then call them via GOSUB whenever the rest of the program needs to search or sort data. Duplicating 10 or 20 (or more) lines of code every time you want to execute one of the sorting or searching routines takes a lot of programming time away from you. The computer should be your slave; you should not be a slave to it. Subroutines will make your programs more manageable and will ultimately help you write better programs faster.

> By using subroutines instead of duplicating the same lines of code throughout a program, you also save disk space.

Organizing Routines

Even if you don't have to execute the same routine more than once, grouping a routine into a subroutine makes a lot of sense: it helps organize your program. Listing 17.10 shows a complete program with three subroutines. The subroutines perform the following tasks:

1. Ask the user for a list of numbers.

2. Sort the numbers.

3. Print the numbers.

As you can see, the first part of the program is nothing more than a calling procedure that controls the execution of the subroutine. By breaking your program into modules such as this program does, you can help zero in on code later if you want to change something. If you want to change to a different sorting method, you can quickly find the sorting routine without having to trace through a bunch of unrelated code.

INPUT

LISTING 17.10 A PROGRAM THAT USES SUBROUTINES FOR EVERYTHING IS EASIER TO MAINTAIN AND UNDERSTAND

```
 1: ' Program with subroutines
 2: CLS
 3:
 4: DIM Values(10)
 5:
 6: GOSUB AskForData      ' Get user's list of numbers
 7: GOSUB SortData        ' Sort the numbers
 8: GOSUB PrintData       ' Print the numbers
 9:
10: END
11:
12: AskForData:           ' Gets 10 values from the user
13:     PRINT "** Number Sorting Program **"
14:     FOR i = 1 TO 10
15:         INPUT "What is a number for the list"; Values(i)
16:     NEXT i
```

continues

LISTING 17.10 CONTINUED

```
17:    RETURN
18:
19: SortData:               ' Sorts the 10 values
20:    FOR pass = 1 TO 10
21:       FOR ctr = 1 TO 9
22:          IF (Values(ctr) > Values(ctr + 1)) THEN
23:             t = Values(ctr)
24:             Values(ctr) = Values(ctr + 1)
25:             Values(ctr + 1) = t
26:          END IF
27:       NEXT ctr
28:    NEXT pass
29:    RETURN
30:
31: PrintData:
32:    PRINT
33:    PRINT "After the sort:"
34:    FOR i = 1 TO 10
35:       PRINT Values(i); " ";    ' Print list with a space between the
                                   ' numbers
36:    NEXT i
37:    RETURN
38: END
```

 By indenting the lines of a subroutine to the right by two or three spaces, you help set apart the subroutine from the rest of the program.

Figure 17.8 shows the result of this program. Of course, the user has no idea that this program is much better organized than one that doesn't use subroutines. However, if someone ever has to change this program, that person will be glad that subroutines were used to help group similar code into modules.

Nested Loops

 As with almost all statements, you can nest two or more loops inside one another. This section explains the concept of nested loops using QBasic's FOR loop. Anytime your program needs to repeat a loop more than once, use a *nested loop*. Figure 17.9 shows an outline of a nested FOR loop. Think of the inside loop as looping "faster" than the outside loop. The inside loop iterates faster because the variable In goes from 1 to 10 in the inside loop before the outside loop's first iteration has completed. Because the outside loop doesn't repeat until the NEXT OUT statement, the inside FOR loop has a chance to finish in its entirety. When the outside loop finally does iterate a second time, the inside loop starts all over again.

FIGURE 17.8.

Entering, sorting, and printing with subroutines.

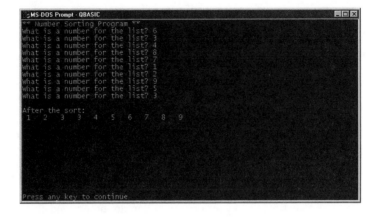

17

FIGURE 17.9.

The outside loop determines how many times the inside loop executes.

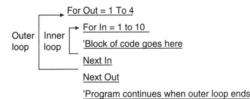

Figure 17.9's inner loop executes a total of 40 times. The outside loop iterates four times, and the inside loop executes 10 times for each of the outer loop's iterations.

Figure 17.10 shows two loops nested within an outer loop. Both loops execute completely before the outside loop finishes its first iteration. When the outside loop starts its second iteration, the two inside loops repeat all over again.

The blocks of code inside Figure 17.10's innermost loops execute a total of 40 times each. The outside loop iterates four times, and each inner loop executes, first the top and then the bottom, in its entirety each time the outer loop iterates once again.

Be sure that you match NEXT with FOR statements when you nest loops. Each NEXT must go with the most recent FOR before it in the code. QBasic and Visual Basic both issue errors if you write a program whose inside loop's NEXT statement appears after the outside loop's NEXT statement. If you omit the NEXT variable, QBasic aligns each NEXT with the most recent FOR for you, but adding the NEXT statement's variable often helps to document the loops and more clearly show where a loop begins and ends.

FIGURE 17.10.

Two or more loops can nest within another loop.

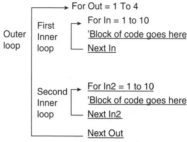

Summary

The techniques you learned in this hour will be useful throughout your entire programming career. Sorting, searching, and subroutines are needed for useful data processing. The computer, thanks to your programs, can do these mundane tasks while you concentrate on more important things.

The next hour describes a different kind of programming language from the ones you've seen so far. Programmers don't use scripting and batch languages to write complete applications but these small languages do help control a system or application.

Q&A

Q How do subroutines improve a program's accuracy?

A A program is easier to write and maintain when you group routine code together in subroutines. The subroutines help you focus on specific parts of the program that you need to change or fix if bugs exist in the code. When your whole program is comprised of small routines, in subroutines, you make your code more modular and you help ensure that code in one part of the program doesn't affect code in another part of the program.

Workshop

The quiz questions are provided for your further understanding. See Appendix A, "Answers to End of Chapter Questions," for answers.

Quiz

1. What is an accumulator?

2. True or false: The following statement is an accumulator statement:

   ```
   Num = Num - 1
   ```

3. What is the difference between the terms *ascending sort* and *descending sort*?

4. Why is a third variable needed when you want to swap the values of two variables (assuming the language doesn't support a Swap statement)?

5. Which sort is the easiest to write and understand?

6. True or false: A counter statement is a special kind of accumulator statement?

7. What is the simplest kind of search technique?

8. Which is more efficient: the binary search or the sequential search?

9. What is the difference between a QBasic GOTO and GOSUB statement?

10. How can you improve the efficiency of a sequential search?

17

Hour **18**

Batch, Macro, and Scripting Languages

Some programming languages exist not for you to write applications in, but to use for control of the operating system and to control other applications. For example, you can automate common operating system tasks so that, with a single keystroke, you can trigger a series of operating system commands that execute as though they resided in a program. In addition, Windows programs such as Lotus 1-2-3 for Windows and Microsoft Word offer macro languages that enable you to collect a series of program commands in a single module, not unlike a program, and when you issue the command to start that module, the commands automatically execute as if you were at the keyboard typing them yourself.

Some Windows applications even support a Visual Basic–like interface that lets you not only collect the application's own commands, but also enables you to build a complete application in Visual Basic that controls the application, creates and manages data within the application, and produces output. You'll learn all about these automation languages in this hour.

The highlights of this hour include:

- How the batch language automated older DOS tasks
- How mainframe programmers control the operating system
- What macro languages common Windows applications support
- When keyboard-based macros are appropriate
- When to use Visual Basic for Applications
- How to use the Windows scripting language

Batch: The One That Started Everything

NEW TERM From the very first PC (the original IBM PC), MS-DOS supported a *batch language* that automated certain DOS tasks. Today, DOS windows inside Microsoft Windows 98 still support batch files. *Batch files* contain commands from the batch language. A batch file is not actually a program like a C program; it is never compiled because the operating system executes the batch file interpretably. Although interpreting batch commands takes longer than executing compiled code, batch files are rarely long enough to take very long to execute, especially given the speed of today's computers.

Even if you could compile a batch file, the batch file's execution speed is limited to the speed of the operating system in handling the batch commands. In other words, if the operating system takes a moment to delete a file as is often the case (the operating system must perform several checks before it deletes a file), compiling the file deletion command will not speed up the process but only speeds up the ability of the operating system to read the command.

> Some third-party software developers have developed batch file compilers. The compilers don't speed up execution, necessarily, but programmers could distribute the compiled batch file with an application to control the startup and shutdown of the application without the users being able to change the batch file as they could do if a regular, interpreted batch file were used.

Batch File Usage

Batch files always end in the .BAT filename extension. You can execute batch files directly from the DOS prompt, from the Windows Start, Run dialog box, and you can even assign an icon to a batch file and execute the batch file from the Windows Start menu or from the desktop. By selecting the icon, Windows automatically opens a DOS window and begins executing the batch file.

The most typical command that is found in a batch file is the name of a program. Whenever DOS encounters a program name in a batch file, at a point in the batch file's execution, DOS executes the program. For example, a DOS program stored in the file EDIT.COM comes with Windows. EDIT.COM is a DOS-based text editor. Any program that ends in the .COM or .EXE filename extension begins executing if you type its filename (with or without the extension) at the DOS prompt or in a batch file. If the word EDIT or EDIT.COM appears on a line in a batch file, DOS will start the DOS editor at that point in the batch file's execution. When you exit the editor, the batch file resumes its execution and continues if other batch commands are in the file.

DOS, unlike Windows, never allows two programs to run at once and one batch command never executes until the previous command is completely finished and control is returned to DOS from that previous command.

As with all programs that end with the .COM or .EXE filename extension, batch files, all of which end in the .BAT extension, execute when you type their name with or without the .BAT extension. Therefore, you can start executing a batch file named DOIT.BAT from the DOS prompt by typing DOIT or DOIT.BAT (you can also mix uppercase and lowercase letters as DOS does not distinguish between them).

Starting with Windows 95, if a DOS batch file contained the name of a Windows program, the Windows program executed. Therefore, you can not only execute DOS programs and commands from within a batch file but you can also trigger the execution of a Windows application.

18

JCL: The Original Batch File Language

If you've ever worked in a mainframe environment, you've heard the term *JCL* (for *Job Control Language*). JCL to a mainframe is like the DOS batch language to a PC. JCL controls the automatic execution of mainframe programs and commands.

JCL has been around since the 1960s. If you go to work for a large organization that uses a mainframe, you'll certainly need to know some JCL. Some college programming degrees still require a class in JCL for mainframe-based degrees. Although you may never have to master all the ins and outs of JCL, you'll almost certainly encounter JCL at some point and will probably have to change the JCL in programs that you run across and use.

Reviewing the Batch Language

Although you'll never have to become a batch command wizard, just for a review, Table 18.1 lists a few of the more common batch commands that DOS supports.

TABLE 18.1 SOME COMMON BATCH FILE COMMANDS

Command	Description
Any DOS command	Any valid DOS command, such as COPY or FORMAT, works in a batch file.
Any program name	Any executable program or batch filename (with or without the file's extension) works in a batch file.
call *batch file*	Pauses the current batch file and begins another, just as Visual Basic uses Call to execute a procedure. When the called batch file completes its task, control returns to the current batch file. If you don't use call but place a batch filename as a command in another batch file, the first batch file's execution stops as soon as the named batch file begins. The call batch command makes the second batch file operate as a subroutine.
cls	Erases the DOS window.
echo	Specified as either echo on (the default) or echo off and determines whether DOS displays each batch command onscreen as the batch file executes. Turning off the echoing of commands keeps the screen clear of clutter but also makes debugging batch files more difficult.
pause *message*	DOS displays the message following the pause and displays Press any key to continue on the next line. The batch file pauses and waits for the user to press a key before continuing with the next command. pause is useful when the user has to indicate that an action has occurred, such as a disk being put in a disk drive.
rem	Remarks that document the batch file. The remarks will appear during the execution unless you've turned off the echoing of commands.

Suppose you want to send a wide directory listing to your printer. You might create a batch file named PRDIR.BAT that contains the commands shown in Listing 18.1.

LISTING 18.1 BATCH FILES DON'T HAVE TO BE LARGE TO BE HELPFUL

```
1: rem Wide Directory Print
2: echo off
3: pause Turn on your printer
4: dir c:\/w>prn:
```

When you run PRDIR.BAT from a DOS window or when you assign a Windows icon to the batch file and execute the batch file, the following output occurs on the screen:

OUTPUT

```
c:\>rem Wide Directory Print

c:\>pause Turn on your printer
Press any key to continue . . .
```

After you turn on your printer and press a key, a wide directory listing of your root directory will print.

Given that batch files are in use much less today than before because the DOS environment is much less important today, mastering the batch language is less critical than before when DOS was the most common environment in which you executed programs. So why do we bother discussing them? Primarily because the nature of batch files is easy to grasp and other kinds of scripting languages work in a similar, interpreted manner. Also, some programs, such as some games on the market, do still come in a DOS version, although most programs are Windows-compatible. In addition, some people still prefer to work with DOS commands more than visual tools such as Windows Explorer for some things. For example, deleting a series of files, in a folder, that have similar names is easier to do using DOS wildcard characters than using the Windows Explorer.

Not only games, but also some utilities such as virus scans and disk-repair programs are sold today for the DOS mode only. The multitasking of Windows sometimes causes these programs to report incorrect results so their authors return to the DOS mode for the program's execution. If you know a few batch commands, you can wrap some commands around the program and create backup files, clear the screen, or possibly process two or more disk drives using the utility without intervening as you'd otherwise have to do.

Macro Languages

There is not one single macro language. Many software applications support their own unique, nonstandard macro language. At its most basic level, a macro language may do nothing more than imitate keystrokes the user of the application might type. The macro, therefore, is a keystroke-recording feature. Once you record a series of common keystrokes in a macro file, you then can trigger those keystrokes by executing the macro within the application. Almost all today's Windows applications enable you to assign a new toolbar button or create and assign an Alt+*keystroke* to a macro so that you can start a macro's execution with a single click or keystroke.

The Need for Macros

Suppose you find yourself saving a backup of a Word document to drive D: every few minutes. The original document appears on C:, and the built-in Ctrl+S keystroke saves the document to C:, but just for safety you want to save the file to drive D: once in a while so that a second backup is available.

The following lists the steps you must perform, including the necessary menu commands and values you might type, to perform such a backup save to drive D:

1. Select File, Save As. The Save As dialog box appears.
2. Press the Home key to move the text cursor to the beginning of the default file-name. The file normally saves the file in the current folder and disk although you are going to override that location.
3. Type d:\ so that Word will save the file on the D drive.
4. Click Yes to override your previous backup file on D. (This assumes that you've saved the file at least once before in D's root folder.)
5. Click the OK button to save the file. The default disk drive and folder will now be on D so you must restore the default to its original location.
6. Select File, Close to close the file from Word's work area.
7. Select File, 2. The 2 on the File menu will be the second-to-the-last file you edited which was the file in its original location before you saved it to D. You are now working, once again, with the original file from drive C and you've placed a copy on drive D.

Notice the last two commands had to close the document and reload it from drive C. Otherwise, your edits would all go to D after you'd saved the file to D and you would not have two copies being saved during your word processing session.

Using a Keyboard Macro

NEW TERM   If you use Microsoft Word, you can follow along with this series of steps to see the screens that appear. Performing these seven steps every few minutes to save the backup file and still keep the original file in its original location is tedious indeed. Instead of typing these keystrokes over and over, let Word record them as a keyboard macro that you can easily trigger. A *macro* is an interpreted set of commands that an application supports for tasks that you automate. Word, as well as most Windows applications that support macros, will enable you to record your keystrokes in a macro file and later play those keystrokes by executing the macro's commands.

Here are the steps you would use in Microsoft Word 97 to record the macro:

1. Select Tools, Macro, Record New Macro. Word displays the Record Macro dialog box shown in Figure 18.1.

Figure 18.1.

Word can record your keystrokes and store them in a macro file.

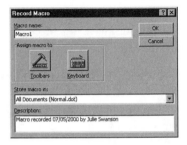

2. Click the Keyboard button to assign the macro you're about to record to a keystroke combination.

3. Press Ctrl+D or another keystroke that you want to use to trigger the macro. If the keystroke is already assigned (such as Ctrl+S, which is already assigned to File, Save) Word tells you about the previous assignment and gives you a chance to replace the previous assignment or type a new keystroke.

4. Press Enter to begin recording the macro. Word places a small, floating Stop Recording dialog box on your screen.

5. Perform your macro's step-by-step commands. If you are following along with this example and are creating a macro to save the current Word documents back on drive D, perform the keystrokes listed in the previous steps.

6. After you've finished typing all the macro's commands, click the Stop Recording button on the floating dialog box to let Word know that the macro is completed. (Word will not save the click of the Stop Recording button in the macro.)

When you press the macro's keystroke, Word runs the macro as if you were at the keyboard typing all the keystrokes yourself.

The keyboard macros are probably the easiest to create because you only need to type the keystrokes that you'd normally type and select the commands you'd normally select to place that command in the macro. The macro can contain *any* keystroke you'd normally use in Word, even keystrokes that enter text in a dialog box or move the focus from one control to another.

Obviously, creating generic keyboard macros is not always trivial. In other words, for a keyboard macro to work, you must ensure that the application is ready to receive those exact keystrokes. Using the previous example, if you had never saved the document to drive D, Word would not prompt you to replace the originally saved backup with the new

18

version (in step 4 of the file-backup steps). The macro assumes that the prompt to replace the backup file will always appear, and if that prompt does not appear, the macro will still assume the prompt is onscreen and will try to select the Yes button when none appears. Such bugs are not always easy to find and generally require a new macro that works in some situations or possibly you may have to replace the original macro with a brand new one that does not assume the same environment.

In addition, keyboard-recording macros are just that; they record *keyboard* actions but not *mouse* actions. No mouse clicks or moves are recorded with the keyboard macros so you must use only keyboard commands when recording macros. The graphic elements and windows that you might normally use might differ each time you run the application so you should not and cannot perform a mouse action while recording a macro.

> Most properly written Windows applications provide keyboard-equivalent ways of performing mouse actions. Therefore, you can use the keyboard in a recorded macro to do almost anything you might otherwise do with a mouse.

Every keyboard-based macro language is different for every application because every application has somewhat different keystroke requirements for issuing commands. For example, Lotus 1-2-3 uses a different set of menu commands than Excel to print a worksheet. Therefore, keyboard macros differ from program to program.

Non-Keyboard Macros

NEW TERM Not all macros are keyboard based, however. In addition to keyboard-recording macros, many macros provide additional commands that you can issue that go beyond the simple selection of menu options. Again, each application may support its own set of macro commands, but Microsoft thought enough of Visual Basic to standardize Visual Basic among all applications a few years ago. The result was *Visual Basic for Applications*, or *VBA*.

Even non-Microsoft products have began to provide support for VBA as the internal macro language for the application so that eventually, if the VBA trend continues, all applications could, in theory, support the very same macro language. (The keyboard-recording macro capabilities will probably remain and will differ among the applications, however, because the menus among applications are always somewhat different.) The next section explains more about VBA.

Visual Basic for Applications (VBA)

Microsoft has offered Visual Basic for Applications for several years in its major software packages, such as the Office products. The problem in the beginning was that no VBA standard existed. Therefore, even a Visual Basic programmer did not automatically know the VBA language because VBA differed not only from Visual Basic, but also among the software programs that used VBA.

Beginning with Visual Basic 5, Microsoft began to combine both Visual Basic and VBA, as well as all the products that support VBA, so that a Visual Basic programmer now knows not only Visual Basic but also VBA. VBA now follows the same standards and conforms to the same rules, syntax, commands, functions, procedures, and control capabilities as Visual Basic. As a matter of fact, when you want to write a VBA program to control Word in some way, the screen that appears in Word looks just like a Visual Basic screen (see Figure 18.2).

FIGURE 18.2.

When you write a macro in VBA to control an application, you use Visual Basic's own environment.

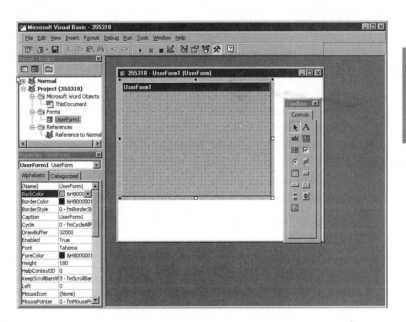

18

The VBA environment doesn't supply all the bells and whistles, such as a profiler tool and extra controls, that the standalone Visual Basic development package supplies (see Hour 24, "The Future of Programming," for a description of profilers and other tools), but the fundamental language tools are all there for VBA that you find in Visual Basic.

Given that Visual Basic for Applications is now identical to Visual Basic, Microsoft is moving away from the term VBA or Visual Basic for Applications and is starting to use only Visual Basic for all Visual Basic–based implementations. Nevertheless, this tutorial will continue to use VBA or Visual Basic for Applications to distinguish the Visual Basic you use to control applications from the Visual Basic system that you use to write standalone Windows applications.

You might wonder how VBA can supplement and add functionality to a Windows application. Excel supports VBA, but with all the worksheet power and commands that Excel already provides without VBA, how could a VBA program controlling an Excel environment and worksheet add any benefit to the Excel user?

Suppose at the end of the month, an Excel user consolidates 25 division's sales report worksheets into a companywide summary worksheet. Such a consolidation of cells could be tedious, but certainly requires only fundamental Excel skills. To automate the task, the employee could easily record a keyboard macro to load each of the 25 division worksheets and update the summary worksheet.

In the previous section on macros, you learned some of the problems with keyboard macros. The most critical part of using a keyboard macro successfully is making sure that the macro runs in exactly the same environment and with the same set of worksheets and columns each time. The keyboard macro has no room for ambiguity. For example, what if one division was to shut down for remodeling one month? The keyboard macro that always expects and consolidates all 25 divisions would either consolidate a blank worksheet or one that doesn't even exist producing an error.

Because Visual Basic is a complete programming language, the employee who needs such a consolidation report might want to create a series of controlling commands that are not as literal as a keyboard macro. Perhaps the VBA code could read in each worksheet and, if data other than zeros appear for the totals, add that worksheet to the summary but ignore any worksheet that had zeros for totals (which indicates that the division had no activity for that period). Such a VBA macro, which is actually a Visual Basic program with code capable of analyzing worksheets, would come in handy.

When you use VBA in an application, the VBA language is identical to Visual Basic but some extensions to the language must be made available by the application's authors as well. For example, the fundamental Visual Basic language supports variables, controls, and data files but contains no direct support for worksheet files or cell processing. Therefore, the Excel implementation of VBA will provide some support for reading and writing worksheet cells and data files.

For example, in Excel, a collection of worksheets can appear in the same workbook. VBA distinguishes the worksheets from one another using a subscript. `Worksheets(1)` would be the first worksheet, `Worksheets(2)` would be the second worksheet in the workbook, and so on. You can access a worksheet by name instead of by the subscript by placing the name in parentheses such as `Worksheets("Division1")`. A single cell or range of cell are referenced by the `Range` keyword so the first cell in a worksheet named `Division14` would be `Worksheets("Division14").Range("A1")` and the cell value works just like a variable or control property because you can assign to or from the cell. To place the value of `25` in the cell, you could write this assignment statement:

```
Worksheets("Division14").Range("A1") = 25
```

All the Visual Basic–based event procedures work and you can even design a visual interface to a worksheet by adding controls to a form that respond when the user clicks a command button or selects from a list box. The event procedure code that you write for the event procedures might process worksheet cells instead of variables as a standard Visual Basic application might process, but the idea is the same. Therefore, you have all the power of a full-fledged Windows programming language with a visual interface that is capable of manipulating Excel worksheet data.

NEW TERM Each Windows application that supports Visual Basic for Applications provides its own object model. The *object model* is the collection of objects that are specific to that application. For example, Word would have document objects that can contain special attributes such as boldfaced text and Excel would have worksheet objects as described previously. VBA uses the application's object model to store, retrieve, and analyze data in the application's format.

18

Scripting in Windows

NEW TERM Although Windows doesn't support the same kind of batch language that DOS does, Windows 98 does provide a start with a controlling language called *Script* or *Windows Scripting Host* (*WSH*). WSH is a set of commands you can store in a file that controls Windows applications and provides some functionality with controlling activities that take place in Windows.

NEW TERM One of the places where the Windows scripting language helps the most does not fall in the typical automated command and program-launching category. Windows scripting has played a major role for several years in controlling dial-up access to online providers. Online services such as The Microsoft Network and America Online require different protocol commands. *Protocol* refers to the way that one computer communicates with another. America Online requires a certain stream of characters to be sent to its computers when someone dials up AOL from home with a PC. The Microsoft Network requires a series of different characters. Not only must your PC be able to communicate the proper protocol to the service you are dialing, but also other dial-up factors may be required. Perhaps you must dial a certain combination of digits to access a long-distance carrier before you dial up an online service if that service is in another calling area.

Creating a communications script file can be tricky because by its very nature, online communications is fairly technical. The Windows scripting language comes with its own help file located in your Windows folder called Script.doc. You can open this file by using WordPad. In Script.doc, you will see that the script language looks a lot like C in the way that the language supports multiple procedures. Fortunately, the script language is even easier than C because the scripting language supports high-level communications commands such as the `waitfor` command that watches your communications port and waits for a signal to come through from the remote computer.

Listing 18.2 shows the script file necessary to communicate with the CompuServe online service. You don't have to write this file yourself, fortunately; instead, the file comes with the CompuServe service when you install the CompuServe access software.

LISTING 18.2   A SCRIPT FILE CONTAINS A UNIQUE COMMUNICATIONS LANGUAGE

```
 1: ;
 2: ; This is a script file that demonstrates how
 3: ; to establish a PPP connection with CompuServe,
 4: ; which requires changing the port settings to
 5: ; log in.
 6: ;
 7:
 8: ; Main entry point to script
 9: ;
10: proc main
11:
12:     ; Set the port settings so we can wait for
13:     ; non-gibberish text.
14:
15:     set port databits 7
16:     set port parity even
17:
18:     transmit "^M"
19:
20:     waitfor "Host Name:"
21:     transmit "CIS^M"
```

```
22:
23:    waitfor "User ID:"
24:    transmit $USERID, raw
25:    transmit "/go:pppconnect^M"
26:
27:    waitfor "Password: "
28:    transmit $PASSWORD, raw
29:    transmit "^M"
30:
31:    waitfor "One moment please..."
32:
33:    ; Set the port settings back to allow successful
34:    ; negotiation.
35:
36:    set port databits 8
37:    set port parity none
38:
39: endproc
```

Even though you may not understand script commands, you can glance through Listing 18.2 and fairly easily follow the script. The script first sets some communications port parameters and then transmits a ^M character (^M mimics the Ctrl+M keystroke first required by CompuServe when you make a connection). When CompuServe sends the user ID request to the user's PC, the user's ID and password (stored in system variables named $USERID and $PASSWORD respectively, set up when the user first installed CompuServe) are sent to the CompuServe computers. Once logged in, final communications port settings are specified. When the script file terminates, the user is logged into to CompuServe and controls the session from that point on.

Most online communication services supply their own script so you'll rarely have to write a script file for communications. Nevertheless, if you want to access a company mainframe or a friend's PC, you may want to create a script file, possibly by making a copy of one that already exists and modifying the copy, so that you can automate the protocol needed to access the remote PC.

All script files require the .SCP filename extension.

When you want to automate an online session, study Script.doc to learn the scripting language that controls protocol and study any examples that exist on your PC (use the Windows Start menu's Find command to look for any files that end with the .SCP extension). You are probably better off modifying an existing script file than starting anew with your own until you become better acquainted with the script language.

Beginning with Windows 98, the Windows Scripting Host gained new commands so that users and programmers could take the Windows automation beyond online communications. The WSH now has the ability to work with Windows objects such as the file system, icons, and windows. One of the most powerful new features of WSH is its ability to support ActiveX objects so that the language can manipulate and work with virtually any Windows application's objects. (Hour 19, "Internet Programming Concepts," explains more about ActiveX controls.)

> The ability to work with ActiveX objects gives the WSH language the ability to manipulate worksheets, word processor documents, and even database tables.

Unlike the scripting language you saw earlier that controls online communication connections, the WSH supports *several different scripting languages*. In the next hour's lesson, you will see examples of VBScript, a scripting language based on Visual Basic. In addition, WSH will execute script files written in JavaScript (sometimes called JScript), as well as others. The future of Windows scripting is uncertain due to the new nature of the language but programmers will often be able to supplement their applications with installation scripts and system-management scripts that prepare the user's computer for the application.

Summary

Several interactive languages exist to control system functions. These languages such as DOS's batch language, JCL, and the Windows scripting languages, enable you to automate a series of commands to make your use of the system and common tasks such as logging into online services much simpler. If you find yourself typing the same operating system commands, consider automating the task with a scripting language.

Not only can you automate operating system tasks but also many applications include an automation macro language. For example, you can automate the Microsoft Office products by recording the keystrokes of commands that you type. You can also write background applications in Visual Basic for Applications, a language that is finding its way into many Windows applications.

The next hour describes how you can use your programming skills to write Internet applications.

Q&A

Q **How often will I have to write a script file to communicate with another computer?**

A Rarely, if ever. Some power users and programmers never write script files and many don't even know that script files automate online protocol. Communications script files used to be more important than they are today because online services supply their own, and even Windows comes with several script files that enable you to communicate with remote computers more easily than you would be able to without the script files.

Q **How important is it for me to learn a scripting language?**

A Now that the scripting language has become powerful enough to work with system and ActiveX objects, and now that Windows supports script language such as VBScript and JavaScript, you may begin seeing non-communications scripts appear with Windows applications.

In addition, you might want to automate operating system tasks that you used to perform using step-by-step commands. There is a small script language war waging VBScript against JavaScript and the ultimate winner isn't obvious yet. Perhaps even another script language will appear that takes over completely. In the meantime, learning one of the scripting language, especially if you've already written Visual Basic or Java programs, will supplement your programming skill set.

18

Workshop

The quiz questions are provided for your further understanding. For the answers, see Appendix A, "Answers to End of Chapter Questions."

Quiz

1. What kinds of commands are possible in the batch language?

2. What purpose does a batch file's name serve in its execution?

3. True or false: A Windows icon can trigger the execution of a batch file.

4. What is the mainframe equivalent of the PC-based batch language?

5. What does *VBA* stand for?

6. What two kinds of macros are usually available in applications?

7. How do you usually save keystrokes in a macro file?

8. True or false: The VBA language is compatible with Visual Basic.

9. How does the object model help VBA applications control applications?

10. What kind of tasks has the Windows Scripting Host language generally controlled through the years?

HOUR 19

Internet Programming Concepts

The Internet is no longer a fad. It is a vital part of business, entertainment, and general communication. As time passes, the Internet becomes more active and supports more features than ever before. You can obtain the latest news, analyze real-time stock quotations, listen to radio broadcasts, and talk on an Internet phone to someone in another country.

All Internet activities require underlying programs. Several ways exist to write applications for the Internet. In this hour, you will learn how to develop Internet applications. Internet programming technology changes rapidly. The technology that you learn today will probably change tomorrow. One of the ways to stay abreast of Internet programming is to master the terminology first and this hour's lesson focuses primarily on the terms that you'll need to know to master Internet programming.

The highlights of this hour include:

- Why Internet programming is so important today
- How the Internet handles connections between computers

- How data travels around the Internet and locates its destination
- Why Mosaic browsers changed the nature of the Internet
- How to use the HTML language to generate and format Web pages
- Why scripting languages have become important for Internet technology
- How to add an ActiveX Web browser to any Internet application that you create in Visual Basic

Internet Programming Considerations

After you understand Internet-related terminology, you'll have little trouble understanding the technology required to program Internet applications. It's impossible to understand Internet-based programming if you don't have a grasp of the hardware and software technology related to Internet communications.

> Keep in mind that the Internet isn't a network but a network of networks. Think of the *Internet* as being an *interconnected network*. The most important aspect of Internet communications requires locating the correct computer at the other end of an intended message.

Because communication between computers is the ultimate goal of the Internet, whether the data is text, graphics, numbers, sound, or video, the data is always sent along a serial wire from one computer to the next until the final machine receives the signal. Unlike a printer cable, the cables between computers, which in most cases are ultimately phone cables, transmit only a single bit of information at a time. Binary 1s and 0s are all that travel the lines between Internet computers. Fortunately, the programming languages behind many Internet applications hide the low-level binary data foundation of Internet communications.

> **NEW TERM** Although communications technology ultimately sends only one bit at a time back and forth between two computers, almost all Internet connections are *full duplexed*, meaning that you can issue commands and send them while the remote computer sends results to you from a previous request of yours. The speed of today's computers makes this possible. Although the wire only allows one bit at a time to be sent from either computer, the Internet connection can combine these single bits at high-speeds to make it appear to the user that data is travelling back and forth at the same time.

Internet Connections

Several ways exist to connect to the Internet. Modems are still one primary contact for end-users. Many businesses install high-speed connections to the Internet. Some users even receive Internet signals from high-speed satellite dishes. The serial method of data communications means that the faster the connection, the faster a user will receive and transmit Internet data.

Your Internet applications won't need to distinguish between the ways that a computer interacts with the Internet. The type of connection is unimportant except that you must keep in mind that not all users will have fast Internet access. Therefore, as you develop Internet applications, remember to keep your applications as efficient as possible. Graphics and video can take awhile to load on the user's machine if the connection is slow. The Internet applications that you write should enhance Web pages, not make users less likely to view the Web page due to the sluggish load time.

NEW TERM The way that a computer correctly receives the signal that another computer sends to it is via *point-to-point* connections, often called *PPP* connections. Switches exist all along the communication routes between Internet connections. The exact combination of switches must be made all along a data path between two computers connected to the Internet when a signal is to travel from one Internet machine to another.

> This PPP connection is used not only for sending and receiving email, but for communicating all Internet information back and forth between computers. Web pages and Internet programs themselves must travel an appropriate set of switches before they appear on the computer which is to receive the signal.

19

Internet Communications

NEW TERM When one Internet-based computer communicates with another, as happens when an Internet server transmits an Internet program in the form of a Web page, the data is rarely if ever sent all at once. Instead, the server breaks up the message into *packets* of data. The short packets enable the receiving machine to collect the packets and relay the proper receipt of the packet before the server sends the next packet. Error-correction is made simpler and a bad packet transmission can be re-sent before too much time passes.

The routing of data to and from Internet computers works a lot like the air travel between cities all over the world each day. Many people might, for example, travel from Chicago to New York, among other towns, but not all travel at the same time. Instead a small group, or packet of people, travels throughout the day on different flights.

NEW TERM Billions of packets travel from computer to computer every few minutes. The biggest challenge isn't the transmission or receipt of packages but that the proper recipient gets the packet that was sent to that recipient and not another. Often, a computer doesn't receive a packet but sends the packet down the line to the next computer on the Internet. The way that a packet gets to its proper location is through a value known as a *packet address*. Each computer connected to the Internet has its own unique Internet address just as each postal address is unique. If a computer receives a packet but the packet's address doesn't match that of the computer, the computer sends the message on down the line until the packet address matches the intended computer's Internet address. Fortunately, data transmits at the speed of light (even though modems do their best to slow things down at times!) so the transmission of data packets occurs quickly enough to make the Internet a viable communications tool.

Unless you write extremely low-level Internet applications, you will rarely need to concern yourself with packets and packet addressing. The previous discussion simply informs you of how Internet computers communicate between each other. If you ever need to write system-level programs that perform connections to various addressed Internet computers, you now have a high-level understanding of the connection and packet processes.

The Need for Simple Navigation

NEW TERM If you've traversed the Internet the past few years, you probably explored *home pages*. Home pages are graphical Internet screens with hot spots that you click to move around the intricate Internet's Web pages. Your Web browsing software takes you on a journey through an intricate graphical maze (a spider web of interrelated connections, hence the term *Web*). An Internet *site* might contain several Web pages; the first screen that you visit for any site generally is that site's home page. The home page often contains links to other pages on the site and to other home pages on the Internet.

For example, if you visit Microsoft's Web site at www.microsoft.com, you'll see Microsoft's home page. The mouse cursor changes shape when you move it over a hypertext link to another page or to a definition box, which pops up when you click the mouse. Figure 19.1 shows Microsoft's home page.

 This 24-hour tutorial doesn't require you to be an Internet guru to understand Internet programming concepts. Nevertheless, it's assumed that you've used the Internet enough to understand home pages and maneuver around the *WWW* (*World Wide Web* or just *Web*).

FIGURE 19.1.

Web pages are graphical and often connected to other sites.

19

NEW TERM Each page that you see on the Web is located *somewhere* on someone's computer. How in the world does your Web browser find the correct page? Each Web site contains a unique address called the *URL* (*Uniform Resource Locator*). Instead of requiring that you type each page's URL (which can become quite lengthy), the current page's hypertext links direct your Web browsing software to the next URL that you want to display. Literally, surfing the Web is as easy as flipping through pages in a book.

 The Web works a lot like the Windows hypertext help system. By clicking hypertext links (sometimes called *hot spots*) or by directing users to another page, you can maneuver throughout the World Wide Web just as you do with online help. Instead of viewing another help screen from your

> application's directory, however, you could be viewing an Italian museum's images of its masterpieces.

The URL Web page addresses are not the same as the Internet computer addresses that you read about in the previous section. A computer at one Internet address might contain several Web pages that the computer serves to others surfing the Web. The Web page addresses often begin with the prefix http://, such as http://www.microsoft.com, although the prefix is usually no longer required by most Web browsers.

The first Web browsers on the market were known as Mosaic browsers, named after the first true Internet graphical browsing program called Mosaic. Students at the University of Illinois at Urbana-Champaign created Mosaic for the National Center for Supercomputing Applications (NCSA). Mosaic took the Web one giant leap forward, making Web crawling (Internet style, of course!) accessible to anyone with an Internet connection and the Mosaic software. The Mosaic-based browsers are still in use, notably with Microsoft's Internet Explorer and Netscape's Navigator, although today's browsers have greatly extended the Web-page programming language that you'll learn about in the next section.

HTML Programming

NEW TERM A Web page might contain text, graphics, icons containing hot spots that the user clicks, and multimedia content. One of the goals of Web page designers is to make Web pages appear uniform no matter what kind of computer the user uses (or, more accurately, which *platform* the user uses, which might be a PC or a mainframe with one of a number of operating systems). The *HTML (HyperText Markup Language)* is a machine-independent language that Web developers use to design Web pages. A page's HTML listing is actually a set of text commands that, when viewed with a Web browser, produces a Web page that conforms to the look the author intended.

Following an HTML Example

Listing 19.1 contains some of the HTML commands that produced Figure 19.1's Web page.

LISTING 19.1   HTML COMMANDS

```
 1: <html>
 2: <head>
 3: <meta http-equiv="Content-Type"
 4: content="text/html; charset=iso-8859-1">
 5: <meta http-equiv="PICS-Label"
 6: content='(PICS-1.1 "http://www.rsac.org/ratingsv01.html" l gen true
    comment "RSACi North America Server" by "inet@microsoft.com" for
    "http://www.microsoft.com/" on "1997.06.30T14:21-0500" r (n 0 s 0 v 0
    l 0))'>
 7: <meta name="KEYWORDS"
 8: content="products; headlines; downloads; news; Web site; what's new;
    solutions; services; software; contests; corporate news;">
 9: <meta name="DESCRIPTION"
10: content="The entry page to Microsoft's Web site. Find software,
    solutions and answers. Support, and Microsoft news.">
11: <meta name="MS.LOCALE" content="EN-US">
12: <meta name="CATEGORY" content="home page">
13: <meta name="GENERATOR" content="Microsoft FrontPage Express 2.0">
14: <title>Welcome to Microsoft's Homepage</title>
15: </head>
16:
17: <body bgcolor="#FFFFFF"
18: style="margin-top: 0px; margin-left: 0px; margin-right: 0px">
19:
```

Take a moment to see how Listing 19.1's HTML commands produced Figure 19.1's Web page. The Microsoft home page is fairly advanced so the HTML listing looks a little forbidding. Nevertheless, as you compare the HTML code to the home page, you'll see some ways that the HTML language produced parts of the Web page.

NEW TERM The terms within the angled brackets, (< and >) are called *tag references* (or *tag commands*). Tag references are central to the HTML program. Many commands contain a beginning and ending tag (a forward slash, /, always precedes an ending tag). A non-bracketed text item is a literal constant, such as a title that is to appear on the Web page. The tags primarily determine the placement of figures, the format of text, links to other Web sites, and table information when different sets of data are to appear on the same page. For example, <TITLE> marks the beginning of a title and </TITLE> marks the end. Many of the tags in Listing 19.1 are formatting tag codes that specify font style and size instructions for the Web browser.

Tags don't contain formatted text; they offer formatting instructions that your Web browser is to follow. Therefore, when your Web browser sees the <CENTER> tag, your Web browser knows to center the text that runs up to the subsequent </CENTER> ending tag.

19

When you navigate to a Web page, the remote server sends to your browser only the HTML text and responds to the commands by formatting text appropriately and placing links and graphics images where the HTML dictates they should appear. Your browser first receives the full HTML page and then receives whatever graphics images and multimedia content are needed to complete the page. Browsers provide a Stop button that you can click to keep from receiving graphics and multimedia images for those times when you don't want to wait on them but want to read the text that has already been sent to your browser. In place of the images and multimedia content, your browser places an icon that lets you know where the image would appear if you had let the image load to your computer.

Understanding HTML

Many Web sites are a good deal simpler than Microsoft's Web pages. Don't get bogged down in HTML commands at this time because even simple HTML commands can produce quite attractive and complete Web pages. For example, consider how simple Listing 19.2's HTML code appears. You should have little trouble following the HTML commands even if HTML is new to you.

 Not only can simple HTML commands produce visually appealing Web pages, many times you don't even have to use HTML to produce a Web page today because many HTML page designers exist that buffer the HTML text from the page that you produce. For example, FrontPage is a product with which you drag items onto a screen from a toolbox and type text in text boxes to create your Web pages visually. FrontPage then translates the page you laid out into HTML commands for you. Microsoft Word and other word processors can often save documents (with formatted text as well as embedded tables, graphics, and multimedia) as HTML pages that Word translates to HTML code.

LISTING 19.2   SIMPLE HTML COMMANDS CAN PRODUCE ATTRACTIVE WEB PAGES

```
1: <HTML>
2: <HEAD>
3: <TITLE>Your Page Title</TITLE>
4: <TITLE>,</TITLE>
5: </HEAD>
6: <BODY>
7: <CENTER>
8: <H1>Fancy, yet simple!</H1><P>
```

```
 9: </CENTER>
10: <HR NOSHADE>
11: <CENTER>
12: HTML is the key to attractive Web pages. Your Web pages will
    carry with them text, images, and multimedia content that the
    HTML code formats into the resulting Web pages.
13: <CENTER>
14: <IMG SRC="Beany.gif" ALT=" ">
15: </CENTER>
16: <H1><I><A HREF=www.microsoft.com>Click here to see Microsoft's Web
    site
17: </A></I></H1><MARQUEE >This text scrolls across the
    screen<?MARQUEE><P>
18: </BODY>
19: </HTML>
```

Figure 19.2 shows the resulting Web page that Listing 19.2's HTML commands produce. As you can see, the Web page is attractive and fairly complex despite the simple HTML code that created it.

FIGURE 19.2.

A nice Web page that requires only simple HTML code.

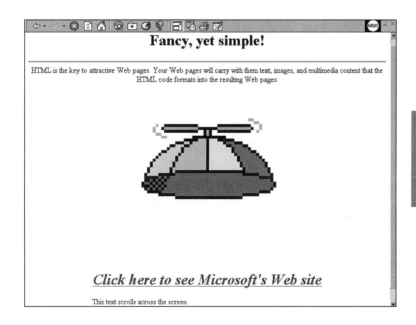

Developers add to the HTML language constantly. As the Web becomes more complex, the needs of the HTML language expands. For example, HTML did not originally support tables of information but tables are now standard. One of the most important additions to the HTML language was the ability of a Web page to become active using an embedded program. You'll learn how to embed a program directly inside HTML code in the next hour's lesson.

> The next time that you log on to the Internet, locate your menu option that lets you view the HTML source code. If you use Internet Explorer, the source display command is View, Source and if you use Netscape Navigator, the command is View, Document Source.

Transferring a packet of HTML code, such as that in Listing 19.2, is much less time-consuming than transferring a graphics image of the entire Web page. Your Web browser reads the HTML commands and then formats the text or graphics images according to their instructions. Although your browser must be more capable than a simple graphics viewer, your CPU's time is much less precious than modem downloading time.

Although several tools exist to create Web pages using modern graphical cut-and-paste methods, you can create a fancy Web page simply by using a text editor and knowing the HTML language. Often, programmers use graphical tools to lay out the overall Web page and then use a text editor to hone the HTML source code to finalize the page. Several good texts dedicate themselves to the HTML language. If you are interested, here are some of the best:

- *Sams Teach Yourself HTML in 10 Minutes* from Sams, written by Tim Evans
- *How To Use HTML 3.2* from Ziff-Davis, written by Arpa, Jian/Mullen
- *HTML Quick Reference* from Que, written by Larry Aronson

THE INTERNET: FROM TEXT TO MULTIMEDIA

The World Wide Web isn't the Internet—it is only a tool that dynamically links Web sites to one another and makes for uniform Web retrieval and navigation. The Internet is defined as the collection of interconnected computers all over the globe.

When the Internet first appeared, users had a difficult time locating information on other computers connected to the Internet. One had to be a master of the UNIX operating system to use the Internet effectively. Successful Internet usage required a mastery both of your own computer's hardware and operating system, as well as a fairly in-depth knowledge of Internet connections and an understanding of more hardware than was covered in the first part of this lesson even. All Internet retrievals required sitting at a text-based terminal and issuing commands to get to where you wanted to go.

In the early 1980s, computer users realized that additional tools were needed to make the Internet usable for more people. Not only were early text-based navigation tools cryptic to use, but they were also machine-dependent. An individual user could not often go to another computer and access information using a common interface. Internet developers began linking their information together into a simple hypertext system that enabled users to jump from topic to topic.

Given the transition of computers in the late 1980s from a text interface to a graphical user interface thanks primarily to Windows, the development of Mosaic in late 1993 finally provided the necessary commonality and graphics access to give Internet users a mouse-driven, graphical Web browsing vehicle. In addition, the Web solidified the Internet as a tool usable by the masses—both computer literate users and novices.

The New ActiveX Control

NEW TERM Even as little as two or three years ago, Web page designers often had to write Web page controlling programs in C or C++ to embed Web browsing technology in applications. No longer is that the case. Many Web-based ActiveX controls now appear in Web applications and the trend is increasing. An *ActiveX control* is, fundamentally, a small program that you can embed inside any ActiveX control-reader container. Many Windows applications support ActiveX technology so that you can extend the application by inserting the ActiveX control in the application.

For the Internet developer, ActiveX controls are important because Web browsers such as Internet Explorer support the inclusion of ActiveX controls. Therefore, if a Web page contains an ActiveX control, the user can interact with that control. You can place common Web page functions inside an ActiveX control that you write and then include that ActiveX control in all Web pages that are to use that function.

19

The ActiveX control works like objects. ActiveX controls support characteristics and behaviors you control in your program.

Perhaps the most interesting use of ActiveX controls for the Web page developer is Visual Basic's Internet control. To add Internet access to *any* Visual Basic application, you only need to drop the Internet browser control into your Visual Basic application's form window. Instead of worrying with how to connect the application to the Web, you only need to add the Internet browser ActiveX control using the Visual Basic Application Wizard. (See Hour 14, "Programming with Visual Basic," for a discussion of the Visual Basic Application Wizard.)

After you select the Internet browser and set the default home page, the Application Wizard adds the Internet control to your application. You can complete the application as you wish but when you or your user runs the application, the View, Web Browser menu command immediately opens the Web browsing window shown in Figure 19.3 and logs the user on to the Internet, if needed, using the user's default Internet service.

FIGURE 19.3.

Insert a Web browser easily in your Visual Basic applications by including the Internet browser ActiveX control.

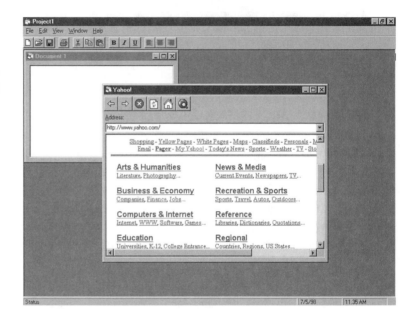

Scripting in Internet Applications

Web browsers such as Internet Explorer support not only HTML pages but also other languages and applications. The Internet Explorer browser is actually little more than an ActiveX container. Therefore, any application that can present itself to the Web browser as an ActiveX control appears inside the Web browser.

In addition to HTML, ActiveX controls, and Java programs that you'll learn about in the next hour, Internet Explorer can also support special scripting languages called JavaScript and VBScript. These special scripting languages enable you to embed controlling code inside HTML code that interacts and reacts to other objects on the Web page. Whereas JavaScript is similar to the Java language, VBScript is similar to Visual Basic. For example, Listing 19.3 shows a partial listing of a VBScript program. The code is virtually identical to Visual Basic's programming language. The HTML tags show that programmers embed VBScript right inside HTML code. The scripting languages give more analysis power to the code behind Web pages.

LISTING 19.3 VBSCRIPT IS BASED ON THE VISUAL BASIC PROGRAMMING LANGUAGE

```
 1: <SCRIPT Language="VBScript">
 2:     Call PrintWelcome
 3:     Call ModMessage
 4:
 5: Sub PrintWelcome
 6:     If Date() = "2/2/99" Then
 7:         document.write ". . . .Kathy's Birthday!"
 8:     End If
 9:     If Date() = "2/5/99" Then
10:         document.write ". . . .Eric's Birthday!"
11:     End If
12:     If Date() = "5/17/99" Then
13:         document.write ". . . .Michael's Birthday!"
14:     End If
15:     If Date() = "7/25/99" Then
16:         document.write ". . . .My Birthday!"
17:     End If
18: End Sub
19: Sub ModMessage
20:     Document.Write "<BR>This page was last modified:
        "+Document.lastModified +"</FONT><BR>"
21: End Sub
22: </SCRIPT>
```

You'll feel right at home with VBScript as you learn more about Visual Basic. (If you prefer Java, introduced in the next lesson, you may prefer to use JavaScript over VBScript.) VBScript is useful when you want to add key Visual Basic features to a Web page, such as pop-up messages, input boxes, loop-through calculations, and so on. VBScript, despite its foundation in Visual Basic, doesn't replace Visual Basic's ActiveX documents but instead loads the ActiveX documents into an HTML page for execution. Therefore, VBScript is the medium through which HTML documents locate and execute Visual Basic ActiveX document applications.

19

VBScript wasn't originally designed to be used solely as a launcher for ActiveX documents—in fact, VBScript was around before ActiveX. The loading of ActiveX documents into HTML pages is one of VBScript's many jobs, but for a VB6 programmer, the ActiveX document is perhaps VBScript's most important job.

Summary

One of the first steps in learning to program Internet applications is to learn how the underlying communications technology works. Although you may never directly manipulate packets and PPP connections, those concepts are vital to understanding terminology and hardware requirements that you may face in the future as an Internet programmer.

HTML is the code that formats Web pages so the pages properly display text and graphics. HTML is the container and formatter of all that appears on the Web page including scripts and Java code. Adding Internet browser technology is one of the foundations of today's applications due to the importance of the Internet. You can use the Visual Basic Application Wizard to insert a browser in the middle of virtually any Visual Basic application for which you want to add online capabilities.

The next hour describes how the Java language works to activate Web pages.

Q&A

Q Doesn't the always-changing nature of the Internet outdate the terminology as soon as I learn it?

A Sometimes. The low-level foundation of the Internet, however, doesn't change with time. The connection of computers to one another, the point-to-point destinations, the addressing, and the packet distribution has remained the same for several years and should continue to do so for some time. The programmable layer of the Internet changes rapidly but an understanding of the underlying hardware is vital for anyone wanting to master online programming technology.

Q Should I use a Mosaic-based browser?

A In a real sense, all current browsers are Mosaic-based. When you view an HTML-based Web page with text and graphics, you are utilizing the technology made solid with the Mosaic browser. Therefore, all Web browsers today are grounded in the Mosaic technology and most of the browsers in use today have extended the browser's capabilities far beyond those of the earlier Mosaic browsers.

Workshop

The quiz questions are provided for your further understanding. For the answers, see Appendix A, "Answers to End of Chapter Questions."

Quiz

1. Why is the Internet known as a *network of networks*?

2. How do switches produce point-to-point connections?

3. True or false: When you send a file to another Internet computer, the file travels all at once to improve efficiency and error-checking.

4. How does a packet find its destination?

5. What was the first browser to support HTML technology?

6. True or false: HTML is a formatting language.

7. How does being an ActiveX container extend the abilities of Web browsers?

8. Name two popular scripting languages.

9. Where does a program written in a script language appear?

10. How can you easily add Internet browsing capabilities to a Visual Basic application?

19

HOUR 20

Programming with Java

The world of Web pages gained an unexpected boost in capabilities when the Java language was introduced. Originally designed to be used for embedded applications such as inside computer modules in automobiles, Java quickly became the standard language used to activate Web pages. Java almost single-handedly rescued static HTML-based Web pages and turned the Web into an interactive medium with which users can interact with changing Web pages.

If you plan to work as a programmer on Web-based applications, you will have to learn Java. Java is simple to learn, however. The inventors of Java used C and C++ as their model language. Java is a small language. Its strength is in its size because small programs can load quickly along with HTML pages to present interactive Web pages to users on the Internet.

The highlights of this hour include:

- What Java is
- How Java programs travel with Web pages
- Why Java programs are small
- How Java compares to other OOP languages such as C++

- How visual programming environments, such as Visual J++, improve the Java programmer's efficiency
- Why Java programs compile differently from programs in other languages
- How to extend the built-in Java classes for your Java programs

Introducing Java

The colorful, Mosaic-like browsers changed the Internet by taking its technological development out of the exclusive hands of scientific, corporate, and educational researchers. (See the previous hour, "Internet Programming Concepts," for a discussion of why Mosaic is so important in the history of the Web.) The new Web browsers made the Internet accessible to anybody and everybody with their simple to-and-fro navigational tools and appealing graphical nature. Soon, millions of users all over the world were moving back and forth between Web sites as easily as they moved from page to page in their word processors.

The Mosaic browsers filled its job requirements better than anyone could have imagined. Yet, within two or three years, the Mosaic browser was considered obsolete due to the static nature of its screens. In other words, despite the colorful and cross-linked pages that Mosaic makes available for the world, the pages don't have enough action in them to keep users occupied; more important, the browser technology is too static to make Web sites truly come alive.

Think about this: As PCs became faster, more graphical, and began supporting multimedia, viewing only pictures and text was at first unique online but then became dull quickly. Users needed more interaction to keep their attention online.

Users seem to want more from the Internet than just a distributed set of interconnected graphical screens. Despite the Web's hypertext nature, those hypertext links simply take you from one page to another without doing any work for you except eliminating the need to type long Web page addresses. Users want real computing power coming at them from the Web sites they visit. For example, instead of reading about the rules of baseball, you might want to see a baseball game in action or get an introductory graphical tutorial on the basics of the game.

Java, developed by Sun Microsystems in the mid-1990s, changes the way that Web sites operate. Java is a programming language with language features similar to C++. Instead of using Web browsers to view data, the browsers seamlessly download programs written in Java and *those programs execute on the user's computer* as opposed to the remote server serving up the Web page. When you view a Java-enabled Web page, you see not only the usual graphical page, but you'll also be able to interact with Java programs that run on your own computer, brought to your computer via the Web's connection.

 Don't make the mistake of thinking that all the sounds and animation you've seen on the Web represent Java technology. For example, when you listen to a Web page's sound file, your own computer's sound-producing software is probably playing the sound data that comes from the Web site to your browser. Java takes computer interaction a step further than that, as you'll see in this hour.

You can write two kinds of Java programs:

- *Java applets* are small programs that travel with HTML code and execute on the Web user's computer.

- *Java applications* are complete standalone programs that don't require a Web browser or HTML to execute.

Most Java programs so far appear as Java applets. After all, the primary goal of Java is to place executable code on Web pages so that users gain more interactivity with Web sites. In addition to writing applets that appear in Web pages, you can also create standalone programs that execute without the need for a Web browser. For example, if you wanted to write a rental property management application that runs independently of an Internet connection, you could select Java as the programming language you use to develop the application.

Java Provides Executable Content

20

When working with Java, you'll often hear and read about executable content. Executable content is what Java is really all about. A Web page contains executable content via HTML commands in the form of a Java applet. Any Web page's content is executable on the target user's computer. Figure 20.1 shows an overview of an HTML document with two embedded Java applets.

When the end user enters the URL that displays the page shown in Figure 20.1 (or when the user clicks hypertext links to navigate to the page), the user's Web browsing software loads the HTML code, formats the page's text according to the HTML tags, displays any graphics images that appear on the page, and loads the executable content (as applets) so the content can execute. The executable content executes either immediately or upon a predetermined event, such as a mouse click over a hotspot on the Web page.

FIGURE 20.1.

HTML serves up Java's executable content.

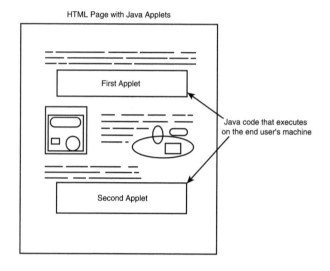

The best method of running Java applets is not always obvious to the end user. The user might think she is viewing a busy Web page when, in reality, an applet is providing animation. The look of that animation is smooth because the animation software runs on the user's computer. Because of the applet, the speed of the animation is not dependent on the download time or on Internet traffic.

As you'll see in this hour's code, the <APPLET> tag indicates that a Java-enabled applet appears inside HTML. The Java code follows the <APPLET> tag until the closing </APPLET> appears. (<APPLET> replaces an older tag, <APP>, that early releases of Java required.)

You will only be able to run applets if you have a Java-enabled browser, such as Microsoft Internet Explorer 3.0 or later or Netscape Navigator 2.0 or later.

Before Java-enabled Web pages, the user did have some interaction with the remote site. Nevertheless, that interaction was severely limited. Web page animation was controlled by the user's animation software. If a computer system had no software that could display animation, that feature of the Web page was lost for that system's user. If the user was to interact with the remote site in a question-answer session, such as order-taking, the user would often have to fill in the form completely before error-checking could be done to any of the user's responses. The user would have to trigger any and all interactions with the remote site; the response would then be limited to the remote site's speed and the current traffic flow on the Internet.

 CGI (*Common Gateway Interface*) programming provides the primitive interaction you often see on non-Java Web sites.

Surely, you have traveled to a remote Web site, downloaded software, and then logged off to execute that software. Java makes this process seamless. When you travel to a remote site, the Java software applet runs without you doing anything at all. In addition, the software applet automatically downloads itself to your PC, runs when you trigger its execution, and then goes away when you leave the Web site without taking up permanent disk space. Think of the possibilities for software developers; your users will be able to test-drive your software without running an installation program and without having to remove the software when the demonstration concludes.

Multi-Platform Executable Content

Now that you've seen how Java-enabled Web sites appear to the user, think about the requirements of such executable content. When you write a Java-based Web page, you want the code to work on the end user's remote computer *no matter what kind of computer the remote user uses*.

NEW TERM Whereas most language compilers, such as Visual C++, turn programs into machine-dependent executable programs, Java development tools don't go quite that far. All Java compilers compile your Java code into a special machine-independent module. The Java compiler compiles the code into this in-between stage called *bytecode*. Your Java-enabled Web browsing software then translates this compiled bytecode into instructions that your computer executes.

No computer can really read bytecode but each computer's Java-enabled browser can. In other words, given a Java applet's bytecode, a PC can run the applet using a Web browser and a UNIX-based minicomputer can run that very same bytecode by using its own Java-enabled browser such as HotJava. Each Web browser actually interprets the machine-dependent bytecode and then translates that bytecode into machine-specific instructions that a particular computer can understand (see Figure 20.2).

20

NEW TERM Figure 20.2 shows the Java compilation/translation scenario. You'll use the Java language to produce bytecode for a *virtual machine*, and not a specific machine, because the bytecode is machine independent. The bytecode is sent to the Web page that is to contain the applet, and when the end user requests that Web page, the user's Web browser reads the bytecode and automatically interprets the bytecode into code readable by the user's computer. The user is unaware that all this took place; he simply displays the Web page and sees the executing applet along with the rest of the Web page's content.

FIGURE 20.2.

Your Java session produces compiled byte-code that subsequent computers translate to run the program.

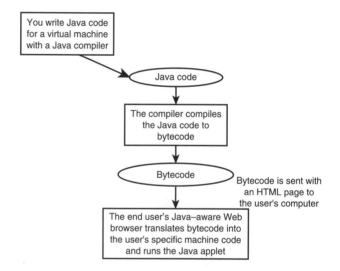

The Web browser automatically runs the Java applet. Some applets run automatically, and some run in response to a user event such as a mouse click. It's important that you realize that the user doesn't necessarily know or care that a small program is running. To the user, the Web page simply does more than one usually does and responds much more quickly, as fast as the user's computer can translate the bytecode's executable content. All traces of the program then go away when the applet ends, or when the user leaves the Web page.

Java enables the fastest response time possible for a user's interaction with a Web page. Although the user still has to wait for the Web page to download, and although the user still has to wait for the bytecode to get to the computer, the applet (comprising the Web page's executable content) executes as quickly as the user's computer can run the applet.

The user is no longer bound to download time once the computer gets the executable content. All other forms of Web page interaction, such as Web page interaction written in CGI, are slaves to download response time and current Internet activity.

Java Usage Summary

As a newcomer to Java technology, you might appreciate a summary of the process one goes through when viewing a Java-enabled Web page with a Java-aware Web browser such as Internet Explorer. Here are the steps that occur:

1. You log on to the Internet, using your Web browsing software.

2. You see your Web browser's default home page.

3. You enter a Java-enabled Web site's URL.

4. The serving computer sends the HTML document to your Web browser.

5. The HTML-based document's <APPLET> tag informs your Web browser of the Web page's Java-based executable content.

6. Your Web browser downloads graphics images from the server, if any graphics appear on the Web page.

7. Depending on how the Java applet is to be triggered (either automatically or by a user's event), the server will also send the bytecode to your computer when the time is right.

8. Your computer's Web browser interprets the bytecode and executes the Java executable content.

9. When you leave the Web page, the executable content goes away. (Some Web browsers will keep the Java code in memory for awhile in case you return to the page.)

Whereas the previous steps were based on the user's perspective, this would also be a good time to explain what you, the Java programmer, will go through to create Web pages with Java applets. Here are the general steps you'll follow:

20

1. Start your Java compiler.

2. Write the Java applet.

3. Create the HTML Web page that will contain the Java applet. Use appropriate tags to indicate the applet and its parameters.

4. Compile the Java applet. Your Java development system will place the applet in its appropriate location needed for the HTML Web page that will contain the applet.

5. If the compiler finds errors, fix them and recompile the file.

6. Test and debug the applet.

7. Store the applet and HTML on your Web server, where they will await an Internet user's request.

Security Issues

Security should always be your concern when writing online applications. In practice, Java-enabled applets could be prone to security problems if the proper precautions aren't in place. After all, when you visit a Java-enabled Web page, you aren't always sure if an applet is running or what exactly that applet is trying to do to your computer's disk or memory.

Fortunately, Sun Microsystems developed Java from inception to be a network-based programming language. Therefore, security is inherent in the language, both for the developer and for the Internet user. What follows are some of the security-related protections built into the Java language:

- A Java applet is not allowed to venture into the end user's memory areas where it doesn't belong.

- A Java applet cannot create, read, rename, copy, or write files on the end user's file system.

- A Java applet cannot connect to additional machines on the end user's network.

- Applets cannot call system routines on the end user's system.

> You can locally load and run a Java applet from your own browser by loading an applet from your own disk drive or network. In the case of a locally loaded applet, the applet does generally have permission to read and write to the local file system. In addition, some applet viewers do let the end user specify a list of files that a Web applet can access.

As you can see, Java developers do understand the need for security and the most obvious security footholds are barred from an applet's access. As more people write Java applets, additional security concerns are sure to enter into the picture.

Give Java a Spin

Now that you know more about Java, you can take a look at a Java-enabled Web page. Use Internet Explorer 3.0 (or later) or Netscape's Navigator to locate the Web site at `http://www.msnbc.com`.

This Web site first analyzes your PC to see if you've visited MSNBC before. If not, a short download of a Java-based applet (along with ActiveX controls to sweeten the Web site even more and make it more powerful) occurs. After the download completes, you'll see a colorful newspaper-like Web page control that details current news events of the day. The Java applet controls the news ticker that flashes across the screen. Figure 20.3 shows the resulting page and the location of the Java-based news ticker.

FIGURE 20.3.

Java applets can enliven a Web page.

The Java-based news ticker

Visual J++: A Sample Java System

Several implementations of Java exist. One of the most popular, due to its similarity with the Visual Basic development environment, is Visual J++, one of Microsoft's newest languages. The Visual J++ technology supports the entire Sun Microsystems–developed Java language. Visual J++ is a programming platform used to develop Java-enabled applets and standalone applications. Visual J++ includes not only a Java compiler (the tool that translates your Java programs to bytecode), but also an editor, debugger, and online documentation provider. (The end of this section explores Visual J++'s features more fully.)

Therefore, if you already know Visual Basic, you'll feel at home with Visual J++ once you learn the Java-based language. Figure 20.4 shows a sample Visual J++ session. The numerous windows and screen elements are the same as Visual Basic's because both use a standard interface called the *Microsoft Visual Studio.*

20

FIGURE 20.4.

*Visual J++,
Microsoft's Java
implementation, uses
the same environment
as Visual Basic.*

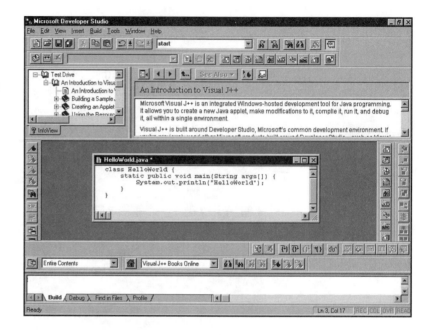

Actually, all of Microsoft's current languages use the Visual Studio platform.
Therefore, the programming tools remain the same although you can write
programs in different languages.

Several Java-based programming systems exist on the market and Visual J++'s big
advantage is that its visual interface is so similar to the other Microsoft languages that
you might use. The early Java compilers were command-line based. Surprisingly, the
graphical nature of computers and the Web did not make it to the Java language development tools until programmers used Java for about a year. In late 1995 and early 1996,
graphical Java development tools such as Visual J++ began to appear on the market.

Keep in mind that Visual J++ is not a Java replacement, nor is Visual J++ a competing
product to the Java language. In fact, Microsoft makes it clear that Visual J++ implements the very same Java technology developed by Sun Microsystems. Other vendors
sell their own implementations of the Java language, such as Borland's JBuilder and
Symantec's Café. Therefore, when you work with Visual J++, you are working with the
Java language, just as Visual C++ programmers write code in C++. Visual J++ is a complete development platform, or program development tool, with which you can create
Java-enabled applets.

To give you a better idea of what a full-fledged Java programming system can offer, here are just a few Visual J++ features you'll run across if you use the Visual J++ platform (competitors might offer some, all, or more of these kinds of features):

- The Visual J++ editor contains a word processing set of powerful text features including the usual search, cut, and paste, as well as multipane viewing, moving, and copying between windows, bookmarks, a full-screen viewer, and advanced windowing features.

- Visual J++ contains a complete online help system that includes all available documentation, including a version of Microsoft's Books Online technology.

- You'll want to take advantage of Visual J++'s interactive debugger. Online debugging enables you to specify breakpoints and examine data contents at any point in your program. You'll learn about online debuggers, such as the one in Visual J++, in Hour 22, "Debugging Tools."

- Microsoft's famous wizard technology enables you to build your initial Java applet or application just as you did with Visual Basic's Application Wizard in Hour 14, "Programming with Visual Basic." After the wizard creates the application shell, you can fill in the missing pieces to customize your own Java program requirements.

- You can use the Visual J++ applet viewer, JView, to test the applets and applications that you write before sending those applets out to the Web with your Web server.

- You can create dialog boxes and menus with the Resource Wizard.

- The included Java wizards can also create your initial HTML Web page containing your Java-based executable content.

- Visual J++ integrates the COM (Common Object Model) so that you can integrate external applications, such as a working Excel spreadsheet, into your own Java applet.

- ActiveX technology is an integrated part of Visual J++ and you can create applications that combine Java applets and ActiveX controls.

Java Language Specifics

Java is not a difficult language to learn. Java includes several pre-built procedures that you often use to perform standard operations such as I/O. Java programs are typically small because the smaller the applets are that you write, the faster those applets will load and run on the user's machine. Java is an OOP language and is identical to C++ in many ways. Both languages have common keywords, comments, and built-in functions. Java's

20

OOP nature means that you can extend language objects that others write to complete applications faster.

> Java developers borrowed heavily from C++ for Java but did improve upon many features. For example, Java, unlike C++ (or C), supports the string data type. Java also supports true arrays (C++'s arrays are actually pointers to memory that can complicate the programming process).

Java Example

Listing 20.1 shows a very simple Java program so that you can familiarize yourself with the format of the language. Right away you should recognize the C++ elements that you read about in Hour 16, "Programming with C++."

LISTING 20.1   JAVA IS VERY MUCH LIKE C++

```
 1: //**********************
 2: // A simple Java applet
 3: //**********************
 4:
 5: import java.applet.*;   // Required support files
 6: import java.awt.*;
 7:
 8: //----------------------------------------------------
 9: // Main class
10: //----------------------------------------------------
11: public class Simple extends Applet
12: {
13:   public void init()
14:   {
15:     resize(320, 240);     // Applet's window size
16:   }
17:   //-------------------------------------------------
18:   public void paint(Graphics g)
19:   {
20:     // Change subsequent text color to red
21:     g.setColor(Color.red);
22:     // Write a simple message in the window
23:     g.drawString("Very simple!", 75, 100);
24:   }
25: }
```

NEW TERM   Listing 20.1 is simple and displays the message Very simple! in red on the screen, 75 *pixels* (or *picture elements* which are the dots on the screen) from the right edge and 100 pixels from the top of the screen. The screen in this case would be whatever Java-enabled Web browser the user has who views the page with the HTML code that contains this applet.

Before going into the specifics of Listing 20.1, take a moment to consider these points:

- All Java programs are case sensitive. Therefore, if you initially name a variable `intSum`, don't refer to that variable later as `INTSUM` because Java will not recognize that both are the same.

- Java is a free-form language. You can indent and include lots of whitespace to make your programs easier to read and maintain.

- A semicolon generally follows each complete executable line. No semicolons follow comments or braces, however. Also, a class or procedure's definition line (the first line in a class or procedure) doesn't end with a semicolon because these statements define classes and procedures but don't execute or produce output.

- A pair of braces encloses a group of lines that Java treats as a single block of code. Generally, a block can appear anywhere that a single statement can appear. The braces also designate start and stop points for procedures.

These Java coding principles apply to small as well large Java programs. When you first begin writing Java programs, you may forget some of these coding conventions. A full-featured Java compiler like Visual J++ will catch simple syntax errors during and after you write your applet.

Analyzing the Code

The details of Listing 20.1 are easy to understand. All text that follows a double-slash, `//`, is comment text. In Listing 20.1, comments help divide the sections of the applet from one another as well as document some lines in the code.

The `import` commands in Listing 20.1 appear in almost every Java program that you'll write. The `import` command is analogous to the C and C++ `#include` preprocessor directive except that `import` is a Java command and not a language directive. `import` inserts classes from special class packages provided by your Java compiler. Remember that in OOP, a class defines an object. A *class package* is a collection of classes that are logically grouped together. For example, graphics routines often appear in a class package. You can use the graphics objects from the class as long as you import that class package.

20

The `import` command follows these two formats:

```
import specificPackage.specificClass;
```

```
import specificPackage.*;
```

When you know the name of a class that you want to use, you can specify that name inside the `import` command. The `specificPackage` is the name of the class package from which you want to import the class named `specificClass`.

The second format of `import` uses the `*` wildcard character to specify that you want to import *all* classes from a class package. Listing 20.1 uses this `import` format for its imported classes. The `java.applet` class package is a necessary class for you to use when the applet is to be embedded in a Web page. Therefore, you'll always import `java.applet` and all its classes at the top of every applet that you write. The `java.awt` class package contains many graphics routines that enable you to send output to a Web page's applet window. Instead of printing text onscreen, your applet must *draw the text* pixel by pixel. Listing 20.1 contains a `drawString()` function that is a class procedure defined in the `java.awt` class package.

The following line from Listing 20.1 defines a class named `Simple`:

```
public class Simple extends Applet
```

The opening brace that follows this `public` statement makes up the body of the applet's `Simple` class and the class doesn't terminate until the closing brace. A statement such as this `public` statement must appear in your applets because your applet is actually an entirely new class, from the predefined `Applet` class, that you are extending. In this example, the applet is taking the generic class called `Applet` (defined in the `java.applet` class package) and extending the class by naming the copy `Simple`; the code in the body of `Simple` is the added functionality for this newly extended class. Without the added code, `Simple` would be no different from the built-in `Applet` class and the applet would appear in the Web page but could do nothing. The new code is what makes the applet perform.

NEW TERM
The next few lines in Listing 20.1 define a new method called `init()`. (*Methods* act much like functions except that you apply the methods to objects such as the screen window object.) In reality, the listing is redefining a method that already exists. When the subclassed `Applet` became `Simple`, a method named `init()` came with the `Applet` class but does nothing except prepare the applet to run. `init()` is a method that's applied to the `Simple` class. Every Java programmer *must* redefine `init()` and almost every Java applet includes the `resize()` function in the body of `init()` as done here:

```
public void init()
  {
    resize(320, 240);    // Applet's window size
  }
```

The resize() method simply informs your class of your applet's window size in the target Web page. You can also insert any other code inside init() that you want executed right after the initial loading of the applet. resize() requires two arguments: an x- and a y-coordinate. Enter the coordinates in pixels. In Listing 20.1, the resize() function is defining the Java applet's window size (the window will appear inside the Web page on the user's machine) as 320 pixels wide by 240 pixels high.

The paint() method should appear in every applet that you create and paint() should follow init(). Your applet executes paint() every time your applet window needs redrawing. If the user hides the applet's window with another window and then unhides it, the hidden portion must reappear and paint() determines what happens every time the window is redrawn. As long as you've supplied a paint() method, and you must, you can be assured that your applet window will reappear properly with the text, colors, and whatever else that paint() puts on the window.

In Listing 20.1, the paint() method looks like this:

```
public void paint(Graphics g)
  {
    // Change subsequent text color to red
    g.setColor(Color.red);
    // Write a simple message in the window
    g.drawString("Very simple!", 75, 100);
  }
```

> Unlike init(), paint() requires an argument inside its parentheses. The argument is a value that the paint() method operates on. Although Graphics g is a strange argument, the argument represents your Web page's graphical applet window. Whatever paint() does to the value named g happens to your applet's window.

The setColor() method, therefore, sets the color for all text that will subsequently appear on the output window, g, until another setColor() appears. Although the window's background remains gray (you can change the background color also if you want), text that appears will be red. After the applet sets the text color to red, two red words appear in the applet's window due to this line:

```
g.drawString("Very simple!", 75, 100);
```

drawString() is a commonly used Java method that sends text strings to the applet's window. drawString() respects the color set by setColor() so the text, Very simple!, will appear in red. Notice the g before the method name. You could, if you opened

20

several different windows with an applet, send text to different windows by prefacing `drawString()` with each window's designated context name such as g used here for this application's single window. The two arguments that end the `drawString()` method indicate how wide and high, in pixels, the text is to appear.

You now know all there is to know about Listing 20.1's applet. You should be proud of yourself. As you can see, Java programming isn't difficult to understand but some of the statements can be tricky due to the inheritance situation brought on by OOP.

Summary

The goal of this lesson was to introduce you to the Java language. Java activates Web pages by sending small active applications, called applets, along with Web pages. Part of that introduction has to be a language overview. Unlike more traditional programming languages such as FORTRAN and Visual Basic, a Java program is almost always part of something else, most notably a Web page. The program travels with the Web page to the user's machine and executes using the user's own computing power.

You may not understand much of the Java language yet, but you can understand a simple Java program better now that you've finished this lesson. An applet is actually a subclass, or an inherited version of a predefined class that comes with the Java compiler. You add functionality to the Java `Applet` class to make the program your own.

The next hour doesn't describe a specific language, but rather, describes how the programming industry works. You'll learn about various jobs in the market that require programming and data processing skills and you'll see how the business of programming works.

Q&A

Q Do I embed my Java program code directly inside the HTML code on my Web page?

A No. HTML is only for formatting a Web page's appearance and for placing the applet in the correct location but your compiled applet, in bytecode, travels along with a Web page to the destination computer. HTML always appears and downloads in source code format whereas a Java program always downloads in bytecode format. Therefore, the two files must travel separately to the end user's computer.

Q Can a user stop my Java program from executing?

A Certain Web-based security features can keep Java applets that arrive with a Web page from executing on the user's machine. Although the Java language includes built-in security controls to keep Java authors from invading a user's machine from the Internet, the user can still keep the applet from executing by setting certain browser options.

Workshop

The quiz questions are provided for your further understanding. For the answers, see Appendix A, "Answers to End of Chapter Questions."

Quiz

1. True or false: The faster the user's computer is, the faster the Java applet that appears with the Web page runs.

2. True or false: The faster the user's computer is, the faster the Java applet downloads on the user's machine.

3. What HTML tag designates that a Java program applet is located on the Web page?

4. What is bytecode?

5. Why is the concept of a virtual machine important?

6. How does the Java language provide security support for the end user who views Java-enabled Web pages?

7. What is the purpose of the `import` command?

8. How do you send text to the screen in a Java applet?

9. Why is the `paint()` method important?

10. What is the difference between Java and Visual J++?

20

HOUR 21

How Companies Program

This hour attempts to give you an idea of how companies program computers. The focus is on the larger companies with big data processing staffs working on one or more mainframes, minicomputers, and microcomputers. You will also learn about the smaller companies and how they deal with programming staffs and other types of computer personnel.

Companies must coordinate their programming efforts to make the best use of their resources. This doesn't always mean that every program wanted by every person gets written. Actually, the allocation of programming talents is one of the data processing manager's primary tasks. You will learn about the different types of available jobs and their titles, and how those people interface with one another. After this hour, you will better understand the wording of the want ads for computer professionals, and you will get an idea of the experience needed to obtain the different jobs in the computer industry.

This hour's lesson is useful to you even if you want to work for a smaller company or start your own. The larger companies have honed the usage of data processing within the corporate umbrella, so seeing how larger companies take care of their programming requests will help you make decisions regarding the computer department you end up in.

The highlights of this hour include:

- What company computer departments are called
- Who pays for a computer department's expenses
- Which programming degree is best: a two-year or four-year degree, or a technical certificate
- How to get computer experience without a degree or training
- Why a Programmer doesn't always write programs
- What programming-related jobs exist
- How to perform a structured walkthrough
- Why data processing departments move programs into production

Data Processing and Other Departments

NEW TERM A company's data processing department often goes by several names. It is known as *DP*, *Data Processing*, *Information Services*, *Information Systems*, *IS*, and *MIS* (but usually not, strangely enough, by that acronym's meaning: *Management Information Systems*). No matter what the company's employees call the computer department, it is commonly in the center of almost every major new project the company takes on. When a company expansion, acquisition, or merger is about to take place, the data processing department must prepare for the additional computing resources needed. When an engineering project begins, data processing supplies the analysis programs for the engineers (although some engineering departments prefer to write their own programs and keep the central DP department in charge of the business side of the company). Whatever new direction a company takes, its data processing staff is usually involved in some way.

As Figure 21.1 shows, the data processing department writes programs for every other department in the company. Unless the company itself is a software-writing company (such as Symantec or Microsoft), the company's main focus is not going to be software development. The company has other objectives, but the computer department supplies the computer systems needed to keep the other departments working as effectively as they can.

FIGURE 21.1.

The data processing department writes programs for the rest of the company.

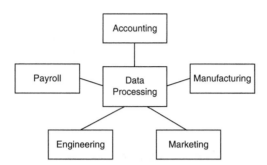

Such a corporate setup is natural. In the early years of business computing, the computer department was placed in the accounting department and governed by the accounting staff. The problem with putting the computer department under direct control of accounting is that accounting will tend to write computer systems it needs and the engineering, marketing, and upper management departments might take a back seat. This doesn't mean that the accounting department would selfishly hoard the computer resources, but the accounting bias would be natural because part of the accounting department's own budget was set aside for the computer and its people.

It was realized in the late 1960s that the data processing department was not directly tied to any one department such as accounting, but instead, computer people worked for the entire company because they developed programs that the entire company used. Therefore, standalone computer departments started appearing on the company's organizational charts. Organizations began viewing their computer departments as individual cost centers that required their own budget and autonomy. Figure 21.2 shows how the typical data processing department fits into today's organizational charts. As you can see, the data processing department is located on the same level as accounting, payroll, engineering, and the rest of the departments.

FIGURE 21.2.

The data processing department is evenly ranked with the company's other departments.

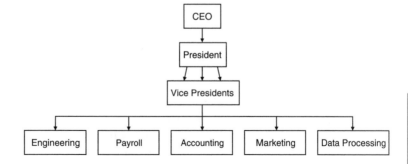

21

Despite the fact that the data processing department is now autonomous in most companies, that autonomy still doesn't ensure proper allocation of computer resources. A data processing department's resources consist of the hardware, peripheral material such as paper and tapes, and people. The people are the most expensive resource in a data processing department. Their office space, desks, supplies, personal computer equipment, telephone, benefits, and payroll costs all add up to a tidy sum.

No matter how much money a company makes, it cannot allow unlimited spending for the computer resources just described. There must be some check on the money spent in data processing. Unlike other departments, whose worth is measured in dollars received by outside customers, the company itself is the only customer of its data processing department. (Many of the accounting-related departments, such as payroll, often have a similar support role in a company.)

Paying for the Data Processing Department

NEW TERM   There are two approaches for budgeting data processing costs. They are *overhead* and *chargeback*. Overhead is the typical way in which other internal support departments are paid. The sales department's cost is paid for by goods sold (the commissions are commensurate with the sales). The engineering department's costs are paid for by breakthroughs made and eventually sold to the public. Unlike engineering and sales, the data processing department fits an internal niche, somewhat like the payroll department, in that it does nothing to generate outside revenue (unless, as mentioned earlier, the company is a computer software company).

Understanding the Overhead Approach

Most internal support departments, such as data processing, are paid for with overhead funds. That is, each department's budget includes a little extra for overhead expenses (lights, desks, paper, telephones, faxes, copying, secretarial, and data processing usage). By collecting some of each department's overhead budget, the company can pay for the data processing resources.

This overhead method of paying for data processing costs doesn't always work well. Overhead is fine for departments such as the accounting department's general ledger group, but the data processing department's skills are more in demand than are other departments'. Without checks and balances of some kind, all the other departments will want programs written with little regard to cost (after all, they've already paid their share of the overhead expense). The computer department can't hire an unlimited supply of programmers just because it receives endless requests for programs.

> There isn't enough incentive with the overhead method to curb unreason-able data processing requests. Under this method, departments from all over the company will constantly hound the computer programmers for more programs.

Understanding the Chargeback Approach

Companies have been turning away from the overhead approach to another approach called chargeback. With chargeback, the data processing center is given no funds from the overhead account (which immediately lowers the overhead expenses for all the other departments). When a department needs a program written, that department requests the program from data processing. The data processing personnel estimate the cost of writing the program and send that estimate back to the original department.

It is then up to the requesting department to accept or reject the charge for the programming. If the department wants the program badly enough, and it has the funds in its budget, that department's management can then transfer those funds to the data processing department's budget. DP then begins to work on the program.

One of the biggest advantages of the chargeback method is that a department cannot ask for the world unless it is willing to pay for it. Its own limited resources keep it from requesting more than it really needs.

> The money being transferred is really *money*. It is made up of internal funds that already belong to the company being passed from department to department. The company is still out the cost of the computing resources, but when it comes directly from the requesting department's budget, that department puts its own check-and-balance system in place to determine whether its data processing requests are reasonable.

The nice thing about chargeback is that the data processing department works like a miniature company within the company, supplying services as long as those services are paid for. The company doesn't have to worry about skyrocketing data processing costs; after all, if the money is already in a department's budget and that department wants to spend it on data processing, there is nothing wrong with that. The department will not

21

have those funds to spend on other things, and departments have the right to determine how they spend their own budgets.

REWARDING COST-CONSCIOUS DEPARTMENTS

At the end of the year, the data processing department often finds that it has made a profit from the other departments. Because the profit is really internal funds, that profit is often distributed *back* to the departments that paid for data processing services at the end of the year. The portion of the refund each department gets is proportional to the amount of data processing dollars that department spent during the year.

In this way, the departments know they are spending only as much money as the DP services cost; if they went outside the company for the same services, they would surely pay more because outside DP services would have to make a profit. The profit made by the internal DP department is redistributed back to the company.

NEW TERM Often, the data processing department hires contract programmers when the company's requests grow. If the DP department predicts that its workload will increase for a while, such as when another company is bought by the parent company, the data processing department hires contract programmers. A *contract programmer* is hired to program for a fixed time period. Whether the time is six months, a year, or longer is negotiable.

Generally, contract programmers are paid a large salary because the company doesn't have to pay for the contract programmer's benefits and retirement. There are software companies that hire programmers full-time, giving them benefits and insurance, and then those companies do nothing but hire out their programmers to other companies who need contract programming. Don't rule out an opportunity for contract programming if you are looking for a job. The pay is good, the experience is better, and often a company eventually hires the contract programmers it uses if they turn out to be productive workers.

Computer Jobs

Several times a year, leading magazines and newspapers list the job outlook for the coming year, five years, and ten years. For the last decade, computer jobs have been high on the lists for the best job environments, highest pay, long-term stability, and so forth. That trend will continue for many years. Despite advancements, computer technology is still in its infancy because there are a lot more programs to write than those that have been written in the past.

Companies sometimes allow data processing managers and personnel to work in more relaxed conditions than other departments. Whereas a company's accounting department reports in at 8:00 a.m., clocks out for exactly 60 minutes for lunch, and leaves at 5:00 p.m. on the dot, its DP staff might not all arrive and leave at a uniform time.

The reason working conditions can be more relaxed is that programmers, analysts, and computer technicians often need to pursue a problem or programming task until its conclusion, even if that means staying awake in the computer room for 20 hours straight. Programmers love to burn the midnight oil. As Hour 3, "What Is a Program?," points out, programming is not a science yet, and it might never be one. A large part of programming reflects a person's style and involves a personal commitment to a project. There is a creative side to programming that programmers often find addictive. A programmer who drags in at 11:00 a.m. might be doing so because he stayed up until 4:30 a.m. trying to debug some code for the company.

DP managers understand that the creative spirit that programming brings often comes in spurts. When a programmer gets involved on a programming project, she spends more voluntary overtime than any other type of worker would consider. The trade-off seems to be worth the relaxed attitude in many programming organizations.

Another primary advantage of the programming field over many others is its equal opportunity. Because the business computer industry didn't really begin until the mid-1960s—when the idea of equal pay for equal work was coming into acceptance—equal opportunity was already a part of the computer industry. There are many female, minority, and handicapped employees in data processing departments, from the lowest-paid job to the highest, and the norm has always been for their job and pay to be equal to those of others among them.

Job Titles

You should understand the kinds of jobs that are out there for programmers. Then when you look at the help-wanted ads in newspapers, you'll have an idea of the qualifications and experience needed for the different jobs that are advertised.

21

The titles described in this section are fairly common in the computer industry, but they are not necessarily universal. Whereas the title for a job in one company might be *Programmer Analyst*, another company might give the same duties a title of *Senior Programmer*. The specific titles mentioned here, although open to change and interpretation, are common enough to describe most of the responsibilities and titles in most computer departments.

Degrees and Certificates

Most computer jobs require some kind of degree or certification (except for the first one, Data Entry Clerk, described later in the section "Data Entry"). There is debate as to whether a two-year associate degree or a four-year bachelor's degree is best. The four-year degree is always better in one respect: you are more founded in the theory behind how computers work and will be able to learn new computer skills faster because of it. However, a four-year degree keeps you out of the work force two years longer than a two-year degree, and two years is a long time in the rapidly changing field of computers.

A two-year programming degree simply doesn't give you enough time to learn much about foundational computing theory. In two years, a college will teach you as many hands-on skills as possible. You'll pick up one or two programming languages (as opposed to four or more in a four-year curriculum). However, you'll find that you can enter the programming marketplace at the same job rank and get paid just as much as someone with a four-year degree. The drawback to a two-year degree is that you will not progress through the ranks as fast as someone with a four-year degree.

Perhaps the best of both worlds is possible. You can get a two-year degree, go to work for a company in an entry-level programming job, and get the last two years part-time to finish a four-year degree (most four-year colleges give credit for classes taken for a two-year degree with only a few exceptions here and there). Often a company will pay for, or at least supplement, its employees' continuing education.

If you have time and money to spare, and who doesn't, (seriously, there are always scholarships, grants, and loans), consider getting a second degree, either an additional two-year degree or a master's in a field other than programming. A second degree will augment your programming skills. In addition to understanding programming, you will be able to apply those programming skills more readily to an area such as accounting or engineering.

Certification

One of the newest kinds of degrees in the computing scene is not a degree at all. Instead of a degree, a technical certificate shows that you are well skilled in a specific area of computing. Microsoft, Novell, and several other companies offer certification training classes and testing sites. After you adequately pass the certification test for a specific area, you are then certified by the corporation offering the certificate. Job applicants in the computing industry are much greater in demand if they are certified. Unlike a college degree only, the certificate demonstrates a specific, measurable ability in a high-demand area of computing such as networking or operating systems.

> The certification tests are rigid and difficult. That's a good thing (if you pass one) because it demonstrates true proficiency in a subject matter. With a certificate, your minimum skill level is known in advance by those hiring.

Data Entry

 Some computer jobs don't require any programming skills. On the low end of the computer ranks fall the *Data Entry Clerks* (often called *Data Entry Operators*). Data Entry Clerks typically need only a high school diploma or its equivalent and some keyboarding skills. Data Entry Clerks, except for the ones who have been with a company for a long time and have often received pay raises, make the lowest salaries of any of the computer jobs in the company.

The life of a Data Entry Clerk is simple; he sits in front of a computer screen typing data into the computer. Typically, as Figure 21.3 shows, all the Data Entry Clerks type on terminals (keyboard and screen combinations) attached to a central computer, usually a mainframe. Eight hours a day, five days a week, the data entry department enters data.

FIGURE 21.3.

Data Entry Clerks normally enter data into the same computer.

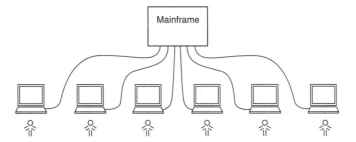

21

A company's data-entry requirements are massive. Payroll figures, sales figures, government figures, competing statistics, market trends, industry trends, projections, and so forth all must be factored into the company's working atmosphere. The computer programs that process a large amount of data need to enter it somehow. The larger the organization, the larger the data needs; some companies have hundreds of full-time Data Entry Clerks.

At first glance, you might want to stay away from such a job. The data-entry position, however, can be a powerful first step into a computing career for some people. People with little or no computer training who need experience can begin as a Data Entry Operator. While with the company, they can show a positive attitude, meet others within the company, and receive the typical company insurance and benefits. If the clerk pursues the proper training, she can move into higher programming positions.

As mentioned earlier, a company will often pay for some or all of an employee's part-time education. Therefore, a Data Entry Clerk, with no programming background at all, can take night classes to begin training in programming skills. After he finishes a degree, or is trained adequately enough, the company can move him into one of the entry-level programming jobs. Such a person might never have been able to get a programming job if he had not started out in data entry.

Programming

A person with knowledge of programming, either a self-taught programmer who has a degree in another area, a person who received programming training in a two-year or four-year institution, or a certified programmer, will bypass the data-entry job and move straight into a job related to actually programming. The first job title given to a new programmer hired fresh out of college (or one with little professional programming experience) is usually *Assistant Programmer* (also known as *Junior Programmer* or *Programmer I*). Assistant Programmer is generally considered the entry-level job for anyone without experience as a programmer in another company.

A person typically doesn't remain an Assistant Programmer for more than six or eight months. The job is really a trial period so the company can determine the employee's work attitude, skills, and general benefit to the company. An Assistant Programmer does no new programming. Instead, she works on programs others have written, often doing routine program maintenance. During the trial period, an Assistant Programmer learns how the company operates, gets acquainted with the other computer personnel, and generally "learns the ropes" of the company's working environment.

After a person stays in the Assistant Programmer role for a while, he is usually promoted to *Programmer*, along with a small raise and a pat on the back. The Programmer title means that the company expects good things in the coming years and has trust in the person. It is rare for a person to hold an Assistant Programmer title for several years and still be with the same company.

The Programmer earns a respectable salary for someone with little experience. As mentioned earlier, the computer field pays well, and its titles tend to command higher pay when ranked with similar experience titles in other departments. Therefore, if a person graduates with a programming degree at the same time as someone with a different type of degree, and they both go to work for the same company, the programmer usually has a higher salary after the first year. Of course, this depends on many factors and doesn't always hold, but on the average it does.

The Programmer does little more than the Assistant Programmer. The title of Programmer is a little misleading. The Programmer's primary job is to work on programs written by others, maintaining them and modifying them when the need arises. The Programmer rarely gets to write a program from scratch for the first year or two.

After a year or two of success, the Programmer's supervisor will begin to have the Programmer write programs from scratch. Of course, the specifications of the program (the flowchart, output definition, and possibly pseudocode) will already be done and the programmer only has to implement those specifications into a new program. After a while, the Programmer's attitude and on-the-job learning can justify moving into a more advanced job with the title *Senior Programmer* (sometimes called a *Programmer Analyst*).

The Senior Programmer is primarily responsible for writing new programs after being given specifications to follow. The Senior Programmer doesn't have to worry much about maintaining older code because the new Assistant Programmers and Programmers take care of that. (There is nothing wrong or unfair about maintaining programs, but when you train for writing programs, you cannot wait to get your hands on new programming projects.)

The Senior Programmer title usually commands a pay raise (over the normal annual cost-of-living raise) and maybe an office of his own instead of sharing an office with another Assistant Programmer or Programmer. A person is a Senior Programmer for a few years, writing code and getting to know the workings of the company, its users' needs, and the base of programs already in existence.

After a few years of success (the time is based on an individual's abilities, but two to three years is typical), the company will probably give that programmer the next higher programming title (along with a raise): Programmer Analyst.

21

A Programmer Analyst begins to work more closely on the front-end of programming: the program design. Hour 4, "The Program's Design," explains a lot about the analysis and design steps that must take place before you can write a program. Although Programmer Analysts don't do a lot of design work, they work closely with those who do. By working with designers (whose jobs are described in the next section), supervisors can learn just how apt that Programmer Analyst will be at program design. The Programmer Analyst does more programming than analyzing, but she does receive on-the-job training for the next step up the organizational ladder.

Analysis and Design Staff

NEW TERM When you make it to the next level of job, *Systems Analyst*, you know you've made the big time. You'll probably never have to write another program again; instead, you'll analyze and design programs that others will write.

Isn't it strange that you train for a long time to be a computer programmer and work hard at programming for several years, just so you don't have to program anymore? Actually, the programming experience is a must for the high-level Systems Analyst. Without the understanding that programming brings, one cannot design systems for others to program.

The Systems Analyst is the liaison between the users and the other departments who need data processing work performed. As Figure 21.4 shows, the Systems Analyst talks to both the users and the programming staff. The users don't understand computer requirements; they only know what they want (or what they think they want). The users must work with the Systems Analyst to design the needed computer system. The Systems Analyst has worked in the company for many years. The Systems Analyst understands the needs of the programmers and the needs of the users in the company. The programmers might appear too technically oriented to the users; sometimes the users themselves don't even know what they want. The Systems Analyst must be able to produce the output definition and logic design through numerous conversations with the users.

FIGURE 21.4.

The Systems Analyst is the go-between for the users and the programmers.

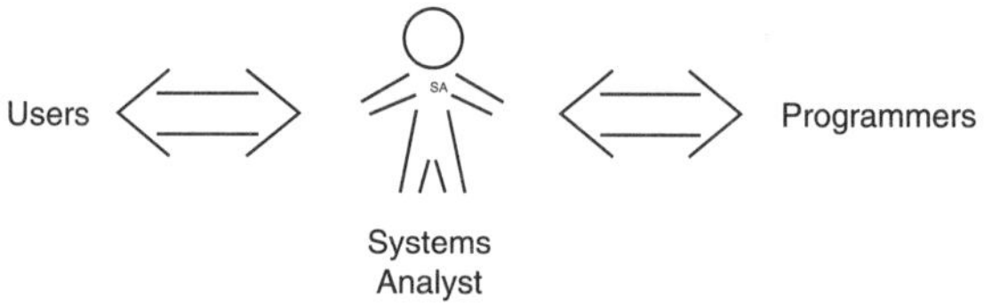

Users ⟺ Systems Analyst ⟺ Programmers

NEW TERM The job of the Systems Analyst is one of the most respected jobs in the computer industry. The Systems Analyst is paid a lot and often has high-level benefits only available to supervisory-level positions within the firm. Often, a person becomes a Systems Analyst and retires from that position instead of moving to another job. Some companies reward years of excellent performance by promoting a Systems Analyst to *Senior Systems Analyst*. The Senior Systems Analyst often does nothing different from the other Systems Analysts, however, and the new title is more of a "thank you" from the company than anything else.

> In smaller programming departments, one person might wear lots of hats, but that person's job title doesn't accurately reflect the range of jobs performed. For example, some companies have only two or three people in the entire computer department. All of them might program and also perform systems analysis and design duties. Smaller companies give you the opportunity to perform a wider range of programming tasks, improve your skills, and give you the opportunity to gain an understanding of the responsibilities of lots of job titles. Larger companies, however, usually offer better benefits, pay, and job security, but it will take you longer to broaden your skills.

Internet and Network-Related Jobs

NEW TERM The online world has created its own set of job positions, many of which overlap those you've read about in this hour. Programmers today often create Web pages by writing HTML code to format Web pages or by writing Java applets that work on pages sent to others. Although the programmers who write programs for the Internet have their own specific titles, such as Web Designer, HTML Coder, and *TCP/IP* (an abbreviation for the communications protocol used by Internet programs) Analyst.

NEW TERM The huge collection of networked computers generates its own set of jobs as well. You will see jobs with titles such as LAN Designer and WAN Specialists, as well as managers of these positions and technologies including security officers who patrol the network for unauthorized access. *LAN* is an abbreviation for *Local Area Network*, a network that links two or more computers located in the same area, floor, or building. *WAN* is an abbreviation for *Wide Area Network*, which is a network that spans more territory than the usual one-building network.

Due to the newness of these positions, most companies link these jobs to other positions. For example, a Java Specialist might have the same corporate status and pay scale as a Programmer or Programmer Analyst although the Java Specialist would concentrate on the online Java language only.

21

Demand plays a big role in the pay scales and corporate level of all computer-related jobs. For example, in the last half of the 1990s, the people with Internet-related skills received a bonus to their pay levels because of the need for their skills, although these employees' corporate status might be equal with a Programmer Analyst position.

Management Possibilities

By the time a person has been a Systems Analyst for a few years, he or she understands the company and the data processing department very well. The Systems Analyst knows most of the users and all the computer people in the company because the Systems Analyst has interacted so closely with users and programmers for so long. A person at the Systems Analyst level might decide that he is ready to move into a management-level position.

The higher salaries offered in the computer field can be a mixed blessing. When you've been in data processing for a few years, your salary becomes much higher than that of others who have been with other departments for the same amount of time. A person who makes it to Systems Analyst and then decides that computers are no longer a challenge often finds it difficult to move to another position within that company. Companies rarely let people move to a position that requires a pay cut; such employees soon miss the money they were used to, and they start looking elsewhere for a job. The Systems Analysts find themselves locked into a job from which they cannot escape if they stay too long. Their only recourse when this happens is to move to a completely different company.

Often, a Systems Analyst decides that he or she is ready to move into management. One of the first management-level job titles in data processing is that of *Supervisor*. Supervisors manage a small group of programmers and analysts, directing projects from a management point of view (making sure their people have adequate resources to do their jobs, are properly evaluated for raises, and so forth). Data processing departments normally prefer their Supervisors to have data processing experience. That is why so many Supervisors are promoted from within the ranks of Systems Analysts.

From a supervisory position, you might next move into a job called *Data Processing Manager* and be responsible for several Supervisors and their projects. The head manager of a data processing department is typically called the *Director*. The Director is usually even in rank with the Vice Presidents in other departments of the firm.

One of the advantages to moving into a supervisory or management position is that you can often move to non-DP departments within the company as a Supervisor or Manager. Before reaching a management position, your job rank and salary would make you overqualified for positions within other departments.

Structured Walkthroughs

The programming standards within the company are most often in focus during a walkthrough. A structured walkthrough has nothing to do with structured programming. A structured walkthrough is a review of a newly written program by some of the programming staff.

You might recall from Hour 4 that a program follows these steps when the programmer is finished writing it:

1. The programmer tests the program at her desk and tries to get as many bugs out as possible.

2. The programmer passes the program on to the user for testing (often, a parallel test is performed).

3. The user puts the program into use.

Now that you are familiar with the roles of the programming staff, you might be interested to know about an extra step that often takes place between steps 1 and 2. When the programmer is satisfied that the program is as accurate as possible, he prints listings of the program for several people and prepares for the structured walkthrough.

In the structured walkthrough, several other Programmers and Systems Analysts get together with a copy of the original listing, with the Programmer in the room, and they pick apart the program in detail trying to find errors, weak spots, broken standards, and poor documentation. Along the way they make suggestions on how to improve the code.

A structured walkthrough often produces what is known in the industry as *egoless programmers*. Programmers are often known for their egos; a good structured walkthrough often shows that a program is not as well written as the original programmer might have thought at first.

21

The structured walkthrough is not an attempt to point fingers. Its only purpose is to produce the best code possible. The other programmers are not going to be critical of the programmer personally; after all, they are going to be at the center of a future structured walkthrough themselves.

After a programmer implements many of the suggestions from the structured walkthrough, the programmer usually finds that he agrees that the program is better written than it was originally. After many such walkthroughs, the programmer develops better programming skills and the company acquires better programs.

Putting a Program into Production

Figure 21.5 shows all the steps needed to get a program into use by the user. When the user is finally convinced that the program works as well as originally asked for, and the user is convinced that the parallel testing went smoothly, the program is then moved into production.

FIGURE 21.5.

The steps for designing, writing, and installing programs.

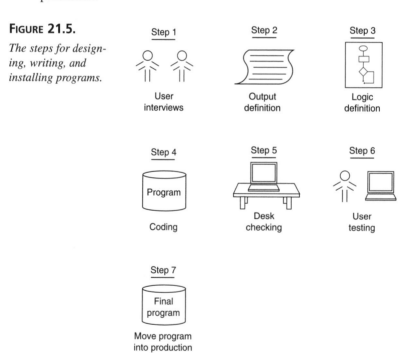

When a program moves into production, it is considered complete. The user begins to use the program in a working, non-test environment. The program's results are considered reliable within reason. (Over time, a program's reliability improves as it is used and continues to work well.)

Being in production hardly implies that the program needs no changing and updating over the years. Nevertheless, a production program is one that is considered fixed and usable until a user makes a request to update the program or scrap it for a completely new one. If changes are made to a program that is in production, the Systems Analyst goes back to user interviews and determines what the user wants. The entire systems analysis and design stage is then repeated for the revised program. Depending on the extent of the changes, a program's revision might take more or less development time that its ancestor program took to write. As you have read throughout this entire book, the maintenance of programs is critical in our ever-changing world. If you write your code better, by supplying more documentation and closely following your company's programming standards, then you will have a better chance at locking in your career in the computer field.

"I WANT JOB SECURITY!"

Job security is an overused term. Often, you hear programmers jokingly talk about the cryptic code they write so that "only they will be able to understand it." Modern programmers are only too aware of the fact that the better employers seek programmers who write clear, clean code, are more concerned with proper programming, and follow as many of the company's programming standards as possible.

Some people can write programs very quickly, but the spaghetti code they produce is unreadable for future maintenance. Don't fall into the trap of thinking that speed is more important than clear programs.

Many companies have formal procedures for moving programs into production. When a program is ready to be moved into production, the programmers finalize the program's documentation and prepare a source code file with a filename added to the production program list's records. That program is then stored on tapes and disks in what are known as production areas.

PC programming languages sometimes come with *version-control modules* that keep strict track of versions that programs go through as programmers update them and release new versions of the software.

21

Some mainframe systems don't even enable programmers to change a program once the system is instructed to treat that source program as a production program. Programmers are able to make copies of the program's source code, but the program is read-only and cannot be changed. If an update has to be made, the programmer copies the source code and makes changes to the copy. After the updates are made and the new version is ready for production, the production records are changed to reflect the new source code. From that point, the production system treats the new version of the code as the production version, but the original remains in place as a backup.

This tight control over production source code enables a company to ensure that it always has an unmodified copy of every program used by every user in the company. Without such control, a programmer could write a program, compile and test it, and install it on the user's system. When installed, the programmer might inadvertently change the program. Because it is virtually impossible to reproduce source code from compiled code, the data processing department would have no way to generate the original source code if the users wanted a change made to the program they are using.

Consulting

Many programmers find an enriching life as a computer consultant. Too many businesses and individuals buy a computer thinking all their problems will be solved, and they don't realize the amount of training that is often needed to use the computer effectively. There has been a growing niche for computer consultants over the last several years, and you might find success as a consultant yourself.

As a consultant, you can be a hero or a heroine to your clients. So many times, computer consultants rush to help someone with a problem getting a report completed, only to find that the client is inserting a disk upside-down or forgetting to press the online button on the printer. The computer is still a mystery to a vast number of people.

As a consultant, you can take on as much or as little work as you want. Many programmers moonlight as consultants, sometimes finding that their consulting business grows enough to do it full time. They might give up the benefits that a company can provide, but they like having full say over what they do.

Getting started as a consultant takes little more than word-of-mouth coverage. Offer to help your accountant, attorney, or anyone you know who uses a computer. Tell them that you'd like to start doing some consulting and that you'd be glad to give them an hour or two free of charge just to see how they like the work (and how you like the work). Often, these initial free calls turn into a long-term proposition that is good for both you and your clients.

Summary

You now have an understanding of computer departments and their people. There are many jobs in the computer industry, both for entry-level and advanced programmers. A computer job is a fun, well-respected, and needed occupation; you'll be glad you're a part of the computer industry.

Understanding the job levels and job promotions can be confusing, especially because many companies follow a unique promotion and title scheme. Nevertheless, the general order of jobs that a programmer follows from the beginning to end of her career is similar across many companies. The online and networking worlds have increased the nature of jobs and improved demand to further complicate the industry and make the roles of programmers even more interesting.

The next hour describes the debugging tools programmers can use to help reduce debugging time and that decrease the time between program idea to implementation.

Q&A

Q Why is the concept of production programs so important?

A The company knows that all programs in production are the final versions of each software release for each program ever written and used within the company. In other words, the production programs are those programs actually used by the company. Other programs might be in process and are still being written. Other programs might be used by individuals but not sanctioned by the company's data processing department and therefore, not part of the released software.

Q When a company makes a change to a production program's source code, does the compiled and revised program replace the current program being used?

A The revised program will also go into production but not replace the original program. The original program version is never removed from the production set in case the revision has problems and the company has to revert back to the original program.

Workshop

The quiz questions are provided for your further understanding. See Appendix A, "Answers to End of Chapter Questions," for answers.

21

Quiz

1. What does MIS stand for?

2. Who does the data processing department's programmers write programs for?

3. What is the most entry-level computer-related position found in large organizations?

4. What do entry-level programmers typically do?

5. What does a Systems Analyst do?

6. What is a structured walkthrough?

7. True or false: A company should keep all source code for all programs that it moves into production.

8. How can computer personnel ensure job security?

9. What is the difference between a LAN and a WAN?

10. Why is the pay for Internet-related jobs usually better than for other DP jobs even though the jobs' ranks might be the same as more conventional computer positions?

HOUR 22

Debugging Tools

Programs are easy to write. *Correct* programs are a different story. Locating program bugs can be difficult. Fortunately, most language distributors supply debugging tools to make your life easier as a programmer. Although the compiler locates syntax errors for you, logic errors often take extra time to locate and you must be the one to locate such problems before your users locate the problems. For example, when a payroll amount comes out incorrectly due to a bug, you will need to locate the problem as soon as possible.

The debugging tools of programming languages have become sophisticated indeed. One of the very first built-in debugging tools appeared in QBasic. This hour shows you how to access some of QBasic's debugging tools because you can try them now. Although in today's world the QBasic debugger is primitive, you do get good exposure to the capabilities of debuggers by studying the debugging tools in QBasic. When you obtain Visual Basic, you can try the more powerful debuggers described later in this lesson.

The highlights of this hour include:

- Why debugging tools are so vital for today's programmers
- How to interpret QBasic's Debug menu
- How to single-step through a program
- When to step over procedures during a debugging session
- How to use the Immediate window to view the contents of variables
- What breakpoints are
- How today's Windows programming languages support advanced debugging operations

Practice Debugging with QBasic

When you start QBasic and click the Debug menu, several strange-sounding menu options appear. Table 22.1 describes each of these menu options. These are the debugging tools that come with your copy of QBasic. Although they are considered relatively primitive in today's visual programming world, the most sophisticated debugging tools in the most sophisticated, visual, Windows development language don't offer many more tools than QBasic.

All the terms in Table 22.1 will become clear if you follow the examples in the next few sections.

TABLE 22.1 QBASIC'S DEBUG MENU TOOLS

Menu Option	Description
Step	Enables you to single-step through your program, executing one procedure at a time.
Procedure Step	Enables you to step through your program, executing one procedure at a time (requires that your QBasic program be written with multiple procedures).
Trace On	Turns on (or off) the program's tracing operation so you can monitor the execution order of the program's lines.
Toggle Breakpoint	Turns on or off a breakpoint at a given statement.
Clear All Breakpoints	Erases all breakpoints you currently have designated.
Set Next Statement	Causes the statement at the cursor to be the next executed statement.

For a review of the kinds of errors that can happen, see Hour 3, "What Is a Program?."

Type a Program

QBasic and enter the program shown in Listing 22.1. The listing has some intentional errors. One of the first things you'll notice as you enter the code is that the very first line has a problem. Obviously, the remark is not specified correctly but go ahead and type the line as it appears in Listing 22.1.

The QBasic system tells you that a problem exists as soon as you press Enter with the error message box shown in Figure 22.1. As with most languages, QBasic monitors your program as you type it to catch minor syntax errors. In addition, when you type a function's first line, QBasic automatically types the terminating END FUNCTION line for you. Go ahead and fix the misspelled first remark in the program and continue typing the rest of the code.

FIGURE 22.1.

QBasic and other languages locate syntax errors as you type your program.

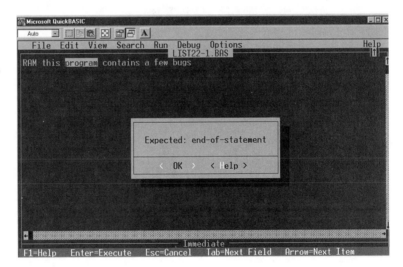

You can often turn off the monitoring of syntax errors. Sometimes you might want to brainstorm parts of a program and you don't want error messages to appear because you are simply entering several placeholder lines to fill in later. To turn off the syntax checking in QBasic, you can select Options, Syntax Checking. Selecting Options, Syntax Checking once again turns on the syntax checking when you're ready to resume your normal programming.

Even if you turn off the syntax check monitoring as you enter a program, the language still locates syntax errors when you run (for interpreted programs such as QBasic programs) or compile them.

LISTING 22.1 A SIMPLE QBASIC PROGRAM THAT CONTAINS ERRORS

```
 1: RAM this program contains a few bugs
 2: REM
 3: REM Two procedures exists in this code
 4: REM
 5: REM This code is rather advanced due to the function
 6: REM procedures that it contains.
 7: REM
 8: REM Just as the dollar sign, $, designates a string
 9: REM variable in QBasic, the exclamation point, !,
10: REM designates a single-precision value.
11: REM
12:
13:    DECLARE FUNCTION netPay! (rate!, hours!, raxRate!)
14:    DECLARE FUNCTION revStr$ (s$)
15:
16:    CLS
17:    INPUT "What is your name"; nam$
18:    PRINT "your name backwards is "; revStr$(nam$)
19:    PRINT
20:    REM Initialize some payroll values
21:    rate = 6.70
22:    taxRate = .31
23:    PRINT "In a payrollll system, assume the following values:"
24:    PRINT "Rate:"; rate
25:    PRINT "Hours:"; hour
26:    PRINT ; "Tax rate:"; taxRate
27:    PRINT USING "& $####.##"; "The net will be";
28:    PRINT netPay!(rate, hours, taxRate)
29: END
30:
31: FUNCTION netPay! (rate, hours, taxRate)
32: ' Function computes net pay based on values passed
33:
34:    grossPay = rate * hours
35:    netPay! = grossPay * (1 + taxRate)
36:
37: END FUNCTION
38:
39: FUNCTION revStr$ (s$)
40: ' Function that reverses whatever string is passed to it
41: ' This function expects a string value and returns a string
42:    b$ = ""   ' String to build on
```

```
43:   FOR i = LEN(s$) TO 1 STEP -1   ' Step back through the string
44:      b$ = b$ + MID$(s$, i, 1)
45:   NEXT i
46:   revStr$ = b$   ' The return value
47: END FUNCTION
```

The QBasic editor handles separate functions that you write in a strange way. QBasic separates functions as soon as you type them into different QBasic editing windows. Unlike Windows 98 windows, you cannot view multiple QBasic windows at once because only one QBasic program window is open and all code must appear in that one window. Therefore, as soon as you type the code for a separate function (the code that appears between FUNCTION and END FUNCTION statements), QBasic stores that function in a window named for that function. After you type Listing 22.1, to view the function named netPay for instance, you'll have to select View, Subs (QBasic calls both functions and subroutines *subs*) to display the window in Figure 22.2 and then select netPay from the list.

FIGURE 22.2.

QBasic separates subroutines and functions so you must select the one you want to work with.

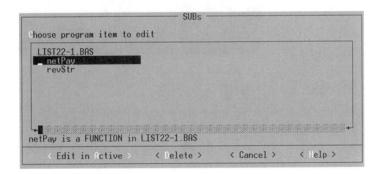

Given these anomalies of the QBasic editor, you can now practice debugging the program using the debugging tools that come with QBasic. Again, please understand that even though QBasic is old and text-based, most of today's Windows-based program debuggers work in a similar manner.

The initial remark is the only syntax error in the program. Therefore, you'll have to use some sleuthing skills to correct the logic errors that remain. When you run the program, the results are almost correct but you'll see some strange things take place. The goal of this eclectic program is to accomplish these two tasks:

- Reverse the characters in the username and print the backward name
- Calculate payroll values based on variables assigned in the program

The program handles the reversal of the user's name just fine. The payroll figures, however, are incorrect as Figure 22.3 illustrates. Although you might be able to correct these problems quickly without the aid of the debugger, use the debugger to help you locate the problems.

FIGURE 22.3.

This output contains some bugs.

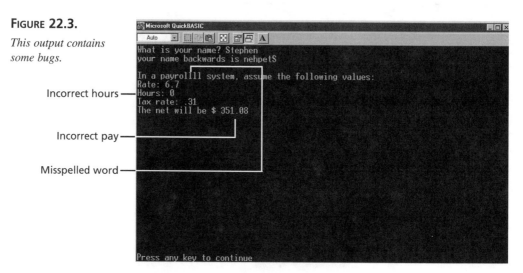

Incorrect hours

Incorrect pay

Misspelled word

Single Stepping

The first problem is the misspelled word, payrollll. Sure, you could search the entire program for the word, but get used to using the debugging tools because some Windows programs that you work on might contain thousands of lines of code. One of the slowest but most comprehensive methods you can use to debug a program is to walk through the program one line at a time using the single-step feature.

To step through this program, select Debug, Step to begin the stepping. (F8 is the shortcut key.) Each time you press F8, another line in the program highlights as QBasic runs the program. (The debugger skips remarks because remarks are not code.) The highlighted line is the line that is currently executing. Keep stepping through the program, pressing F8, watching the highlighter move through the code. When the program needs input, you will see the output screen and you can type the requested name. (You can always view the output screen, at any time during the debugging, by pressing F4 if the output screen is hidden at the moment.) As you step through the program, you'll see the loops and the jumps that the program makes as it follows the QBasic instructions in the program.

Eventually, you'll get to the misspelled text in the PRINT statement as shown in Figure 22.4. Here's one of the amazing things about debuggers: You can, interactively, change code as the program runs in single-step mode. Therefore, you can correct the spelling to payroll and then single-step through that line. Press F4 and you'll see that QBasic wrote the correctly spelled word to the output window.

FIGURE 22.4.

You'll eventually step to the incorrect statement.

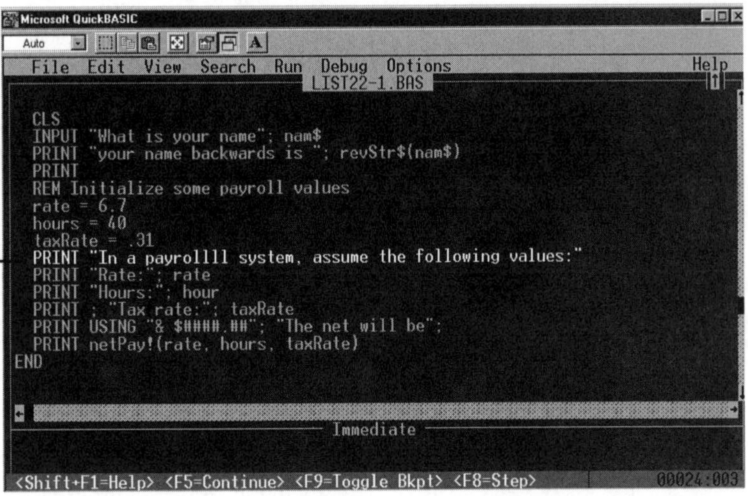

Incorrect statement ——

```
Microsoft QuickBASIC                                              _□×
Auto  ▾ ▨▨▨▨ ▨▨ ▨▨ A
  File  Edit  View  Search  Run  Debug  Options              Help
                          LIST22-1.BAS

  CLS
  INPUT "What is your name"; nam$
  PRINT "your name backwards is "; revStr$(nam$)
  PRINT
  REM Initialize some payroll values
  rate = 6.7
  hours = 40
  taxRate = .31
  PRINT "In a payrollll system, assume the following values:"
  PRINT "Rate:"; rate
  PRINT "Hours:"; hour
  PRINT ; "Tax rate:"; taxRate
  PRINT USING "& $####.##"; "The net will be";
  PRINT netPay!(rate, hours, taxRate)
  END

                          Immediate
<Shift+F1=Help> <F5=Continue> <F9=Toggle Bkpt> <F8=Step>    00024:003
```

Your ability to change programs while in single-step mode is sometimes limited. For example, if you modify a statement that changes the structure of a program (such as changes in the structure of a loop or a definition of a new variable in the middle of the program), some languages require that you restart the program from the beginning. The program cannot incorporate such a major change into the current execution.

For now, press F5 to complete the program's execution after fixing the misspelling. The next section explains how to step through the program faster.

Skipping Procedures

The Procedure Step option on the Debug menu enables you to execute complete subroutines or functions without walking through each line in them. Single-step through the program once again and get to the following statement that prints the name backward:

```
PRINT "your name backwards is "; revStr$(nam$)
```

This statement calls the revStr$() function. Therefore, if you continue single-stepping through the program when this statement is executed, you will single-step through each line in revStr$().

This code seems to work so there's no reason to waste time stepping through procedures that already work. At this point, instead of pressing F8 to step through the procedure press F10 (F10 is the shortcut key for Debug, Procedure Step).

Although the entire revStr$() procedure executes, the procedure executes at its normal speed and you won't be bothered with the single-stepping through the code. When the procedure finishes, control is returned to you in the main code and then you can continue single-stepping through the program.

Printing Variables

As you debug a program in QBasic and in most other programming languages, you can view the contents of any variable at any time. Notice that QBasic has two windows, a program window and one named Immediate. The Immediate window enables you to enter any valid QBasic statement, before, during, or after a program's execution, and the results of your typing appear in the output window that you can view by pressing F4.

Suppose that you step through several variable assignments and computations and you want to know what's currently in a variable at that point in the program. In Listing 22.1's output, you know that a problem occurs when the hours worked are printed because zero appears for the hours worked. Something about the initialization of the variable that holds the hours worked, or something about the printing of that variable, has a problem.

You can test the value of the variable named hours as soon as the program assigns 40 to it in the following statement:

```
hours = 40
```

Of course, 40 *has* to be in hours due to this direct assignment, but something's wrong somewhere because the output of the hours value produces only a zero. Therefore, after you single-step through the assignment of 40 to hours, go ahead and click the mouse cursor in the Immediate window and type the following statement:

```
PRINT hours
```

The value of 40 prints as you can see from the output window in Figure 22.5. Therefore, hours seems to be initialized properly. (The problem with the Immediate window is that its output appears along with the program's normal output, but with only one output window, this is the only way QBasic can show you your Immediate window results.)

FIGURE 22.5.

The Immediate window results appear along with your program's output.

Hours is correct

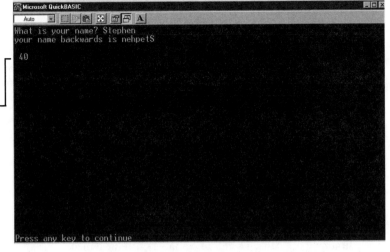

Press F4 to return to the editing window where you can continue to single-step through the program. As soon as you step through the Print statement that prints the hours, check the output window to see whether zero still prints for the hours. It does; therefore, something's wrong with the value being printed.

One of the nice things about the Immediate window is that your commands stay in the window and a scroll bar enables you to scroll back to previous commands that might have been scrolled out of the window. Locate the PRINT command you typed earlier for the variable hours (you can probably still see the command without scrolling the Immediate window) and click the command to place the text cursor on the command. To reissue the command, simply press Enter with the text cursor on that line and QBasic will execute the PRINT once again. Press F4 to see the output window and the correct value of 40 still prints. The code did *not* overwrite the variable but the code does still produce a zero with this PRINT statement:

```
PRINT "Hours:"; hour
```

Ah, perhaps the problem is now clear. This PRINT statement prints a different variable. Instead of hours (plural), the PRINT prints hour (singular). Perhaps you noticed the problem long ago, but in a huge program, such misspellings can often go unnoticed for quite awhile. The debugger helps you determine whether the variable's value has been damaged before that point or whether the PRINT itself is wrong as is the case here.

The Debug, Trace On command is rather useless in today's world of fast computers. This option enables you to execute the program and watch each highlighted source code line execute, one after the other, as the program runs. The speed of computers today, however, makes programs run too fast for the trace to be of much use. The single-step and procedure step commands are much more beneficial.

Setting Breakpoints

NEW TERM A *breakpoint* is a location in code where you have determined, in advance, that the program is to stop. You can set one or more breakpoints. When you set a breakpoint at a certain line and then execute the program, the program runs normally up to the breakpoint and then the program halts. The program does *not* terminate all execution but only halts. Therefore, variables still have their values, files might still be open, and the program is only temporarily ceased.

To set a breakpoint in a QBasic program, locate the line where you want the program to halt, click the line to place the text cursor there, and press F9 (the shortcut key for Debug, Toggle Breakpoint). To turn off a breakpoint, locate the cursor there once again and press F9 again.

> You can turn off all breakpoints that you've set in a program by selecting Debug, Clear All Breakpoints.

When the program reaches a breakpoint and halts, you can single-step through some code, procedure step through the code, use the Immediate window, or press F5 to complete the execution of the program. If you set more than one breakpoint, the program will continue when you press F5 as usual from the previous breakpoint until halting at the next breakpoint reached.

The net pay is incorrect in Listing 22.1. Probably a good place to set a breakpoint might be at the following PRINT statement that prints the net pay:

```
PRINT netPay!(rate, hours, taxRate)
```

The only problem with this is that the PRINT calls a function named netPay!() and the result of the function prints but the code for the function resides in the netPay!() function. Therefore, instead of placing a breakpoint at the PRINT, you should place one inside this function that computes the net pay to determine the problem with the calculation.

As you can see, debugging is a skill that you learn to hone over time. The program's structure and the language help determine the best approach when you begin to debug.

Select View, Subs and select the `netPay!()` function code to view. The function primarily consists of these two computations:

```
grossPay = rate * hours
netPay! = grossPay * (1 + taxRate)
```

Set a breakpoint at the first statement. A red bar appears through the line to indicate the breakpoint. Now, run the program by using the F5 key. The program executes normally, asking you for your name, and then halts at the breakpoint's line.

When Microsoft designed Visual Basic, it used many of the same shortcut keys for the Visual Basic debugger as for QBasic. Therefore, F9 sets breakpoints in Visual Basic code and F8 single-steps through Visual Basic code. Other languages, such as Visual C++, use similar shortcut keys.

Something is wrong with one or both of these calculations because the net pay is incorrect. Press F8 to single-step through the first statement. Click the Immediate window and print the value of the `grossPay` variable using the following statement:

```
PRINT , , , grossPay
```

The commas place the Immediate window's gross pay amount far to the right of the screen so you'll know which value came from the Immediate window. A `268` appears and seems reasonable. Therefore, the problem must be in the next statement.

Single-step through the second calculation. Sure enough, now that you analyze the only statement that's left, you realize that you should not add one to the tax rate because that's assuming a tax rate of 131%. (Taxes are not *that* bad yet!) To compute the rate correctly, you must multiply the net pay by 1 *minus* the tax rate because the net pay is the result of the gross pay after all taxes are taken out.

After you change the plus sign to a minus sign, rerun the program to see that a correct net pay of `$184.92` appears. Congratulations!

As you step through a program, you can actually change the order of program execution although doing so does not always make debugging simpler. During a halt at a breakpoint or during a single-step session, you can click on any line in the program and select Debug, Set Next Statement. That statement will execute *next* no matter which statement would normally follow in the execution order. You cannot execute a statement in a different subroutine or function procedure. Generally, the Debug, Set Next Statement is beneficial when you want to skip over a few statements that you know have possible bugs to see how statements later in the program execute. The skipped statements might initialize valuable variables needed later, so use this option with care.

Other Debugging Tools

When you use programming environments more powerful than QBasic, such as Visual C++ or Visual Basic, most of the debugging aids are similar to those that you now know. The Windows environment enables the debuggers to take on even more powerful features, however. For example, the output window can be different from the Immediate window so that your temporarily printed values will not steal screen real estate from your program's regular output.

The following list is a partial sample of some of the features you'll find in most of today's Windows debugging systems that come with Windows programming languages. Many of these features are mirrored or are supported in a lesser manner in QBasic as you learned throughout the earlier sections of this hour's lesson:

- You can analyze variables at runtime (as you can do from QBasic's Immediate window) and view those variables in a window separate from the output. For Windows programming languages, you can also analyze the contents of control values. Therefore, you can easily check to see which value has been stored in a text box or command button property.

- You can change the contents of variables during the execution of the program (as you can do from QBasic's Immediate window) so that the rest of the program acts as though the code had assigned those values.

- Set breakpoints throughout the program.

- Set *watch variables* that halt the program's execution when the watch variables receive a specific value or range of values.

- Skip statements that you don't want to execute during debugging (as you can do with QBasic).

22

Figure 22.6 shows one of the nicest features of Windows-based debuggers. When you halt a program during a single-step session or with a breakpoint, you can view the contents of a variable just by pointing to the variable. The value in the variable appears in a pop-up window at the mouse pointer's location.

FIGURE 22.6.

The debugger can pop up a variable's value.

curGrossPay contains
312

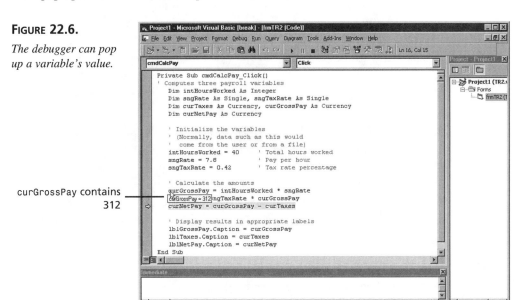

NEW TERM In addition to the usual fare of debugging features, you can also retrace your steps through a program. When you need to see exactly which parts of a program have executed up to a breakpoint, you can look at the *call stack*. The call stack appears in a dialog box and shows all procedures that have executed in the program to this point. If you double-click a procedure name, the code window opens to that procedure and all variable values are still intact so that you can see what values have been computed.

Figure 22.7 shows a call stack dialog box that displays over a Visual Basic code window. In addition, a Debug toolbar appears so you have one-button access to common debug operations such as viewing watch window variables and stepping through code.

FIGURE 22.7.

The call stack's dialog box retraces your pro-gram's procedures that have executed.

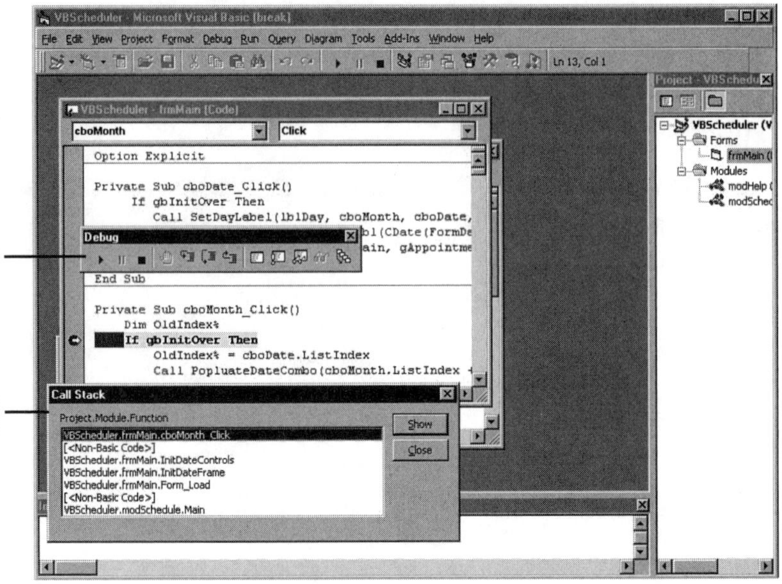

The Debug toolbar ──

The Call Stack dialog box ──

Summary

This lesson showed how you can use powerful debugging tools to locate problems with your programs. You used the text-based QBasic debugger to learn the skills related to debugging, but those same skills will transfer rapidly to other languages. Learning how to debug pays dividends when you need to track bugs. Although the debugging tools can-not locate specific logic bugs on their own, they make locating logic bugs easier for you to do.

One of the most powerful aspects of the debugger is its interactivity with the program during a breakpoint session. When your program reaches a breakpoint, all the values ini-tialized and computed to that point are still live. Therefore, you can view variables to see whether their intermediate results contain the same values you expect. Also, you can change a variable's value in the middle of the program's execution and watch how the rest of the execution reflects that change.

The next hour describes what happens after you debug an application and you're ready to distribute that application to others. Application distribution can be involved if you are sending applications that are multifile projects as most of today's Windows programs are. Nevertheless, as you might expect, the tools that come with today's programming envi-ronments make the distribution easier.

Q&A

22

Q How can single-stepping help me debug a program when it takes so long to step through a large application?

A By executing a program one line at a time, you can analyze variable and control values at your pace. Remember that you don't have to single-step through every statement but only the statements that you want to analyze. After you view values, you then can run the rest of the program or set a breakpoint later in the code and run the program at normal speed to that set breakpoint. Single-stepping not only helps you ensure that data values are correct but you can also monitor the execution of a program to make sure that the program's statements execute in the order that you intended.

Q Can I debug a compiled program?

A Unfortunately, the debugging tools only work with source code. The source code is needed to display variable names and locate program statements. As a good programmer, you will keep a copy of all source code you compile into a user's programs so you can locate and fix bugs that the user finds.

Workshop

The quiz questions are provided for your further understanding. For the answers, see Appendix A, "Answers to End of Chapter Questions."

Quiz

1. What kinds of errors does the programming language locate for you?
2. What kinds of errors can a programming language *not* locate for you?
3. True or false: You can turn off the monitoring of syntax errors that can occur when you type source code.
4. What key is used for single-stepping through most programs?
5. What is the purpose of the QBasic Immediate window?
6. Why is the tracing feature of QBasic not as helpful as it once was?
7. How can you change the order of execution in a program that has stopped at a breakpoint?
8. What are watch variables?
9. How does a Windows-based programming environment improve upon QBasic's debugging tools that you learned about this hour?
10. What is a call stack?

HOUR 23

Distributing Your Applications

After you write a program, test it, and then debug it, you must get your program into the hands of those who will use it. One of the problems with the software industry is a lack of installation standards for new software. Although Windows provides some uniformity for installing software, not all software producers conform to that standard and not all software could even be made to conform to the Windows Control Panel's Add/Remove Programs feature.

This lesson introduces you to the problems associated with software distribution. You want to be sure that your users have an easy time installing the programs you write. In addition, those programs have to work after they are installed. Today's distribution tools help a lot when it comes to creating distributable software. This lesson takes a look at how one software product, Visual Basic, creates a customized installation for you.

The highlights of this hour include:

- Why installation issues can be complex
- How to start QBasic programs automatically from a Windows icon
- How wizards simplify the creation of installation routines
- Why compiling the application is so critical to proper installation
- Why version control is important
- What an installation wizard does for you
- How an installation wizard stores the install files it generates
- Why an uninstall routine is important

Issues Surrounding Software Distribution

The hardest part of software distribution is not selling the product. More computer-related stores are now open than ever before. Even discount stores and warehouse chains carry software as if software were a staple item for our daily lives. Software companies are looking for new titles to distribute and new programmers to write the code. Software mail-order catalogs are numerous. The business of computers today gives you many avenues in which to market your product.

Just because you wrote a program that works on your computer with your software settings certainly does not mean that the program will work on others' computers. For happy users, you must make sure that the program installs on the user's computer and that the program will run after it's installed.

QBasic Is Too Easy

Despite the fact that QBasic is outdated using a text-based environment, programs that you write in QBasic are some of the easiest to distribute to others. The lack of a compiler means that, as long as the user has QBasic installed on his computer, any user can run any program you write. Often, programmers who write QBasic programs distribute the QBasic file along with a batch file that copies the file to a directory.

 QBasic makes a good introduction to program-distribution aspects that you'll learn about this hour. Nevertheless, QBasic does *not* make for a good programming language that you use to write programs you distribute to others in most cases. You cannot compile a QBasic program so anyone can easily change the source code that you must distribute. Also, QBasic is an

> interpreted language that runs more slowly than compiled languages. Lastly, the text mode of QBasic means that the program cannot connect to Windows programs in any way.

The problem with QBasic is that the QBasic language doesn't come pre-installed on today's computers. In Hour 8, "Your First Language: QBasic," you saw what steps were necessary to locate the QBasic programming language on your Windows CD-ROMs and copy QBasic to your hard disk for actual use. QBasic is no longer part of the Windows installation, so you must manually install the language.

The benefit that comes with QBasic, the fact that it appears on every PC-compatible computer in the world that runs Windows, does not outweigh the fact that the user must go through tedious steps to install the product. Therefore, other than a great learning tool, and a good tool for writing short and simple text-based programs for yourself, QBasic is not a good language to use for programs that you write for others.

> Even if you can assume that the user has QBasic on her computer, the user must always start QBasic and load your program before the program executes. Such steps are tedious for the average user. You can create a batch file and link that file to a Windows icon to start a QBasic program automatically, but there is no simple way to create an installation script that does that for you.

In case you want to run QBasic programs from a Windows icon for your own use, here is one way to do it:

1. Select the Windows Start button's Settings, Taskbar & Start Menu option.
2. Click the Start Menu Programs tab.
3. Click the Add button to display the Create Shortcut dialog box shown in Figure 23.1.
4. Type `QBasic /RUN` *programName* (where *programName* is the name of your QBasic program) and click Next. The `/RUN` option tells Windows to load QBasic and run the program without requiring the user to select File, Open and then Run, Start.
5. Select the Windows Start menu option where you want to place the program's icon and click Next.

6. Type a title for the icon and click Next. Windows adds the icon and closes the dialog box.

7. When you select the icon, QBasic starts and automatically begins running the program.

FIGURE 23.1.

You can make a QBasic program respond to a Windows icon selection.

Windows Application Distribution

 This section walks you through one of the most common distribution methods of Windows software in use today. The Microsoft Visual Studio supports a standard distribution system that collects all files related to a Windows project and packages those files into a distributable set of disks, CD-ROM, or networked distribution. The Visual Studio even creates an *installation script* that controls the entire program installation when the user installs the program.

> The Microsoft Visual Studio is certainly not the only product that creates standard installation scripts for the Windows programs that you write. Nevertheless, almost all Microsoft languages, including Visual Basic, Visual C++, and Visual J++, use the Visual Studio interface and the distribution system. If you end up using a non-Microsoft language or a different installation distribution system, the steps you go through will not match those of this lesson exactly but the general nature of the system will mimic that of the Visual Studio system.

Your First Step: Compilation

As mentioned earlier, you will need to compile whatever Windows application you distribute. The compiled file is a final executable file with the .EXE filename extension. All the related Windows application modules and forms work together to form the executable file. Although auxiliary files might still be necessary, such as a Microsoft Access database file used for initial data, most of your project's files combine into the executable to make distribution easier.

A compiled application is more secure than a distributed source project. If you distribute the source code (the project and its related files), anyone with a Visual Studio language, such as Visual Basic, can modify your work. However, most people couldn't even run the source code because most do not have Visual Basic to load and run the source code. Therefore, a compiled file is necessary so that all can use your application.

23

Your compiled application runs much faster than the application running within Visual Basic's development environment. You want your application to run as quickly and smoothly as possible without your users doing more than necessary. The compiled executable file makes the application's execution simple.

Before you compile your application, make sure that you've debugged the application as much as is feasible and that you've eliminated as many bugs as possible. As you learned in the previous hour, "Debugging Tools," you cannot run the debugger on a compiled file.

When you're satisfied that you have your program running as accurately as possible, the Visual Studio File, Make option actually performs the compilation. Other programming platforms use a similar, if not identical, menu option for the compile. Visual Studio then displays a Make Project dialog box that is little more than a File Open dialog box. You need to select the folder where you want to store the compiled application and the name for the executable file. (The project will have the executable filename extension .EXE.)

Before clicking OK to start the compilation, you can set compilation options by clicking an Options button to display the Project Properties dialog box (see Figure 23.2). The dialog box lets the programmer specify version information for the compiled application that is common information needed by developers. If you plan to release several versions of the software, the version numbers let you determine the order of versions. You can specify the version information from the development environment's Project Properties dialog box so you don't have to specify versions just at compile time. The version numbers and description information stay with the project's source code.

FIGURE 23.2.

*Set the compiled pro-
ject's options in the
Project Properties dia-
log box.*

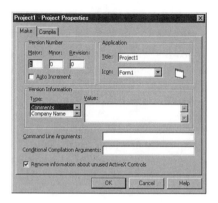

The Icon entry designates the icon that indicates the application on the Windows Start menu and on a taskbar button. Generally, you leave the primary form name in the Icon field. The form's Properties window contains an Icon entry from which you can select an icon for the form and, therefore, for the compiled application.

NEW TERM   A Compile tab (also common among all companies' compilers) displays the Compile Options page shown in Figure 23.3. To optimize the compiled project to make it run as quickly as possible, you could set options such as the Compile to Native Code option. (If you compile to *p-code*, a special intermediate language used by some compilers such as Visual Basic, the application requires that your users keep a runtime Visual Basic–based DLL file in their System folder. Native code runs faster and requires fewer files.)

FIGURE 23.3.

*You can control the
compile options.*

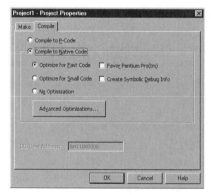

If you select any of the options that appear when you click the Advanced Optimizations button, you forsake some of the runtime error checking but gain execution speed.

When you close the Project Properties dialog box and click OK, Visual Studio compiles your code. Assuming that no compile errors exist, Visual Studio creates the .EXE file (you'll see the compilation status in the upper-right corner). You can exit Visual Studio and run the application by selecting the Start menu's Run option after locating the .EXE file. The form's icon that you selected appears in the taskbar when you run the program.

Of course, your users will not, at first, be able to run your application as easily as you can because the application is already loaded on your system. The next section shows one tool that automatically creates an installation script for your users so they can install your application with minimal trouble.

23

Deploying Your Application

In Visual Studio, beginning with release 6, a special wizard exists that walks you through the creation of a Windows-based installation for your application. Although you might not have a Visual Studio-based product now, and although you might use a different vendor's product in the future, you can learn a lot about such products by following the walkthrough described here.

Visual Studio's Package and Deployment Wizard does a lot of work for you, including the following:

- Compiles the application and compresses the files.

- Creates a setup program that your users can use to install the application.

- Determines the best fit for installation of floppy disks, creates the numerous setup disks, and splits files across multiple floppy disks for extra-large files. The Package and Deployment Wizard tells you in advance how many floppy disks the setup requires.

- Copies your compiled application to a hard disk so that you can install the application over a network or onto a CD-ROM creator.

- Sets up your application for distribution across the Internet for Internet Explorer users.

The Package and Deployment Wizard generates a list of several files needed for the setup. A single Setup.exe doesn't come out of the setup routine. Often, a Windows application requires .DLL and .OCX files, and those files reside in the targeted setup area (floppy disks or a hard disk) with the compiled program and the Setup.exe program.

Most installation programs that contain the installation script for any given application are named Setup.exe.

Starting the Package and Deployment Wizard

Before you can run the Package and Deployment Wizard, you must load your application's project into the Visual Studio environment. Therefore, if you use Visual Basic, you would load your Visual Basic project files as if you were going to work on the application.

Only after you have debugged and compiled your project are you ready to create the installation module. The installation routine, the Package and Deployment Wizard, will compile your code one final time if you've made an edit since your most recent compilation. Figure 23.4 shows the opening screen of the Package and Deployment Wizard.

FIGURE 23.4.

Use the Package and Deployment Wizard to create a Setup.exe file.

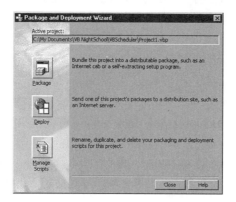

The first Package and Deployment Wizard option, which is the option you'll probably select most of the time, creates a standard Setup.exe routine that your users can install. The Package and Deployment Wizard can prepare this installation routine on a disk, floppy disks, CD-ROM writer, or in special .CAB files that you can send out over the Internet for online distribution. The second option sends the install routine to an Internet server that can install the application remotely.

During the installation-creation routine, the Package and Deployment Wizard creates a script file that describes the setup routine. In subsequent sessions, you can either modify a setup script that you've already created before, or create the setup from the original project. The third option on the Package and Deployment Wizard's opening window lets you manage your installation scripts.

Due to the size of most Windows applications today and the abundance of CD-ROM recorders, few applications come on disks.

The Wizard's Options

The first option generates the most common forms of an installation routine for most applications. It is this option that most other software installation routines follow. After you click the first option, you'll see the window shown in Figure 23.5. Unless your application requires external ActiveX controls or database files, you can keep the first option selected.

FIGURE 23.5.

Determine the kind of setup package to create.

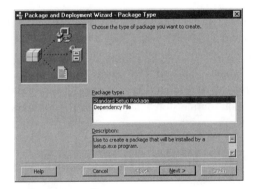

If you want to set up an ActiveX control, you need to select the Dependency File option so the wizard can collect the proper files in the order the application needs them. Without telling the wizard that other dependent files must appear in the project, the wizard would be unable to collect all the necessary files.

The Installation Location

You'll need to specify a folder on your own computer where you want the distribution files saved. The Package and Deployment Wizard needs to know where your final setup application should go. The directory you select should be empty so that other installation routines don't get in the way. Therefore, as a developer, you will have many folders on your disk drives with each folder holding one complete set of installation files for each application that you write. You should document these folders so that you can later go back and collect the proper files you need for applications that you distribute to others.

By saving the installation to a new and empty folder, you'll know when the wizard finishes that all the files in the directory are there as the result of the wizard.

The Dependency Files

One of the most powerful features of an installation-creation system, such as the Package and Deployment Wizard, is that the wizard can scan your project file to determine which program files your application needs. (The wizard can't determine which database drivers are needed if your application contains any data-related controls, so you'll have to select them from a dependency-file screen.)

A dialog box such as the one shown in Figure 23.6 appears after the wizard finishes collecting all the application's files that you've specified. Make sure that you look through the files to determine that every file your application requires is listed. You might need to add (by clicking Add) more files, such as Readme.txt or a database file. Additional database support files might be needed and you would need to add those database files to the file list so the installation routine stores the database files along with the installation files in the setup package.

FIGURE 23.6.

Look through the files to make sure the Package and Deployment Wizard collected the files your project needs.

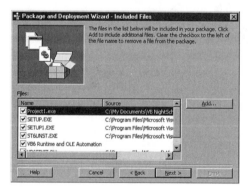

Selecting the Location

The Package and Deployment Wizard's next dialog box requests distribution information. You can create a single distribution file or request that the setup routine be placed across multiple floppy disks or other kinds of media. After you determine how you want the Package and Deployment Wizard to divide your installation routine, you can display the Installation Title screen to type your installation project's title that appears in the installation dialog box that the user sees. After clicking Next, the Start Menu Items dialog box appears as shown in Figure 23.7.

FIGURE 23.7.

You can determine the way the application will appear on the end user's Windows Start menu.

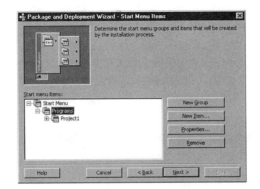

23

From the Start Menu Items dialog box, create the submenu that will appear on the installed PC's Start menu. Clicking the New Group button and displaying the Add Group dialog box enables you to add new menus to the user's Start menu group of menus. You can specify the application's submenu items that might include a Readme file you want to add to the project or an auxiliary program, such as a system utility.

Completing the Wizard

Several additional screens might appear depending on your installation options. A screen called the Install Locations screen determines the locations of each of the installed files. Although you'll want the majority of the files installed in the folder that the user selects during the installation procedure, as specified by a system variable called AppPath, you can select individual files in the Package and Deployment Wizard's list and send those files to an alternative folder, such as the user's Program Files folder (specified by a system variable called ProgramFiles).

As you can see, installation systems such as Visual Studio's Package and Deployment Wizard require numerous decisions. With those decisions, however, comes complete control over how and where your application arrives on the user's system.

Click Next to select any files that you want to designate as shared files. A file might be shared not only by other users (as would be the case for a database file the application might access) but also by other programs on the computer as might be the case for ActiveX controls that your project contains. Designate which files are shared by clicking next to each shared file and placing a check mark in the box next to that file.

One of the finishing touches of the Visual Studio Package and Deployment Wizard is a screen that asks what you want to call your installation's script file (see Figure 23.8). By creating a script file, you will not have to answer the long list of wizard queries that you've had to answer to this point the next time you create the installation routine. In addition, you can modify the script without having to redo the installation screens if something changes in the installation process, such as the removal of a shared file.

FIGURE 23.8.

Save your installation script so you do not have to re-create it later.

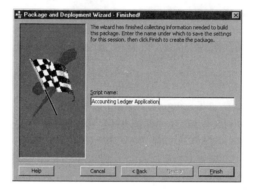

When finished, the Package and Deployment Wizard builds the installation script, creates the installation routine, and places that routine in one or several files depending on the options you selected. When finished, a Setup file will reside on your PC that you can distribute, in one or several files, which will install and re-create your application on other computers.

After Generating the Setup

After your installation wizard generates a setup routine, test it. To test the routine, run the generated Setup program to make sure that no bugs appear and the final application runs smoothly on the computer.

NEW TERM If you really want to test the setup routine, run the Setup program on a computer that has never contained your application. Even better, make sure that the computer doesn't even have a copy of the Visual Studio language you are using. By testing your application on such a *clean machine*, you help ensure that your application installs properly on users' computers. Some business copier centers allow you to rent PCs and such PCs are good candidates for installing your software if you are allowed to install new software on the computers there.

The simplest way to test the generated setup routine is to choose Run from the Windows Start menu and find the Setup.exe file. Click the Run button to start the application's setup. A typical setup installation will occur. The Setup program will analyze the target computer to ensure that no programs are running that might conflict with a file that is about to be installed.

> If you cancel the Setup program at any time before it completes, it closes after removing any files copied to that point. Therefore, if you cancel the process at any time, Setup removes all traces of the application's setup.

23

Uninstalling the Application

Installation wizards such as the Package and Deployment Wizard not only generate the installable setup routine, but also an application uninstaller that lets users uninstall all the application's files at any time. The Package and Deployment Wizard works in conjunction with the system Control Panel's Add/Remove Programs icon. Therefore, if users want to remove the application from the system, they only have to follow these steps:

1. From the Start menu, choose Settings, Control Panel.
2. Double-click the Add/Remove Programs icon.
3. Select the application from the list of installed applications. After verifying that the user wants to remove the application, the uninstall routine takes over, and removes the program and all its related files from the user's computer.

The Package and Deployment Wizard stores the uninstall information in the same directory as the application. The file that contains the removal instructions is named ST6UNSTLOG and holds the necessary details for the Add/Remove Programs system utility to do its job. Not all files should be removed, especially system files that might be shared by other programs. Before removing such potentially needed files (such as ActiveX controls), the removal utility displays a warning dialog box that lets users decide how to remove such files.

Summary

This hour's lesson was more technical than many of the previous ones but creating an installation script is not actually straightforward. Fortunately, Windows utility programs such as the Visual Studio Package and Deployment Wizard make the work simpler. Not only can you specify the files needed to install, but also the wizard handles auxiliary files such as database and ActiveX files your application needs as well as creates an uninstall program so your users can properly remove the application from their systems.

The next hour concludes your 24-hour introduction to programming by discussing some of the issues related to the world of computing and explores some of the tasks you'll face as a programmer.

Q&A

Q Should I always offer an uninstall routine?

A By providing a way for your users to uninstall your application, you help your users get rid of old versions of the software when new ones come out. In addition, the user knows that all traces of the program go away when the user implements the uninstallation routine. All traces of a Windows application rarely go away when a user has to attempt to remove an application manually without the automated help of an uninstaller.

Workshop

The quiz questions are provided for your further understanding. For the answers, see Appendix A, "Answers to End of Chapter Questions."

Quiz

1. Why is it not a good idea to distribute QBasic programs to others these days?

2. How does the lack of a compiler make QBasic less desirable as a language?

3. True or false: Given QBasic's interpreted, text-based mode, you cannot link a QBasic program to a Windows icon.

4. What is an installation script?

5. What filename extension do compiled programs use?

6. What filename is often used for the primary installation file of an application?

7. What kind of media (such as disks) can an installation system often use for distributing the application?

8. Why do installations rarely come on disks these days?

9. Why is testing the installation on a clean machine so important?

10. How do you create an uninstall routine?

HOUR 24

The Future of Programming

What's in store for you as a programmer? One thing is certain and that's *change*. Change occurs rapidly in computing. The face of programming has dramatically changed since computers were first invented and the rate of change is increasing. Today's programming tools were not even dreamed of ten years ago. New languages such as Java often crop up to handle new technology like the Internet.

This final lesson shows you what tools are available to help you become a better programmer. More important than the tools, however, is proper coding that is easily maintained later. The Year 2000 (Y2K) problem is showing programmers exactly how vital documentation is.

The highlights of this hour include:

- Which tools you might use to improve your programs
- How a profiler helps you improve a program's efficiency
- Why efficiency doesn't mean your programs have to lose their main-tainability

- How version control tracking can help a company maintain its database of source code programs
- Why Windows resource management is important
- How the Y2K problem came to be
- How to avoid problems such as Y2K in the future
- What other resources are available to improve your programming skills

Some Helpful Tools

As you develop more programming skills and work with more programming language environments, you will run across tools that you will want to add to your bag of coding tricks. The following sections briefly describe tools that you might run across as a programmer that you'll want to look into.

Profilers

 One programming tool, called a *profiler*, analyzes parts of your program and determines exactly which parts are sluggish. It is thought that 90% of a program's execution time is spent in less than 10% of the code. Of course, this rule of thumb is probably not scientifically provable but its concept is understandable.

Perhaps a sorting algorithm is inefficient and needs looking into to speed it up. Perhaps you are performing a sequential search when a binary search might be faster. Perhaps a calculation is inefficient and you can combine operations to make the program compute results more quickly. A profiler can analyze the execution of your program and tell you where the time is being spent during the execution.

 Speed and efficiency are great factors, but don't forsake proper programming techniques if doing so means eking out a microsecond or two of machine time. You'll learn in the section "Y2K's Implications," later in this hour, just how harmful a lack of proper program coding and maintenance can be. Clear code should be paramount in your coding. Computers are getting faster, not slower, so you know that your program will never run *slower* than it runs today. Some scientific and financial calculations, for example, get extremely complex. To clarify your code, you could break such calculations into several statements, storing intermediate calculation results along the way. Although it might be more efficient and execute a few microseconds faster, if you combined all the calculations into one long expression, this expression would later be difficult to debug or change if a problem arises. Therefore, unless a system's speed is critical (as might be the case in

> some medical or space exploration programs), don't make your code too
> tricky to be maintained later.

Many of the major programming languages on the market either have a profiler or their authors are producing one. A balance can be met between efficient code and clear, maintainable code. Sadly, programmers don't use profilers enough. Often, a program contains a sluggish section that could use some honing that would not risk the code's maintainability. The backlog of programming jobs right now and in the foreseeable future also keeps programmers from taking the time needed to check the execution profile of their applications.

Version Controllers

Version control used to be important only in the mainframe world where programming teams wrote computer information systems for large groups of people within the company. Perhaps one department might use a version of the software that contains more features than the other department programs contain. The programming staff developed a way to keep the versions straight. They assigned unique version numbers to each program sent into production that was used by the company.

Now, PC languages are getting into the act by providing version control software that enables programming departments to track versions of software. The version control tracks versions of distributed programs and keeps track of all source code that goes out to end users. Companies are seeing the need for such control on their PC software because so many data processing chores are being ported to the PC for client/server computing where the data might be stored on a networked mainframe, but processed on the PCs connected to the mainframe. Such a distributed system of programs can get confusing, so the version tracking software keeps things in order.

When the programmers complete an application for a department, the programmer can use the version control software to log every file related to the project. Software such as Visual Basic includes version control called *SourceSafe* as an option every time you save a source program. A dialog box such as the one in Figure 24.1 appears asking if you want to add the program to the source code version control, which means that you want to track the software in the version control system and assign a unique version number to the files in the project.

FIGURE 24.1.

PC software requires version control tracking just as mainframe software does.

Generally, not just anyone can, or should, add software to the version control system. Usually, a System Administrator or a DP Security Officer will control the adding of programs to version-tracking systems such as SourceSafe to maintain integrity and to make sure that all the software in the version-tracking system has been approved for storage there.

By requiring the proper authority, programming departments can help keep incorrect software out of the version library so that a user is not assigned the wrong program during the program's distribution.

Keep in mind that the version control is *not* the same version-tracking values that you saw in Hour 23, "Distributing Your Applications" when compiling a program (see Figure 24.2). Although you can assign major and minor version numbers to a compiled program, it is the source code that must be monitored with secure version control software. As you'll see with the Y2K problem later this hour, the source code is the only sure way that a company has of modifying the program at a later date, so the proper version of source code must always be tracked to ensure that the source code ends up assigned to the proper department that uses the compiled version of the code.

Major version number

Minor version number

FIGURE 24.2.

Monitoring of compiled software is less important than monitoring source code.

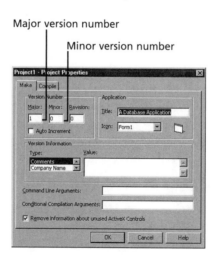

> One of the advantages of version control is that you can release a new version of an application and, if the user finds serious bugs, you can restore an older version of the software. The version-tracking system will keep track of each version you release and will enable you to easily retrieve previous versions when needed.

Resource Editors

A Windows programming language brings its own requirements to the table. Tools exist to help the Windows programmer that were not needed in the DOS environment and make no sense in the mainframe world.

NEW TERM   One such tool is called a *resource* editor. A Windows resource is just about anything used in Windows. A resource might be an icon, a text string, a bitmap image, a menu, or a dialog box. As you work with programming languages, you will manipulate such resources. Resources appear in an application's project in a file that ends with the filename extension .RES.

24

Several ways exist for you to use resources in your Windows applications. You can, for example, designate an icon to use for the end user's installation of your application. The user can click that icon to start the application. You might want to create your own icon. A tool called the *resource editor* can help you create and edit icons and other Windows resources. Visual Studio contains a resource editor that appears as a dialog box, as shown in Figure 24.3, which lets you add, delete, and edit resources in your application's project.

FIGURE 24.3.

The Visual Studio resource editor keeps track of your project's resources.

Will Programming Go Away?

For several years, people have been predicting the demise of programmers. As those predictions get older and more numerous, the demand for programmers has grown tremendously. The need for programming seems to be increasing at a rapid pace.

NEW TERM   In the mid 1970s, *Management Information Systems (MIS)* were going to be the answer to all computing needs. Each company would have MIS in place and all data needed by the company would be at each computer user's fingertips. That kind of data filtering was to be so vast and efficient that ordinary and more specific programs would not be needed. Obviously, the promise of MIS was not only over-predicted but never materialized.

CASE Tools

NEW TERM In the late 1980s, *CASE (Computer-Aided Software Engineering)* was going to replace programmers. Instead of having coders who knew one or more programming languages, programming teams would master CASE tools. CASE is like a program generator, only instead of helping programmers write programs, CASE tools help the DP staff create programs starting at the initial design level. A Systems Analyst can use CASE from the inception of a program request to the program's movement into production.

CASE is a massive program on the computer that the Systems Analyst can use for the initial output design, data definitions, logic definition (some CASE programs even draw flowcharts from a flowchart description entered by the Systems Analyst), and program generation. CASE often produces code based on the Analyst's logic definition, but heavy programmer intervention is needed to implement any but the most general of programs and to ensure the project's overall success.

CASE's proponents promised that it would revolutionize the programming environment and decrease the time and resources needed to produce a finished program. (Most of the newer programming advances promote quicker development time and easier maintenance as their primary goals.) The promise of CASE, however, never materialized. Although CASE has achieved some success, it has yet to produce the advances in software development that were originally hoped.

> The CASE products of the 1980s were not bad tools. The problems that resulted from them were due to the fact that CASE helped Systems Analysts and programmers do faster what the Systems Analysts and programmers already did incorrectly. Pre–object-oriented programming (OOP) methods suffer from difficult maintenance and documentation problems that OOP does not introduce. CASE could not eliminate the inherent problems that non-OOP programming contains. (OOP has its own set of problems as well, however, but it is viewed as an improvement over other traditional methods.)

> Think of CASE as a program that helps you and others design and write programs. CASE is good for handling the minute details throughout the system's development, so you and the other programmers and Systems Analysts can work on implementing all the user's requests.

In recent years, programmer's tools have certainly become sophisticated as you've seen throughout this entire 24-hour tutorial. Some even feel that wizard technology, such as the Visual Basic Application Wizard, will become so powerful that programming will become little more than answering a series of questions.

The reason that programmers are needed more than ever is that computer technology keeps changing along with the programming tools. The early PCs brought new challenges to programs because of their lack of speed and their high demand. As PCs got faster, people networked them together and to mainframes, so distributed client/server programs were needed. Windows required much more effort to program than the simpler, text-based DOS mode. The Internet brought a new set of requirements for programmers that was not dreamed of before.

As you can see, programming demand keeps increasing because the nature of computing keeps changing and becoming more complex. That's the trend that will probably continue for years to come. Programming language developers are recognizing that new tools are needed not to replace programmers but to help them perform their ever-complex jobs.

UML: Data Modeling

NEW TERM Microsoft is joining several other vendors to solidify a new program-modeling language called *UML*, or the *Unified Modeling Language*. The UML provides a uniform definition of modeling a program. Therefore, a company that models one program can share that model with companies that are writing similar programs. The models are not code but are definitions of the applications.

The UML is most useful, initially, for database designers and database application writers to share the components of each database and to transfer those components between computers. The concepts of the UML, however, will also be applied to program designs.

UML will benefit the following five areas of computing:

- **Reuse:** After a company completes a design, that design can be reused.
- **Tool interoperability:** The UML design will be usable by different programming and database systems. Therefore, a UNIX-based HotJava programmer will be able to use the same UML model as a Visual Basic programmer.

24

- **Team development:** The UML tools are usable in a team programming environment.

- **Data resource management:** Resources that appear along with the required data in the UML design are tracked along with the UML's objects.

- **Dependency tracking:** If files are required by other files in the design, the UML keeps track of those dependents.

As with the other design tools of the past, the UML will not replace programming but should enhance programming and enable the design of a system to be used with other systems to improve programmer productivity.

Y2K's Implications

The Y2K problem offers an interesting case study for newcomers to programming. The term Y2K, also known as the Year 2000 problem, is given to the bug that directly blames computer technology for a glitch that happens at midnight, December 31, 1999. At the time of this writing, Y2K has yet to occur. Many predictions are being made about the impact of Y2K, including the following:

- A few bugs in programs will appear that are easily and quickly fixed.

- A modest shutdown of banks and industry computers might occur until all the bugs can be traced and repaired.

- A major shutdown of services will occur, including utilities, blanketing the world and causing a change in the way people live for several weeks to several months or years.

The third scenario offers some interesting implications if it happens in the fullest sense, including worldwide riots, famine, and war. Very few people predict the latter, but after learning more about the Y2K problem, you can see why they believe in the possibility of a shutdown of services.

You might be reading this before or after the year 2000 begins. If after, you know how Y2K actually affected the world. No matter how the problem shows itself, this discussion is going to demonstrate why, from a programmer's point of view, the problem even exists. Also, you will gain a better understanding of the need to write clear and concise programs that are well-documented for subsequent maintenance.

To compound the problem, the year 2000 is a leap year but 1900 was *not* a leap year. Therefore, programs that use a two-digit date and assume that the first two digits are 19 will not properly go from February 28 to February 29 but will instead change to March 1st.

The Reason for Y2K

When computer memory was expensive and computers were slow, mostly before the 1980s, programmers often stored the year as a two-digit value. Therefore, 1978 would be stored as 78. Old habits die hard. As computer hardware got more powerful and memory prices dropped, many programmers still used the two-digit year number. Newcomers to programming would maintain programs written earlier and would keep the two-digit year value automatically.

Most current system software, hardware, and languages, for both the PC and for larger computers, have properly handled four-digit year values for a long time. Nevertheless, programmers did not begin using four-digit years consistently until the Y2K problem reared its ugly head, and some perhaps still use two-digit year values for reports and other trivial programs. Even though computers are in place that don't conform to a two-digit year, those computers run software written by people who might not have thought through all the problems caused by a two-digit date change.

Around 1995, people began to seriously ask what would happen to computer programs in the year 2000 when the two-digit year went from 99 to 00. Consider the simple scenario of an accounting program that computes past-due balances using two dates. Subtracting one date from another gives the number of days past due. If the year changes from 99 to 00, however, a *negative* value results in the calculation. Therefore, the customer will no longer show a past-due balance, but a *credit*! Such a result makes the customer feel good, but consider the company, such as a credit card company, that has hundreds of thousands of accounts that might show a balance at any one time. Those customers would all be owed money due to the incorrect date change.

If the programmers had assumed a four-digit year value from the beginning, the Y2K problem would not be a problem. Going from a value of 1999 to 2000 poses no problem and calculations based on the date will still function properly.

The debate about whether programmers should have used four-digit dates is moot at this point. Many did not use four-digit dates, so the problem exists. In the early days of computers, memory and speed simply could not be sacrificed for four-digit year values and when computers had the capabilities to handle the extra space, programmers didn't think about the ramifications of the second millennium.

More important than whether they should have considered the Y2K ramifications is that programmers should write clear, concise, and well-documented program code. After the Y2K problem plays out, if it has not already by the time you read this, other problems will pop up down the road that people would not have expected. One cannot predict every possible scenario. Companies are bought and sold. New data types are required. Programs must be adapted to new technologies. Therefore, the true problem with Y2K is not the specific Y2K values themselves but the difficulties companies have trying to modify programs that are in production. Some source code has even been lost and the executable code cannot be easily edited, so new source code that supports four-digit dates must be written to replace what was already in place.

HARDWARE AND Y2K

Some PCs still are in use (those that are called *AT-class machines*) that, when rebooted, will use 1900 as the year when 2000 comes. Such date problems are easily corrected from DOS or Windows. More serious hardware problems can occur, however, on hardware devices that are used in industry to control metered flow—as is the case for gas, water, and electric power.

Hardware switches often control the flow of a meter. Many such switches might have been created to work with only two-digit year values. When the time comes for such a switch to turn on or off on a given date, and the switch thinks the date is now 100 years *earlier* than the actual date, the switch could possibly fail. Hence, the doomsday scenarios that are common in the Y2K discussion.

NEW TERM Everybody agrees that the hardest-hit systems will be those that are *legacy systems*; legacy systems are those programs written years ago that are still in use. Numerous COBOL programs written in the 1960s and 1970s, for example, still run daily on company mainframes around the world. Many companies put new software in place regularly and they update their computers to react to the changing and growing needs of the business. Such companies probably will not feel the impact of Y2K as much as organizations that do not respond to change as easily.

Some believe that one organization uses more legacy hardware and software than any other: the Internal Revenue Service. The IRS will likely be hit, and hit hard, with Y2K if the predictions are true.

Fixing Y2K

Fixing Y2K is not trivial in many cases. As mentioned in the previous section, lost source code harms some companies that have to re-write a program from scratch to implement four-digit year values. Many different problems, too numerous to list, will need to be fixed to correct the problem and make systems Y2K-compliant.

Consider what happens if a company realizes that an accounting data file is in use that uses only two-digit year values in a date field. The following steps must be taken to correct the file:

1. A new program must be written to read each record in the file and write a new file with a correct four-digit year.

2. All programs that read, write, and modify the data file in any way must be corrected or re-written to handle the new date format of the file.

3. All subsequent dates must be entered into the program as four-digit dates for the data to be properly separated by date.

4. Extra disk storage might be needed if so many records exist in the file that the storage medium is filled up by the two extra digits in each record.

5. All programs that interface to programs that access the data file must be reviewed to ensure that two-digit year variables are not passed into the system.

If this is the effort required just for a single data file, think of how intense the Y2K problem will be for several hundred, or even thousands of data files and database tables. The cost of repairing Y2K is not definable even if Y2K appears in its mildest scenario that makes only a small and short-term impact on the computers in use during the year 2000.

As you write programs in the future, keep the Y2K problem clearly in focus in all that you do. You cannot predict what problems lie ahead so make your code as easy to modify as possible. Document your work even if you think you are the only one who will ever modify the code because, after a few months pass, your own code will seem foreign to you.

While coding, keep asking yourself the following questions:

- If someone must change this program feature, what can I do to make the code as clear as possible?

- How can I code this so that anyone can look at my code later and know what I'm doing?

- How much better can I comment this code to enable future programmers to zero in quickly to whatever they might have to change?

24

- Have I broken my code into enough small procedures so each procedure performs one and only one task? Can a programmer modify my procedure without adversely affecting another feature of the program any more than necessary?

Only if you continually ask yourself these kinds of questions can you ensure that one of your programs will not be a culprit in the next Y2K-like problem.

Your Training Needs

Only if you keep up with industry changes can you help ensure that problems such as Y2K do not occur in the future. Programmers continually hone their skills to keep up with the changing technology in languages, operating systems, software, and hardware. As you learn more about programming, you should consider sharing your knowledge with others through training, consulting, writing, or teaching. You will find that your own programming skills improve when you teach them to someone else.

The need for training is never as apparent as it is in virtually every programming department in the world. Programmers are often called to offer a training class for others who do not possess some needed skills. In-house training enables a company to keep a cap on its training costs and control the material being covered.

Your own computer training does not stop. The computer industry changes rapidly. The skills you have today can be obsolete in ten years, so part of your job is to continue your own training. It is incumbent upon you to stay up with current trends if you want to secure your computer position in the future.

INDUSTRY STANDARDS

Not every new breakthrough in computer hardware and software becomes an industry standard. You do not have to be on the *bleeding edge* of technology (a programmer's pun describing very new and unproved technology), learning everything there is to learn. You do not even have to be on the *leading edge* of computer programming innovations. For instance, object-oriented programming is now considered by the industry as the best way to program, yet the majority of computer programmers haven't learned how to program with objects. They might or might not have to master OOP depending on where their jobs take them and the language they must master in their companies. The future seems to be heading towards using OOP languages in most situations, however. There is rarely a need to stay on top of the latest trends because today's breakthrough might be tomorrow's flop.

You will find your own niche in the computer field. Specialization is almost a must these days. It is so very difficult to master everything. Some people choose to specialize in networking, Internet programming, Web page design, object-oriented programming, or graphical user interfaces. As you learn more about programming, you will find the area that best fits your own interests and you will master that area.

Each month, take a trip to your local library or bookstore to scan the shelves for the latest computer magazines. Try to read one good computer book every month or two. Every six months, research a new topic of computer programming to improve your skill levels. Most computer people find that self-study is not a job they balk at; the field of programming is exciting. It never gets old. The new innovations everywhere you look are always exciting and hold promise of powerful computing power in the future.

Now that you have a more solid foundation than almost any other beginning programmer has ever had, you are ready to direct your education toward more specific goals. You should now begin tackling a programming language in depth. Mastering a programming language takes a while, and people learn at different rates. Nevertheless, the biggest problem budding programmers face is that they jump in too fast. After reading *Teach Yourself Beginning Programming in 24 Hours*, you will not have that problem; you will be surprised at how well this book's concepts prepare you for your programming future, whether that future is just for fun or for a career.

Computer books are known for their series approach. As you already know, the *Sams Teach Yourself in 24 Hours* series is designed to teach you the basics of a subject in as little time as possible. The *Sams Teach Yourself in 21 Days* series is also designed to teach a topic to a newcomer but the topic is taught in more depth due to the added time. As you browse the bookshelves, you'll also see special editions of *Sams Teach Yourself More* books designed to add content to earlier books in the series. In addition to the highly successful *Sams Teach Yourself* series, you'll want to use the *Unleashed* books to master the advanced aspects of a programming language.

The following Sams Publishing titles are a sampling of some books that you might want to look at to improve your skills as a programmer. These books were specifically chosen to get you up to speed in a specific area of programming:

- *Sams Teach Yourself PCs in 24 Hours*: Introduces you to PCs and explains the hardware and software associated with the popular computers. If you've programmed only on larger computers, or are still one of the many who are PC-phobic, this book will put you at ease and explain the essentials of PCs.

24

- *QBasic Programming 101*: If you want more practice with QBasic than this book was able to provide, you can learn the entire language in this comprehensive tutorial.

- *Sams Teach Yourself HTML in 24 Hours*, *Sams Teach Yourself Visual Basic in 24 Hours*, *Sams Teach Yourself Java in 24 Hours*, and *Sams Teach Yourself C++ in 24 Hours*: These books are the perfect next step from this book to take you more deeply into the language of your choice.

- *Sams Teach Yourself Visual Basic in 21 Days*, *Sams Teach Yourself C in 21 Days*, and *Sams Teach Yourself C++ in 21 Days*: These books take you far into the languages to prepare you for your career or hobby.

- *Moving from C to C++*: Written for C programmers and designed to take the C programmer into the OOP-based world of C++.

- *Visual Basic Unleashed* and *Visual C++ Unleashed*: These books assume some familiarity with the respective languages and dig deep into the language to provide you with a comprehensive reference and study aid for the languages.

To keep up with the latest in programming titles, regularly check out Macmillan Computer Publishing's Web site at www.mcp.com.

Summary

Programming tools go far beyond just the languages themselves. Throughout this 24-hour tutorial, you've seen examples of languages and programming tools that help you be a better programmer. This hour showed you additional tools that programmers can use, especially Windows programmers, to become more productive programmers.

The most important part of programming is writing clear and concise code so that others can maintain your programs when needed. The Y2K cloud might have a silver lining: Programmers are learning what it takes to modify older code; hopefully, the Y2K problem will earn the respect of today's programmers and teach the importance of proper documentation and clear code.

After you've mastered programming, what's next? Keep mastering! Continuing education is almost as vital in the field of computers as it is in the medical profession. The rapidly changing computer technology requires that programmers stay on top of current trends by reading books and magazines and taking courses when possible. Share your knowledge with others to help improve the programming community and reduce the backlog that the computer industry faces. Knowledge shared is knowledge improved.

Q&A

Q Are CASE tools available for PCs?

A Some CASE tools exist for PCs, but they are primarily used on mainframes where a huge program that is used by hundreds or thousands of users must handle the company needs. Although extremely advanced programming is now being done at the PC level, especially enterprise computing that is made possible by client/server models, CASE hasn't found a good foothold in the door of PC programmers. Probably the failure of CASE in the 1980s has made PC programmers afraid to try it. Newer tools, such as UML, will probably be more common in the arena of PC development.

Workshop

24

The quiz questions are provided for your further understanding. For the answers, see Appendix A, "Answers to End of Chapter Questions."

Quiz

1. What is a profiler?
2. Which is more important: program efficiency or program maintainability?
3. Why is the version control library important to a programming department?
4. What are two possible Windows resources?
5. What is a resource manager?
6. Why does the demand for programmers increase even though tools become more powerful?
7. What does *Y2K* stand for?
8. What is *legacy software*?
9. What is *CASE*?
10. How does the Y2K problem affect programmers before, during, and after the year 2000?

APPENDIX A

Answers to End of Chapter Questions

Hour 1

Answers

1. Information provides useful facts and figures on which you can base decisions. Data is comprised of raw facts and figures that must be processed into some other form to be useful.

2. True.

3. A program is a set of instructions that tells a computer what to do.

4. False; computers make mistakes all the time, but the reason usually involves people who, somewhere before, entered incorrect instructions or data into the computer.

5. A computer is not a thinking machine, but people can think. The computer is useful for performing the same boring, repetitive task over and over, but people are best used in decision-making positions where their insight is valuable. Computers free people up from mundane jobs. In

addition, the computer industry has boomed into an industry worth billions of dollars and, directly and indirectly, millions of jobs.

6. The hardware is the least expensive component of a computer information system.

7. False; the price of software, people, data, and procedures is going up over time. Some software drops in price, but the overall price of software that businesses and people purchase for their computers is rising because the number of programs in use increases.

8. Computer programs process data and produce information. If the program receives bad data, the output will also be bad in most instances.

9. The Data Entry department provides the data input into most companies' computer systems.

10. Companies must put security procedures, personnel procedures, backup procedures, and training procedures into place before they can maintain an adequate computer information system.

Hour 2

Answers

1. Large jobs require large computers. In spite of the rapid advancement in C capabilities over the years, large supercomputers and mainframes are still required to handle the computing tasks of large organizations and companies.

2. Transistors are less expensive to operate than tube-based electronics and they take far less power and maintenance. Therefore, transistor technology enabled more businesses and organizations to purchase and run computers that otherwise could not afford them. That proliferation of machines in so many people's hands spurred competition among computer companies and advanced programming technology.

3. The CPU, the Central Processing Unit, is the brain, or the actual computer inside a microcomputer. All other devices attached to a PC exist to communicate in some way or store data for the CPU.

4. False; perhaps society will always need faster computers as information needs continue to grow. For the time being, having much faster computers allows for the accurate prediction of weather in time to save lives. Other uses, such as medical simulations and research, require constantly improved computer speeds. Besides, think about how much better games can get if computers get even faster!

5. Supercomputers run so fast they generate extra heat that needs to be removed, so the computers can continue to run properly and at top speed.

6. Client/server computing refers to the combination of supercomputers, mainframes, minicomputers, and PCs, in virtually any configuration, used to communicate as a

single massive computing architecture. Users can keep their individual PC programs and operate at their desks using programs such as word processors, or those same PCs (the clients) can interact with the larger computers (the servers) to access and update the data stored on those larger systems.

7. The operating system is the interface between your computer's hardware and software. The operating system interprets commands from the user and from the executing programs and interacts with the hardware when needed.

8. True; Windows is just a program, although Windows is a huge program that manages the system resources and controls the execution of other programs as well.

9. Today's programming tools require many computer resources. If you, as a programmer, are writing to the average computer out there, you must realize that by the time you finish your program, computers can be faster than they were when you started writing your program, but that doesn't mean your users will have the faster machines. The software you write must compete against the other programs out there and must not consume extra resources that would take away from the speed of other programs running at the same time. Although computers are getting faster, you must write to the average computer out there. Programming languages themselves can consume massive resources, so you need a computer that can handle the demands of programming languages as well as execute the programs you write and test at the same time those languages are loaded.

10. When the computer executes a program, the computer follows, step-by-step, the program's detailed instructions. The executing program must be loaded into memory before the computer can run it.

Hour 3

Answers

1. You can purchase a new program and use it, purchase a program and customize it to suit your needs, or write your own program.

2. By writing their own programs, businesses can be assured that the programs do what is needed.

3. Programs are not written in human language but in a programming language.

4. Human languages are far too ambiguous for machines to understand.

5. Computers only understand the machine language comprised of 1s and 0s.

6. False; programmers might only know one programming language well and that's all the programmer needs to know if the language is a modern-day language that can produce the programs needed.

7. The CPU can only execute instructions loaded into memory. The CPU cannot execute instructions still residing on a program on a disk drive.

8. Syntax errors and logic errors appear in programs.

9. Syntax errors are the easiest to locate. As a matter of fact, the computer programming language will spot syntax errors for you.

10. Compilers produce faster programs than interpreted programs.

Hour 4

Answers

1. Proper design details every item that appears in the final program. Without a proper design, the programmer spends much more time in the program-writing stages modifying and changing the program to suit the programmer's wishes.

2. The programmer must first define the program's output.

3. True.

4. Top-down design produces all of a program's details but does not order those details.

5. The user may not have the computing power to run your visual design tools or the user may not even have computer equipment yet. You may not have a license that allows you to install the visual design tools on a second system.

6. A flowchart decision symbol can produce only two values.

7. A decision symbol should include a yes or no question.

8. True.

9. Pseudocode uses text only whereas a flowchart combines both text and graphics to detail program logic.

10. The final step in creating a program is the actual programming stage.

Hour 5

Answers

1. Word processors tend to wrap lines of text and your program should not be word wrapped.

2. Line editors and full-screen editors are both still in use.

3. Full-screen editors are more common than line editors because they are easier to use.

4. Menus provide lists of commands you can perform so that you don't have to memorize commands as you did in the days when line editors were the norm.

5. A debugger is an integrated tool within most of today's programming languages that you can use to help locate and correct program bugs.

6. A profiler is a tool that lets you analyze programs to determine where inefficiencies reside.

7. Structured programming is the opposite of spaghetti code.

8. The three structured programming language constructs are sequence, decision, and looping.

9. Excess branching causes your program to jump all over the placing making the program harder to analyze, understand, and maintain later when you must make changes to the program. The more structured your program is, the faster you will finish the program and the easier the program will be to modify in the future.

10. Parallel testing is the use of the program while, at the same time, the previous program or manual procedures are still in place. Beta testing is offering the program to users to help test and locate bugs.

Hour 6

A

Answers

1. Only one-eighth of a character will fit in a bit. A bit is a representative of an on or off state of electricity.

2. A byte is equivalent to one character.

3. It takes eight bits to make a byte.

4. PCs use ASCII tables for character translation.

5. Computers can only perform addition. All other mathematical operations must be simulated through addition.

6. Assembler language replaced the 1s and 0s of machine language.

7. COBOL is considered to be the best programming language for business.

8. COBOL is considered more self-documenting than FORTRAN.

9. APL requires special hardware to produce the language's symbols and the language is so cryptic that programmers stopped trying to learn it as other languages came on the scene.

10. The United States government created ADA for contract and internal programmers.

Hour 7

Answers

1. Pascal supports structured programming techniques the best, although all of today's modern languages do allow for full structured programming.

2. C replaced Pascal as the most popular language of the 1980s.

3. The limited memory and disk storage offers perfect environments for small languages such as Pascal and C.

4. C++ is the new and improved C language.

5. C and C++ provide support for numerous operators.

6. C++ was the first wide-spread language to support OOP.

7. True.

8. Windows programs were originally written in C.

9. Visual Basic is a Windows-based programming system for Windows.

10. False; the best language to use varies from individual to individual, company to company, and application to application.

Hour 8

Answers

1. You must copy QBasic's files from the installation CD-ROMs.

2. QBasic locates some errors as you enter a program and some as you run the program.

3. Remarks are used to document the program for programmers.

4. A variable holds a data value.

5. False; PRINT prints only to the screen.

6. Variables can hold one and only one data value at a time.

7. The dollar sign indicates that the variable holds character data.

8. QBasic follows a predefined order of operators that you can override with parentheses.

9. False; QBasic supports only short filenames that conform to the eight-character limit.

10. CLS erases the QBasic screen.

Hour 9

Answers

1. When outputting numeric values, QBasic often leaves a blank space where the plus would go.

2. False; negative numbers don't need the blank because the negative sign fills the place where the blank would go.

3. A semicolon causes subsequent output to appear right next to the output value just printed.

4. An internal function is a built-in routine that does something such as space output.

5. SPC() inserts a fixed number of spaces between values and TAB() forces output to appear in a specific column.

6. The USING clause formats output.

7. The INPUT statement gets values from the user at the keyboard.

8. Use the LINE INPUT when you need to receive a string value that might contain a comma.

9. True.

10. If you do not prompt the user, the user will have no idea what kind of input you need.

A

Hour 10

Answers

1. Conditional operators return a true or false value that determines how two values relate to each other, whereas the mathematical operators perform calculations.

2. A loop is a block of one or more statements that repeat.

3. True.

4. False; if the FOR loop's control variable initially exceeds the final value in the FOR statement, the FOR loop never executes, but execution of the program will resume right after the NEXT statement.

5. The variable following NEXT is optional.

6. You can use the EXIT FOR to terminate a FOR...NEXT loop earlier than its normal termination.

7. The FOR...NEXT loop is best to use when you want to loop a fixed number of times. Use the DO loop when the loop is controlled by a conditional value.

8. The DO...WHILE continues to loop while a certain condition is true and the DO...UNTIL continues to loop until a certain condition is true.

9. Your data and personal preference will determine whether you use a DO...WHILE or a DO...UNTIL. If the majority of times the conditional test will be false, the DO...UNTIL loop may make more sense to use over the DO...WHILE. Remember, though, that you can make either kind of loop work in almost any case.

10. The placement determines whether the loop will execute at least once no matter how the conditional values compare.

Hour 11

Answers

1. All arrays, no matter how many elements they have, have one and only one name. You don't distinguish array elements from each other by name, but by their numeric subscript.

2. You can step through all elements in an array inside a loop, such as a FOR loop, and the loop controls the incrementing of the subscript.

3. An array is in memory and is simply a table of variable values. A disk file is for long-term storage of data that stays on the disk after you power down your PC.

4. The DIM statement reserves space for arrays.

5. The ERASE command erases every element in an array.

6. False; the number of rows has nothing to do with how many columns of data a file contains.

7. True.

8. False; the append mode always adds to a file, or creates a new file if one did not exist before.

9. The file handle is a number that you assign to a file when you open the file. After you assign a file handle, you don't have to access the file by name for the rest of the program and your coding is made easier.

10. The EOF() function tests for the end of file.

Hour 12

Answers

1. The BEEP command buzzes your PC's speaker.

2. The hertz value, indicated by the number you specify, determines the tone of the sound that the SOUND command produces.

3. The PLAY command supports its own miniature language so that a single PLAY command can produce an entire song.

4. The term *pixel* is a shorthand form of *picture element*.

5. The standard VGA graphics card supports 640 pixels by 480 pixels.

6. True; use the SCREEN command to place your screen in a graphics mode before drawing graphics.

7. True; but the LINE and CIRCLE commands are much easier to use and more efficient.

8. Two points define a line.

9. Two points define a box from one corner to the opposite diagonal corner.

10. The LOCATE command determines where the next PRINT will print.

A

Hour 13

Answers

1. A control is an item that interacts with the user in a graphical user interface.

2. A property determines how a control looks or behaves.

3. An event is an action that takes place with or by a control.

4. A Windows program is comprised of a set of files, often called the project files, that combine to form one application.

5. It is the property values that distinguish one control from another.

6. A hot key is a keystroke combination, usually containing the Alt key, that activates a control or menu action.

7. The control that is currently highlighted, or active, is said to have the focus.

8. The user can click a control or press the control's hot key to receive the focus.

9. The control's name will be part of the event message passed to the application.

10. Windows handles the filtering of all events.

Hour 14

Answers

1. Using Visual Basic's Application Wizard, you don't have to write any code to embed Internet-browsing capabilities in a Visual Basic application.

2. True; the Application Wizard creates only the shell of an application, and you must add code and controls that make the application specific to your needs.

3. The default names that Visual Basic assigns controls are not good because they give no indication of the control's purpose. Therefore, a name that you assign such as lblTitle shows two things: the control is a label and it holds a title.

4. When you double-click a toolbox control, Visual Basic places that control in the center of the Form window where you can specify the control's properties and move the control to its final location on the form.

5. Use the Menu Editor to add menus to Visual Basic applications.

6. The properties in the Properties window always belong to whatever control is currently selected on the form.

7. You can use Visual Basic's built-in debugging tools to help debug any programs you run from Visual Basic's environment.

8. A compiled Visual Basic application that runs outside of Visual Basic's environment executes faster than one that you run inside Visual Basic's environment.

9. The procedure is private, which means that only code from the current form module can access the procedure. The procedure is a subroutine, so control returns to whatever code was executing before the event that triggered this procedure occurred. The event that the procedure responds to is a scroll bar that has been changed.

10. False; many procedures are general purpose and do not apply directly to specific controls on a form. You'll place these general procedures inside a code module that you can copy into any application that has need of the routines in the module.

Hour 15

Answers

1. C is a compiled language which makes it much faster than QBasic's interpreted language. In addition, C's small command set and extensive collection operators make C more efficient than most compiled languages.

2. A header file is a source code file, supplied by the C compiler, that is included in your program during the compilation.

3. All C programs have a `main()` function.

4. C does not support a `string` data type.

5. True; C recognizes string literals enclosed in quotation marks.

6. You can store string data if you declare a character array to hold the null zero-based string.

7. The semicolon should not appear after the first line's closing parentheses. The semicolon immediately terminates the relational test so that the `printf()` executes no matter what the value of `sales` is.

8. C includes several operators that shortcut similar operators in other languages. For example, C includes increment and decrement operators as well as compound assignment operators that update variables.

9. Braces help group statements together, such as a function's beginning and end as well as the body of `if` statements and `for` loops.

10. `\n` is a control character and consumes only one character in memory.

Hour 16

Answers

1. True.

2.   A. A bug exists because the programmer failed to close the first comment.

    B. You could rewrite the code like this in C++ (notice you don't need to worry about unfinished comments in C++):

```
// Perform a data check
   if (a < 50)
     { flag = 0; }  // False
   else
     { flag = 1; }  // True
```

3. A class defines the way objects look and behave.

4. The `iostream.h` header file defines I/O in most C++ programs.

5. You use the `class` statement to define an object's data members and member functions.

6. Only member functions within the class have direct access to private data members or private member functions.

7. A class defines an object's data members and member functions. An object is a specific instance of a class.

8. C++ programmers often use the cin and cout objects, along with << and >>, to perform standard input and output.

9. Polymorphism allows for operator overloading because, with polymorphism, objects from different classes respond to the same operators in different ways.

10. Inheritance enables the programmer to create new classes from existing classes and add capabilities to the newly inherited classes.

Hour 17

Answers

1. An accumulator is an assignment statement with the same variable on each side of the equal sign. The variable is being updated, or changed, by the accumulator assignment.

2. True; but only in the strictest sense of an accumulator's definition (see answer #1). The same variable, Num, resides on both sides of the equal sign but the variable is actually being decremented and not incremented in the accumulator-based assignment statement.

3. All values appear from the lowest to the highest in an ascending sort, whereas, all values appear from the highest to the lowest in a descending sort.

4. Without the third variable, the first assignment statement would wipe out one of the values in the two variables you are attempting to swap.

5. The bubble sort is the easiest to write and understand.

6. True; a counter assignment is an accumulator assignment statement that adds only one to the value of the variable being updated.

7. The sequential search is the simplest kind of search technique.

8. The binary search is more efficient than the sequential search.

9. GOTO is an unconditional branching statement; GOSUB performs a temporary branch but eventually returns to the current place in code.

10. Sort the values in an ascending sort before you perform a sequential search to improve the search's efficiency.

Hour 18

Answers

1. The batch language supports operating system commands as well as includes extra commands that control batch file execution.

2. B; the programs do what they need them to do.

3. True; you can attach a Windows icon to a batch file so the batch file begins executing as soon as the user selects the icon.

4. Mainframe users often use JCL (Job Control Language) to automate operating system tasks.

5. VBA stands for Visual Basic for Applications.

6. Major Windows applications support keyboard-based macros and macros written in Visual Basic for Applications.

7. Applications can often record keystrokes that you type as you build macro-based commands.

8. True.

9. The object model includes support for the application that uses the VBA program.

10. The Windows Scripting Host language controls online communications.

A

Hour 19

Answers

1. The Internet is not just a bunch of individual computers connected together by phone. The Internet is a series of networked computers connected to other networked computers. This tangled web-like network makes it possible for you to communicate to virtually any computer system in the world.

2. For one Internet computer to communicate with another, several things must take place at lightning speed. When you are talking in an online chat room to someone in another country, a single wire does not exist between your two computers. Instead, many wires between many computers exist to make the communication possible. Many switches go on and off to form the needed path between two computers that need to communicate.

3. False; sending a huge amount of data at one time turns out to be quite *inefficient*. If an entire file is sent at one time and an error occurs towards the very end of the

communications, the entire file must be re-sent. If, instead, the file is broken into packets, each small packet can be sent, checked, and then re-sent if needed.

4. Each packet has a packet address that directs the packet to its destined computer.

5. The Mosaic browser was the first browser to support HTML.

6. True.

7. An ActiveX object is a programmed object with characteristics and behaviors. In practice, an ActiveX object works like an embedded program in another program that can contain the object. Therefore, a Web browser that can contain ActiveX objects allows the execution of those objects inside the Web browser.

8. VBScript and JavaScript are two of the most popular scripting languages.

9. Script code goes inside HTML code.

10. Use the Visual Basic Application Wizard to add browsing capabilities to any Visual Basic application you write. You'll have to do no programming because the wizard inserts all the code needed for the application to display the browser, log on if needed by the user's system, and traverse to the home page you request.

Hour 20

Answers

1. True.

2. False; generally, the machine's speed has little to do with how fast a Web page and its components, including the applets that you send with the Web page, load from the Internet. The server and the user's connection speed determine the download time.

3. The <APPLET> HTML command tag designates that a Java applet appears with the Web page.

4. Bytecode is the compiled version of a Java applet. The bytecode is not truly compiled, as a compiled C program would be, because you don't know the kind of target machine that the Java applet will run on.

5. When you write Java applets, you compile them into bytecode, which is machine independent. In other words, the machine that recognizes bytecode does not really exist but is a virtual machine. When a user uses a Java-enabled Web browser, the Web browser, no matter which kind of computer the browser runs on, interprets instructions from the bytecode and produces the applet.

6. Java cannot access the user's internal memory because such memory is protected by the language from access. Also, a Java applet cannot connect to networked

computers that might be attached to the user's own machine. Finally, a Java applet cannot read, modify, create, or rename files on the end-user's machine.

7. The `import` command loads class packages that define various classes and methods you can then use and extend in your Java programs.

8. You draw text on the screen instead of writing the text. Methods (methods act much like functions except that you apply the methods to objects such as the screen window object) such as `drawString()` draw text strings on the applet's window.

9. `paint()` determines what happens when the user forces a redraw of the applet window.

10. Java is a programming language and Visual J++ is an implementation of the language.

Hour 21

Answers

1. MIS stands for Management Information Systems.

2. The DP department writes programs for the entire company.

3. The Data Entry Clerk is often the most entry-level computer position in a large company.

4. Entry-level programmers often maintain code written by others.

5. A Systems Analyst designs applications.

6. A structured walkthrough is a meeting with other Programmers and Systems Analysts who look over a programmer's code and make suggestions for improving it.

7. True; the source code is what programmers use for program maintenance.

8. Job security comes from a job well done in most cases.

9. A LAN is a network that covers a few PCs connected together in an office, on a floor, or in a single building. A WAN may span several buildings and even cities and countries.

10. In these times, Internet demand is high. That demand puts an upward pressure on salaries for those with Internet programming skills even though the personnel is at the same level as others in the DP department.

Hour 22

Answers

1. Programming languages locate syntax errors as you type the code or when you run the program.

2. Programming languages cannot locate logic errors. If a payroll amount comes out wrong, for example, the programming language cannot determine that you used an incorrect calculation.

3. True.

4. The F8 key is almost universally used to single-step through a program.

5. The Immediate window enables you to view values of variables during the execution of a program.

6. Today's computers are too fast to watch the real-time execution of most programs line-by-line.

7. You can specify that program execution is to step over code and begin at any statement in the current procedure.

8. A watch variable is a variable that you've designated that triggers a breakpoint if a specific value or range of values appear in that variable during the program's execution. You can designate more than one variable to be a watch variable in a program.

9. One of the biggest limitations to the QBasic debugger is its capability to run only in a single window at one time. In a Windows-based debugger, your output window is not polluted with debugging values that you send it from an Immediate window; instead, the Immediate window's values appear in their own window.

10. The call stack is a list of all procedures your application has executed to the current breakpoint.

Hour 23

Answers

1. QBasic no longer comes installed on people's computers although they can, through some file-related operations, load QBasic onto their computers.

2. In source code format, your programs are not as secure as they would be if you could compile the programs. The user can change the code and bugs can appear.

3. False; you can connect a QBasic program to a Windows icon and the program will automatically begin when the user selects the icon.

4. An installation script is a file that an installation system uses to specify all files and how they are to be installed on a user's computer.

5. Compiled programs use the EXE filename extension.

6. The primary installation filename for most applications is Setup.exe.

7. Most installation systems can store an application's installation files on just about any media available, including diskettes, networks, and the Internet.

8. The large size of most Windows applications requires much space. The installation would require too many diskettes to be cost-effective.

9. The clean machine ensures that files needed for the installation don't appear on the computer prior to the installation. If the installation omits a needed file, you're more likely to realize that the file is missing than if you installed the application on a machine that you created the application on or on a machine to which you've installed the application at least once before.

10. A good installation-creation program, such as Visual Studio's Package and Deployment Wizard, will create the uninstall routine for you so that all files are properly removed when the user wants to remove the application.

Hour 24

Answers

1. A profiler shows you where your program is sluggish so that you can improve the efficiency of the inefficient sections.

2. The ability to maintain a program is much more important than its efficiency in most cases.

3. Version control software provides a reliable means of recording which source code is distributed to your users.

4. A Windows resource might be an icon, a bitmap image, a text string, a menu, or a dialog box.

5. Resource managers are programming tools with which you can add, delete, edit, and create resources for your applications.

6. Computing changes rapidly and that rapid change requires new programming skills to meet the demand.

A

7. *Y2K* stands for *Year 2000* and refers to the bug that appears in some computer software and hardware in the year 2000.

8. Legacy software is older software still in use.

9. *CASE* stands for *Computer Aided Software Engineering* and refers to a product that programming departments can use to help design complex software products.

10. The Y2K problem is going to take a while to fix and all the bugs will not be fixed before 2000. Nevertheless, the primary lesson learned from Y2K is not that programmers should use four-digit year values. Instead, the lesson is that programmers should write code that is easily maintained in the future to meet changing conditions in which the company uses the program.

INDEX

mcp.com

The Authoritative Encyclopedia of Computing

Resource Centers
Books & Software
Personal Bookshelf
WWW Yellow Pages
Online Learning
Special Offers
Site Search
Industry News

▶ Choose the online ebooks that you can view from your personal workspace on our site.

About MCP   Site Map   Product Support

Turn to the *Authoritative* Encyclopedia of Computing

You'll find over 150 full text books online, hundreds of shareware/freeware applications, online computing classes and 10 computing resource centers full of expert advice from the editors and publishers of:

- Adobe Press
- BradyGAMES
- Cisco Press
- Hayden Books
- Lycos Press
- New Riders
- Que
- Que Education & Training
- Sams Publishing
- Waite Group Press
- Ziff-Davis Press

mcp.com
The Authoritative Encyclopedia of Computing

Get the best information and learn about latest developments in:

- ■ Design
- ■ Graphics and Multimedia
- ■ Enterprise Computing and DBMS
- ■ General Internet Information
- ■ Operating Systems
- ■ Networking and Hardware
- ■ PC and Video Gaming
- ■ Productivity Applications
- ■ Programming
- ■ Web Programming and Administration
- ■ Web Publishing

When you're looking for computing information, consult the authority. The Authoritative Encyclopedia of Computing at mcp.com.

Order Your Program Disk Today

Instead of typing the code you find in *Sams Teach Yourself Beginning Programming in 24 Hours*, you can load the programs from a companion disk and forget about the tedious typing errors that plague so many first-time programmers. As you learn programming with this book's text, you will appreciate not having to fight the keyboard as you type, edit, and test each program.

As a bonus, you will also receive a set of *Tutorial Example Programs*, a new concept that beginning programmers will find invaluable as they move into intermediate and advanced QBasic programming. The disk contains over 200 programs that highlight *every* QBasic command and function. As you progress with QBasic, learning more of its advanced commands, you will be able to turn to this TEP companion disk and find a program that spotlights any QBasic command, no matter how common or obscure.

Disks are available in 3 1/2-inch format. The cost is $15 per disk. (When ordering from outside the U.S., please add $5 for extra shipping and handling and draw funds from a U.S. bank, or please use a money order.)

Just fill in the blanks on this page or a copy of this page, and mail it with your check or postal money order (sorry, no credit card orders) to:

Greg Perry
QBasic Companion Disk
P.O. Box 35752
Tulsa, OK 74153-0752

Please print the following information:

Number of disks: _____ @ $15.00 = _____

Name: _____

Address: _____

City: _____ State: _____

ZIP: _____

(On foreign orders, please use a separate page to give your mailing address in the format required by your post office.)

Checks and postal money orders should be made payable to **Greg Perry**.

(This offer is made by the author, not by Macmillan Computer Publishing.)